BEST
FOOD
WRITING
2004

BEST
FOOD
WRITING
2004

Edited by

HOLLY HUGHES

Foreword by
JEFFREY STEINGARTEN

Marlowe & Company
New York

BEST FOOD WRITING 2004

Published by
Marlowe & Company
An Imprint of Avalon Publishing Group Incorporated
245 West 17th Street • 11th Floor
New York, NY 10011-5300

AVALON
publishing group incorporated

Library of Congress Cataloging-in-Publication Data is available.

ISBN 1-56924-416-2

9 8 7 6 5 4 3

Designed by Michael Walters and Susan Canavan
Printed in the United States of America
Distributed by Publishers Group West

Contents

The Meat of the Matter

Eating Out

Appetites

Foreword

by Jeffrey Steingarten

I t is an honor to introduce *Best Food Writing 2004* in this fifth year of its publication. Not since Alice Waters wrote the foreword in 2000 have our distinguished editor, Holly Hughes, and her publishers been able to find anybody worthy of succeeding Alice. Until now. In just four short pages I will explain why we write about food, why I do so, how we're getting on, and how we might improve.

We write about food for all the noble and twisted reasons that all writers write; most of us are more preoccupied with food than other writers are with their subjects—for reasons ranging from aesthetic and animal pleasure to the fact that cooking, eating, and growing reach as deeply into our natures as sex or love, and sometimes more. But above all, nearly every food writer is on a mission. We are trying to make food better.

Ask most people why they become food writers (or chefs or farmers) and they'll answer with a story—a narrative full of foreshadowing and surprises, a series of random events woven into an inescapable and inexorable narrative. My grandmother and her four sisters were wonderful cooks. I once shopped with them for the lungs of a cow. Did I mention that on the day of my mother's funeral, I made my first chocolate mousse? Upon hearing this, the readers will exclaim, "Aha!" Having undergone two completely successful long-term Freudian psychoanalyses, I can assure you that childhood experiences have no effect whatsoever on the adult personality. Contrary to what you may have read, the child is not father of the man. Many other types of stories are possible. In some cultures, karma is the preferred source of cause and effect. For me, it's neurology.

Eight or so years ago, a friend whose hobbies include undermining my preoccupation with gastronomy sent me a copy of the journal *Neurology*. In it was a paper by two Swiss doctors who claimed to have discovered what they named the Gourmand Syndrome, in which "an excessive interest in fine food" can often be traced to a lesion in the right frontal hemisphere of the brain. Their breakthrough patient was a prominent political journalist in Zurich who had once been indifferent to what he ate. One day he suffered a stroke in the right frontal hemisphere. As he recovered, he began talking incessantly about food, displaying culinary knowledge that nobody imagined he had. In six months he returned to journalism. The newspaper had held his job open, yet against everybody's advice, he persuaded his editors to let him write instead about food. He succeeded famously.

But surely I don't have a lesion. Or do I? Ten days later I was lying on a table in the Cantonal Hospital in Geneva, being slid into an MRI machine. The diagnosis? For now I can say only that maybe I switched from being a lawyer because of neurons and synapses. Maybe.

How are we doing? Is food writing getting better and better? Yes and no. The greatest food writing remains at the same stratospheric level. Is Alan Richman funnier than Robert Benchley or Mark Twain? Does Calvin Trillin create better sentences than A. J. Leibling? Is Jonathan Gold's judgment of restaurants more reliable than Grimod de la Reyniere's? Could Adam Gopnik whup Duncan Hines? Am I superior to Brillat-Savarin as a lawyer-writer-gastronomer? Well, maybe, but only sometimes.

No, it is the average that has grown so much finer. Food writing attracts so many more intelligent souls than it did twenty years ago; browse through the better food Web sites, such as eGullet, and you'll meet budding talents who, considering their longing to get published, can be hired for a peppercorn.

Today it's much harder to get away with shoddy practices.

We're so well traveled that the third-hand ethnic adaptations in, say, Craig Claiborne's truly pioneering *New York Times Cookbook* now only make us smile, smugly. Scientific explanations must now be at least as enlightening as Harold McGee's or Shirley Corriher's. We can no longer rely on what recently passed for food history in the charming prose of Waverly Root and the anecdotes of James Beard (remember the poisonous-tomato myth?). What I mean to say is, really good food writing has grown much tougher to do since I got into the racket.

On the other hand: As food history has so quickly become professionalized in the Anglo-American academic world, it has sometimes turned dry or tendentious and consequently less interesting. In some universities, food history has become a subset of gender studies, and we all know what that can mean. Narrative history seems to have become unfashionable in the academic world; could an American academic have written Felipe Fernández-Armesto's brilliant *Near a Thousand Tables* and kept his job? Somehow the field has gone from sloppy to technical, skipping the delightful middle ground.

Also on the other hand: It's been the fashion for five years or so for editors and publishers to recruit noted novelists (and famous non-fiction writers) to write about food. The results have been mixed. Most vaunted fiction writers can't face the seemingly trivial job of describing the food in itself; instead they talk about everything around it. It's embarrassing (and for a man other than Hemingway, wimpy and effeminate), to describe food closely, to use phrases like "perfect puffy pillows of pasta." Something comparable happens when an otherwise rigorous non-fiction craftsman writes about food as though he's on vacation and needn't bother with research.

None of the really good minds in our field—the Ray Sokolovs, Corby Kummers, Paul Levys, John Thornes, Nancy H. Jenkinses, and at least a dozen others—ever forget the point: It's the food, stupid.

How can we do it better? If American food writing has drooped in the past thirty-five years it is in the art of writing recipes. This excellent series has not been a neutral influence. As Holly wrote in her introduction to the inaugural volume, "I realized that two of the most common types of food writing—the recipe piece and the restaurant review—would end up being underrepresented in this collection. Many perfectly interesting recipes are so focused on the technical cooking information that elegant prose style is almost beside the point."

Recipes are too often written in the style of auto-repair manuals. The fault lies with all of us. Perhaps the next volume in this series will devote a short section to recipes as literature. Everybody, including me, swoons over Elizabeth David's beautiful recipes, even though you can't cook from them unless you know ahead of time what the dish is supposed to look and taste like before you start. Yet when did you last read a cookbook review that evaluated the style of the recipes?

I once taught a three-hour course at the Culinary Institute of America's Napa Valley campus on "The Recipe as a Literary Form." Pretentious, you say? I'm sure that if the day hadn't been so warm and if the students had had brains in their heads they would not all have fallen into deep, hypnotic states within fifteen minutes. But I am not discouraged. Occasionally, I've played with writing the same recipe in a multitude of ways besides the ubiquitous, increasingly tiresome imperative: active and passive (which Alice B. Toklas uses charmingly); past, present, and future; first person singular and plural ("first I strangled a cabbage . . ."); second and third persons; and variations on the imperative, from the harsh Alsatian voice ("You vill chop now . . .") to a more loving tone ("Squish the tomatoes with your hands until no large pieces remain. This should be quite enjoyable . . ."). The latter comes from the pizza recipe in my last book.

I used to tell a few jokes in every recipe. The beauty part is that you may give your readers a smile or two during their often-solitary confinement in the kitchen. The disadvantage is that very few jokes stay funny when you read them repeatedly. Instead, let's try to write our recipes as though they were literature.

JEFFREY STEINGARTEN is the food critic for *Vogue* magazine and the author of *The Man Who Ate Everything* and *It Must've Been Something I Ate*. His essays have received numerous awards from the James Beard Foundation and the International Association of Culinary Professionals. He lives in New York City.

Introduction

by Holly Hughes

T his year, it seemed that everybody I knew was on either the Atkins diet or the South Beach diet (or at any rate, they all *said* they were on those diets), and eating out was becoming totally joyless. The only person who'd admit to being interested in food anymore was the mother of one of my daughter's baseball team-mates who wanted to talk non-stop about her raw food regimen, while the rest of us eyed the post-game Krispy Kremes with sur-reptitious guilt and longing.

It was with great relief, then, that I turned to food magazines, cookbooks, and websites where I was reassured that people are still eating food, enjoying food, and obsessing over food as much as ever. True, there was plenty written about meat (so much so that I've included an entire section on it, "The Meat of the Matter"), but thankfully these were articles about loving meat, not about fearing carbs. Looking to fill the "Eating Out" section, I found hardly any pieces about stuffy high-profile restaurants, but lots fea-turing unpretentious local joints. Perhaps this is a function of the economy, or of a bunch of food editors all jumping onto the same bandwagon; if you like, blame reality TV. Still, it made me wonder if maybe America is finally getting bored with the one-upsmanship of trophy dining—*so* twentieth century. I certainly noticed fewer adoring profiles of big-name chefs in the food press; instead I found several wonderfully detailed narratives of the actual process of cooking (grouped in "Cooks At Work"). Apparently it's still okay to be enthusiastic about food. Whew.

The deeper I got into this year's reading, however, the more I began thinking about who these folks are who write all this stuff. Why would anyone choose to become a food writer? It's incredibly hard to make a living at it, for one thing. There's no category to honor food writing in the Pulitzer prize lists. And yet, I kept receiving hopeful submissions, of widely varying quality, from writers all over the country. Visit eGullet.com and you can scroll through dozens of wonderful essays written by food-writing hopefuls. And a plethora of food-themed weblogs have sprung up on the Internet, with tempting names like chocolateandzucchini.com, meathenge.com, mylatestsupper.com, iwasjustreallyveryhungry.com, and nicecupofteaandasitdown.com. They're just what you'd expect from internet writing—sloppy, unfiltered, ungrammatical, self-involved prose (folks, don't give up your day jobs)—but all the same, isn't it curious that there's such a large community of people out there who have so much time to think about food?

What is a food writer, anyway? I asked several of this year's contributors, and just about all of them started out as something else—chef, dishwasher, journalist, novelist, university professor, sportswriter, lawyer, advertising copy writer . . . the list is as long as our table of contents. Things may be changing: I know recent college graduates who aspire specifically to be food writers, and more and more culinary schools have added food writing to their curriculums. But still, there's no set career path for being a food writer, because there is no set definition of a food writer. Among our contributors, Peter Reinhart is a former priest and bread baker, Louise DeSalvo a feminist literary critic and biographer, but start talking pizza and they're fellow fanatics. A world-traveling bon vivant like James Villas is as different as possible from a regional social historian like John T. Edge, yet both write brilliantly about the food of the American South.

If we can't agree on how to define a food writer, maybe that's because we haven't yet agreed on what food writing is. Molly O'Neill's soul-baring diatribe in the *Columbia Journalism Review*, which leads off this book, is a devastating critique of the state of food writing today. She laments how food journalism is compromised by its symbiotic relationship with food sellers—restaurants, hotels, market chains, food product conglomerates—a tortuous relationship that's further illuminated by Mimi Sheraton in her candid memoir *Eating My Words* (excerpted here as "My Times at the *Times*"). The public would indeed be well served by writers trained to be investigative journalists, nutrition experts, and business critics as well as cooks. Robb Walsh's "Sex, Death and Oysters," Joe Dolce's "The Deal With Raw," and Jonathan Gold's "A Snail's Pace" demonstrate how a good writer can take a hard look at the food we eat and still whet your appetite.

I admire O'Neill's high standards, but I can't help but think that food writers have other roles to fill, too. In an America that's becoming more and more homogenized, for example, hometown newspapers owe it to their readers to celebrate local tastes, to champion area businesses, even if that means being a bit of a booster. It's the local papers who, this year, published so many stories about close-to-home food shopping that I had to add an entire new section called "To Market, To Market." When New Orleans's Brett Anderson writes about the last days of New York's La Caravelle, or Charlotte's Kathleen Purvis reviews a host of Manhattan barbecue joints, resolutely sticking to the local angle makes all the difference between a puff piece and a real story.

In times like these, too, we could all use more entertainment, and food writing that does that for us deserves a hand. Steve Almond's *Candyfreak* was the book I most often recommended to friends this year, and not only because there's a secret candy freak in all of us. Yes, this book is a fascinating account of struggling independent candy manufacturers, but what really makes it special is Almond's dark, mad humor (I'm talking laugh-out-loud-till-you-embarrass-yourself-in-public funny). Exuberant, funny writing makes Jason Sheehan's "Way to Go" so much more than a restaurant review. Julie Powell's "A Menu Marathon" slyly pokes fun at the pretensions of food magazines; who cares if you don't actually learn anything about cooking from it? Andy Borowitz isn't a food writer at all—he's a political satirist, and a wickedly funny one at that—but he happens to write about food in "Manning the Stove," and it's a hoot.

If we're asking food writers to be high-minded, why not let them range over the whole gamut of academic disciplines? Both the quarterly journal *Gastronomica* and the literary magazine *Tin House* are full of articles with a cultural anthropology slant; Laura Shapiro uses food to study social history in "Something From the Oven." And what about the psychology of eating (see Louise DeSalvo's "Appetite") or of cooking (Dan Barber's "The Clean Plate Club")?

I'd also argue for the value of food-writing-as-memoir. First-person essays like Greg Atkinson's "Forming a Palate," Matthew Amster-Burton's "Learning to Cook; Cooking to Learn," or Amanda Hesser's "Fundamental Pleasures" all get at something very fundamental about the nature of the culinary pursuit, at why it *matters*, in a way that objective journalism couldn't. Every piece in the section I've titled "The Family Meal" is part memoir; how else could a writer explore how eating together shapes a family? Even in more journalistic pieces, like Bruce Feiler's "My Life as a Hand Model," Matt Lee and Ted Lee's "New Wave Cooking: Do Try This at Home," and Andrew Todhunter's "La Carte", the first-person point of view works precisely *because* the writer himself is front and center, walking us through his efforts to accomplish something unusual. And although the first-person voice is often a lazy way to write a restaurant review, sometimes it rises beautifully above the whole messy fray: Read the final piece in this collection, by Min Liao, and you'll see what I mean.

When a food writer is at the top of his or her game, in fact, he or she can do it all at once. Take John Thorne's "Conflicted About Casseroles": what begins more or less as a book critique branches out to become culinary history, memoir, and recipe deconstruction, all borne along on the engaging stream of Thorne's conversational voice. I know more than one person who'll say that it was John Thorne's work that inspired them to take up food writing, and I totally see why.

Maybe that's the answer: Writers become food writers because that's what they want to write about. They bring whatever talents they have to the table. It could be as simple as that, or as complicated as that.

Well, if that's what these gifted folks want to write about, then that's what I want to read about. I hope you do, too.

The Food Biz

Food Porn

by Molly O'Neill
from the *Columbia Journalism Review*

The most discussed food article of the
year was this gutsy essay by Molly O'Neill
(formerly of the *New York Times*, now at
The New Yorker), an unflinching look at
where culinary journalism has been and
where it may be going. Smart, thoughtful,
passionate, it's a must-read.

On a balmy May evening in 1997, I was at a bookstore in
Santa Barbara, California, signing copies of my third cookbook. It wasn't my best book, and nearly every chapter of it had
previously appeared in my food column in *The New York Times
Magazine*. Nevertheless, nearly two hundred people waited to pay
me homage—as well as $26.95 for the book.

The magazine was one of the most powerful platforms for food
writing in the nation and, to the people in line, I was a rock star.
My mother, a sensible Ohioan, was with me that night and she was
appalled. She stood near as fans gushed admiration for my prose
and recipes.

Finally, as if unable to contain herself another second, my
mother interrupted one woman's compliments and asked: "Do
you actually cook that stuff?"

"Of course not," replied the customer, who looked like my
mother, tall, lean, with a white cap of stylishly coiffed hair. "Every
week I cut them out of the magazine and promise myself I will
cook them. Don't we all?"

The laughter that erupted was a deep ah-ha-ha-ha. It was a
truth-telling sort of laughter, the kind that started rising among

women in the late 1960s when, after cooking through both volumes of *Mastering the Art of French Cooking*, they began reading books like *The Feminine Mystique* and forming consciousness-raising groups.

The sound of it made me feel like I'd eaten a very, very bad clam.

I meant to be a journalist, a sort of latter-day Finley Peter Dunne, writing about the triumphs and inequities of private life as he had those of the public one. For more than twenty years I tried to tease the extraordinary from the mundane, and to use the familiar—the sprig of basil, the bottle of olive oil—to usher readers into social, geographic, and cultural worlds where they otherwise might not go.

But the people lining up to buy my book didn't see me as an interpreter of everyday life. They saw me as the high priestess of a world that exists almost exclusively in the imagination, the ambitions, and the nostalgic underpinnings of American culture.

And they were not mistaken.

It was a painful reckoning. But it was important, and it was timely. Some of the most significant stories today—the obesity epidemic, water purity, the genetic manipulation of the food supply as well as its safety and sustainability—are food-related. And while science and business writers, as well as general assignment reporters and a growing number of food scholars have and should continue to address these issues, food writers are uniquely suited to the discussion.

In addition to training and experience particular to the edible world, food writers enjoy a rare and intimate bond with readers. Shared tastes imply shared values and aspirations. A food writer is, therefore, trusted to disseminate the issues that can affect what readers put in their mouths.

And never before has interest in food been as avid or as widespread as it is today. Fifty years ago, for instance, fewer than twenty food magazines were published in the United States. Last year, 145 food magazines, quarterlies, and newsletters were produced in America and, if the circulation that each claims is accurate, a total of 19.7 million people read regularly about food. TV's Food Network claims that 78 million households subscribe. The number of books about food and wine sold each year continues to climb from the 530 million that *Publisher's Weekly* reported were sold in 2000. So the opportunity for food writers today is unprecedented in audience size alone.

The question is this: Will food writers pander to these readers or will they seize the chance to be better journalists?

Unfortunately, recent history—including my own—favors the former. In general, entertainment, rather than news and consumer education, has been the focus of food stories for nearly a decade. Food porn—prose and recipes so removed from real life that they cannot be used except as vicarious experience—has reigned.

Food writers have always walked the dangerous lines between journalism, art, and their role as handmaiden to advertising. But we have not wobbled quite so regularly in nearly a half century as we do today. Food has carried us into the vortex of cool. There, the urge to become part of the story is stronger than the duty to detach and observe and report the story.

ROOTS

Traditionally, there were several schools of food writing and each served as social arbiter. In the gentlemanly tradition of gastronomic prose, the food writer was a sort of everyman's "Jeeves," the one who knew all. The domestic science branch of food writing was the voice of an über-Mom. The merging of these two sensibilities was part of what created food-writer chic in the final years of the twentieth century.

As early as the 1840s, when food writing first appeared in American newspapers, culinary writers were already established as more than cooking instructors. They were trusted to describe the world, as explorers had in the earliest written accounts of food in America. They were also relied upon to supply guidelines for upward mobility. The first cookbook published in America, known as *American Cookery*, was written in 1796 by Amelia Simmons, presumably a member of the serving class, and gave clear instruction on cooking for the gentry. The cookery writing by abolitionists, ideologues, and dietary religionists also primed the culture to look to food writers for life advice.

That advice began to appear regularly in newspapers in the late 1880s. An enormous wave of immigration had brought people who wanted to live and eat like Americans, and newspaper publishers wanted each of them to read their papers. Women with sights set on the middle class needed instruction in living accordingly, and given the rise of suffrage and increased female literacy, newspapers were happy to oblige. Another social and economic change—the shift from making everything in the home to mass production—was also an incentive to publish food stories. Food, fashion, and fiction that were heart-rending, or inspiring, or an object lesson for gender or class training were as heady as free chocolate to Victorian ladies—and to the advertisers who wanted to reach them.

As nonpartisan commercial journalism grew, so did a code of ethics designed to protect its editorial integrity. Except in women's news. "During the time that women's pages were emerging, journalism was becoming more independent politically, and objectivity was emerging as the dominant journalistic ethic," says David Mindich, a professor of journalism at St. Michael's College. "But the women's pages were not included in the objective mix. Even into the twentieth century, women's pages were not seen as real journalism."

In fact, until the early 1940s, newspaper food writing was generally the province of home economists or reporters who'd failed elsewhere. Then, in the unprecedented prosperity of the postwar era, food began moving up the social scale.

RIPENING

Since Pliny, stories about food have located the reader in time and then, by evoking distant lands, exotic flavors, or lives unlived, taken the reader elsewhere.

For almost as long, gastronomic writing has also sought to ease readers' anxieties and to affirm their ambitions. Therefore, the aspirations of those who read food stories influence their style and content.

As the middle class grew after World War II, a reconciliation began between elite cuisine and the meals of everyday people. The concerns of those who cook (traditionally, women) and those who savor but do not cook (traditionally, men) became more similar. The polarization between continental taste (once considered the gold standard of cuisine) and American taste (once thought to be an oxymoron) began to subside.

These changes were reflected in the pages of *Gourmet* magazine and in the food coverage of the *New York Times*, and they suggest that a new audience—if not a nascent mass market—for fine food had taken root.

When *Gourmet* was introduced in 1941 it was conceived not as a food magazine, but as a general interest one. The early *Gourmet* was aimed at a small social elite that could afford to hunt, fish, and travel, and that viewed fine dining much as it did art, theater, or opera: as something one need only appreciate in order to possess. During its first decade, the magazine sounded as if it were written by and for members of "a pre-war London gentleman's club," wrote the food historian Anne Mendelson in an analysis of sixty years of *Gourmet* that appeared in the magazine's September 2001 issue.

The food advice that appeared during the magazine's first decade wasn't aimed at people who cooked; it was crafted for people who considered themselves connoisseurs. But by the 1950s, the magazine began to recognize people outside the old club. Its travel stories became more service-oriented; its recipes more accurate and concise; its tone less pompous and more practical.

As if to balance the shifting class lines of the postwar era, food was romanticized, primarily in nostalgic ways. In fact, according to Mendelson, the most important part of *Gourmet*'s identity in the 1950s was "an intense fixation on the past as the standard of meaning."

But even in the whirl of their purple prose and gossamer tales of edibles gone by, food writers promoted a fundamental shift in the way America began to view dinner in the 1950s. "Food acquired a . . . gloss of snobbery it had hitherto possessed only in certain upper-income groups," writes Nora Ephron in an essay called "The Food Establishment" that appeared in her 1967 book *Wallflower at the Orgy*. "Hostesses were expected to know that iceberg lettuce was déclassé and tuna fish casseroles de trop."

The photographs in *Gourmet* reflected this change. When I was growing up, an elderly neighbor subscribed to the magazine and I remember leafing through it before I could read, studying pictures of quiet streets dappled with light, charming doorways, and wide open, unpopulated vistas. But by the late 1960s, when I perused *Gourmet* while waiting in the orthodontist's office, there was a picture of girls in miniskirts outside a pub in London, and one of a long-haired boy careening around a fountain in Rome on a Vespa. There was a picture of people eating paella—people I wanted to know.

By 1968 good food was no longer remote and rarefied in *Gourmet*; it no longer revolved around a "romantic glorification of the past," wrote Mendelson. Good food was young. It drank. It showed thigh. It probably rubbed elbows with the Beatles. "Food became, for dinner-party conversations in the sixties, what abstract expressionism had been in the fifties," writes Ephron.

This evolution from food-as-fuel to food-as-aesthetic-experience was mirrored—if not urged along—by the food coverage in *The New York Times*.

From the nineteenth century until nearly the middle of the twentieth century, the *Times* published a single weekly column dedicated to food, and its titles, "The Household," "Hints for the Household," and "Timely Hints for the Household" suggested whom the column was written for.

In the late 1930s, however, food information in the *Times* became newsier and appeared under the heading "Food News of the Week." And while most stories maintained a dowdy and dutiful tone, a few suggested that food was social climbing. In 1940 a story by Dr. O. Gentsch, for instance, declared cooking "one of the greatest arts."

The best evidence that food had arrived, however, was the anointing of its own specialist. The term "food writer" first appeared in the *Times* on March 12, 1950. Given the intimate connection between food writing and the food industry, it may be no coincidence that the phrase made its debut in a story by Jane Nickerson about a press trip to the manufacturing plant of Tabasco sauce in Louisiana. Interestingly, Nickerson was the one of the first to apply news-side ethics to the food report.

When Craig Claiborne became food editor at the *Times* in 1957, he continued the trend, banning press trips, free meals, and gifts (other than food samples and cookbooks) for those who wrote in his pages. With an undergraduate degree in journalism and culinary training from École Hôtelière, the venerable Swiss hotel school, Claiborne treated food pages as if they were part of the news report. He also reformatted recipes and lifted them from within stories to an adjacent space, making them easier for aspiring cooks to follow. Many were, in fact, learning to cook from books, cooking classes, and the food section of the paper and, by melding culinary criticism, consumer information, and education, Claiborne became their guide. His authority rested, in part, on his gentlemanly reserve, on the fact that he was the paper's first male food editor. However, his most significant contribution, the four-star restaurant rating system with its protocol of multiple, anonymous visits, was not a result of his gender, but of his training as both a journalist and chef.

Claiborne's tenure at the *Times* spanned nearly thirty years. In 1976 food was broken out into its own section, called "Living," a rubric that suggested both simple sustenance and "really living," as in "the good life."

By then, Claiborne was established as one side of a gastronomic trinity that also included Julia Child, a.k.a. The French Chef on PBS, and James Beard, the cooking teacher, cookbook writer, and impresario.

Between them, they brought journalistic muscle as well as style and joy to the subject. In addition, each personified some of the characteristics that defined food writing until the last decade of the twentieth century; they embodied, in other words, the traits and qualities that lent cachet to culinary expertise. Claiborne's air of impeccability and unflagging curiosity engendered absolute trust in his readers. He also commanded a respect among his colleagues that had not previously existed. Beard's memoirist approach to food writing lent mystique to daily life and created an emotional resonance with readers. Child was a clown who made cooking fun and, week by week, demonstrated the delight of being wholly human and less than perfect.

Not one set out to be a food person. Beard imagined himself in the theater, Child wanted to be a spy, Claiborne had writerly ambitions. Food was Plan B for all of them. Each, therefore, exuded the delight and wonder of the amateur, a feeling that

resonated with the counterculture's antiestablishment, anticorpo-
rate cosmology. Food was fun and relatively lawless when I started
writing about it. The hurdle between being a culinary illiterate and
having food savvy was not particularly high. There was plenty of
room for idiosyncrasy, but most of all, the writers who shaped my
generation—primarily Claiborne, Child, Michael Field, M.F.K.
Fisher, Richard Olney, and Elizabeth David—exuded the excitement of discovery.

I wanted to be all of them, with a slice of Woodward and Bern-
stein on the side. My fantasy was fated. The "foodie stories" (such
as a chef profile, a report on an ingredient or cooking technique)
had slowly been eclipsing "news" stories (such as a report on
famine or food poisoning or a culinary event with news value) for
almost forty years.

The change seemed insignificant at first. In 1940, for instance,
the *New York Times* Index listed a total of 675 stories about food.
Of those, 646 were news stories and the remaining twenty-nine,
or 4 percent of the total food editorial that year, were "foodie"
stories. This percentage remained constant through the 1950s, but
in 1960 news stories about food slipped to 91 percent while
"foodie" stories rose to 9 percent. Ten years later, the percentage
of "foodie" stories rose another point to ten. By 1980, 36 percent
of the food stories in *The New York Times* had no news hook.

The shift largely occurred in the Claiborne era, and it was as
much a reflection of the culture as it was of his influence; nevertheless, the shift was one of Claiborne's deepest regrets. As I was
preparing to begin writing the weekly column about food that
Claiborne had formerly written in the *Times* magazine, I invited
him to lunch and asked his advice.

He told me that although I might want to write like Proust,
my audience just wanted to eat dinner. He advised me never to
run a column that lacked either a news element or an anecdote
that touched a universal chord. "When you remove the news you
lose the vitality of a story, its ability to touch real lives, its slow and
incremental way of reflecting the world," he said. "Before you
know it, you have the god-awful pretension and solipsism that
trivializes the entire subject and can only, in the end, compromise
the reporter."

Three years after Claiborne joined the *Times*, in 1960, 244 stories about food appeared in the paper. By the year 2000, 1,927 food stories were published in the *Times*. Eighty percent of them were foodie stories, 20 percent had news value.

ROT

I belong to what may be the last generation of Plan B food writers. I was a poet and a painter and I worked in restaurants to support my art. It was unusual for a woman to rise through the ranks of the hard-drinking, hard-working, blue-collar men that cooked in restaurants when I began working in them. My ascension was inextricably linked to the fact that I couldn't drink as much as my colleagues and by 10 PM was usually the only one who could read the orders and organize the subsequent proceedings. Possessing physical endurance and a college degree probably aided my ascent as well. I read voraciously, traveled, studied cooking in Paris and, because I was one of only several women chefs, my name became known in Boston, where I lived in the late 1970s—recognizable enough for *The Boston Globe* to ask me to write a story about pancakes. Earlier, I'd not have considered it: food writing would have been an embarrassment. But the times had changed. Within days I was the world's leading pancake expert—and a food writer.

When my first story appeared, the editor of *Boston Magazine* called and offered to turn me into a "great" food writer. I was young and stupid and arrogant enough to believe him, which was my good fortune: I got to work for a brilliant and difficult editor who understood how important food was to readers and the necessity of exhaustive reporting. In the five-year journalism apprenticeship that followed the decade I spent learning to cook, I was forced to report news stories, business stories, science, wine, travel, trend, and human-interest stories, and to write profiles. Unimpeachable ethics were assumed. Once, when I was still living around the corner from her in Cambridge, Julia Child told me, "You have to earn the right to all this fun somehow, dearie."

But the line that separated information-with-a-commercial-agenda from objective information was clearer in those days. A reporter who passed on freebies, discovered her own stories, and found three sources for each assertion had a reasonable chance of maintaining an independent view. Or so I thought. In fact, only part of the relationship between food writers and the food industry is blatant; other parts are all but invisible.

After extensive research for her 1986 book, *Perfection Salad*, a cultural history of how home cooking was hijacked by science and industry, Laura Shapiro concluded: "Food coverage is either written by the food industry or at the service of the food industry."

Food stories were, after all, first included in newspapers and magazines to attract the readers most likely to buy the products that were advertised in those pages. In the early twentieth century, when food processing began on an industrial scale, advertisers quickly realized that recipes using their products were potent selling tools. Food manufacturers established test kitchens that created thousands of recipes—using everything from gelatin to canned soup—and distributed the concoctions to food editors. To publications lacking the resources to create their own recipes, these handouts were a boon.

Marketers were not concerned by newspapers and magazines that shunned their free copy, meals, or junkets: if thousands of people are suddenly enamored of, say, the molded and gelled "Perfection Salad," then the recipe and its acolytes become a "trend" worthy of being noted in loftier publications.

Entering the food fray at the height of its bohemian chic, I was, of course, morally superior to food concepts that issued from industrial kitchens. I knew that an average of 20,000 new food products are introduced in the United States each year, that an average of $10 million to $12 million is spent to advertise food products, and that up to $50 million is often spent to introduce a snack item. I understood that my job was to question anything those dollars bought.

Nevertheless, even as I protected the public from nefarious comestibles—writing, for instance, about the dysentery-like reaction that a dietary fat substitute produced among the food writers attending its introduction ceremony, or exposing the synthetic truffle oil that had more in common with petroleum than it did

with expensive subterranean mushrooms—I was already participating in the most successful marketing campaign of recent
memory: olive oil.

The International Olive Oil Council, a consortium of olive
oil producers, exporters, and importers, was founded in 1959
expressly to increase olive oil sales by expanding its consumer
base from the ethnic fringes of American society into its mainstream. With an annual budget of about $1.5 million, says Fausto
Luchetti, the former director of the IOOC, "We understood
very clearly that we could not afford to compete with large
brands in America, and we spent that money almost exclusively
to influence the taste makers."

In the 1980s, the council began a major push. It publicized
dietary health research that championed olive oil and sponsored
seminars in tantalizing spots abroad to disseminate and debate that
information. The IOOC hired some of the country's most influential food and health writers to speak at these symposia. It hired
other food writers to lead trips to the Mediterranean to investigate olive oil production as well as olive oil-based cuisine and the
olive oil life-style.

I attended several of these events. Some of my closest food-
writing friends consulted for the council. I didn't write about the
events directly, but over time I found myself cooking more often
with olive oil and that shift was obvious in the recipes that I published. In 1994 I wrote a feature story about America's romance
with Mediterranean food, fashion, and décor.

The story was legitimate. But was the phenomenon bought and
paid for by the olive oil council? Maybe. Or maybe olive oil was
in the air and sun-baked Tuscan colors were on the walls of more
and more homes, and I was doing my job, responding to public
appetite.

Either way, the incident resides in the shady spot between being
an ethical journalist and being an arm of the food industry's marketing machine. Such gray areas—those that exist between education and promotion, as well as between personal friendships and
professional relationships—are what people seeking to influence
opinion are most apt to exploit today.

More shadowy land lies in the area of justifiable boosterism. Do

I, for instance, mention olive oil because it is delicious or because I believe the health claims associated with it? Or do I leap to believe the claims because I've been seduced by the Mediterranean mystique?

In 1982 "olive oil" appeared 483 times in the publications tracked by Nexis. Last year, the oil had 8,161 mentions. In that same period, olive oil imports rose from $8.4 million dollars worth to the $64.3 million worth that will be imported this year. Many in the persuasion business believe that for every dollar spent on food-related public relations three dollars would have to be spent on advertising to achieve the same results. Linda Luca, an advertising executive for McCann-Erickson in New York City who oversees $40 million worth of food advertising each year, regularly counsels clients to supplement their ad campaigns with public relations efforts aimed at food writers and editors.

"They are the ones who disseminate information, who usher taste from the high end of the food chain to the mass market," she says. "The food editor is the one you trust for what you put in your mouth."

If Luca is correct, the power to affect at least $900 billion worth of buying decisions resides in the fingers of food writers as they race across keyboards toward deadlines. That is the total amount America spent last year on conventional and specialty groceries, restaurant meals, and fast food. According to Competitive Media Report, a total of $12.3 billion was spent advertising food and restaurants.

Food is big business, and from that vantage point alone writing about food is serious business. The food and health connection is also serious business—and whether they are equipped with the skill to read and interpret scientific data or not, food writers have a profound influence over readers' food choices.

From the beginning of newspaper food coverage, the pages have been home to dietary fads and weight-loss schemes. Horace Greeley was himself an acolyte of Sylvester Graham, whose vegetarian moralism makes that of say, Dr. Dean Ornish, appear to be downright sybaritic. But it may be nothing more than the mists of time that differentiate the dietary faddism of that era from the fads promulgated by food writers today. After being diagnosed with hypertension and counseled to reduce his salt intake, for instance, Claiborne wrote a guide to cooking without salt called *Craig Claiborne's Gourmet Diet* in 1980. Based on the medical establishment's assumption that forswearing salt could stave off hypertension, Claiborne echoed the American Heart Association's position and rallied the public to join his low-salt life-style. Thus was a low-salt food industry born before further research revealed that although cutting salt consumption is critical for people who have high blood pressure, reducing it prior to the onset of high blood pressure generally does little to lower the chance of developing the disease.

More recently, food and health writers baptized the low-fat life-style and a wildly lucrative segment of the food industry was created to support it. In an article called "What If It's All Been a Big Fat Lie?" that appeared in *The New York Times Magazine* on July 7, 2002, however, the science writer Gary Taubes suggested that dietary fat theory was not science but an amalgam of poorly controlled studies, preconceived notions, and an assortment of private and commercial agendas. Even as the fat debate continues, the "low-carb" life-style is ascending in food and health pages.

Health myths are one of the aspects of food studies that Andrew F. Smith, who teaches culinary history at the New School University in New York, addresses in his paper, *False Memories: The Invention of Culinary Fakelore and Food Fallacies*, which he presented to the Oxford Food Symposium in 2000. Undocumented assertions, he writes, are the norm, rather than the exception in food writing for several reasons. Historically, food preparation has been passed along via an oral tradition and stories recited change over time, some information is dropped and other aspects added. In his studies, Smith has found that food stories are vulnerable to additions born of journalistic enrichment, logical error, local boosterism, individual puffery, and commercial promotion.

Food writing is also frequently guilty of "presentism fallacies," or the undocumented belief that because something is true in the present it has always been so, as well as "temporal jingoism," or the conviction that food is better today than were the victuals of earlier times.

These problems are symptomatic of work done by people whose enthusiasm is not quite matched by what Smith calls, "a canon of knowledge." George Lang, a restaurateur and author, was more direct in his assessment. "Culinary history is a collection of questionable happenings," he wrote in 1980, "recorded by persons of dubious credibility."

But the creation of hundreds of university-based food studies courses is already beginning to lend more intellectual rigor to food research and, by inference, food writing. "When I got into this field twenty-five years ago, there were about a hundred people who were writing seriously about food," says Smith. "Now, not a week passes that a decent food book doesn't come out of the academic or commercial press, and there are three to four thousand people working on food-related research."

A new generation of Plan A food writers, then, is already taking shape—people who not only have a working knowledge of the existing literature and traditional food-writing mistakes, but who are also educated to think analytically and apply science, history, and economics to food writing.

REGENERATION?

In addition to the need for renewed rigor, food writing also faces other challenges. The current cultural landscape needs less wistful nostalgia and more food coverage oriented to the here and now. The times also seem to beg for more authority and less autobiography.

This will require some subtle recalibration of the six components of food writing—reportage, education, guidance, interpretation, criticism, and motivation—a process of de-emphasizing some of the elements that have over the past twenty-five years become more pronounced.

Led as much by Claiborne's frequent profiles of them in *The New York Times Magazine* as by the era's idealization of "working-class heroes," American chefs began to be viewed as trailblazers and life-style gurus in the late 1970s. And the celebration of the amateurism of the early Claiborne era began to give way to a celebration of professionalism.

Chefs, and by association food writers, became stars, an image bolstered by the habit of dressing sex up in gourmet drag in food stories. Books such as *Blue Skies, No Candy*, the 1976 novel by Gael Greene, the restaurant critic for *New York Magazine*, that chronicled the awakening of a young woman's appetite for good sex and good food, brought an outlaw aura to food writing. The mystique of food writing received another boost from *Heartburn*, Nora Ephron's 1983 novel whose heroine is a cookbook writer.

But even as the profession came to be seen as a sexy life-style arbiter, food writers had, by the early 1980s, begun to respond to public taste rather than lead it. In part, this was because food became news during the decade and covering news is, by its nature, reactive. Nouvelle Cuisine unseated traditional French cooking, and America finally began to mint its own tastemakers—native-born chefs. In California, New Orleans, New Mexico, Boston, and New York, American cooking was being elevated to "cuisine."

At first, these happenings were reported in excited trumpet blasts—it was so cool to see the small town of Food becoming Food Nation! But as the decade waned, food writing began to sound arch. The detachment was an understandable response to the 1980s ethos: although more and more people were turning gourmet, the conversion had less to do with sensual engagement than it had to do with status and the appearance of living like a sybarite.

The pursuit of lean body mass was, after all, second only to the pursuit of lucre in the early 1980s. Treadmills and Stair-Masters gobbled rare leisure hours, liquid diets were vogue, and both anorexia and bulimia were on the rise. Food writing became voyeuristic, providing windows into a world of unattainable bodies and unimaginable disposable income and time, an unreal world.

There is a fine line between soothing readers' anxiety and becoming the Victoria's Secret of the Fourth Estate.

This world was increasingly attractive to advertisers. *The New York Times* began publishing the first freestanding magazine supplement on food in 1979. The appearance of the advertising-driven insert signaled that food had become a comfortable atmosphere for advertisers such as automobile, liquor, and credit-card companies. Food, in other words was not just food, it was a life-style. And, as the decade progressed, the taste for living high on the food chain trickled into the middle class from the wealthier spheres and spread from both coasts into the nation's center. At the same time, dietary health concerns became more pronounced, everyday life became more frenetic—and fine homemade meals became the stuff of dreams.

Given the dissonance between food fantasies and everyday eating, the birth of food porn was all but unavoidable. Waxing sentimental may have been questionable art, but as a counterpoint to the technological changes that clicked through the culture over the past three decades, nostalgia served an important role. Likewise, first person singular was a reassuringly human voice; it was also a logical extension of the confessional mode that was popularized in the feminism of the 1970s.

Some social analysts believe that citizens of an increasingly violent world watch crime shows to feel safe. Reading food writing offers a similar sort of reassurance. People tell me that they read my cookbooks "like novels," to enter an alternate reality where cooking is slow and leisurely and imbued with a comforting glamour.

The upper middle class is willing to pay dearly for these feelings. By the mid-1990s, it was not uncommon for people to spend much of their disposable income on fancy food and wine, traveling to eat, and building kitchens large enough to accommodate crowds: cooking was becoming a spectator sport.

When reporting a story for *The New Yorker* several years ago, I found that the less people cook, the more money they spend on cooking appliances. Like the people who stood in line to buy my cookbook, people bought professional-grade ranges in the hope that they would one day use them.

It should not have been surprising when, in the final decade of the twentieth century, food writers became the voice of an idealized past, issuing bulletins from a land where pies cooled perpetually on windowsills. Even so, I was startled in 1990 when an editor at *The New York Times* proposed cutting six words—"the mad arc of Norah's knife"—from a profile I'd written about M.F.K. Fisher.

Fisher had written the words about a cook who had worked for her family and had later murdered her own husband. The editor said that mad knives were not good for my image. "Let's leave the raging knives to the news side," said the editor. "We need you to be the princess of our little patch of blue."

There is a place in newspaper food sections, and food magazines for cheery, revisionist, nostalgic waxings, for songs of dew-kissed baby lettuces, for Proustian glances back, and for personal opinion. It is impossible, after all, to write about food without writing about the self. But there is a line between soothing readers' anxieties and becoming the Victoria's Secret of the Fourth Estate.

Today that line is as fine and brittle as a thread of spun sugar. It divides vibrant, responsible, and useful food journalism from words written at the service of the food industry, food writing that reflects the reality of its era from food writing that is a fantasy.

The affluence that prompted the mass-marketing of epicureanism and the emergence of food porn in the last half of the twentieth century has given way to economic uncertainty and dietary trepidation. Already, editors and writers are struggling to adjust to the changed atmosphere.

The public's response to Michael Pollan's best-selling book, *The Botany of Desire*, and the acclaim that Eric Schlosser garnered for his *Fast Food Nation* suggest that readers are, once again, hungry for solid reportage, fearless analysis, independent opinion, and knowledgeable interpreters and guides.

The fact that neither Pollan nor Schlosser identify themselves as food writers is a sad commentary on the trajectory of the genre over the past decade. But the talent to retake the journalistic high road exists—and more food experts capable of tackling the difficult and controversial subjects that begin (or end) at the table are being trained in university-based programs every day.

The stories to prove their mettle—all the instances and variations of the convergence of health, environmental, and legal concerns around food—are waiting to be documented. Together, they could unravel the current American food chain as certainly as *The Jungle* did nearly a hundred years ago.

With the support and encouragement of their editors and

publishers, food writers can take a leading role in each of these discussions. We also need to merit the support. And to understand that readers are hungry for joy and passion, hungry for the writers they trust in a nearly familial way to distill scientific and economic information, as well as interpret fashion, manners, and mores.

My Times at the *Times*

by Mimi Sheraton

from *Eating My Words*

Sheraton's entertaining, frank autobiography spilled the beans on her tenure in one of America's most coveted food-writing jobs, chief dining critic for the *New York Times*. With clear-eyed candor, she recounts the professional pressures that lay behind all those fabulous restaurant meals.

I t's okay to slap a man in the face, but you don't have to cut his cheek with your ring. Remember, have a little *rachmones* . . ." With that advice, enforced by the Yiddish word for compassion, Abe Rosenthal anointed me food critic of the *New York Times* in August 1976.

"Let's have a celebration lunch!" suggested Larry Van Gelder. "I say it's hot dogs from Nathan's for all."

It was the perfect choice, not only because I passionately love hot dogs (the closest I come to a junk food predilection) but mostly because the Nathan's Famous branch then on Times Square harked back to my childhood days at the Coney Island original, where I had a prophetic first exercise in concentrated, comparative tasting. To celebrate graduation from elementary school, a group of us were out for a night of rides and carousing, and we began to argue about the relative merits of hot dogs at Nathan's and the nearby Feltman's, where, legend has it, the American hot dog—a frankfurter served on a warm bun—was invented by the owner, Charles Feltman, in the 1870s. Before the evening ended, we had made four round-trips between the two, downing eight specimens each just to be absolutely sure of our verdict. Even if I could remember the winner it would be moot, as Nathan's Famous is the only option still standing, Feltman's having closed in 1954. Yet in that simplistic comparison, I unwittingly began a technique I would resort to when rating loftier fare such as caviar, truffles and cheese as a professional food critic.

We sized up the hot dogs by appearance (bright burnished red and sleek, not gray-brown or wrinkled), aroma (fresh and spicy, *not* not stale or sour), texture (meaty, tender and snappily juicy, not mealy, dry or rubbery), flavor (smoky beef, peppery and garlicky) and after-flavor (no bitter or medicinal lingerings). For the sake of purity, we tried them with and without rolls and mustard. (Ketchup and relish were never authentic dressings for a New York wiener and I don't recall Nathan's or Feltman's ever serving sauerkraut.)

Despite my earlier experiences as a restaurant critic, I felt a special burden descend upon me, awed as I was by the *Times*'s reputation for seriousness and because of its power, which put much at stake for both restaurant owners and customers. I was clear about my main allegiance being to the public, but I also wanted to give owners a fair shake; I not only followed the *Times*'s rule about a three-visit minimum before writing a restaurant review but often went six or eight times and in one case twelve, just to be sure.

In the seven and a half years that followed, the reviews I most enjoyed were those in which I reported on very good restaurants not generally in the public eye, none more so than the one in which I gave three stars to Rao's on August 19, 1975. A tiny corner bar in Spanish Harlem, formerly an Italian neighborhood, Rao's had eight tables and a clientele that included mobsters, journalists, sports figures and assorted neighborhood types who hung around the bar in undershirts. Dick and I were introduced to it by our friend and local Democratic New York state assemblyman, William F. Passannante, who wisely introduced me as Mrs. Falcone. Looking much as it does now with its year-round Christmas decorations and photos of celebrity patrons on the walls, it was run by chef-owner Vincent Rao, who cooked wearing a ten-gallon hat, and his wife, Anna, always an immaculate vision in starchy whites. The food, Italian-American classics such as seafood salad, meatballs, pastas, lemon chicken and sausages and peppers, was sublime and I wanted to write about the place.

After my third visit, I announced myself, and Frank Pellegrino, nephew of the owner and the manager of the dining room, said it would be all right for me to write a few lines. I said that I would write as many lines as I wanted to and did. The result was that Rao's telephone rang off the walls to such an extent that a few callers were told where they could go, and eventually, the receiver was taken off the hook. Feeling this would all blow over after their August vacation, the Raos and Frank were surprised—and, ultimately, delighted—that it did not.

Shortly after the review appeared, I had a call from Lt. David Durk, of the New York City Police Department, reminding me of his book, *The Pleasant Avenue Connection,* written with Ira J. Silverman and Arlene Durk. It was a novel based on his work as an undercover detective investigating organized crime and he pointed out that Rao's used to be the site for "mob sit-downs," where matters of vital importance were decided, a sort of raffish credential, I thought. Such activities hardly drive the public away as proven recently when a customer shooting at Rao's brought a renewed flood of requests for reservations. I even teased Frank Pellegrino about having staged it to renew luster to the restaurant's increasingly tame reputation.

I always resisted the temptation to keep a few choice finds for myself by not reviewing them, preferring to get credit for the discovery.

Another review I counted as a triumph was the four-star rating I gave to Vienna '79, a suave, modern Austrian restaurant on East 79th Street. I had not heard about it until a year after it opened, but the food was so elegantly and lightly rendered yet full of authentic flavors, all in a stunning setting devoid of the usual Vienna Woods kitsch, that I felt it deserved the rating. I never made the automatic judgment that one ethnic cuisine was categorically better than any other and tried to approach each visit to each restaurant as though I had never been there before, totting up the score for all visits at the end. To be fair, on a first visit I regarded every restaurant as eligible for four stars and even awarded them to Hatsuhana when it was new and innovative and prepared the most impeccable sushi.

Star ratings were the subject of intermittent debates as they were used in no other criticism at the *Times*. It was begun by Craig Claiborne, following the Michelin tradition. For a while I agreed with those who thought it childish, finding it annoying to deal with and feeling that readers should make their own judgments after reading the reviews. Also, when a rating was low, many would skip the review altogether, thereby missing details that might have proven interesting. I soon changed my mind, first because readers seem to love seeing stars, but also because they represent an instant, reductive score. If the ratings are decent, restaurateurs like them, too, as an easy way to succinctly report an accolade in an advertisement or in a window. More important, however, I came to realize that having to reduce my opinions to an exact score made me more diligent about deciding how I truly felt.

"When a critic shows up unexpectedly at a restaurant and is recognized, what can the chef do to improve the food on such short notice?"

The short answer is, "Just about everything."

And that's why I became obsessed with preserving my anonymity for as long as I possibly could. Any food professional like a chef, a restaurateur or a food writer who claims that little can be done is either a fool or a liar: a fool because he or she cannot know very much about cooking techniques. More likely, such a person is a liar who is loath to admit otherwise because that would make his or her job less pleasurable or, perhaps, even impossible if a publication cannot afford such costly research and so allows its critic to accept free meals. (My expenses ran about $95,000 in 1983, my last year at the *Times*.)

The longer I reviewed restaurants, the more I became convinced that the unknown customer has a completely different experience from either a valued patron or a recognized food critic; for all practical purposes, they might as well be in different restaurants.

Although legendary after only three years in existence, Le Cirque, in its original home in the Mayfair Hotel, received just two stars in 1974 from one of my predecessors, but its standing as a celebrity circus under the direction of owner Sirio Maccioni was out of proportion to its respectable rating for food. Judged by the gossip column names who gathered daily to blow air kisses and stuff their pockets with petits fours before leaving, it might have rated an entire constellation of its own. Shortly after I joined the *Times,* but six months before I became the restaurant critic, Pierre Franey took me to lunch at Le Cirque and introduced me to Maccioni and his then chef-partner, Jean Vergnes.

Eighteen months later, I safely slipped passed Sirio, Vergnes and the effusively corny, croupier-like maître d', Joseph, eagle-eyed for celebrities but blind to unprepossessing interlopers. In the course of about six visits, I was subjected not only to meals that ranged from very good to merely passable, with a watery sauce on the house's famed spaghetti primavera (snobbishly off the menu and so ordered only by the in crowd), duck that tasted of stale grease, lamb delivered well done when ordered rare, oversalting of everything and grainy soufflés.

The real travesties were the service and general treatment: seating us at cramped corner tables near the kitchen door, even though many others were available; keeping early arriving guests at the bar until our party was complete (forgiveable only in an inexpensive restaurant where turnover is crucial); and on one occasion, seating friends before we arrived and then putting us at a different table where we waited for thirty minutes before discovering Joseph's carelessness or, really, his lack of interest. Pepper mills and cheese graters were not offered to us, nor were nightly specials—the glowing, roseate red mullets, the fragrant white truffles—incredibly enough shown to regulars seated right next to us as though we did not exist. At the last dinner, when the captain presented the dessert wagon, he called out, "What kinda pastry do you want, lady?"

Reducing Le Cirque to one star in August 1977, I earned kudos from many who had shared my fate and brickbats from its most vocal fans as well as from Sirio, who complained to Franey and Craig Claiborne, but to no avail.

Le Cirque was not the only blatant example of why a critic should remain unknown. One evening at the Four Seasons restaurant, where I expected to be recognized, our guests arrived twenty or twenty-five minutes ahead of us as prearranged. Also according to plan, after a few minutes, they ordered appetizers of smoked salmon and pâté. Just as the captain started to slice a dried-out tail end of salmon on the tableside gueridon, Dick and I arrived. Recognizing us, the captain spun the cart toward the kitchen, returning a few minutes later with a whole new side of salmon that he began to slice—in the choice middle, yet—as he greeted us. "Good evening, Miss Sheraton, Mr. Falcone . . . Nice to see you here."

"Especially nice for our friend who ordered the salmon," I answered.

Through the years, fresh breads and cakes replaced stale ones at several places when I appeared even if it was too late in the evening for new cakes to be cut. Wilted floral centerpieces were replaced by brighter blossoms. Once, I spotted the homemade tortellini I had ordered being carried into a new East 58th restaurant from its sister restaurant with its older, superior kitchen across the street. *Fatta in casa* indeed, but in which *casa*?

But none of these top the abysmal experiences I encountered at Régine's, which I rated "Poor" in January 1982. We arrived on a Saturday night for a second anonymous visit to this bustling New York branch of the Parisian supper club directed by the henna-haired social dominatrix, Régine. Euro-trash and local climbers could hardly wait to get in. It took weeks to wrest an eight o'clock reservation for this busiest night. The reservation was in the name of Mr. Lawrence, as in Lawrence Van Gelder. Steering us through the jam-packed room, the maitre d' acknowledged the reservation but sighed, "Oh, I don't know where I'm going to seat you. We are inundated with royalty tonight!" Then, in an aside to a captain he whispered, "The king will be here at midnight with six bodyguards . . ."

Not a very popular king, I thought with glee, realizing that great copy was in the making. We were inched over to a tiny table where two of us were seated in the aisle so that our chairs would be kicked rhythmically by the passing parade. What followed was agonizingly slow and distracted service and food that included over-the-hill shellfish, rubbery quenelles, acrid duck pâté and pastry with the texture of Uneeda biscuits. On this and two other visits I ordered a soufflé and each time was given the extraordinary excuse that the soufflé oven was not working. Recalling the ritual four questions asked at the Passover seder, I thought of a fifth: "Wherefore is a soufflé oven different from all other ovens?" Or could it possibly be that the kitchen didn't want to bother making soufflés for unimportant guests? At the end of the evening, our captain asked if dinner had been satisfactory and when we indicated it was not, he shrugged and said, "Well, you can't fight City Hall!"

At a lunch one day when the captain ignored me and two women friends, we, in desperation, ordered desserts from a waiter. When he failed to deliver, we caught the captain's eye only to be told, "If Madame knew how to order properly from a captain instead of from a waiter, perhaps she would get things promptly." I was often assured by many in the field that such reviews taught New York restaurateurs a lesson and that service had improved and, skeptical though I tried to be, as I gradually became known I almost was convinced of that. But proof that little had changed came by way of Ruth Reichl's first review of Le Cirque in the *New York Times* in 1993, shortly after she became the third critic to follow me. Her report of meals at Le Cirque, before and after being known, seemed to echo many of my long-ago experiences at that restaurant and Régine's, complete with references to royalty.

The instances of a chef or a manager doing nothing special for recognized critics are few, limited to those practitioners who think they are doing everything right, or to others impervious to reviews. Those in the know were always extra polite, served larger portions of the best cuts, kept busboys refilling water glasses after every sip and surrounded us with enough servers to perform a heart transplant. In a few old-style Italian restaurants, mushrooms—apparently symbols of elegance—were heaped over everything.

Salt was another giveaway. I preferred not to have chefs gratuitously protecting my health and often faulted kitchens for undersalting. When I was recognized, therefore, my food often was so bitingly salty that I returned it, undoubtedly causing the chefs to wonder if I really knew my own mind and palate. Some were reported to complain to colleagues, "First she says there is not enough salt, then that there is too much." Exactly!

When food is cooked to order, much can be done with it and often is, especially at the expensive, trendy establishments. But even in the least expensive Chinese restaurants, cooks can choose only the best ingredients properly cut, and stir-fry them in a well-cleaned wok with fresh rather than re-used oil, then add authentic seasonings not tempered to the American palate, all big steps toward curing the most common flaws in presenting that cuisine. That last consideration about authentic seasoning applies not only to hot and spicy seasonings in Hunan, Sichuan, Mexican and Indian dishes but to garlic in Italian food, lard in German and some American dishes, cilantro and lemongrass in Southeast Asian specialties and more.

In addition, all fish, poultry and meats that are not prepared in advance can be cooked as ordered—rare, medium or well-done. Such requests accounted for some of the longest waiting periods I suffered when recognized, as, for example, a steak accidentally done past my requested rare being served to another diner, while a second was started on the grill for me. The much hyped but long-gone Palace on East 59th Street, known more for its high prices than for its excellence, had an ostentatious Louis-the-Last decor reminiscent of better dress departments in Saks Fifth Avenue and Neiman Marcus. It was two years old and still a hot topic when I reviewed it in 1977, and I invited the *Times*'s wine writer, Frank Prial, and his wife, Jean, to join us, so that he could critique the wine list. On this, my second visit, we were made from the start and were accorded lavish service except for the inexplicable hour-and-a-half wait between a fish course and the roasted duck with green peppercorn sauce I ordered. Months later I learned from a former kitchen worker that it had taken three ducks to get one cooked to the rosy-red, medium-rare perfection deemed suitable for me. True to the restaurant's reputation for high prices, my check was relatively the biggest I have ever racked up—about $850—primarily because during the duck-induced pause, Prial tiptoed through and ordered from the pricey, exceptional wine list.

Even on short notice much can be done to improve many prepared dishes shortly before they are served if the chef deems it necessary for a critic or a highly prized client. Soups and the gravies or sauces of stews and braised meats can be thinned or thickened and their seasonings corrected, while more of better ingredients can be added (like clams to clam chowder), or a fresh vegetable garnish prepared. With any sort of meatloaf or pâté, dried end slices can be eliminated (as with the Four Seasons salmon), or they might be served to unknowns, or whole loaves can be started if the cut ones have been around too long. In extreme circumstances, say, when a dish is scorched or otherwise beyond repair, the critic may be told that the last portion has been sold—hard to believe when it occurs at a 12:30 lunch, as it once did.

In 1984, when I wrote on this subject for *Vanity Fair,* I received a call from Adi Giovanetti, the proprietor of the prominent Il Nido. "Signora, you don't know the half of it," he said. "There is a lot more that we can do, especially if you order an appetizer. That gives us plenty of time to fix the main course."

For these reasons and more, and following examples set by the Guide Michelin and my predecessors at the *Times,* I tried to remain anonymous. And fueled by the romantic notion of undercover agents in disguise, I believe I was the first restaurant critic to collect a wardrobe of wigs. One was an auburn pageboy affair with straight bangs that I dubbed the Greenwich Village Lady Poet. A second, the Five Towns Macher, was done up as a silver-blond bouffant cascading over one eye. The third was a long, loose, comb-down of black hair that partially obscured my face in the style of an anguished activist, perhaps more Mimi Montag than Susan Sontag. I usually went to dinner directly from the *Times* or from my home and, not wanting colleagues or neighbors to know what my disguises looked like, I awkwardly donned them in taxis with only a small purse mirror to check results.

Despite perfect eyesight, I bought several pairs of eyeglasses, accessories no one associated with my face. I had them fitted with nonprescription lenses that were tinted, the better to obscure my glance as I studied the room. That last was a lesson I learned during a breakfast at Lou Mitchell's in Chicago's financial district, where this super coffee shop attracts early-bird workers from the mercantile and stock exchanges. Standing on the long waiting line, I tried to figure out the pattern of action. After a few minutes the manager approached, offering me the little box of Milk Duds distributed to ladies-in-waiting and asked, "So where is your place?" When I looked confused at the question, he continued, "I figure you must be in the business because of the way your eyes are working the room."

I made reservations in fictitious names or in those of friends dining with us. When the names were totally fake, I sometimes forgot which I used. Dick and I overcame that touchy situation by expressing embarrassment at the desk and apologizing for not being able to recall who we were dining with and suggesting that a peek at the reservation book would help. The ploy always worked, although it made us appear to be having a precocious senior moment.

Sometimes I paid for meals with the credit cards of dining companions, but usually I paid in cash, necessitating thrice weekly advances from the *Times* cashier, who always seemed grumpy at my requests, as though I was profligate with his money. At first, such advances were always in twenty-dollar bills, creating large bundles and a suspicious modus operandi, so I began placing advance orders for different denominations. At first I feared that paying cash would be a giveaway, but I needn't have worried; it was (and remains) a fairly common way to hide unreported income, both for customers and those restaurateurs who might be so inclined.

Fellow diners were warned not to call me Mimi, with Clara or Louise suggested as substitutes, because I feared a staff member might be alert to that name, if to nothing else. Alas, the few incurable Mimi-sayers were never invited again. Intermittently, word would get back to me that some lay diners deliberately used that name for precisely the reasons I avoided it. There were even more brazen types who used to call in my name for a hard-to-get reservation and to receive special treatment, and some who, once there, announced they were me or my assistant, hoping for a free meal. A few wisely suspicious restaurateurs knew I did all of my own eating and called the *New York Times* operator (who would not give out staff telephone numbers), asking that I call them so that they could check on the imposters.

One such attempt at securing a difficult reservation was made by my cousin, the painter and art dealer Wallace Reiss. Knowing I would not ask for special consideration on anyone's behalf, he called asking for a table at Le Cygne right after I gave it four stars, announcing that he was my cousin. "That's what they all say, monsieur," was the answer he got, and deserved. A great cook and a passionate food lover, Wally and his wife, Irene, sometimes accompanied us on review forays. Inevitably, as we approached the entrance he would whisper, "I hope they recognize you so we get great food."

Evidence of similar chicanery was rarely more telling than at a charming little Cuban restaurant on Cornelia Street in Greenwich Village, run by a young American woman who had studied that cuisine. Our companions that evening were two of our closest friends and most experienced Green Berets, Shirley and Sidney Cohlan, both pediatricians who, it often seemed, took care of every child in New York, our son included. Sure enough, when we entered the restaurant they realized that the chef-owner had been their patient. Not wanting to blow my cover, or to be rude, they introduced us as Mr. and Mrs. Anderson. I decided that I would use the advantage to get a line on the owner and I asked how business was.

"Oh, just great," she said, "and it's going to get much better. Last week, Mimi Sheraton was here."

"Really?" I answered. "That must have been exciting for you. Was she nice? Did she like the food?"

"Very nice," she answered, "but of course she doesn't make up her mind until she has been at least three times, and then you don't know until you read the review."

Happy that she at least had some details correct, I made two subsequent visits as Mrs. Anderson, then gave the restaurant two stars. When the owner called to thank me, I departed from my practice of not revealing myself even after a review appeared, in case I had to return or encountered the owner or a staff member in another restaurant.

"Do you remember the night the Cohlans came in for dinner?" I asked. "I was with them when you said I had been in the week before. What made you think that other woman was me?"

"My press agent brought her and introduced her as you. I pay him based on the number of press people he brings in," she answered.

"If I were you I would fire him," I advised.

At another dinner at Il Cortile on Mulberry Street in Little Italy, James Greenfield was dining with friends who knew the owner. When they introduced Jimmy as being at the paper, the owner said, "You must recognize the woman sitting two tables behind you . . ."

Looking around, Jimmy said he did not.

"Oh, you just don't want us to know . . . It's Mimi Sheraton."

"I see her every day and I swear to you that is not Mimi Sheraton," Jimmy reported saying, doubting that he was believed.

Confusion about my identity resulted in other amusing occurances, none more so than at a sushi restaurant near the *Times* building. Since my reviews were submitted on Tuesdays for the Friday "Weekend" section, where they then appeared (and still belong), Abe Rosenthal, the executive editor, looked for the chance to beat the crowds to a top-rated place, especially for Japanese or Indian food, cuisines he had acquired a taste for as a foreign correspondent in those countries. Seeing a two-star review for this nearby sushi outpost, he made a reservation as always, saying it was for the editor of the *New York Times*. When he arrived, his greeting from the owner was, "Ah, Mimi Sheraton, we are happy to have you here." Nothing he said could dissuade the smiling, bowing staff, who apparently did not recognize Mimi as a female name, and so addressed him by my name for the entire evening despite his efforts to make it clear that he was *the* editor, A. M. Rosenthal, and that Mimi Sheraton was, *merely,* the restaurant critic and a woman. He was at my desk by ten the next morning, laughing over the tale, but not without a certain smirk of resentment at his own name ringing no bells.

The Top Ten

by Patric Kuh

from *Los Angeles* Magazine

> Like it or not, just about every restaurant reviewer has to churn out an obligatory annual round-up article. In Patric Kuh's deft hands, however, this series of capsule write-ups become snapshots defining the L.A. dining scene at that evanescent moment of time.

The restaurant scene in Los Angeles is flourishing in a way it hasn't since the arrival of Spago. Here are the newcomers that are helping to usher in a new golden age.

All cities are defined by their restaurants, but L.A. more so than most. Here a particular address can bring the expanse of Los Angeles into vibrant, if brief, focus. The clamor of a dining room can give us an early glimpse of who we are to become. In the mid 1970s, when Jean Bertranou led a veritable revolt from behind the stoves of L'Ermitage on La Cienega, restaurants defined the epochal changes taking place. Breeding ducks with Michael McCarty in the high desert, hosting the likes of Paul Bocuse, encouraging young guns such as Wolfgang Puck to remain in L.A., Bertranou helped pry the city from the era of Perino's and sent it confidently into the age of Spago.

We are experiencing a renaissance again. Over the past 18 months we have seen a flurry of restaurant activity that has all the makings of a golden age. We might no longer expect dining rooms to capture our times so much as be their antidote. We live in a state of electronically induced anxiety. We are constantly reachable and pageable, exposed to scrawled text, bounced–back messages, rolled-over minutes, incompatible equipment, rebooted screens, and system-down funk. Restaurants are where the frayed ends of daily life can be spliced; the restaurant table is where the scrawl stops.

To imply that the restaurants that make up our Top Ten are sanctuaries is to place them in the hushed atmosphere of yesteryear. Daylight floods these rooms; none is cosseted in dark red velvet. Their elegance is not underlined at every opportunity but presented, as true elegance must be, as a throwaway gesture. Tradition is implicit, not spelled out on menus. I'm thinking of the silver-plated water coasters at A.O.C., the brothel couch at Opaline, the potato chips at the bar at Sona, the rustle of olive leaves in the courtyard at Bastide. All are flecks in the overall experience and yet are the details that convey the soul of each establishment. That is the way of restaurants. They offer their freeze-frames amid balsamic tastings, ladled soups, and foamed essences. They reveal their emotions in fleeting instants.

A.O.C.

One rarely sees the word *levant* anymore. It describes the shores of the eastern Mediterranean, from Greece to Egypt, where young English lords on their grand tours would sow oats and see ruins. It's due to be dusted off. Many of today's cooks base their styles on the products of this broad region, and none does so with more heart, skill, joy, and oomph than Suzanne Goin. A.O.C., an acronym for *Appellation d'origine contrôlée,* the French laws that govern wine and a few other goodies like *lentilles du Puy* and blue-legged chickens from the Bresse region, is the second restaurant of her partnership with Caroline Styne. Devoting the menu to small dishes has liberated Goin from the strictures of the appetizer–main course–dessert format and allowed her to offer her passions sampler-size. A salad of beets, tangerines, and mint snaps with acidity; a plate of escarole, radicchio, anchovy, and mustard is a testament to intelligent cooking. Grilled quail with pomegranate and pine nuts, lamb skewers with feta salsa *verde,* fried *tetilla* cheese with quince paste and *romesco*—with these delights one dips a toe into turquoise waters and eases right in. *Dinner nightly. 8022 W. 3rd St., 323-653-6359.*

BASTIDE

When Alain Giraud walked into the Paris offices of Andrée Putman to discuss the design of his L.A. restaurant, he talked to her about the *cantou*, the immense fireplace that anchored his grandmother's kitchen deep in provincial France. It was under that massive flue, where in winter months farm implements could be fixed, dried beans shelled, meats smoked, and stories traded, that Giraud's culinary sensibility was formed. If you take the primal power of that scene and suffuse it with the light, sound, and flavors of Provence, you get the essential nature of Giraud's cuisine.

His is the antithesis of fusion cooking. In his native Correze, one didn't draw on another continent; one wasn't even curious about how they did things in the next village. With years of experience behind him in such noted kitchens as Le Grand Vefour in Paris and Citrus in Los Angeles, Giraud has returned to a style that is brilliant in its refined rusticity. The result has something ageless about it. When ingredients come together, they glow with meaning and renewed tradition, and like the first berries and early summer's *fromage blanc,* their union seems positively preordained. *Dinner Monday through Saturday. 8475 Melrose Pl., 323-651-5950.*

CHLOE

Jeff Osaka grew up in Crenshaw, Christian Shaffer in Culver City. They worked as chefs for many years at different restaurants before meeting at the short-lived Drake's in Venice. When they found it shuttered one morning, they decided it was time to open their own place. Chloe is named for Osaka's three-year-old niece and abuts the Ballona Wetlands; if the restaurant wasn't in one of the last small beach towns in Los Angeles, it would be among the most talked about in the city.

This is one of those great little spots where, at the start, an abundance of heart made up for a shortage of finances. Osaka's brother did the electrical wiring; Shaffer's grandfather built the wine rack. They bought the paint at Home Depot. The result is two tiny dining rooms, one in front of the small bar, with its coveted stools and cushion-strewn banquettes, and another in a converted apartment out back. The cooking is marked by a devotion to technical perfection and a palpable pride of workmanship that is evident in dishes like goose rillettes with pickled shallots, roasted *poussin* with sage stuffing and pan sauce, and calf's liver with *cipollini* onions and applewood-smoked bacon that is get-down-on-your-knees-and-testify good. All are brilliantly executed, light of touch, and fluent in the idioms of today's table. *Dinner Monday through Saturday. 333 Culver Blvd., Playa del Rey, 310-305-4505.*

EM BISTRO

Pragmatism runs in Charles Nuzzo's family. His "Uncle" Nick Durante, who owned a speakeasy on the Passaic River in New Jersey, once told him that the keys to restaurant success were "good soup, good coffee, and a clean john." EM Bistro, the restaurant Nuzzo opened last year, would seem to be on solid ground. It not only incorporates the basic requirements Uncle Nick described but sweetens the enticement with the work of one of the city's most talented and unheralded cooks, Anne Conness.

A Georgetown University English major and refugee from the WB network's postproduction department, Conness was in her thirties when she applied herself to the craft of professional cooking. She studied and worked under some of the city's best chefs, including Mark Peel and Alex Scrimgeour. But it was her time with Makoto Tanaka, who owns Mako restaurant in Beverly Hills, that seems to have marked her most. "I remember watching Mako butcher fish," she says. "Oh, he had such style."

It is no surprise, then, that a sense of Japanese restraint runs through Conness's American-inspired cuisine: steamed mussels with lentils and curried leeks, John Dory with chanterelles and succotash, a steak with creamed spinach and fries. The restaurant's decor is modish Barbarella, with globe cluster lighting and deep, comfortable chairs in an atmosphere that's casual and civilized. EM breathes an easy confidence because there's a fine cook in the kitchen and an extremely practical owner at the door. *Dinner Monday through Saturday. 8256 Beverly Blvd., 323-658-6004.*

GRACE

Along banquettes in a muted Caltrans shade of orange sit the spiky-haired, the toned, and the all-knowing peering over their Oliver Peoples pince-nez. To their delight, Neal Fraser, who in

1995 started the Beverly Boulevard restaurant row with Boxer, twirls a baton of concepts and styles in the air like a marching-band drum major, exulting in the risk and handling it with finesse.

Vegan risotto, tenderloin of boar, saddle of rabbit on a saber-handled skewer that looks as if it were picked up in the gift shop of a Spanish airport, braised short ribs with langoustines, flights of soup, trios of fish, jellied doughnuts—if these dishes amount to a magical sequence, it's one that's kept from shooting right off its sprockets by, of all things, a blue-collar approach to the cooking. Fraser often works in the short-sleeved vest of the diner cook. It's who he is. Not a guy swathed in 300-thread-count Egyptian cotton but one who could tear a ticket from a spinning order wheel and bark, "Food's up!" *Dinner Tuesday through Sunday. 7360 Beverly Blvd., 323-934-4400.*

NOÉ

Some restaurant openings put one in mind of a cotillion, though it is not a deb but the talents of a chef being presented to society. Others showcase a willed comeback. Noé falls into the latter camp. Robert Gadsby closed his first restaurant, Gadsbys, in the mid 1990s and did something few chefs can afford to do. He took time off and went inward. Now, assumptions questioned, passions charged, he has re-emerged fully energized with Noé, a short stroll from the Walt Disney Concert Hall.

Though professionally precise, Gadsby's cooking draws one in by limning his many experiences. This man hounded Thomas Keller for a job at Rakel in New York and submitted to French discipline under Joel Robuchon when the Michelin-three-star chef was still at the Hotel Nikko in Paris.

Delicacy is Gadsby's hallmark, greens are his accents, and inventiveness crackles throughout his best dishes. A mimosa salad might serve as an example for the rest: The egg whites and yolks are chopped separately and not fridge cold, alluding to the finest caviar service while remaining modest. The pineapple infusion his Jamaican mother called tea is a palate cleanser. Broad in inspiration, exact in execution, the cooking at Noé signals a new downtown destination and a welcome return. *Dinner nightly. Omni Hotel, 251 S. Olive St., 213-356-4100.*

OPALINE

If George Saintsbury, the author of the 1920 wine classic *Notes on a Cellar-Book,* had a shaved head and wore natty suits, he might look like David Rosoff, the owner of Opaline. What are these descriptions that Rosoff writes in his fantastic wine list? "Lithe and graceful" for a German red. "Painfully beautiful" for a Chambolle-Musigny. They're love notes, admissions of vulnerability, confessions of a romantic, perhaps. They're certainly attempts to put into words the fascination of wine.

Opaline's classic formality has no visible connection to the past. A votive and abstract interior is anchored by an architectural column of light and big windows that look onto Beverly Boulevard. The hostess wears a newsboy cap, the man with long hair and a T-shirt beams as his wine is decanted, and the baby in the carriage seems to be enjoying the evening as much as anyone else.

In Jason Travi, Rosoff has a new chef who has hewed a sly menu that's alert to the requirements of showcasing the wine list but pushes each selection to be the best it can be. A deep red broth of rabbit with a *mirepoix* and braised veal cheeks with a tartlet touched with *mostarda di Cremona* bring out the meaty funkiness of a full-bodied Gigondas. A pumpkin flan from pastry chef Julien Wagner leads one naturally to the sweet—calling, perhaps, for a half bottle of Müller-Catoir Auslese. Recently I asked Rosoff to suggest a wine that would get me from the aperitif through the next two courses and lead me to a third. "Ah, the transition wine," he said like a man mulling over one of the more pleasant decisions in life. He suggested a Touraine rosé, and it was rangy and grand. *Lunch Monday through Friday; dinner Monday through Saturday. 7450 Beverly Blvd., 323-857-6725.*

ROCCA

James Beard once celebrated the practicality of a short-order cook who pressed his hash browns on the griddle with a can of coffee. Rocca chef Donald Dickman has his own way of working. For chicken *al mattone,* traditionally weighed down with a brick, he places a large can of tomato paste in a pan. It's a symbol of how the native New Yorker has internalized the culinary values of Italy, where all is simplicity, where the rind of a ham might be the meat that flavors a *brodo* and pasta water is the perfect liquid for stretching out a sauce.

Dickman's business partner is Don Dikmak, who's at the door. Dickman came to L.A. in the mid '80s and was soon employed by Michael Roberts at Trumps, where he made such signature dishes as a Brie quesadilla with sweet pea guacamole. His career can be seen as a trajectory from inventing dishes intended to shock with their newness to re-creating those that come in on a whisper of tradition. For Dickman the light went on in a tiny restaurant in Modena, where over a four-hour lunch he came to understand the poetry of Italian minimalism. At Rocca the portions are small but intense, allowing one to savor ricotta gnocchi, *bucatini* carbonara, butternut squash tartelloni, and pork cheek ravioli bathed in broth. It's genuine rustic Italian, and you can get there on the Big Blue Bus. *Dinner nightly. 1432A 4th St., Santa Monica, 310-395-6765.*

SONA

They don't think of you at Sona; they obsess over you. The tap water is filtered; the bread sticks are made from 100-year-old Puglian starter. A camera in the dining room transmits a live feed to the kitchen. The attention to detail verges on mania, and the result is unforgettable.

David and Michelle Myers, chef and pastry chef, respectively, have transformed a no-luck corner location on La Cienega into a quartz-like cube, where the decor has been purged of the extraneous and the food has been distilled to its essence. Theoretical, yes. Deconstructed? That, too, and yet Myers's skill is in warming up an intellectual approach to cooking. His version of modern food is suffused with something much older, the sense, say, of a Sunday table. Ascetic but not austere, linear but not stark, conceptual but somehow generous. Revel in the confit Scottish wild salmon with truffled gnocchi and red wine oxtail *jus*; applaud the hand-pulled Austrian strudel with sour cherries and black beer ice cream. Remember, you are being watched. *Dinner Tuesday through Saturday. 401 N. La Cienega Blvd., 310-659-7708.*

WÁ SUSHI & BISTRO

In L.A., "where do you go for sushi?" is a conversational gambit, an icebreaker. While we have our share of fine purveyors of the stuff, it is easy to fall into mediocre establishments serving fish-draped rice bowls one suspects are a means of getting rid of fillet ends and doling out salads with "secret" sauces drenched in nothing more than sesame-seed oil and rice wine vinegar. These and other abominations can slip in behind the ever-cheerful first greeting.

So when a great new place opens, word gets around. Wá Sushi is the restaurant of three longtime Matsuhisa chefs, Toru Takenaka, Tomofumi Igawa, and Hiroyuki Imai, who opened farther up La Cienega just below where it crests onto Sunset. Its minimall setting comes pretty close to what people who've never been to L.A. might imagine the city to be: an actors' head-shot studio surrounded by gyms. You might have to step over a personal trainer stretching a client on the stairs as you climb to the second-floor landing.

But with the first morsel you experience that jolt of clarity that makes people talk. The sushi here has an almost Shaker austerity: oysters with *ponzu* gelée; salmon with nothing but salt, lemon, and shiso; scallop with a microcube of *yuzu* rind. The concentrated flavors broaden with hot dishes such as grilled Santa Barbara shrimp with torched *uni* and an exquisite tear of beurre blanc. You linger. You look at the lights snaking up La Cienega. The city hums with energy. The decades compress. You can think you're at the spot Marlowe passes in *Farewell, My Lovely* when he says, "We went west, dropped over to Sunset, and slid fast and noiseless along that." *Dinner nightly. 1106 N. La Cienega Blvd., Ste. 201, 310-854-7285.*

My Life as a Hand Model

by Bruce Feiler

from *Gourmet*

In the spirit of the late, great George Plimpton, Bruce Feiler goes undercover to get the inside story on the sly business of making food commercials. Ever wonder whose hands those are, pointing, cooking, and serving those mouth-watering goodies?

T he bell peppers need more Vaseline. The Swiss cheese needs more baby powder. With just seconds to go before the cameras roll, assistants are placing hunks of cheese, piles of peppers, and bottles of olive oil around a stand-in pizza. The bottles refract the light and lend long shadows to the scene, as if it's sunset on a hillside in Tuscany. A brawny prop guy appears and begins brushing baby powder onto the cheese so it doesn't sweat, and another spreads Vaseline onto the bell peppers, then sprays them with water, forming delicate beads that cling longer to the skin.

"This is called a romance shot," says executive producer Rick Katzen. "Don't ask me how come the lighting says sunset, but the peppers look like they're still covered in morning dew."

On this bright spring morning, I'm standing in the cavernous studio of 50 Mile Radius [now Nadel Productions], in Manhattan. It looks like a cross between James Bond's gadget factory and a *M*A*S*H* emergency room. Director Bruce Nadel, famous for his Red Lobster lemon squeeze, is shooting a commercial for Donato's, a Midwest-based pizza chain owned by McDonald's, featuring their new Philly cheesesteak pizza. This first setup will be followed by an "appetite appeal" shot, in which cheese drips invitingly off a slice.

In the kitchen, about a dozen food stylists are preparing pies. There are 30 empty crusts, 50 onions, 100 bell peppers, and 3 trays of prebrowned cheese dollops (called scabs or spiders) standing at the ready. Each of the onions and peppers is being meticulously sliced and the winning rounds lightly browned in an oven. Each slice of steak is being sprayed with soy sauce and Kitchen Bouquet, then placed on a small griddle.

The lead food stylist takes a crust covered with lightly melted cheese and gingerly places each individual onion and bell pepper ring on top, being careful to tuck the steak into the peppers to give the pie more depth. Then she takes tweezers and situates about a dozen of the prebrowned scabs in strategic spots. The reason? The pie will continue to cook under the television lights, and everything is deliberately undercooked so it won't turn gray too quickly.

Finally, the cry goes up: "Hero's ready!"

Onstage, the assistants step aside, and in comes the perfect pizza. Nadel grabs his handheld camera and begins a near swan dive into the heart of the pie, curving, contorting, and getting millimeters from the tips of the peppers so the pizza looks like the Austrian Alps in *The Sound of Music,* all colorful, green, and alluring.

Ten seconds later Nadel abruptly quits. "Heat!" he cries, and assistants leap in with heat lamps and goggles, blasting the pie with white-hot light.

Suddenly we're underneath the space shuttle before it takes off. When the cheese begins to bubble and the scabs begin to ooze, Nadel starts again. Once more we go through this routine; then the pizza is done.

It took 45 minutes to prepare the pizza; it took 45 seconds to shoot it.

Now James Furino walks onto the set. A lithe, forty-something drummer and onetime stand-up comedian, Furino is one of a select few supermodels who command double union scale per day ($839.40) for using their hands. Furino is supposed to chop the steak for the pizza. But there's a twist: His hands will not be shown. The only thing you will see in the finished commercial is his chopping motion.

Later, Rick Katzen explains. In shots in which the hand is

meant to be the stand-in for the customer—lifting the pizza, say, the fingers appear. But in shots in which the hand is meant to be *preparing* the food, the hand is not shown. To put it bluntly: Advertisers don't want customers imagining that some minion in the kitchen is actually touching their food.

Nonetheless, hand models like Furino are still hired because they can do almost anything—and be almost anybody. "I've been Matthew Perry's hands. I've been Regis Philbin's hands. Once I was almost Michael Jackson's hands."

"Why did you lose the job?" I asked.

He cracked a stand-up's smile. "My hands were too dark."

I'd been mildly obsessed with my hands ever since I'd learned how to juggle and do mime as a teenager. The muscle and dexterity I developed stood me in good stead in the early '90s, when I spent a year performing as a circus clown. When I first started to learn about food, I realized that hand control was a big part of cooking—slicing, chopping, even serving. We learn these skills by watching cooks we love, by watching restaurant professionals, and, if truth be told, by watching television. What better way to find out how television advertising slyly shapes the way we view food, I thought, than to become a hand model?

As best as anyone can remember, the idea of hand modeling for commercials began to gain currency in the 1950s. Kraft regularly used hand models in the 1960s. "It was live," says Carmen Marrufo, "so if the cheese melted, it was a big problem." Marrufo, the undisputed queen of the cuticles, has been a hand-model agent for more than three decades. She has watched as the business grew steadily, peaking in the 1980s. The rise of computer graphics, the increase in shoots abroad, and changing tastes have tempered the market. These days, Marrufo keeps only a handful of clients who have the skills to work with food.

"What about me?" I asked, presenting my hands.

Marrufo held my hands delicately in hers. "Your hands are beautiful," she said. "But the key is not their appearance. It's how well you move them."

"But will they work?" I insisted. "Am I qualified to goose the Pillsbury Doughboy?"

Marrufo looked at my hands again. She smiled. "I can make you a star."

My big break came the following week, at the studios of Arf & Co., in Hoboken, New Jersey. Director Alex Fernbach was shooting a commercial for Freschetta Brick Oven Pizza. A gentle, philosophical man who was born in France and raised in New York City, Fernbach, 52, could be the Jacques Derrida of food commercials.

"The challenge of food photography," he said, "is that fundamentally the equipment doesn't scale with the food. If you want to take a picture of a car, or two people, you're far enough away that you won't interfere with the attitude or lighting of your subject. But say you're looking at a wonton."

For decades, he noted, food was presented in commercials in a direct way: Here is a sandwich; here is a bowl of soup. Today, that food has to be presented laden with emotion, whether surprise, or comfort, or sophistication. But the emotion must not be overt—it must be subtle, communicated ineffably by the image on the screen.

"A big part of commercials used to be the 'bite and smile,' " Fernbach said. "Someone had to register the delight of biting into the food. Nowadays we must convey that emotion in different ways."

In this commercial, even though you're eating a pizza pulled from your freezer, you must *feel* as if you're eating a pizza pulled from a brick oven. To do that, Fernbach's team built a brick oven, which they filmed first. On top of that, they layered in some flames. Today, they are shooting a baker's peel sliding into the oven, retrieving the pizza, and lifting it toward the camera.

To do this, they need a hand model. Furino was hired for this job, too, but after a few takes, it was time for the understudy. I step into place, standing directly underneath a 1,000-pound film camera mounted on a computerized rig. In front of me is the pizza, put on a blue screen that will later be replaced by the oven, shot the previous day.

The choreography would go as follows: Fernbach would cue the lights and launch the camera, which would swoop into place, making the kind of noise that trucks make when shifting into reverse. To avoid being decapitated, I had to kneel. As soon as the camera brushed my shoulder, I had to leap to my feet, grab the three-foot wooden peel, slide it under the pizza, jerk the pizza into place, then follow the camera to three spots that corresponded to oven, hearth, and camera. All the finger exercises in the world could not have prepared me for this contortion—or this pressure. At roughly $100,000 a day, this crew clocks in at $10,000 an hour.

"Ready," Fernbach cries, and a technician snaps one of those slate time stamps.

"Lights." I feel as if I'm tucked into a metallic cocoon.

"Camera." I'm staring into a tunnel directly at the pizza.

"Action!" The camera whizzes by my head.

"Now!" I rise from my knees, grab the peel in my hand, slide it under the pizza *(yes!)*, make the slight jerk, and it leaps into place *("Is it crooked?")*, pull it to the first stop *("Did I hit it?")*, slide it toward the second, then lift it slightly toward the third. Suddenly I'm done and the place erupts into applause.

"Not bad!" Fernbach cries, patting me on the back. "Not bad. Look at that smooth turn. A little bit slower to point A, but not bad . . ."

I do another take, and the pizza falls off the peel. In my third take the entire gesture seems smooth. Hardly practiced elegance, but I'm reminded of the advice Fernbach had given me earlier: "If you're comfortable, you're not doing your job."

The next day, the pizza is ready for its closeup, as am I. The pie is nailed to a board as I am charged with taking a pizza cutter, slicing through the crust, bisecting slices of onion and pepperoni, then lifting my arm as Fernbach goes sliding under with the camera.

The big challenge is making the pizza look piping hot. Among the hardest things to shoot in food photography is steam. Food photographers talk about shooting steam the way mountain climbers talk about scaling Everest. Fernbach even outfitted his studio with a hyperpowered air conditioner so he could drop the temperature 20 degrees in an hour, thereby requiring less heat to make steam.

In the old days, photographers made steam by combining the vapors of ammonium and hydrochloric acid, but steam made that way doesn't dissipate and it looks chemical. Later, they began hiding calcium smoke chips around the food. In recent years, they've tried dry ice, cappuccino makers, even theatrical foggers. Fernbach found that one surefire technique of getting steam from, say, a baked potato is to stuff it with a moistened tampon. "The mixture of concentrated moisture and heated surroundings produces the most gorgeous steam," he said. Now there's a tip for the next dinner party.

For the pizza, Fernbach uses an industrial clothes steamer. I position myself on one leg. He calls for the shot, and I cut the crust, slice the onion, slide through the cheese. Then we do it over and over again.

And in the repetition of this gesture, I finally understand what I've been doing. This is a frozen pizza I'm cutting. It goes into your freezer, into your oven, and into your mouth when you don't have time to worry about dinner.

But by putting the object through this complex choreography—pulling it from the flames, sliding it across the hearth, slicing it with a robust thrash—we are taking the most pedestrian item and converting it into a totem of the moment, one that embodies freshness, romance, sex on that Tuscan hillside.

The hands are the element that makes all this possible, because they stand in for the viewers' fantasy of themselves. And in a world of food sophistication, viewers don't want to think of themselves as having passive hands that merely receive the pizza already prepared. They want to have active hands, doing hands, the hands of the chef who kneads the dough, the hands of the pizzeria owner who reaches into the fire, the hands of the hunky waiter with the Armani pout who slices the pie at your table.

The hands embody this myth of the moment. They understand the hour even better than we do. In other words, the hands do what they've always done best: They tell us the time.

To Market, To Market

The Staff and the Stuff of Life

by Laura Faye Taxel

from *Northern Ohio Live*

Writing about food from her Ohio base for 25 years (her guidebook *Cleveland Ethnic Eats* is a local bestseller), Taxel has a Midwesterner's instinct for the solid and abiding things of life—like home cooks, old-fashioned food artisans, and neighborhood markets.

I was standing in line at a bakery in my Cleveland Heights neighborhood. The small, grey-haired woman ahead of me asked for half of a large five-pound loaf of corn rye. The young man behind the counter told her he couldn't cut the loaf.

"Last week," she said, "they did it for me."

"My boss told me not to do it anymore," he replied, "because nobody's buying the other half."

She was crestfallen. I understood her disappointment. It's wonderful bread—moist, dense, and chewy—available only once a week; in fact I was there to get a loaf myself. Frustrated, she complained out loud. "It's only my husband and I. A whole loaf is too much." On impulse I said I'd buy the other half, plus another whole one. "The boss," I promised, "will never know." He shrugged and went to get a knife.

She turned to me, delight filling her face. I explained that with two teenage sons at my house, the half loaf would be gone in an hour. She told me about her kids, who were grown with kids and even grandkids of their own.

It was pleasant to chat with a stranger, getting to know a person in passing, making a friendship that would only last a moment.

This could be the end of the story but it isn't. She chose a few more items. When the sales clerk gave her a total, she instructed him to charge it. "I need your credit card," he replied.

"I don't have it on me," she answered. "My wallet's in my purse and I think I left my purse at my son's house. It's not in the car. So just make me a bill."

"Do you have some kind of special account here?" he asked.

"No, no account," she said, "just write me up something to sign, and I'll send a check." She obviously came from a world and a time where this was conceivable. The boy did not. Neither do I. If I found myself without my wallet, I'd just give up and go home.

She certainly didn't look like a thief, like someone who didn't normally pay for her bread and cookies. She was well groomed, wore nice clothes, newish shoes. And what kind of scam artist would waste time on conning somebody out of $8.62 worth of baked goods?

She patiently explained, as though to a child, that she needed bread for supper but that she didn't want to have to go all the way home to get money, and then come back again. The boy was unmoved, utterly confused about what to do, polite but at a loss for how to help. "My boss," he kept saying, "my boss won't let me do this."

"So go get the boss," said the lady.

"She's not here today. It's only me and the baker. I can't do what you want." And still she didn't give up, give in as I would have done. She stood there, secure in the rightness of her position, the legitimacy of her solution. Then the man behind me in line took out his billfold, peeled off a ten, and gave it to her. She thanked him and paid for her stuff, leaving the clerk visibly relieved. Pocketing the change, she told her benefactor she'd send him a check for an even $10, and asked him to write down his name and address for her.

The third crisis, neither of them having paper or pen, was quickly averted by my contribution of both. "Don't worry," she said to him, "I'll send you the money."

He didn't look worried at all. He looked pleased. This feeling I think was not rooted in her assurances of payback. It was in his own ability to respond, to give, to help. I'd felt the same when I volunteered to take the other half of her loaf of corn rye. Instead of being anonymous and isolated city dwellers, we three had suddenly become neighbors, members of a community in which it's normal to care about one another's welfare, to come to another's aid. And each of us left the store a bit happier than when we had come in.

Not long after this event I heard an urban planning expert speak. He characterized the best neighborhoods for living as those that offer a place, within easy walking distance of your home, where you can buy fresh bread. I knew he was absolutely right.

Table to the World

by John Kessler
from *The Atlanta Journal-Constitution*

John Kessler hit the trifecta with this feature story—a food piece, a business profile, and a human interest tale all in one. Delving into all the many faces of this unique Atlanta food market, he found a story that is bigger than food.

Two things strike you when you walk into the DeKalb Farmers Market. Not just strike you, but reach out and grab you: the smell and the cold.

Jayshri Joshi doesn't notice the smell anymore—that fecund overload of fish guts and wet mops, of mangoes with their memory of the tropics, of chickens roasting and samosas frying. Of cheese, of meat, of half-sour pckles and of people. People riding forklifts and people pushing buggies with drowsy children inside. People sitting in dark, lonely corners stocking boxes of pasta, and people raking their fingers through the cool promise of Georgia green peanuts, looking for the tiniest and sweetest to surface in the pile.

Joshi doesn't smell that smell because after five years of daily exposure, she is inured to it the way cat owners no longer smell their pets in the house. But she feels the cold—the 65-degree temperature that keeps the leaf lettuces pert and the blue crabs feisty in their open bins. She stands at the customer service desk by the door wearing a winter coat and cupping hot coffee in her hand; the coffee, poured from a thermos, is as milky and sweet as Indian chai.

There are no farmers at this farmers market. The food is sold by employees from 30 countries who work in pairs, based on the owner's theory that they need to balance each other's expanding and contracting energy. Behind their blue coats and sometimes stumbling English, they are a collection of people who, before arriving, were bankers and teachers, economists and military officers. They escaped famine and fled the Taliban.

They landed in this world market just outside Decatur, a market that has thrived by catering to immigrants while spinoff Harry's Farmers Market struggled. It is a market so unique on the American landscape that competing grocers and tour groups of preschoolers come to gawk.

Every day 7,000 people come through, and Joshi sees all the regulars. The willowy man in his lime-green caftan who stops shoppers to tell them, "Every day on this Earth is a blessing!" The tall, balding fellow who wants cilantro with roots for some mysterious purpose. The real estate agent beelining toward the cafeteria for his daily date with the steam table. The retiree who rides a bus 80 miles once a week to shop.

Joshi's name tag informs customers she speaks English, Hindi and Gujarati, the last being her native tongue from her homeland in northern India. But everyone speaks English to her. A woman with a singsong Caribbean accent and kinky blond hair offsetting her cafe au lait skin approaches the desk with a bag of pistachios. "These weren't good the last time I got them," the woman says. "Not any good at all. I won't buy more until I try them first." Joshi waggles her head from side to side—the Indian sign of assent—and slices open the bag with a penknife.

"Please, try one," Joshi says. The customer extracts one nut with two inch-long orange fingernails, pulls it from its shell and thoughtfully chews before agreeing to buy. "You can go get a fresh bag," says Joshi.

When Joshi's day is finished at 5 PM, she packs up her shoulder bag and walks home. It isn't far—out behind the market, down a road where kudzu leaps from the woods, hurdles up and over chain-link fences, and reaches its tendrils out to the pavement. Home is a squat apartment block where, suddenly, everyone around speaks Gujarati. The doors to several apartments are open, and plastic outdoor furniture loiters on the common lawn. The smell of Indian spices hovers near the building, finding a welcoming home in the moist air. Inside one apartment, Joshi's sister Rehka Patel is cooking and her brother-in-law, Ashok Patel, is sitting on the sofa watching TV. This is home, a two-bedroom flat the three of them, all market employees, share. Rekha snaps and strips the peas from guwar beans. She drops black mustard seeds into hot oil, causing them to let off staccato pops and a nose-tingling fragrance, and adds the beans. Then she mixes dough. Every night they make fresh flat breads. There's no hurry—dinner's at 8—so Joshi goes to her bedroom to pray by the photo of her late husband.

An Atlanta institution, the market draws loyal shoppers attracted by its eccentric mix of organics and international exotica as well as newcomers and tourists who go for the sheer eye-popping spectacle of the place. After all, where else can you find spelt-flour rotini, bitter melons, lamb testicles, furiously snapping crabs, organic lard and all-natural raspberry-ginger cereal flakes under a canopy of international flags?

Rhode Island grocer Robert Blazer opened the DeKalb Farmers Market as a produce stand in 1977 in the Medlock neighborhood of Decatur. Soon thereafter Blazer brought in his younger musician brother, Harry, to help manage the growth of the market, which had expanded its offerings far beyond produce. It had become a gourmet haven that attracted food enthusiasts from throughout the city. Customers knew the two brothers well—Robert, the soft-spoken introvert with mop-top hair, and Harry, the flamboyant showman with his trademark bushy mustache.

By 1986 the market had outgrown its space, and Robert Blazer moved it to its current 100,000-plus-square-foot location a mile away. It was frequently in the news at that time, and not only for its revolutionary scale. Some former employees filed a class action lawsuit, characterizing Blazer's management doctrine as a "New Age quasi-religious cult." Even Harry Blazer spoke out against the market's management practices and left to found the competing chain of Harry's Farmers Markets. He opened the first location in what *The Atlanta Journal-Constitution* described at the time as "the bucolic community of Alpharetta."

Despite their disagreements, these two brothers not only changed Atlanta's food shopping habits, they created—each in his own way—a widely imitated template for gourmet retailing in America. Chuck Gilmer, editor of the Norcross-based Shelby Report, a national grocery trade publication, credits the DeKalb and Harry's farmers markets with introducing upscale prepared foods to the country ("getting past fried chicken and doughnuts") and with encouraging food markets to expand their seafood and meat offerings. Food retailers flew to Atlanta in the early 1990s to study their innovations.

Harry's dominated the news during Atlanta's go-go expansion and went public in a barrage of national press. The DeKalb market stayed privately owned by Robert Blazer, who has never released sales or revenue figures. Harry's tried to show its concept could work everywhere, expanding to three megastores and six Harry's in a Hurry gourmet takeout shops. The DeKalb market watched its changing neighborhood, adding more Indian and Caribbean products to the increasingly weird mix. Harry's hired celebrity chef Scott Peacock to develop pastries. DeKalb sold samosas, fried tofu and steamed chard in its cafeteria. Harry's spiraled into debt, never turning a profit from 1993 until the younger Blazer sold the megastores to Whole Foods in 2001. DeKalb added 40,000 square feet of space to accommodate its new status as Atlanta's world market. It now employs 470 people from 30 countries, and it's these people who perhaps offer the best clue to its continued success.

During its 27 years, this food store has become a unique kind of town square, in a county where 60 languages are spoken and one out of 10 residents have emigrated within the past decade. Here shoppers can walk alongside their near but unknown neighbors and see what they eat, what clothes they wear, how they interact with their children. In the jostling, noisy interior of this market, side-by-side communities don't dissociate immediately into their separate realities, but combine briefly into an unstable compound—a new culture. And for each of the people whose lives the market has touched, the story always begins with the smell.

Reti Canaj remembers the smell, that first whiff six years ago. She and her husband, Ali, had been in America for only two weeks—refugees who had entered a green card lottery and won. They sold their home for plane fare and left Albania, the poorest nation in Europe, with two small children and three suitcases. They took only clothes, a stainless steel pressure cooker and two kitchen knives. They left their parents and their country, which had lurched from dictatorship and seclusion during the Cold War to financial desperation after the fall of the Berlin Wall. Reti Canaj was a bank manager who saw her clients lose their homes and businesses in pyramid schemes that had wrecked the country's economy.

And so, here she was in Georgia in August, sweltering in a one-room apartment with mattresses on the floor. Her Albanian-American sponsor, Flora, said she would take her to a market to show her something special. And then she added, "Just don't let the smell bother you." Flora took Reti into the market and pointed to the ceiling, where hundreds of national flags hung. "I looked up and saw our flag," Canaj recalls, "and I began to cry. It was like I saw my people."

Canaj, with her university education, didn't speak enough English to find work. She applied for jobs and was turned down. A&P wouldn't hire her to bag groceries. She eventually got work as a maid at a hotel, where a kind manager named Melissa told her not to be disappointed, that life would get better. "I didn't know what that meant, disappointed."

Canaj studied English at home and decided to apply at the market. She was scared of failure and took along her 6-year-old daughter, Silva, to help translate. She rarely spoke English to anyone other than Melissa. The first step was a written test in English and math. Canaj completed the exam and handed it to a Bangladeshi administrator in the market office. The woman flipped through it and said that she had done well, to come back for an interview without her daughter. There might be a job. "At that moment," Canaj says, "I started to be happy."

Canaj has done well at the market—from her first job as a cashier to her current one as co-director of human relations. Now she administers the tests and doles out hope. She works in an office up in a skybox, eye level with the flags. She can look down and see the bustle—children craning their necks by the live crabs, yuppies sniffing cheese, the mad multiculti rush for summer mangoes. And she occasionally sees people with necks craned, looking for their flags. Sometimes they cry. "The Africans," she says, "are usually so happy when they see their flag. They point and laugh."

It is Tuesday, application day. People who want to work at the market arrive promptly at 9 AM to take the written test that Canaj hands out. Usually about 40 people come and take desks in the big conference room. Today's crowd consists mostly of East Africans from Ethiopia, Somalia and Eritrea plus a scattering of Iraqis and Afghans. "We have an extensive cheese department at the market," the test reads. "Some smell sweet and some smell strong. Cheese can be made from sheep, goat or cow's milk." "Do some cheeses smell strong?" "What is cheese made from?"

Canaj sits in her office with her partner, a carefully coiffed Ethiopian woman named Adanech Gebremariam. Canaj and Gebremariam work closely as a pair, as do all the market employees. Canaj wears a white dot on her name tag, which means that she has "expanding energy." Gebremariam wears a black dot for "contracting energy." When employees are hired at the market, Robert Blazer gives them a personality test and assigns them a type. Those with expanding energy are thinkers, ideators, people who come up with better systems to complete their work. Those with contracting energy are doers, brawn to the other's brains, people who know that the best way to do a job is to get it done. Each working pair consists of one white dot and one black dot. "Robert believes you work best when you have good relationships with friends and family," says art department manager Ashley Vinson. Employees are always referred to in pairs. There's Thuy and Tuha in flowers. Latif and Jai in wine. Yussuf and Tesfaye in supplies.

After three years together, Canaj and Gebremariam seem two sides of a coin. They are like spouses who finish each other's sentences, taking a thought halfway, then punting it over for the other to finish. They eat in each other's homes and share recipes. Gebremariam now makes Albanian soups for her family.

The cashiers can identify the thousands of market products by their numeric codes. They are tested routinely for accuracy, and they can differentiate purple-stemmed Vietnamese spinach from loose-leaf spinach. They recognize by sight the tied bunches of yellow root, the shiny fresh water chestnuts, the slender green stalks of meri gai choy and the dirty brown lumps called boniato.

Few people in Atlanta know what to do with these ingredients as well as Dr. Tim Dondero. A medical epidemiologist with the Centers for Disease Control and Prevention, Dondero has lived and cooked in Malaysia, Cameroon, India, Thailand and Jamaica, among other places. Now at home in Druid Hills, he picks a different world destination for dinner every night, consulting his 2,000 cookbooks and his computer files. He is the tall, bald man who periodically pesters the customer service desk for cilantro with roots and thanks them profusely when it comes in. A skilled practitioner of Thai cooking, Dondero grinds the roots with a mortar and pestle for Thai curries and marinades. And as he goes through the aisles on his weekly market visit, his mind switches countries like someone with an ethnic cook's remote control. Click: "These little zucchini are just right for Mediterranean stuffed vegetables." Click: "This Hungarian Swiss cheese is a bargain and makes great fondue." Click: "These snow pea shoots are way too expensive, but I love them." Click: "I buy all my candied fruits here during Christmas to make fruitcake." Fruitcake and cilantro roots: the pantry of a one-of-a-kind cook.

Dondero admits that he may come to the market with a short shopping list but then end up "spending an hour or more wandering around. This place makes me happy, maybe because I get such good associations from it."

As Dondero wanders the market, activity swirls around him. Sophie Smulders escorts 40 children from the Pace Academy preschool on a tour and hoists an enormous bunch of basil in front of one startled kid, nearly engulfing his head. "Here's a good smell," she says cheerily. Jayshri Joshi patiently explains to a peeved customer that she may not exit through the entrance to fetch a shopping cart. A lone crawfish has made a break from the fish counter and crawls across the floor, nearly reaching the promised land of the bread department. Jai Gowkurian rides a forklift through the narrow aisles of the wine department, overseeing a reorganization of the shelves while his partner, Latif Ramanou, talks on the phone in booming West African French. Gowkurian wears the white dot, Ramanou the black.

Mahnaz Nassiri adds shredded carrots and raisins to the "Afghanistan rice" she makes for the cafeteria. Like so many employees at the market, Nassiri has, as she calls it, "a little bit of tragedy" in her past. After her father was killed by the Taliban secret police, she escaped across the border to Pakistan, where she lived for two years in a refugee camp. Now she lives in Clarkston with other family members who escaped Afghanistan, studies English at night, and delights restaurant customers with new flavors. She has adapted her mother's recipes to the needs of the market, to the ingredients at hand. She uses tortillas for Afghan flat bread, and, with egg roll wrappers, she can make a canny duplicate of the scallion dumplings called aushuk.

Everybody who works here has a past life. Joshi was a high school science teacher. Canaj a banker. Gowkurian an army officer in British Guyana, part of the division called to clean up after the Jonestown massacre. "That was a long time ago," he says, not wanting to hesitate for an instant on the memory. But they have one thing in common. They were all hired by Robert Blazer. "Robert has a big heart for immigrants," says Canaj. "We start from zero here. We are like children. Robert has helped a lot of people who came here without anything."

Robert Blazer had only a little retail experience before he went knocking on doors in his Decatur neighborhood in 1977, asking people if they'd like a farmers market. He had worked in his father's discount variety store in Pawtucket, R.I., and persuaded the old man to let him sell a few fruits and vegetables in the basement. While customers upstairs scrounged for cut-rate clothing and housewares, others downstairs rummaged through piles of seasonal corn. Connecting farmers with shoppers, Blazer felt, was his calling.

To the neighbors in Decatur, a fresh market sounded like a fine idea. Blazer opened with one load of fresh produce under a plastic roof in a former greenhouse. Without proper refrigeration on site, he couldn't keep a lone carrot fresh overnight. "The first day was a make-or-break day for me," he recalls. The neighbors, true to their word, bought out the market. When the market's roof collapsed in an ice storm two years later, Blazer didn't have insurance. So he again appealed to his neighbors. They exchanged checks for scrip—$100 here and there—and reclaimed their money in groceries after the market was rebuilt with a sound roof. Blazer made as many improvements to the building as he could, adding air compressors and fans, a checkout annex and an expanded parking area. But he couldn't put proper drainage in the concrete floor; workers with squeegee mops had to pass continuously, as wet-footed shoppers stepped aside. And he couldn't conjure more space out of thin air.

In 1986, much of metro Atlanta watched as Blazer cleared a tract of land in Scottdale and built the current location. And as he subtly shifted the market's focus from gourmet mecca for Atlanta's established middle class to international market, Blazer's credo as a greengrocer—representing the "people who are growing [produce] directly to the public"—became the cornerstone of his business model. By cutting out the middleman, he could keep prices low. His purchasing staff orders directly from nectarine growers in California, salmon farmers in Chile, artisanal food manufacturers in Italy.

Business was rocking after the market relocated, but Robert Blazer's personal life was starting to fray. His first marriage fell apart. His dealings with Harry were growing strained. And his father, with whom he had a number of unresolved conflicts, died. "I was failing in my relationships with people," recalls Blazer, his eyes clouding with the memory of hitting bottom. "I realized that all of us were struggling," he continues. "We had to learn to work well with people—at home and in the workplace. We had to create a future."

He was looking for answers. And he found some in the teachings of Werner Erhard, the controversial founder of est. Blazer became involved in the Forum, a motivational training seminar developed by Erhard, and encouraged his managers to follow suit. Many did, though some were reluctant. In late 1988, eight former employees of the market sued Blazer, claiming they were unfairly fired or forced to resign because they refused to adopt the tenets of the Forum. At the time Blazer refused to talk to the press, but his attorney claimed there was no coercion; a market spokesman called the allegations of religious brainwashing "ridiculous." The suit was settled out of court for an undisclosed amount. Blazer now says the Forum "had some good ideas" and that his only motivation in encouraging his supervisors to attend seminars was to help them. But he was bruised by the beating he took in the public eye and has been camera-shy ever since.

Even after his own brother went into direct competition with the opening of the first Harry's, Robert Blazer feels he emerged from the Forum debacle not weaker, but stronger. His interest in group relationships had grown only more ideological and more personal. In 1988 he wrote a credo, which he titled "The Stand." It greets customers from a plaque between the front doors:

> We declare the world is designed to work.
> We are responsible for what does not work.
> We make the difference.
> No matter how technologically advanced we become, we cannot escape our fundamental relationships with food and each other. The possibility of these relationships is the world market. In this context, the world works for everyone free of scarcity and suffering.
> We commit ourselves to the possibility this world market is for the future generations of this planet.

"The Stand" gave Blazer his first glimmer of the "world market"—not just a physical market with chickens and tomatoes, but a metaphorical market, a laboratory for bettering the human condition through food and commerce. The following year Blazer began to develop his personal management philosophy and his theories of expanding and contracting energies. He won't discuss the particulars, although he is working on a book that will spell it out. But he is certain his beliefs and practices—"the outcome of a certain way of seeing things"—allowed his market to thrive, while the absence of such beliefs sank Harry's. "Harry was trying to prove he was better than us. To build a business, it has to be based in giving something to people. If you give to life, life gives back to you. When all you want is to get something, the positive energy is not present."

Blazer, 55, currently runs the market with his second wife, Barbara. He is still deeply involved in the produce arm of the business; Barbara's imprint can be seen in the cookbooks, dry goods and housewares, and she's had a hand in redecorating the cafeteria. His 18-year-old son, Daniel, a recent graduate of Woodward Academy, is deferring college for a year to learn the family business.

Harry Blazer, who has relocated to Montana, refused comment for this story. Robert Blazer says the two see each other "once or twice a year."

Reti Canaj pulls a Pyrex plate out of the oven in her kitchen. Inside are lamb chuck steaks sizzling in their rendered fat. She puts the lamb on the stove and prepares a concoction that seems strange to non-Albanian eyes: yogurt, eggs, flour, oil, dill and parsley. She pours a good gallon of it over the lamb and returns the dish to the oven.

The Canajs have owned their house in a Tucker subdivision for a year. It has a cathedral ceiling in the living room, arrangements of pastel silk flowers along the fireplace, and a portrait of the founder of the Albanian state hanging by the front door, Gjergj Kastrioti, also known as Skanderbeg. In 1443 Kastrioti raised Albania's double-headed eagle flag and proclaimed, "I have not brought you liberty, I found it here, among you." The Canajs have found a certain degree of liberty in America. Their 9-year-old son, Gersi, can ride his bike safely on their dead-end street. Their daughter, Silva, is a brilliant student at Tucker High who has so far faced down only one B, in advanced placement chemistry. Yet Ali Canaj, with his advanced degree in engineering, works nights at Pep Boys. Reti wishes they had the resources to visit her ailing mother in Albania or her sisters who relocated to Western Europe.

As much as Reti Canaj, a passionate cook, appreciates the fresh foods she brings home from her workplace, she misses the personality of Albanian foodstuffs—the way the green beans filled her nose with a prickly, vegetal aroma when she snapped them, the darkness of the egg yolks, the lamb. "All the houses smell very good over there when people bake meat. That's because all the animals eat actual grass." Nonetheless, her house in Tucker is smelling about as good as a house can. Reti removes the baked lamb dish, called Tave Kosi, from the oven. The yogurt-egg mixture has reduced to a thick, golden custard. She brings it to the table along with green beans she stewed with veal and tomatoes in her pressure cooker, the one she brought from Albania. She serves a vegetable soup that's bright and tangy with lemon and dill, and deep with the flavor of veal bones. After dinner, Canaj pulls out a bottle of Albanian brandy called konjak. It is decorated to look like a wooden log and features a portrait of Gjergj Kastrioti. And she pours shots in tiny crystal glasses.

She often wishes she could return to Albania. She and her husband have striven so much to rebuild their lives. They often feel lost in America. It's all for the children, for their future. "We have to work so hard to keep our family strong," says Reti Canaj, sitting down for a moment, if not exactly relaxing. "But I think that people, if they work hard, then maybe they can find themselves."

Dinner at the Joshi/Patel household usually takes about an hour to prepare, and that is with the help of a squadron of pressure cookers to speed the process along. Every night they prepare a vegetable, papadum crisps, homemade flat breads, yogurt seasoned with spices fried in ghee (clarified butter), and either rice and the Indian lentils called dahl or khichadi, a soft mixture of rice and dahl cooked together. Tonight they've made chapatis, a kind of flat bread that they roll and fold and roll and fold to give them a flaky texture. They cook the chapatis in a flat iron skillet called a tawa until they puff and blister. When the chapatis are all cooked, dinner's ready.

They sit around a small table set against their living room wall; it groans with the above dishes plus chutneys and pickles that emerge from Tupperware containers. They eat everything except the khichadi, which they save for the end, like dessert. When it is time, Rehka Patel fetches the pot of khichadi and the tin of ghee from the kitchen. She spoons out large steaming scoopfuls onto everyone's plate; it is lemon-yellow and fragrant with spice, and has a texture that's a bit like stiff grits. People help themselves to the firmly set ghee, which melts on top of the khichadi and sends buttery rivulets down the sides.

The table, which a minute earlier had been filled with animated laughter, falls silent as they all take their first bite. It is so good—the flavor of home.

Playing the Market

by Sara Deseran

from *7 x 7 SF*

San Francisco's food scene has long had its own wacky gestalt, and its open-air market scene is just one more eccentric component. Food reporter Deseran plays a fly on the wall observing the various players at the upmarket Ferry Plaza Farmers' Market. It's a delicious bit of theater.

The woman buried her nose in a fragrant bouquet of lemon basil, inhaling dramatically. Beneath her straw hat, saucer-sized, owlish glasses magnified her eyes as she rolled them upwards in ecstasy. "Oh, you have to smell this!" she said to the woman next to her, who was wearing a straw hat too, and shoved the bouquet in her face. "It's good for baking," she said with conviction. "I'm going to put it at the bottom of a génoise to perfume it. Very Victorian."

It was 7:45 in the morning at the Mariquita Farm stand, and the hardcore foodies were already making their rounds. (Technically, the Ferry Plaza Farmers' Market doesn't open until 8 AM.) The garlic scapes were selling briskly. It didn't seem to matter that no one knew what they were—the mystery only added to their allure. "You can use them in an omelet," Mariquita's Julia Wiley explained patiently over and over. "They're a bit like asparagus, but they're garlic."

A woman with a Bulgari scarf wrapped loosely around her neck breezed by, fingering the romaine like a swatch of cashmere. She deftly veered left to avoid a hunter green doublewide jogger-stroller paving a trail through the quickly growing crowd. In it, a pair of blonde twin girls from Cow Hollow kicked back, munching contentedly on organic snap peas as their father, the cook in the family, tried to balance a flat of $3-a-pound peaches in one hand. Out of nowhere, a man stepped up and prophetically announced to anyone who would listen: "Fresh tomato. Mozzarella. Basil."—and nothing more.

For anyone who has frequented the Ferry Plaza Market over the past few years, this will all seem like business as usual. In a city where restaurant menus name-drop farms like designer labels (think Frog Hollow and Star Route) and amateur cooks use words like "sustainable," "terroir" and "pan-sear" without missing a beat, food has been catapulted beyond daily sustenance—some might say that it's become a lifestyle.

If that lifestyle is being lived out anywhere, it's in San Francisco, and it comes together in a cultish way at the Ferry Plaza Farmers' Market, run by the nonprofit group CUESA (the Center for Urban Education about Sustainable Agriculture). Although there are almost 80 farmers' markets in the Bay Area, if you're looking for the cream of the crop, the Ferry Plaza is it. In the middle of summer it's an organic utopia, with a huge array of fruits and vegetables that are as beautiful and fresh—and expensive—as anywhere in the United States. (It's not uncommon to overhear the uninitiated gasping when they see a basket of blueberries that costs $5.)

Over the 11 years that it's been in business, the market has become as much of a social scene as it is a place to do the week's shopping. "It's really become a community meeting place—a market square kind of thing," says Patricia Unterman, co-owner of the Hayes Street Grill and one of CUESA's founding board members. Every Saturday, there's a reliable cast of regulars: restaurant chefs; Alice Waters and her entourage ("There are a lot of people that follow her and buy what she buys—I've seen it," says Tatiana Graf, the communications manager for CUESA); the kiss-kiss society set; the stroller brigade; the sporty spandex crew; KQED subscribers with their Mephistos; even the homeless cognoscenti dining on feasts of organic leftovers.

When the Ferry Plaza Market started, there were only two other markets in the city: the Civic Center and the Alemany. Although both of those markets are wonderful in their own right, they're decidedly more funky, catering largely to an immigrant population. The inexpensive produce isn't displayed in wicker baskets;

prices aren't quaintly written on chalkboards. Since the beginning, the Ferry Plaza has drawn a different crowd—well-heeled and mostly white. "These were people who never went to those markets, the people from Pacific Heights and the North End—a different kind of cook," says Unterman.

But CUESA had bigger dreams all along—plans for a more permanent space much like the grand markets in Europe. And this past spring, when the market moved from its more humble digs in a parking lot on Green Street to the Ferry Building, it all came closer to coming true. Sweeping panoramas of the water and the Bay Bridge have replaced a view of cars zooming down the Embarcadero; now there's plenty of room for everyone to sit and enjoy their Hobbs bacon, egg and tomato sandwiches.

To top it off, the old Ferry Building was refurbished into a long 65,000-square-foot hall of gleaming stalls and reopened as the Ferry Building Marketplace. There's been much buzz about the permanent vendors, such as Recchiuti Confections, Hog Island Oyster Company and the Imperial Tea Court. In June, the Slanted Door agreed to join the growing list of restaurants including Taylor's Refresher and MarketBar. Planners have taken pains to keep it as local as possible. It all seems to be coming together to become one big food paradise.

But what fun would it be without a little trouble? Moving the market was like kicking aside a very content anthill. For the first month it was a frenzied zigzag of grumbling and disoriented shoppers. Some regulars threatened to never come back. "People keep asking me, 'What do you think?'" says June Taylor, the goddess of jam, in regards to the new setup. "And I say, what do I think of *Bush*?" Probably the biggest complaint is that the market is no longer configured in a loop. One morning, Peggy Knickerbocker, another of CUESA's 14 board members and part of the core group, was in an argument with her partner because she had insisted on stopping at every single farmer's stand. "I get nervous because it's not formed in a continuous circle anymore," she said, a bit of panic still in her voice. "You get that feeling that you're missing something."

But beyond issues of feng shui, probably the biggest concern is that the market is going to become one huge artisanal food court, bringing in hordes of tourists to load up on toothpick samples.

"It's become food shopping as entertainment," laments Paula Linton, one of the many produce experts at GreenLeaf. "I hate this veneration of the farmer. We've made media stars of the chef, the peach. I just want us to fast-forward to the day when that's just the way it should be—maybe that will happen when I'm dead."

And although some won't admit it outright, the market has cultivated an undeniable bit of elitism. Old-timers are reluctant to share this new market with the inevitable wave of out-of-town gawkers, ferry commuters and other unsavory sorts who can't appreciate a good stinging-nettle pasta.

But CUESA is optimistic that everything will soon return back to normal. (Unterman recalls that when they moved from the market's original parking lot to another one a few blocks over, people were up in arms too. "There was huge anguish when we had to move to the Green Street location," she says.) Already people are beginning to familiarize themselves with the layout. The statue of Gandhi that rises out of the center has appropriately become the place for lost souls to rendezvous. A cell phone is indispensable. And you can always catch entertaining snippets of conversation floating through the lavender-scented air.

"I'm thrilled to be here for the summer tomato frenzy!"

"Are you going to the benefit tonight?"

"Are you going to the GMO protest in Sacramento tomorrow?"

"Do you take Visa?"

People still try to sneak in their dogs, and most everyone is back to their routines: Put a Hoffman chicken on reserve before they run out, pick up some broccoli di cicco at Mariquita, wolf down a Downtown Bakery donut muffin, swing by Knoll Farms for turkey figs, lettuce at Star Route, cheese from Andante, a ploughman's loaf from Delia Fattoria and flowers at White Crane ("He grows his flowers biodynamically and he has artisanal wells," raves Knickerbocker).

As the crowds thicken, walk over to the water's edge and take refuge in the fresh sea air. Be thankful that we can buy spinach that's not in a bag and fruit that tastes like fruit should. And if nothing else, look to Gandhi for a little perspective.

The Mother of All Markets

by Rick Nichols
from *The Philadelphia Inquirer*

Nichols inherited the *Inquirer*'s food column almost by default, but it turned out to be a perfect match—"I like to eat, and I like to use food as a prism to explore broader issues." As a longtime Philly native, he knows what the local fooodways are—and what they aren't.

Soon we'll be heading up to the week-old Wegmans Food Market in Downingtown, but because that's not our final stop we dig up clumps of violets from the front yard. We have a new destination in mind for them.

The Wegmans visit is for reconnaissance, not shopping, though of course we have a short list—organic yogurt, a few shrimp for the pad thai, berries if they look good.

The place is, I've read, the supermarket reimagined, the supermarket on steroids, the mother indeed of all supermarkets, with a floor plan the size of a Wal-Mart, its own French patisserie, bread ovens that burn wood, and cheeses by the hundreds.

It did not sound like the supermarkets of my mother. We'd pull a wagon, when I was young, to a Penn Fruit, the only exotic feature of which (besides the Chung King shelf) was the scent of dill that wafted from the barrel of kosher pickles.

Supermarkets had not been long on the scene 50 years ago, having recently subjugated the corner store and mom-and-pop bakery, the roving produce hucksters and farmers' markets.

Even the celery was different in those markets. At Central Market in Lancaster, in my earliest memory, the displays were tended by farm women in prayer caps who scrubbed each stalk until, amazingly, it gleamed.

Wegmans is a relatively small, 65-store, family-held chain based in Rochester, N.Y. It does more than $3 billion in sales each year. Its fans are loyal and legion: Rochester expats living in Baltimore are happily making the pilgrimage to Downingtown already.

When we pull up, Wegmans' facade is staring flat and blank-eyed. It is in a shopping center east of downtown Downingtown on Route 30, its brick face as generic as any refurbished Acme or Genuardi's.

The energy doesn't hit until you walk through the barn-door-wide doors.

Bushel baskets of sweet red, yellow and orange peppers are tilted invitingly—almost heliotropically—toward the entryway. Asparagus climbs a stepped display rack. Potatoes are framed in stained wooden crates.

It is the farmers' market in captivity, with more wood, reconstructed crates and rustic baskets than in the genuine item.

In moments, we've plopped a huge papaya into our cart, sold by the glistening cube offered by a sampler.

So it goes—at least for a while. We get the non-melting Halloumi cheese they're grilling. I ask for a tub of the roasted glazed Greek figs swimming in a countertop jar. I spoon out a plastic cup of Nicoise olives.

A customer brings a camera to get a shot of the black truffles, locked in a Plexiglas case, for $499 a pound. There are gobo root and baby bok choy, skate wing and cinnamon-cap mushrooms.

The patisserie glitters. The bread is fresh from the wood-burning oven but tends toward a certain sameness—soft and sweet, not unlike the fresh-baked bagels among which I note one dismayingly labeled "French-toast flavored."

It is too much after a while—too many carts jostling (this is the first week, after all), too many acres of aisles. The pizza crust, disappointingly, is puffed like popcorn. I recoil at a sign over a sandwich counter: "Old-fashioned Sub Shop."

We share a juicy grilled salmon BLT and made-to-order pasta primavera, but I can feel the circuits overloading.

In the lounge, there is the look of a Starbucks—contemporary couches and comfy chairs and, on the wall, posters of trattorias on cobbled streets in some magical city that, suddenly, reminds me of the one I work in every day.

I look up, and through the wall-to-wall skylight, the sky is blue, the clouds still and white. They are still, it turns out, because they are painted on the sky-blue ceiling just beyond the translucent panels.

The farmers' market impression of first flush has morphed, in our weariness, into something mildly cloying—the sort of bustling, pretend world of your average Jersey Shore casino.

So we're off, driving a few miles north into the spring-green hills of Guthriesville.

In the cemetery of a country church, we dig little holes around my mother's grave and plant the violets, her favorite flower from my earliest memory.

It is a lovely Sunday afternoon on this gentle rise, the air fresh, the sky blue, the clouds white and shifting in the breeze.

A good day, finally, not so much for shopping as for growing things.

Getting the Goods

by Ann M. Bauer

From *Minnesota Monthly*

Considering herself a storyteller more than an epicure, novelist Anne Bauer returned recently to her home state of Minnesota after a decade away. Her curiosity about how local chefs shop inspired this magazine profile—and led her to discover the food writer within her.

The Twin Cities has seen its share of theme restaurants—huge neon guitars on the walls, trivia games flashing from panoramic television screens, thunderstorms gathering in palm trees and live birds fluttering overhead. The menu might come in the form of a book or appear billboard-style in a flashing electronic LED display. These are places where eating and entertainment overlap, a mixture of dinner theater and Disneyland's whirling teacup ride.

To be fair, the food can be good. Fresh, standard, consistent. It arrives each morning in cardboard cartons sent by the parent company: blocks of standard-issue ground beef, transparent pouches full of cut vegetables, pre-cleaned shrimp in large plastic handle bags.

Scattered among these are the establishments whose only trademark is quality. These restaurants are quieter; they have lasting power. People don't tend to line up, pagers hooked to their pants pockets, waiting three hours for a table. Instead, these restaurants have developed a steady, loyal clientele, educated about food and wine. Their menus, which appear on regular card stock, may vary with the season. And their executive chefs start work early in the day—not cooking, but hunting for grade-A ingredients.

These culinary professionals aren't reading out of manuals, set-ting up bins of ingredients so they can prepare the very same salad that's coming out of kitchens in Detroit and Santa Fe. They're calling brokers, visiting stockyards and fresh fruit markets, hedging bad crops. They are inspectors, comparison shoppers, and extraor-dinary skeptics. Because when your reputation is built entirely upon serving the very finest steak, seafood, or stir-fry, you're under the gun to produce exactly that. Every single time.

THE MEAT MAN

Boyd Freeman started working at Murray's Steak House as a prep cook in 1974. He was 17 years old and had scraggly long hair, which he kept pulled back in a ponytail. Mrs. Murray—the first Mrs. Murray—didn't like it. So he cut it. And from that moment on, she treated him like family. It's a haircut that's lasted a little over 28 years.

These days, Freeman is clean-cut and freshly shaved, and he dresses—as he has throughout his working life—in a white butcher's apron double-tied around his waist. He's had no formal culinary training, no junkets through France. Instead, he's learned hands-on under five executive chefs at Murray's. "Executive Chef" is, essentially, the position he holds now, though the title makes him squirm.

"They just handed me the reins last spring," Freeman says. "But we're still discussing what they're going to call me, how it'll all work. There's talk about my going on salary and being manage-ment. But I'm not sure about that. I've been a union guy my whole life."

No matter what they call him, it's clear Boyd Freeman runs the kitchen at Murray's. He is, for instance, in charge of ordering, inspecting, and carving the $2,500-$3,000 worth of prime meat that comes through the back door each day.

Since 1946, Murray's has occupied the same spot at 26 East 6th Street in downtown Minneapolis, and its name has been syn-onymous with steak. Even as food trends have come and gone—California cuisine, nouvelle, fusion, Tex-Mex—Murray's has gone right on serving its Silver Butterknife, a 28-ounce strip steak for two, guaranteed to be so tender it can be cut with a butter knife. And for 57 years it has been just that.

Boyd Freeman has been nearly as steady. He put in eight years in low-level kitchen staff jobs, but in the early 1980s he happened to get a spot next to Arnie, the meat cutter. "I watched him every day," Freeman says, "and when he retired in 1982, I fell into the job. That's back when we used saws and I was breaking down the whole thing. Bones, byproducts, everything."

This morning, he's not working with a saw. Murray's major supplier, Lombardi's, has refined its Sterling Silver beef line so that it arrives mostly cleaned. But there's still a great deal of knife work to be done.

"Just to keep 'em honest, we go out and do a side-by-side taste testing [with meat from other suppliers] a few times a year," Freeman says. He pulls out his knives—just two of them, one with a thick blade, the other with a rapier tip. He lays them on a square white cutting board. "Last month, I toured their plant in Spring Lake Park to make sure it was up to snuff."

There's less blood and mess than I'd imagined. Lombardi's delivers its product in hermetically sealed plastic packages or white paper, not unlike what we regular consumers find in our local butcher shops. Only these packages are much bigger. Freeman lugs a 30-pound strip loin out of the cooler and slices its packaging open with one sweep of the knife. There is no odor; the meat lies on the board like an enormous tongue—winey red, soft to the touch, nearly two feet long.

He explains that the meat has been locker-aged for 30 days, which breaks down the enzymes and makes it tender. Freshly butchered beef would be tough as rubber. On the other hand, blood in the package would mean it's been stored too long. If Freeman sees a great deal of "purge," he bundles the meat up and sends it back immediately.

"First, you look it all over to make sure it's nicely marbled." Freeman prods and lifts sections of the beef with the tip of his knife. "There has to be just enough fat running through to give it flavor." He cuts off a two-inch fringe of thick white fat and tosses it in the garbage can. "And we're looking for redness in the meat, not dark purple."

It looks pretty uniformly red to me, but Freeman nips and trims, taking an inch here, a half-inch there. Scraps go into the can.

But once the accordion-sized piece of meat is free of fat, bone, and gristle, he will waste nothing.

"I cut off the vein end to make pot roast, hamburger, sirloin tips, or steak-sandwich meat," he says, hacking off about a sixth of the strip loin, then wiping his knife, one side and then the other, on his apron. "And here's the ball piece. This isn't good for steak, so I'll cut it away for braised tips."

He moves like a blackjack dealer, sweeping small pieces to one side of the board with the back of his hand, large pieces to another corner. After about ten minutes, he is left with a scaled-down version of the original piece, and even I can see that this is the best of it. Glistening, uniform, etched with delicate branches of white. "Now, everything's in 14-ounce increments, to make it easier to halve things if we run out during dinner." Freeman slices confidently and weighs the piece he cut away: a quarter-ounce over. He slices again, and this time he hits the 14-ounce mark dead-on.

Less than 30 minutes after he began, Freeman has taken the hunk of raw beef and turned it into roughly a dozen steaks, which he arranges in a plastic bin, covers, and stores in the cooler. Tougher pieces go into another bin, labeled for pot roast and specials. Then he hooks up the cuber (an original, 1950s-style aluminum machine that looks like a giant toaster with teeth), flips the toggle switch, and forces the chunks through.

By four o'clock, Freeman has worked his way through about 20 strip loins. His knives and cutting board are clean, and he is consulting with his sous-chef, Mark, and the restaurant's second-generation owner, Pat Murray. A woman comes through the kitchen door, holding her uniform and carving set, and waves at Freeman. He turns. "That's my wife Marcia. She's been a waitress here for 30 years, and we just celebrated our 21st anniversary." He grins. "Murray's has been very good to me."

THE VEGETARIAN VIGILANTE

Brenda Langton doesn't shop at the Minneapolis Farmers' Market on weekends. She says it's geared toward a less-sophisticated clientele on Saturdays—people who can be fooled into buying wormy, commercial produce simply because it's sitting on a table in the open air. Today is a Friday in July. Cool, dry, the morning light clear and yellow. Brenda stalks up and down the aisles carrying six oversized shopping bags, all empty.

"It's always good to take a quick spin through when you first come to the market, to see everything before you buy," she says. "See, these are the best beans, the really dark green ones. And here they are, way at the end."

Langton opened her first vegetarian restaurant in 1978 and has owned Cafe Brenda, together with her husband, Tim Kane, for the past 17 years. The background page on her website says Brenda began cooking professionally in the early 1970s, which means she must be approaching 50. But looking at her now, you'd be hard pressed to tell. She is delicate in a flowered dress, roughly a hundred pounds of whirling motion—hands, fingers, feet, and head. She darts from stand to stand, waving hello to the people she knows, picking up bunches of herbs and smelling them, rubbing leaves and flowers and sprouts as if she can taste them through her fingertips.

"The Hmong vendors are doing the most wonderful work with greens," she says. We are standing in front of a table that is covered with bouquets of vegetables that have dark leaves, tiny yellow flowers, and thick bands around the stalks. "Here." She points to one. "This is yellow Chinese broccoli. The flowers and stems are edible. Everything. I wish I could take some, but I took delivery from Roots and Fruits [a Minneapolis produce wholesaler] yesterday and I already have so many greens."

She sighs and puts the bunch down carefully. "I can't take any today, but your greens are just beautiful," she tells the elderly man seated behind the table.

We walk about a hundred feet, stopping at three tables along the way so that Brenda can buy four enormous heads of cauliflower, each swaddled in a giant wreath of cabbage-y leaves, three cartons of waxed beans, three of baby cucumbers, and a particular bunch of pea shoots. "I look for the smaller ones. Not too stemmy. Then I just cut them up and add them to stir-fry."

The bulk of her produce comes from trusted suppliers, like Roots and Fruits, that deliver to her door each Thursday. But in preparation for the weekends, Brenda haunts the markets, looking for fresh vegetables she can build specials around. Tiny, marble-sized red potatoes are perfect for stew, she says. And the sharp-smelling slender scallions she finds will be a perfect garnish for fish.

At each vendor she visits, Brenda pulls out a wad of cash and peels off dollar bills—she says she tries to bring exact change as a courtesy—before settling the purchases into one of her bags. By the time we reach the end of the first aisle, she has two bulging bags and has spent just under $30. We cut across, toward the parking lot, where Tim is just driving up to take the first round of purchases back to the crisper and give Brenda two coolers to hold the rest.

As we head back, a hawker from behind a table of strawberries and broccoli in standard green grocer cartons calls out, "Three for a buck, lady!"

Brenda stops to examine the man's goods and wrinkles her nose as she nudges the broccoli's brown leaves. "These are over the hill, dear." She glares at the young man. "The nutrients are gone and they've lost all their flavor."

He shrugs. But as we leave, Brenda's still fuming. "I wish someone would patrol and keep those people out," she says. "They're just selling-off seconds. And that's not what this is all about."

Brenda has built her business around gourmet food and nutritional know-how. She's written several nationally marketed cookbooks and works as a natural foods and diet consultant. She says she often selects items for her restaurant according to their yin/yang properties, because she believes this will improve her customers' health and digestion.

At a stand devoted entirely to root vegetables, she buys an enormous daikon radish that she'll serve with fish, in order to absorb any toxins, such as mercury, and help dissolve fats. Brenda is rabidly opposed to the Atkins diet trend, or any other rigidly restrictive program, and believes that people all over America who follow such regimes are courting kidney disease and osteoporosis. Her theory is that good nutrition is all about balance: pairing vegetables that grow up out of the ground with those that grow down into it, proteins with complex carbohydrates, colorful foods with earthy staples.

She also sees the beauty in food. Holding up a box of baby squashes, she gazes at the fluted orange blossoms growing out of their tips and decides to buy them, simply because she wants to decorate her dinner plates with these flowers. By the time we head back to her car, Brenda has filled the last four bags and bought as much as her coolers will hold.

"I have farmers who deliver directly to me, and a fairly set menu of dishes my customers expect," she says as she climbs behind the wheel. "But I still don't think I could do what I do without this sort of market. I come here to fill in and be inspired. Every time I come, I find myself building a whole meal around something unexpected that I found."

THE SURVEYOR OF SEAFOOD

Rick Kimmes looks like a chef. He wears the checked pants, the double-breasted coat, the tall hat. He received his training at the Culinary Institute of America in Hyde Park, New York, and retains a rigid respect for the uniform (he bristles when he sees chefs hunched by Dumpsters, smoking while wearing their whites). Kimmes carries himself like a captain. But he acts more like a stock trader, at least during the morning hours.

The Oceanaire Seafood Room at the Minneapolis Hyatt Regency, which he owns and operates with partner and dining room manager Steve Uhl, doesn't open for dinner until 5 PM But Kimmes starts work around 6 AM, when the night fishermen dock their boats off the Atlantic coast. Throughout breakfast and the drive in to work, he's on his cell phone.

When he arrives, he heads for two tables in the back of the dining room that were left half-set the night before. There is a slightly soiled tablecloth and a pot of black coffee, set out by Uhl, who beat him through the door this morning. Kimmes walks in with a black four-line telephone, cord dragging on the ground behind him, a stack of paperwork, and a cup. He plugs in the phone, pours himself some coffee, and starts working.

Even before Oceanaire opened in November 1998, founder Wade Wiestling envisioned a restaurant in the middle of the country that would serve fresh fish from all over the world. He spent months building relationships with seafood vendors, learning about seasonality, fishing techniques, and shipping methods.

His goal was to serve fish netted within the previous two to three days, with an ideal elapsed time of 12 hours from sea to plate. He was banking on the willingness of Twin Cities diners to pay a premium for the very finest seafood. And he was right. Even through a sluggish economy, Oceanaire has done a steady business, serving roughly 300 people each weeknight and up to 500 on Fridays and Saturdays.

"Five years ago, this restaurant set a new benchmark by saying people in Minnesota should be able to get fresh seafood on a daily basis," says Uhl. "We post our air bills on the blackboard so our customers can see exactly when their meal came in, date and time."

Indeed, the Icelandic Arctic char and Guatemalan mahi-mahi that Oceanaire served last night arrived just yesterday afternoon; I can read the postmark clearly.

But I really came to talk to Rick Kimmes, who took over as executive chef when Wiestling moved out of the kitchen to expand the Oceanaire concept to other cities (the restaurant now has locations in Washington, D.C., Seattle, Dallas, and Indianapolis). However, Kimmes has been on the phone 90 percent of the time I've been in the building. Each time it rings he apologizes profusely, but the call cannot wait: It's a broker standing on the docks in Gloucester, Massachusetts, with a report on the day's catch; an oyster vendor from Seattle, up before dawn just to take Kimmes's order of 20 dozen large closed-shell; and, once, a fisherman himself shouting over the roar of surf from the pitching deck of his boat, telling Kimmes he just caught an 80-pound halibut and needed to know how much to set aside for Oceanaire.

Finally, around 11:30, there is a lull. The shipment is due in at noon, so we rush to tour the kitchen. The "fish box," as they call it, is a walk-in cooler with a cutting board and sink on one end. It is kept at 32 degrees. It is clean and only slightly fishy smelling—and, at this hour, nearly empty. Uhl pulls out a whole fish on crushed ice and lifts it out delicately by the tail, displaying its freshness. There are one or two trays of king crab legs as long as my forearm.

"We really try to order exactly what we need for the night," Kimmes says, explaining the lack of fish in the box. "I don't want it sitting around, and it's expensive to waste."

But they do toss it, Uhl hastens to say, after three days. No question.

On the cooler door there are four clipboards with logs for fish temperature, cooler temperature, food waste, and a cleaning roster. There's also an envelope marked Fish Tags; Oceanaire keeps all shellfish tags for 120 days (the industry standard is 90) in case of an outbreak of fish-borne disease. This has never happened, and Uhl tells me proudly that Oceanaire's kitchen was used to train University of Minnesota students who are studying to become food and restaurant inspectors.

Noon arrives; there is no shipment. The phone has stopped ringing and Kimmes begins to pace. His sous-chef, Michael, came in about half an hour ago; he has a laptop open and is making up the night's menu. "We have a little in-house printing shop," he explains, checking the order sheet Kimmes made up yesterday and creating menu items on the spot, based on the incoming orders. "Every night we create fresh menus with a few core dishes— things we always have, such as shrimp cocktail—and the items we make because they're in season."

Twelve-thirty. Michael is nearly done with the menu, but still they have no product. Kimmes finally sits at the table strewn with order forms and old menus. This is the toughest part for him. "Ever since 9/11, the airport x-rays every box that comes in from overseas," he says. "That's why we have to take the temperature of everything that comes through the door. We have to make sure it didn't sit on the tarmac for a couple hours, waiting to be checked."

I have to ask. "Does it ever just . . . not come?"

Kimmes sighs and sits back in his chair. "No." He taps his foot. "Once in a while, an oyster we're expecting won't show up. Or a batch of lobsters. It can get really bad during the holiday season, or when there's bad weather. We just wait. And sometimes we get nervous. But somehow, every day at five o'clock, we're stocked up and ready."

About three minutes later, a delivery driver bursts through the door trundling a dolly stacked with cold cardboard boxes.

Cooks at Work

Learning to Cook, Cooking to Learn

by Matthew Amster-Burton
from eGullet.com

This all-food-all-the-time website offers some of the internet's most entertaining reading, and one of its most articulate voices is Amster-Burton, who also writes for the *Seattle Times*. Like many eGullet essays, it touches on fundamental questions about why we cook and why we eat.

Like many of her admirers and detractors, I wouldn't have missed the recent made-for-television movie, *Martha Inc.: The Story of Martha Stewart,* for a free copper skillet. The best scene was the one in which Stewart, played by Cybill Shepherd, is giving a cooking demonstration at K-Mart and tells a querulous customer, "Maybe you just can't cook. There is *nothing wrong with my tartlets.*"

Martha's TV alter ego may be a jerk, but she has a point. The instinct of the novice cook is always to blame the recipe when something goes wrong. And the recipe is almost never to blame.

When we're learning to drive, we don't blame the driver's manual or the driver's ed instructor when something goes wrong. We correctly point the finger at ourselves (okay, maybe at that asshole who cut us off). When we're learning a musical instrument, we don't blame the music teacher when we're having trouble getting the right sound out of the oboe.

Something about learning to cook, however, brings out the codependent in everyone. Since before Fannie Farmer there have been writers eager to reduce cooking to a system of interlocking never-fail recipes and readers eager to believe this is possible.

There is a place for the highly specific recipe: beginner's cookbooks and recipes for things generally considered tricky (pie crust) come to mind. A helpful hint is never out of place (cook the pancakes on the first side until the bubbles on top start breaking). *Cook's Illustrated* and the Dorling-Kindersley books follow this format with great success.

The problem with detailed recipes is that they reinforce a bad assumption: that everything you need to know about making a dish can be encapsulated into a recipe, and that learning to cook is just a matter of picking the right book and following the instructions carefully.

Good cooks are experts at what they do. Being an expert means that most of the task is unconscious: you've internalized all sorts of tiny principles that lead to a successful outcome, and you can no longer call up what many of them are. You can stop and think and break it down, and being able to do that is one hallmark of a good teacher. But you will never, ever break it down completely; otherwise, it wouldn't be a skilled task in the first place.

"A recipe is not your instructor," writes eGullet's Steve Klc. "How realistic is it to expect recipes to fill in all the possible gaps of your knowledge and experience—which you bring to the table along with said recipe—and also those gaps or weaknesses of all other cooks?"

Ever taught someone to drive? Weren't you amazed to realize all the things they didn't know instinctively? The only way to become a good driver or a good cook is practice.

My first car was a 1980 Mazda hatchback with a manual transmission. It was a brutal teacher; the clutch was as touchy as they come. My father took me to a parking lot and explained how the transmission worked. His explanation was terrific. I understood the friction point and what it meant to bring the drive shaft up to speed. I felt ready, and you know what they say: you never feel more ready than just before you blow it. I started the car, depressed the clutch, shifted into first, and stalled out with much jerking and sputtering. This was the first of a dozen consecutive stalls. My brain knew what to do; my feet were useless.

It took six months before I was confident in my ability to get that car into first gear on a hill without stalling. I got rid of the car in 1996 and haven't driven a stick shift with any regularity since. Every time I've needed to do so, however, it has been easy. I didn't have to relearn a thing. I remember that it was once hard, but I don't remember why.

If you've never driven a stick shift, surely you've learned to ride a bike (I was a slow learner here as well), juggle three balls, or play chords on an acoustic guitar. Psychologists understand a lot about how we learn these things, but at some level it will always seem like magic. It was hard yesterday and easy today . . . and I'm not doing anything different.

In their book *The Social Life of Information* John Seely Brown and Paul Duguid make an observation that should have been obvious but was somehow never clear to me: there is a difference between learning *about* something and learning to *do* something. I wrote two weeks ago about learning to bake bread, and before I began I read several excellent baking books which taught me about different types of yeast and flour and how to use preferments to improve flavor. I could have memorized every word in these books and I still would have been a bumbling baker once I got my hands in the dough.

Cookbook publishers want to sell a completely different story: read this book, follow the carefully tested "foolproof" recipes, and bingo, you're a cook! What happens next? The aspiring cook brings the book home and the first five recipe attempts come out terrible. Then they blame the book and its bad recipes (there is something wrong with Martha's tartlets!) or figure they just don't have any talent.

Don't conclude that I'm anti-cookbook, though. I grew up with cookbooks. My mother has a collection of several thousand, and I have about 300. I read them obsessively and use the recipes, but these books don't earn their keep by recipes alone.

"Recipes, obviously, are the most important element in distinguishing one cookbook from another," writes Mark Bittman in the introduction to *How to Cook Everything*. He couldn't be more wrong, unless he means something facile, like, "Italian cookbooks have Italian recipes and Chinese cookbooks have Chinese recipes."

In fact, headnotes, sidebars, and chapter introductions do a lot more to separate the good cookbooks from the bad than recipes.

James Peterson's *Splendid Soups*, for example, has plenty of soup recipes, but it's the sidebars about improvising soups, fixing a dull-tasting soup, and countless other topics that make the book worth owning.

"There are countless cookbooks from which I have never made a single dish but for which I have the highest regard and which I would recommend unreservedly to anyone," writes John Thorne in his *Simple Cooking* newsletter.

Starting your cooking journey with a cookbook full of badly written recipes will lead to frustration. Starting off with a superb beginner's cookbook will also lead to frustration. If you don't get frustrated while learning to cook, you should join the cast of *Touched By an Angel*. In the end, I don't think it matters which kind of cookbook you start with as long as it keeps drawing you back, demanding that you try the recipe again because you just *have* to taste that. The success of *Mastering the Art of French Cooking* is due to this quality. It doesn't have the best recipes—although many are good—but it made readers want to cook. It still does. Can you imagine any other cookbook that would take over the life of an otherwise normal person like Julie Powell of the Julie-Julia Project and compel her to cook every recipe in the book? Powell's Weblog is famously full of kitchen disasters. Her experiment has been running for about nine months, a long enough gestation period for a good cook to emerge.

Anybody can learn to cook, and the payoffs are huge. The first time you say to yourself, "I can't believe I made something so delicious," it's a memorable moment, like not falling off the bicycle. But nobody can magically learn to cook without practice and without making embarrassing mistakes.

It would be hard to name a more influential cookbook than Escoffier's *Guide Culinaire*. By the modern definition, that book doesn't have a single recipe in it, certainly nothing you could get published in a cookbook or weekly food section. More recently, Elizabeth Schneider's celebrated book *Vegetables from Amaranth to Zucchini* has a few detailed recipes but far more like the following:

> At Restaurant Jean Georges, another restaurant where
> wild foods are a signature ingredient, chef Vongerichten

offers Porcini and Walnut Tart with Chickweed: Caramelize onions with walnuts, then puree. Spread puree on disc of thin puff pastry. Top with porcini slices; brush with garlic oil. Bake. Toss together chickweed with lemon juice and grapeseed oil. Serve alongside tarts. (Chickweed is a green; substitute mustard greens or kale if you can't find it.)

There is nothing wrong with Vong's tartlets—or his recipe.

Good Cooking is Trouble

by Paul Bertolli
from *Cooking By Hand*

The stunning production values of this cookbook by Bertolli—chef/owner of the acclaimed Oakland restaurant Oliveto— make it look like another coffee-table celebrity chef album. What is really is, though, is a radical challenge to return to cooking basics, no matter how much more time it takes.

I have never met a skilled chef who didn't have an acute sense of smell. This heightened sense gives one the ability not merely to perceive and identify aromas and bouquets, but to be *stirred* by the way things smell, for better or worse. I first became interested in learning to cook because I had a strong desire to replicate what I remembered having smelled and tasted. I discovered other worlds beyond my mother's kitchen—restaurants—at a fairly early age. My parents liked to take us to a seafood house on nearby Richardson Bay, a backwater of the Golden Gate, for cocktails of Dungeness crab and bay shrimp, fried sand dabs, and San Francisco *cioppino*. Later, I was part of a group that enjoyed the generosity of my high-school English teacher, a cleric whose rich aunt sent tithes directly to his checkbook. For several years, at nearly every week's end we ate at a different restaurant. I discovered broiled lobster, the seductions of sweet butter and soft-ripened cheese, pasta Alfredo, and French reduction sauces. When we got away with it (who could refuse a priest in collar?), we ordered drinks and I discovered how exciting a meal could be when lubricated with old-fashioneds and red wine.

Later on, I started reading about cooking and experimenting

with cookbooks. It didn't take long to discover the disparity between what I remembered having tasted and my own renditions. Even the food I tried that was most familiar to me and more directly accessible, through instructions provided by my mother and grandmothers, never tasted quite the same when I cooked it. Following recipes was frustrating. Trying to match the static words in a book to the leaping events in a saucepan was a clumsy back-and-forth endeavor. Of course, recipes varied in quality, but more often than not, I found them vague, overly general, or outright wrong. Recipes left me with more questions than they answered about the actual process of cooking. I wanted to know why I was being asked to perform a certain step or what to do if things went awry. The reductive efficiency of the recipe offered little clue. It was clear that ingredients could vary across the board, so when instructed to "dice 3 leeks," this raised the question "What size, and in what condition?" Having digested Escoffier's dissertations on the mother sauces and what I could gain of technique from Pellaprat, Pepin, Guerard, Bugialli, Hazan, Ada Boni, and others, I struck out on my own. I substituted ingredients or left them out altogether; I experimented with herbs and oven temperatures, methods and utensils, and levels of reduction. I did my best to correct for deficiencies in flavor or balance, usually by adding *more* of something. In retrospect, some of these meals were abysmal, especially since "more" often resulted in food that no longer resembled itself or the original idea. Nevertheless, occasional successes gave me confidence that following my own nose and instincts would lead me closer to the ideals of my taste memory. I was happiest when improvising.

Later, when I began recording what I had done in the kitchen, I found that I was no more comfortable writing a recipe than following one. Studying my food-stained notes, I was annoyed at having to go back and measure in cups and teaspoons the ingredients that I had originally added according to taste and feel. Any good cook knows how to dose salt in the right proportion to food by the way it feels in the hand. Take that dose, put it into a measuring spoon, and it may come up fractionally short or overfill the brim. When a cook creates a recipe to fit standard weights and measures, the measures themselves creep in to exert control over the cook's better instincts. Precision is lost. Weight rather than volume measurement is the more accurate way to record the amount of any ingredient. But it likewise puts an object foreign to the creative context between the cook and the food. As my friend Richard Olney said, the act of recording a recipe "robs it of the license responsible for its creation." Ultimately it is the reader, the presumed learner, who is left bereft. Subtleties in the way food looks, smells, and behaves are lost when the process of cooking is reduced to a series of simple and efficient steps. Such is the unfortunate legacy of almost all recipe writing.

Still, some measurements are necessary. A cook who fails to provide an ingredients list with a basic guide for quantities would be remiss. But developing a quantified recipe is a long process rich with interesting and informative detail. By moving beyond the rigid confines of the standard recipe format, the writer/cook could add back many subtleties of his own experience that might give the reader a guide for dealing with what happens along the way. This same detail could help the reader understand the "process" well enough to be able to improvise according to his or her own tastes, or in response to the ingredients at hand.

Of course, this thinking about recipes does not apply to all processes in the kitchen. In pastry making and almost all forms of flour confectionery—indeed in any preparation in which the basic ingredients are relatively consistent—precise proportions must be observed in order to achieve good results. It is not a good idea to "wing it" with a cake or with someone's favorite cocktail. Nevertheless, such preparations are not entirely formulaic and call for an equal amount of attention on the part of the cook to the small variables that can make all the difference. It is impossible to communicate in words the precise feel of pasta dough when it is fully kneaded. It's equally troublesome to describe how much moisture and elasticity in the dough will give the eventual noodle its appealing bite. Variations in the manner of incorporating beaten egg white into cake batters can also result in degrees of lightness or heaviness in the finished cake. Regardless of the degree of specificity in any recipe, the difference that makes all the difference lies between the lines. Following a recipe does not absolve the cook from cooking.

While my own early forays into French and Italian cooking had sharpened my mechanical skills, I still felt at a loss for some deeper understanding of what I was doing. Looking around me, apart from a few San Francisco specialties tied to the seasonal availability of certain fish and shellfish, there was no clear food tradition to absorb. America in the thrall of *nouvelle cuisine* and *cuisine minceur,* fast food, and the influences of ethnic cooking was only confusing. In comparison to the Old World, America seemed embarrassingly impressionable. Food writers fascinated with the open restaurant kitchens of the west coast, their grill menus, celebration of local farms, and prophets of the fresh and pure, created the concept of "California cuisine." I am still at a loss to identify a single defining dish that belongs to this "revolution." Professional cooks with credibility either came from northern Europe or looked to it for inspiration. I could only imagine what it might mean to live in a city like Nantes that had a sauce named after it, or in Langhirano, where it took mountain air and a year and a half to age a ham, or in Lyon, where it was considered divine to roast a farm hen in a pig's bladder.

Through a combination of coincidence and fate I began working in restaurants in the late 1970s and after several years of apprenticeship I had the good fortune to land a restaurant job in Italy, the country of my heritage on both sides of my family. I'd grown up on emigrant renditions of Italian food, with no way to judge or question the differences between Italian food in Italy and versions of it made with New World ingredients. By working in Italy, I was able to ground myself in the food with which I was most familiar. I immediately felt drawn to Italy's transparent traditions and the long-established links between the food of a region and nature at its source. I was also intrigued with the intersection of skill and mystery in cooking—the transformations of food initiated through human intervention but only fulfilled by more obscure forces. For how could a mortal man have made this glorious wine, this cheese, and this *aceto balsamico*?

It was through working in Italy and returning time and again over the years to explore the cooking of its various provinces that I discovered what it means to live within a food tradition. I learned to understand the many ways in which simplicity manifests in cooking. Ironically, simplicity represents the trouble that many generations of cooks have taken to arrive at the best expression of their native ingredients. I saw that such simple food lives as much in the most refined dishes of a big-city restaurant as in the rustic menus of an *osteria*. No matter how straightforward or complex the ingredients or the cooking technique, simple food is directly appealing; there is nothing extraneous or fussy about it and the tastes and presentation are clear and unified. I discovered many examples all around me in the homes in which I ate traditional family meals, in markets and restaurants, and in the cellars of vintners, cheese makers, olive oil producers, vinegar makers, and pork butchers. The experience of this simple food was fundamental to my formation as a chef. I learned that olive oil is not just a cooking fat but a culture, that food is determined by place and inseparable from it, and that nourishment around the table is not only a matter of filling one's belly but of taking part in a daily ritual that celebrates and confirms a sense of belonging to the food and to long, recurrent traditions of a place.

Authenticity has its own taste yet its principles are universal. Given that the taste, the process, and the overall effect of particular flavors are bound by place, people and tradition, I do not attempt to duplicate at Oliveto, my restaurant in Oakland, California, the risotto with cuttlefish I ate in Venice, the wild field salads I gathered in Chianti, or the *culatello* I learned to cure in a foggy cellar in Zibello. Instead, I approach my cooking with a similar commitment to present what is grown here, to make food from scratch, to gather in the wild, to maintain my vinegar loft in the quiet of the countryside and my curing cellar in the fog of the Berkeley hills.

Like any active aesthetic practice, cooking is most satisfying when you are creatively involved. Being able to create in the kitchen necessitates learning the language and inner workings of cooking. The painter mixes her color palette to her mind's eye. The musician learns to listen to sound and to play what he hears. Cooks develop an internal memory for scents, tastes, textures, the architecture of flavor, and the path and process toward its consummation. The ever-evolving taste memory is the internal compass that arbitrates the physical steps, maneuvers, and choices a cook makes along the way. When you smell pasta made with fresh wheat you may be impelled to grind your own flour. Your taste for the genuine may temper your impatience at the prospect of waiting six months for your *salame* to ripen. The vivid quality of produce just pulled from the ground may lead you to plant your own radic-chio or carrots. With growing curiosity you may find yourself puz-zling out the savor missing in a braise you've made a dozen times

. . . [I] encourage an open-ended approach that leads you to consider the options and variables dictated by the moment, to chart your own direction, to develop a feeling for food, in fact to *cook*. To those accustomed to cooking more to the letter of a recipe, this approach may appear annoying or problematic. If I knew of a better or easier path, I would have recommended it. But experience has shown that the trouble you take will also be your enduring pleasure.

The Kitchen Detective

by Christopher Kimball
from *The Kitchen Detective*

Founder and editor of *Cooks Illustrated*, host of TV's America's *Test Kitchen*, Kimball approaches cooking with a scientist's empirical technique. His signature obsession for detail could be very irritating, were it not for his refreshingly candid, opinionated, and often very funny tone.

ALL YOU REALLY NEED IS LOVE—
AND 25 GOOD RECIPES

Most cooks I know are constantly looking for new recipes the way some folks are constantly on the lookout for antiques, clothes, computer software, or specials down at Price Chopper. There is nothing wrong with living life vicariously through recipes—we all do it to some extent—but the problem with most home cooks is that they have too *many* recipes rather than too few.

Two hundred years ago, good cooks generally had a relatively limited repertoire, extending to perhaps 50 key recipes. They could make a roast, a cake, a loaf of bread, a few casseroles, etc. As a result, they became experts at what they cooked—they could make buttermilk biscuits, a pot roast, wax beans, or chocolate cake from memory, even with their eyes closed. The point? Well, they soon realized that details mattered, that small variations in preparation yielded different results, and that baking a pie in July was quite different from doing so in February, because the dough was more likely to heat up and become unworkable. They also learned that different cuts of meat behave differently in a pot roast, that yeast is not always a predictable ingredient, and that ovens are not precision instruments and need to be watched closely. Like good musicians, good cooks realized that restricting one's repertoire has great advantages: It allows one to focus on the underlying technique instead of just a new set of notes.

So, my suggestion is to start with a shortlist of 25 recipes that you make most often, and stick with them for a bit. As you get better, slowly increase your range. You will soon learn what a biscuit, a roast chicken, or a chicken soup is really supposed to taste like. That is the first step in learning anything.

PASTA WITH TOMATOES AND ARUGULA

In a small mountain village north of Rome, I was once served a simple dish of pasta with a sauce that had penetrated the pasta itself, flavoring it and bathing it with a silky salve of fruity olive oil, garlic, and herbs. This was a far cry from the usual American spaghetti dinner—a watery mound of pasta onto which is dumped an oily flow of tomato sauce. As we all know, oil and water don't mix.

I was also bothered by the comments of Italian friends who reprimanded me on the subject of the ratio of sauce to pasta. Although they insisted that a small amount of sauce goes a long way, I found that my attempts at lightly sauced pasta simply yielded underdressed, bland plates of spaghetti.

My first thought was to cook the pasta in the sauce itself, not in boiling water. Using a simple, 10-minute tomato sauce, I added angel hair pasta with horrific results. By the time the center of the pasta was cooked, the outside had turned slimy. In addition, the sauce was starchy from the pasta, and it became very dry (dried pasta absorbs a lot of liquid during cooking). When I then added vast amounts of liquid to the pan to thin the sauce, the flavor of the sauce was compromised.

Next, I tried starting the pasta in water and finishing it in the sauce. This method proved superior, because the water rinsed off excess starch, the texture of the finished pasta was good, and the cooking water made the perfect liquid for thinning the sauce. Using fettuccine, I reduced the cooking time in water by one, three, five, and seven minutes, finishing the cooking in the sauce itself. When the pasta spent just a few minutes in the sauce, the results were disappointing: The noodles had not absorbed much flavor. When I precooked the pasta for only a couple of minutes, however, I ended up with the same situation I had started with—slimy pasta. Finally, I settled on cooking the pasta about half the time in boiling water and half in the sauce. This was perfection—the sauce penetrated the pasta and clung to it like suntan lotion. A little bit of sauce went a long way.

Now that I had tested fettuccine, I wanted to test other shapes. Surprisingly, from angel hair to fusilli, it ended up to be the same: Half the cooking time in water and half in sauce produced an amazingly flavorful piece of pasta, although the amount of cooking liquid that had to be added to the sauce varied. I also wanted to try this with other types of tomato-based sauces. Meat sauces were wonderful, as were an amatriciana (tomato sauce with pancetta or bacon) and a ragu, although a puttanesca was less successful. My favorite, however, is still a quick tomato sauce with a handful of arugula thrown in near the end. It's fast, it's easy, and it marries perfectly with the pasta.

Pasta with Quick Tomato Sauce and Arugula

Serves 4

The amount of pasta water you add to the sauce is variable—just be sure to reserve 2 cups cooking liquid before the pasta is drained. This approach is also very good with any meat sauce.

1 (28-ounce) can diced or whole tomatoes packed in juice (not puree), Muir Glen preferred
2 medium garlic cloves, peeled
3 tablespoons extra-virgin olive oil
¼ teaspoon sugar
Salt and freshly ground black pepper
1 pound pasta
2 tablespoons coarsely chopped fresh basil leaves
2 cups arugula leaves, washed and dried
Freshly grated Parmesan cheese

1. If using diced tomatoes, go to step 2. If using whole tomatoes,

drain them and reserve the liquid. Dice the tomatoes into about ¼-inch pieces either by hand or with a food processor. Add enough juice to yield 2 cups.

2. Process the garlic through a press (or mince with a knife) into a small bowl; stir in 1 teaspoon water. Heat 2 tablespoons of the oil and the garlic mixture in a very large skillet or sauté pan (at least 12 inches) over medium heat until fragrant but not browned, about 2 minutes. Stir in the tomatoes and simmer until slightly thickened, about 10 minutes. Stir in the sugar and ½ teaspoon salt.

3. Meanwhile, bring 4 quarts of salted water to a rolling boil in a large pot over high heat. Add the pasta and cook for half of the time indicated on the package. Reserve 2 cups of the cooking water and drain the pasta. At this point the pasta has started to soften but still appears quite raw in the middle. Add the pasta to the skillet (or, in the absence of a large enough skillet, add the pasta and sauce back to the pasta pot) and complete cooking the pasta in the sauce, adding the reserved cooking water as needed to keep the sauce moist, stirring frequently. With 2 minutes cooking time remaining, add the remaining 1 tablespoon oil and ½ teaspoon salt as well as the basil and arugula, and stir to combine. The pasta and sauce will likely look drier than normal but will be moist and flavorful upon tasting. Taste and adjust the salt level if necessary. Serve immediately with cheese and pepper to taste.

VEAL SHANKS REDISCOVERED

I know the statistics. Whereas Americans consume more than 60 pounds of beef per capita per year, we eat less than 2 pounds per year of veal. Perhaps that is because veal and rabbit have that same baby thing going—we don't like to eat cartoon characters, and although baby vegetables are okay, we turn our back on calves. It is, no doubt, a reasonable moral position, but, speaking as someone who raises his own beef and pork, I am not sure that heaven makes moral distinctions between killing and eating animals that are 2 years old versus 2 months. Oh, and rabbit is about the most delicious meat there is—I even shoot my own. So if you haven't thrown this book down in disgust, let's talk about

the best way to cook veal shanks, one of the world's most succulent and satisfying foods.

The shank is the lower foreleg of the animal and is my favorite
cut, as it is incredibly tender when properly cooked. (Osso buco is
made from this cut.) But over the years, I have had mixed results
cooking shanks. Some were perfectly tender after two hours; other
shanks were still tough after three hours of cooking time. I wanted
to discover a foolproof method for determining just when they
were done as well as home in on the best oven temperature.

I have found that long, slow cooking is the best method for most
cuts of meat, the exceptions being lamb and very expensive cuts such
as tenderloin. I have tried a variety of temperatures with shanks and
found that a low 250 degrees is ideal. Low temperatures allow the
meat to cook evenly without overcooking the outer layers before the
middle of the meat is properly cooked. The big problem, however,
was how to determine exactly when the shanks were done.

It turns out that an old-fashioned pot roast held a valuable clue.
When meat's internal temperature reaches a bit over 100 degrees,
the meat starts to lose moisture. The fibers twist like a bath towel,
exuding juices. That's why rare or medium-rare meat is usually
juicier than medium or well-done meat. However, when meat starts
to reach temperatures in excess of 160 degrees, the collagen, those
tough jelly-like ripples in the meat, start to melt, softening the meat
and making it more tender. What I didn't know is that the meat
must reach a whopping 200 to 210 degrees for this process to be
fully realized. Meat cooked to, say, 180 degrees, will still be tough
and dry. That's why many of the shanks I had cooked were still
tough; I just hadn't cooked them long enough. The best way to
measure the internal temperature, by the way, is to use an instant-
read thermometer.

I also noted that both the pan and the shank itself might dramatically change the cooking time. A cast-iron Dutch oven, for example,
will cook much faster than stainless steel. Large pieces of shank cook
slower than smaller, thinner slices. As a result, the recipe below
simply states two to four hours of cooking. (This dish can be held
and then reheated.) Let the thermometer or your fork be the guide.
Continue cooking until the shanks are fully "pot-roasted" and meltingly tender. By the way, this dish is a model for hundreds of similar

recipes. You can use lamb shanks or beef short ribs instead. You can change the herbs or the seasonings to make endless variations.

~~~

Veal Shanks with Olives, Anchovies, and Sage

Serves 4

Be sure to cook the shanks long enough—the meat should be falling off the bone, and the internal temperature should reach at least 200 degrees. This dish can be made earlier in the day and then reheated on top of the stove over low heat (about 15 minutes). If you refrigerate this dish before reheating, any fat will solidify and come to the surface, where it is easy to remove. I like to serve this dish with Seven-Minute Polenta.

4 small to medium veal shanks, 2-inch-thick center-cut pieces
    (2½ to 3 pounds total)
Salt and freshly ground black pepper
2 tablespoons unsalted butter
2 tablespoons olive oil
¼ cup flour
1 medium onion, chopped
6 anchovy fillets, chopped
1 garlic head, cut in half and excess paper removed
½ cup dry white wine
1 cup chicken stock
1 cup canned diced tomatoes, drained
1 cup pitted and chopped Kalamata olives
2 tablespoons minced fresh sage

1. Adjust an oven rack to the center position and heat the oven to 250 degrees. Tie a string around the circumference of each shank (or have the butcher do it for you). Season shanks with salt and pepper.

2. Heat the butter and olive oil in a 12-inch-wide Dutch oven or sauté pan with a lid over medium-high heat. When the butter-oil

mixture is very hot but not smoking, lightly flour the seasoned shanks and then add them to the pot. Sauté for 4 minutes per side, shaking the pan occasionally to stop the shanks from sticking. The shanks should be golden brown on each side. Remove the shanks from the pot and reserve on a plate. Add the onion and anchovies to the pot, stir, and cook for 2 minutes. Add the garlic, wine, chicken stock, tomatoes, and ¼ cup of the olives along with the veal shanks and bring the mixture to a boil. Cover and place in the oven.

3. Cook for 2 to 4 hours or until the meat falls off the bone and is very tender. Remove the garlic head and squeeze out the contents, adding the cooked garlic back to the liquid. (Cooking time will depend on the size of the shanks, your oven, and your pot. You can make the recipe to this point, refrigerate, and reheat later for serving.)

4. Place the pot on the stove and bring the liquid to a simmer. Add the sage and the remaining ¼ cup olives. Cook, uncovered, for 4 minutes. Adjust the seasonings, adding salt and pepper to taste. Transfer one shank to each plate and spoon the sauce over the shanks.

CHICKEN CUTLETS IN FOUR MINUTES?

I am appalled at the lengths to which some folks will go to get dinner on the table fast, gulping down frozen dinners, jarred spaghetti sauce, bad take-out Chinese food, and the ubiquitous Domino's Pizza. I am no food snob—I love a burger as much as the next carnivore—but I am wedded to from-scratch home cooking for reasons of taste, health, and, well, philosophy. So, in order to compete with Lean Cuisine, I set out with a near-impossible task. Could I create a recipe for a homemade chicken dinner that would take 20 minutes or less, including all preparation and cooking?

My first thought was that skin and bones would have to go in order to speed up cooking time. That left me with boneless, skinless cutlets. But chicken breasts can be quite thick, and as such they would never cook in just a few minutes. So after a bit of testing, I decided to slice them in half horizontally to make them thinner and quicker cooking. The next barrier to quick and easy cooking was the unevenness of the chicken breast. I found it necessary to quickly pound the thicker parts of the breast so that the sliced cutlets were an even ¼ inch thick.

A hot sauté pan is fast and easier to manage than a broiler or hot oven. But thin, naked cutlets would dry out quickly in a hot pan. My solution was to devise a simple coating for the cutlets to keep them juicy and add some textural contrast as well. The first choice was dried bread crumbs, but they were a bit dull. A combination of grated Parmesan cheese and bread crumbs was better, providing both flavor and a crispy coating. I then tested egg whites, whole eggs, and then no eggs at all as a coating before adding the bread crumb-cheese mixture. The whites were the winner; the whole eggs made the coating too thick and heavy, and without any egg, the cutlets were bland.

Because of the large amount of cheese, I found a nonstick skillet to be essential. Hot oil is crucial to developing a nice crispy crust. To determine whether the pan is hot enough to add the chicken, heat the pan over medium-high and wait until the oil starts to smoke. Now you know the pan is ready. The cooking time was fast—three to four minutes total—and I could handle four cutlets at a time if I used a 12-inch skillet.

Now that I had a lightning-fast chicken recipe, I wanted to make a whole meal of it. A bed of arugula arranged on the plate with one sliced tomato worked nicely. These are drizzled with extra-virgin olive oil and balsamic vinegar and sprinkled with fresh tarragon leaves. The hot chicken cutlets are then placed on top. Serve this quick dinner with a fresh baguette and a fruity wine, and you have a quick, from-scratch dinner—a whole lot better than any frozen pizza.

Four-Minute Chicken Cutlets

Serves 4

Use very fine textured store-bought bread crumbs for this recipe instead of fussing with homemade. You can skip the bed of greens if you like, although peppery arugula adds a lot to this dish. The idea for this recipe was inspired by New Food Fast *by Donna Hay.*

4 boneless, skinless chicken breasts, rinsed and patted dry with
   paper towels
3 large egg whites
¾ cup freshly grated Parmesan cheese
½ cup fine dried bread crumbs
3 cups arugula or tender greens of your choice
4 small or medium tomatoes
Extra-virgin olive oil for drizzling
Balsamic vinegar for drizzling
Salt and freshly ground black pepper
1 bunch fresh tarragon or basil
4 tablespoons olive oil, or more as needed

1. Cut each individual breast in half horizontally to yield a total
of 8 pieces. Using a flat meat pounder or small skillet, pound the
chicken (smooth-side up) between 2 pieces of clear plastic wrap
to a thickness of ¼ inch. In a small bowl, lightly whisk the egg
whites with a fork. Combine the grated cheese and bread crumbs
in a shallow dish or pie plate. Make a bed of ¾ cup arugula on
each of 4 dinner plates. Slice the tomatoes and place on top of the
greens. Drizzle with the extra-virgin olive oil and balsamic
vinegar and season with salt to taste. Scatter tarragon leaves over
the tomato.

2. Heat 4 tablespoons olive oil in a 12-inch nonstick skillet over
medium-high heat until just starting to smoke. Meanwhile,
season 4 pieces of chicken on both sides with salt and pepper.
Dip each piece into the egg whites and then into the cheese-
crumb mixture, pressing on the chicken to collect a thick coating
on both sides. Place the chicken in the heated pan and cook
1½ to 2 minutes on each side, or until deep golden brown. (Only
3 very large pieces of chicken may fit into a 12-inch pan, so you
will have to cook 3 batches, not 2.) You can cut into a piece of
chicken to check for doneness—it should be just cooked through
and juicy. Remove to paper towels to drain. Repeat with the
remaining pieces of chicken, adding more olive oil when necessary. On each of the 4 dinner plates, arrange 2 pieces of hot
chicken over the tomatoes and arugula. Serve immediately.

HAPPY MEALS ARE MADE AT HOME

Here are some depressing facts: Hamburger Helper's annual sales are $400 million and growing nicely. Teenage boys get 9 percent of their daily caloric intake from soda. The average amount of time Americans want to spend making dinner is 15 minutes. The total number of pots and pans Americans want to use to make dinner is—you guessed it—one.

Yet, I find that serious foodies spend a great deal of time and money traveling to conventions, writing books, and reading magazine articles about the latest hot food item (pomegranate molasses, anyone?), the history of food in the Dark Ages, and how long it took to get through dinner at the French Laundry. Wake up and smell the french fries. McDonald's has won. Ronald has slam-dunked Escoffier—it was no contest. The war is over, and we just lost.

But one thing is for sure. We have not only lost our culinary heritage, we have lost the joy of cooking. Cooking is never really about just the food; it's about the process. It's about having someone in the kitchen when the kids come home from school. It's about making buttermilk pancakes at 6:30 AM before the school bus shows up. It's about baking a loaf of bread for a neighbor who is ill. It's about investing the time to do something for others. It's about learning a new skill. It's about being productive as a human being.

I have a proposal: Let's start at the very beginning. Let's initiate a program in public schools to teach cooking (remember Home Economics?). Nothing fancy, mind you. We'll start with how to boil an egg, how to make pancakes, and how to refrigerate butter properly. Then we can move on to steaming a vegetable, sautéing a filet, or pot-roasting a tough cut of meat.

As I have said a million times, happy meals are made at home. Let's get into the kitchen and get busy. If you go into the kitchen a little more often, I'll even get off my soap box.

Conflicted about Casseroles

by John Thorne
from *Simple Cooking*

> Thorne is yet another cook who loves to take us with him as he putters around the kitchen, tinkering with recipes, testing new techniques, browsing through old cookbooks. His newsletter format gives him room to stretch, to digress, to tell anecdotes, to ramble on—in short, to be John Thorne.

The French name "casserole" has a certain amount of terror for the American housewife. The foreign word startles her and awakens visions of cooking as done by a Parisian *chef,* or by one who has made the culinary art his profession. She, a plain, everyday housekeeper, would not dare aspire to the use of a casserole. And yet the casserole itself is no more appalling than a saucepan. It is simply a covered dish, made of fireproof pottery, which will stand the heat of the oven or the top of the range. And the dainty cooked in this dish is "casserole" of chicken, rice, etc., as the case may be. Like many another object of dread this, when once known, is converted into a friend.

—*Marion Harland's Complete Cook Book* (1903)

How things change. I thought of Marion Harland and this passage when, exactly one hundred years later, I was asked to write a blurb for a new cookbook by Jim Villas, *Crazy For Casseroles:*

275 All-American Hot-Dish Classics.★ Housewives have now so much lost their fear of the casserole that the word rarely if ever "awakens visions of cooking as done by a Paris *chef.*" Quite the contrary. This treasure trove of old familars—tuna noodle casserole, shrimp Creole, cheese strata, Johnny Marzetti, Chicken Divan, frozen chopped spinach casserole★★—summons up the image of a cozy kitchen with steamed windows, the clatter of the table being set, and the soothing aroma of a family favorite emerging hot and bubbling from the oven.

One of the genuine pleasures of *Crazy About Casseroles* is the impression it gives that all Villas had to do was appear at a neighbor's back door around dinnertime to glean another choice recipe for his collection. Think what you might of casseroles, it's hard to imagine any other aspect of our national cooking that would reward the compiler with such rich helpings from family and friends: Three-Soup Chicken and Almond Casserole Scarborough, Lizzie's Low Country Chicken Bog, Hootie's Hot Seafood Shroup, Flossie's Butternut Squash Orange Bake, and Shrimp Royal ("Royal" rather than "Royale," Villas explains, because the first is, in fact, his sister's married name).

The term "casserole," of course, embraces a wide range of American dishes, some of them very old indeed, and many of them containing nothing at which any cook, however fussy, need turn up their nose. Villas includes plenty of these in *Crazy for Casseroles*, but they do not lie at the heart of this book, and they are not the dishes that prompted fellow blurber Jeremiah Tower to paraphrase St. Augustine—"God grant me strength to be chaste, just not yet." This statement, and others like it, signals to the casserole aficionado that Villas is not one to flinch when called on to dive straight into the deep end of the pool.

"If I had to pinpoint the one casserole," he writes, "that the

★ Harvard Common Press, 2003. My quote appears on the back jacket of the hardcover edition but not on the paperback one.
★★ The only truly surprising absence—and it may be, *must* be, in there somewhere—is Green Bean Bake, made with a can of cream of mushroom soup, a dash of soy sauce, milk, and a can of Durkee's French-fried onions. I remember practically swooning when I first tasted this at a supper party back in 1969.

women in my Southern family—mother, sister, aunt, or niece—
prepare at least once a month for all sorts of informal occasions, it
would have to be Poppy Seed Chicken . . . ," which, if you don't
know the dish, is made with chicken meat, a can of Campbell's
condensed cream of chicken soup, a cup of sour cream, a stick of
butter or margarine, and half a pound of Ritz crackers.

This doesn't mean that Villas believes that, when it comes to
such dishes, anything goes. Far from it:

> To maintain the distinctive character of the American
> casserole, I by no means have any objections to the use
> of such traditional components as leftover cooked foods,
> canned broths, soups, and tomatoes, packaged bread
> stuffings, certain frozen vegetables, plain dried noodles,
> pimentos, and supermarket natural aged cheeses. On
> the other hand, nowhere in this book will you find
> canned meats and vegetables, frozen chives or dried
> parsley flakes, processed cheeses, liquid smoke, MSG,
> bouillon cubes, crushed potato chips, or, heaven forbid,
> canned fruit cocktail.

Unfortunately, such distinctions don't survive long under serious
scrutiny—as is usually the case when one attempts to keep a foot
planted firmly in each of two warring camps. In this instance, one
camp is our unselfconscious vernacular cooks, who simply don't
bother to make such distinctions at all; the other is the small
minority of cooks who wouldn't be caught dead making *anything*
with three different kinds of canned soup. Villas is gamely proposing
that there is a happy middle ground between the boobs and the
snobs, a place where reasonable folks—him, you, me—can stand tall.

It's a nice enough sentiment, sure, but it seems to me to lure the
reader out onto awfully thin ice. It's like saying that beanbag furniture and lava lamps are okay, but not, heaven forbid, plaster gnomes
and fake pine panelling. For example, the recipes in *Crazy for
Casseroles* seem to call for enough Parmesan to absorb every ounce
produced in Emilia-Romagna, at least until you decode that interesting phrase "supermarket natural aged cheeses." As it happens, a
diligent searcher can find jars of dry pre-grated Parmesan that

declare themselves "all natural" and aged for any number of months. If *these* are okay, why not processed American cheese?

Similarly, if packaged stuffings are in, why diss crushed potato chips? Those, after all, are made strictly from potatoes, oil, and salt, whereas the former usually sport an ingredient list that requires an advanced degree in food processing chemistry to decipher. And what's wrong with frozen chives if you're happily throwing frozen spinach into every casserole in sight? There are distinctions to be made here, to be sure, but this is not the way to do it.

> Today the word casserole is applied to any deepish pot in which cooking actually goes on, or even to pots more rightly called sauteuses or deep skillets.
> —Irma Rombauer,
> *The Joy of Cooking* (1951)

Those who browse old cookbooks will be aware that the casserole as we Americans know and love it is a recent creation, and one that only vaguely resembles the European dishes that were devised to make the most of what was originally a fragile clay cooking dish. Indeed, as Russ Parsons perceptively observed in a piece on casseroles that appeared several years ago in the *Los Angeles Times,* American manufacturers have so radically "improved"—i.e., changed the composition and qualities of—the cooking dish itself that it, too, has little connection with the Old World original.

What Villas has in mind by the phrase "all-American hot-dish classics" is, as best as I can work out, the product of two distinct moments in the history of our national cooking. The first was the craze for chafing dishes that swept the country in the early 1900s, when it became fashionable to invite guests home for a light late-night meal after an evening at the theater, to be made by the hostess herself at tableside, the servants, of course, having long ago gone to bed.*

---

* If there were any servants to speak of. One of the unspoken advantages of the chafing dish was that it allowed young couples to entertain with style but without the trappings and expense of formal dinner parties.

(Tableside cooking as a mode of casual entertaining replayed itself in the fifties with the arrival of the electric skillet—although the dishes prepared with that were not nearly as fine . . . remember sukiyaki parties?)

Of course, what the chafing dish did was put the finishing touches on a dish that was prepped and often partially cooked earlier in the day. The following recipe—which appears in an extremely short (four-page) chapter called "With the Casserole" in *Marion Harland's Complete Cook Book* (1903)—exhibits just how.

Creamed Chicken & Macaroni

Cut cold boiled or roast chicken into small dice of uniform size, and into half-inch lengths half the quantity of cold, cooked macaroni. Make a good white sauce, season highly with paprika, salt and a suspicion of onion juice. Beat two eggs light and stir into them four tablespoonfuls of cream, heated, with a pinch of soda. Mix well with the chicken and spaghetti; put over the fire in a frying-pan, or broad saucepan, and stir and toss until smoking hot. Serve in a deep dish.

Notice that, unless you count the serving dish, there is no "casserole" in use here at all. However, if Harland's final step had been to combine the sauce, chicken, and spaghetti in an ovenproof dish and put that into a moderate oven until "smoking hot," you would have something amazingly anticipatory of tuna casserole. (Canned tuna was still an imported novelty at the time, but food writers were even then noting how closely it resembled chicken.)

What is important here, however, is that Harland has set the scene for the appearance of our American casserole by completely disregarding any thought that the cooking vessel itself might have something to impart to the dish. Instead, it is the idea of the entrée and main starch of the meal melded in a creamy sauce and brought to table in a single serving dish that becomes the casserole: a simplification that still manages to retain the genteel suggestion of sauceboat and serving platter. This sense of amalgamation—as opposed to the simpler, cooked-together oneness of, say, a beef stew—is a defining quality of this kind of casserole, and it is shared by the many dishes from that era that are made to this day (and, in fact, can be found in *Crazy For Casseroles*). These include Turkey Tetrazzini (1912), Shrimps de Jonghe (1900), Lobster Newburg (1895), and Chicken Divan (circa 1900).

Many of these also share something else: a pleasant confusion between the richness of the ingredients—eggs, butter, cream—and of those who first ate them. These dishes were often given names that implied an association with the rich and famous—or at least with the places where those people ate—which put that fare on the same footing, almost, as a rib roast. And, to an impartial palate, they merited that equal billing. For example, Shrimps de Jonghe (the name of a Dutch family who made this the signature dish of their Chicago hotel restaurant in the early 1900s) deservedly appears in Junior League spiral-bounds to this day. It is easily made and quite delicious.

Shrimps de Jonghe

Serves up to 4 as a main course, 6 or more as an appetizer

2 pounds shrimp, cleaned, cooked, and peeled
½ cup (1 stick) unsalted butter
1 clove garlic, minced
½ cup bread crumbs
¼ cup finely chopped fresh parsley
¼ cup dry sherry
salt and black pepper to taste
a dash of hot pepper sauce

• Preheat oven to 400°F. Cream together the butter and the minced clove of garlic. Blend in the bread crumbs and parsley and moisten the mixture with the sherry. Season to taste with salt, a grinding of black pepper, and a dash of hot pepper sauce, blending this in well. Spread the shrimp in a shallow baking dish and dot with the butter mixture. Bake for 25 minutes and serve hot.

COOK'S NOTE: There has been much fiddling with this recipe over the years. Perhaps the best notion I've come across is to add some chopped onion and celery tops, peppercorns, a bay leaf, and a large pinch of salt to the water the shrimp are boiled in, to pep up their flavor.

Jean Anderson, in her *American Century Cookbook*—one of the best books there is on the unfolding of our contemporary vernacular cooking during the last century—points to a 1916 Campbell's booklet, *Helps for the Hostess,* as the moment when that company first put forth its products as the easy alternative to "long-winded sauces," thus launching the classic American casserole. This is true enough—except that while Campbell's may have had the idea, they lacked, and would lack for some time, the right soup to bring it to fruition.

In *Helps for the Hostess,* cooks were instructed to thicken their soup of choice with a roux of flour and butter, thus plunging them back into the very long-windedness they were supposedly escaping. In fact, none of the Campbell's soups of that era—oxtail, mock turtle, tomato-okra, Mulligatawny, chicken gumbo—had the starch-thickened base necessary to become an instant sauce.

It took the company almost thirty years to follow its own idea to its logical end and introduce the first in a line of thickened soups that would be used primarily as sauces: cream of mushroom soup, in 1934. Cream of chicken soup didn't appear until 1947, over a decade later. And that was the one that *really* lit the fire—Campbell's wouldn't introduce a soup that met with such instant success until the launch of cream of broccoli in 1990.

Today, their bestsellers are, in order of preference, chicken noodle, cream of mushroom, tomato, cream of chicken, and cream of broccoli, with purchasers using *one of every three cans* as a recipe ingredient; with cream of mushroom soup, that figure jumps to eighty percent. (In my opinion, this last is a *very* conservative estimate. Eaten straight . . . well, if your taste in soup runs to mushroom-flavored pancake batter, it can't be beat.)

Even so, it is hard to credit corporate machinations for the adoption of convenience foods as a casserole mainstay, when the evidence can just as easily point in the opposite direction—not only Campbell's own painfully slow stumbling toward the light but the decades that Bird's Eye Frosted Foods had to wait after introducing frozen spinach in the 1930s before anyone noticed how terrific the nasty stuff was in Green Rice Casserole, No-Nonsense Spinach Casserole, and shrimp Florentine.

> At one time a badge of shame, hallmark of the lazy lady and the careless wife, today the can opener is fast becoming a magic wand. . . . We want you to believe just as we do that in this miraculous age it is quite possible—and it's fun—to be a "chef" even before you can really cook.
>
> —Poppy Cannon,
> *The Can-Opener Cookbook* (1951)

This shift in attitude toward convenience foods, rendering them an accepted, even welcomed, component of American home cooking is the second of the two defining moments in the creation of today's casserole. First it became an amalgamation of rich ingredients; now it was streamlined—some might say dumbed down—through the use of canned soups and their like.

The compelling question, of course, is *why* kitchen-proud homemakers so quickly and radically revised their perception of these foods. One possible answer would begin by noting that the rise in popularity in these dishes coincided with an unprecedented surge in home ownership. Housing developments began springing up all around the country in the fifties—an astonishing twenty-five percent of all American homes in 1960 had been built within the span of the last ten years.

As it happens, my parents were a part of this. In 1957, they bought our first house, a three-bedroom garrison in a small development. (A garrison had a second floor that protruded a few inches in the front to give it a "colonial" look.) It was the newest house I had ever been in, which made it exciting, but it wasn't an excitement that would last. My grandparents' home, which was not all that far away and in which I had spent the first five years of my life, was an extremely complex organism—wheezing, stubborn, and surprisingly delicate. The electric wiring dated back half a century; fuses blew at a sneeze. The steam heat rumbled up from a massive furnace in the basement to hiss at you from cast-iron, claw-footed radiators. In the fall, heavy glass storm windows went up; in the spring, these were replaced with freshly painted wooden screens. It was a house that today would be considered a homeowner's nightmare, but my grandfather took all this in his stride. For a child, it was a place of endless mystery and delight—much of this conveyed in my book *Home Body**—and, fifty-five years later, it remains for me the template of what a home should be.

The new house ... well, it was like replacing a friendly old dog with a stuffed toy one—comfortable, unthreatening, endlessly embraceable, but really, nothing at all like the original. This was not merely a matter of newness. The same construction techniques that made these houses easier to afford also meant that more corners could be cut in their manufacture. Ceilings in the new house were lower; windows had shrunk: walls and doors were hollow, where before they had been solid. The overall experience was one of compression. You couldn't call the house cramped, exactly, but it was full of space that never quite made it to spaciousness.

The builders were well aware of this. They took those things and sold them as advantages. Home buyers, it proved, would overlook the fact that a house was cheaply built if it was also cheap to heat and cheap to maintain. In my grandfather's time, a house required continuous care, and owning one meant mastering all sorts of knowledge and performing a never-ending round of upkeep, both indoors and out (or paying someone else to do these things for you).

The houses of the fifties and afterward demanded no such commitment. Curiously, the result was something you might call responsibility deprivation. Here were houses that asked for so little care in a culture still primed with an ethos of devoting time and money to keeping them up. Home owners felt vaguely immoral doing nothing and, with nothing much to do, threw themselves into home improvement to fill the void.

---

* *Home Body* (Ecco Press, 1997). It is out of print, but copies are available from us for $15 each, plus $2.00 shipping.

At first glance, it might seem that there was as little to improve as there was to fix. All the houses in our development came with a garage, a breezeway, and a fully equipped kitchen, with turquoise-colored appliances and, something quite à la mode, a dishwasher and a waist-high oven built into the wall. In fact, there are so many things to like about the place that it would be hard to enumerate them all—from the shiny wood floors to the clean, tight basement with its convenient bulkhead doors. What more could anyone want?

Well, as it turns out, lots of things. The breezeway quickly reveals itself as being a bit too breezy; after a year or two, it gets turned into a sunroom. Fiberglass insulation is unrolled in the attic: an exhaust fan is installed in the kitchen; a large downstairs closet becomes a very small guest bathroom. Half the basement is upgraded into a cheery family room, turning the living room into a showcase for company. Garages get expanded; backyards get swimming pools and privacy fences; front yards get flower gardens and RVs.

This new definition of house proud, I think, helps us make sense of the sea change that made respectable the recipes that *Crazy For Casseroles* celebrates. Like the home owner, the home cook needed no longer shoulder a wearying responsibility—in this instance, the one incurred by dishes made from scratch. Like tract houses, dishes incorporating convenience foods—canned soups, crackers, frozen vegetables—as their foundation were affordable, easy to maintain (they always turned out well) and, with a handful of almonds or water chestnuts tossed in, easily made fancy.

Today, all this is taken for granted. Fifty years is quite long enough for a way of cooking to become a tradition and for the dishes that come out of it to be considered classics. The fact that these even now still manage to teeter at the edge of questionable taste testifies as much to their power of attraction as to the lowering of our standards ("Campbell's soups have done more to debase the cooking of Americans—and their palates—than any other factor," said an unnamed source quoted approvingly by John and Karen Hess in *The Taste of America* twenty-five years ago).

In truth, we're not talking about good taste and bad taste here; we're talking about the fact that things change and that we change with them, whether we are aware of it or not. That makes the issue of goodness a very slippery one, and it's a mistake to trust anything like a quick response to it. Reading an early draft of this essay, Matt recalled a favorite dinner party casserole of her mother's. Shirley herself had gotten it from Jean, a savvy but down-to-earth professor's wife, and it proved so popular that whenever Shirley served it, she, too, was besieged by requests for the recipe.

Jean's Two Meat Two Rice Casserole

Serves 8

6 tablespoons butter
1 pound EACH lean pork and veal, cut into 1-inch cubes
2 onions, chopped
1½ to 2 pounds mushrooms, sliced
2 cans cream of mushroom soup
1 soup can water
⅓ cup soy sauce
4 cups sliced celery
1 cup EACH uncooked white rice and wild rice

• Preheat oven to 325°F. Melt half the butter in a large skillet and sauté the meat cubes over medium heat until browned on all sides. Turn these into a large casserole. Add the remaining butter to the skillet and sauté the onions and mushrooms until both have just started to brown. Blend the soup, water, and soy sauce together until smooth. Wash the rices in two changes of water and add to the meat with the celery and the soup mixture. Stir well. Cover and bake for 2 hours. Serve with a tossed salad and garlic bread.

For the late fifties, the presence of the wild rice, the two kinds of meat, the quantity of fresh mushrooms, the soy sauce, all gave the casserole an air of sophistication. At the same time, the can of cream of mushroom soup immediately assured the hostess that she could approach the recipe without fear. Similarly, it signaled to the other women at the table that this was not the sort of competitive cooking meant to put them on their mettle. Their enjoyment eating it could only be enhanced by the appreciative awareness that, once given the recipe, any one of them could make it just as well . . . which, of course, is exactly why so many asked for it.

In other words, the pleasures inherent in this kind of cooking are essentially, emphatically, *social*. One need only compare the open-handed communality of the cooks in *Crazy for Casseroles* with, say, Madame X in *The Cooking of South-West France*, who agreed to teach Paula Wolfert about the local cuisine while refusing—through distraction and, if that failed, outright deception—to reveal any of her hard-won cooking secrets. Madame X's cabbage and dumpling soup may or may not taste better than Jean's casserole, but the reason one was not shared while the other was—over and over again—had nothing to do with goodness. One of the unalloyed benefits of the nonthreatening, noncompetitive nature of convenience-food cookery is that it radiates a contagious sense of companionship and good cheer.

It was this, I realize now, that captivated me when I first leafed through *Crazy for Casseroles*. I had been completely absorbed by the image of other people happily making and eating this food—something very different from thinking I might want to make it myself. This isn't to say that I wouldn't gladly gorm it down as a dinner guest, which has happened more than once—remember my response to green bean casserole. I might even, in that flush of pleasure, ask, like all the others, for the recipe. But, in the end, I would never use it. These dishes are not what makes me want to cook.

Casserole: a porous dish of clay or earthernware, much used in French cooking. The heat penetrates it slowly and all the juices and flavors of the meats, etc., are retained.

—Artemas Ward,
The Grocer's Encyclopedia (1911)

Artemas Ward's description reminds me—perhaps it is that word "porous"—of my grandfather's house. Maybe it is just that, having used such casseroles, I know that they are an example of form determining function: too fragile to handle high heat on top of the stove or within it, they require the low, sustained heat that, it turns out, retains the juices and flavor of the dish. An old house likewise demands an alertness that shapes our experience of it and, for good or ill, our personality. This can, at times, be annoying, but its reality is such that its absence can make another, newer house feel strangely empty, even sterile.

This must be how I feel about the now ubiquitous, nonporous, high-heat-fired Corningware casserole dishes—which can be (some of them, anyway) used on top of the stove as well as in it, and which can take as hot an oven as you care to put them in— because I don't own any . . . whereas we have several of the old-fashioned clay kind. What these lack in cold perfection they make up for in *resonance*—if I can use that word to convey how an inanimate object can compel your attention and reward it with accretions of experience.

This same term can be usefully applied to a certain sort of recipe as well. Jean's casserole called to mind *baeckeoffe,* a traditional casserole from Alsace, which might not be considered a dinner party dish on its native turf, but could certainly fill that role here. Made with three kinds of meat, marinated and then baked in wine, and brought to table in the cooking vessel, where its seal of flour paste is broken to release a cloud of delicious aromas, it has all the necessary class, enhanced with a touch of drama. It is also rather easy to make.

Baeckeoffe

Serves 8

1 pound EACH boneless stewing pork, shoulder of lamb, and stewing beef
2 pig's feet, split in half (optional-see note)

Marinade

1 tablespoon salt
½ tablespoon black peppercorns
1 sprig fresh OR 1 teaspoon dried thyme
2 bay leaves
2 or 3 garlic cloves, minced
1 or 2 sprigs fresh celery leaves, chopped
several sprigs fresh flat-leaf parsley, chopped
½ bottle dry white wine (preferably an Alsatian Riesling)

Casserole

butter or lard for greasing
3 pounds waxy potatoes, peeled and sliced
2 onions, chopped
2 leeks, trimmed and sliced
4 carrots, peeled and cut into bite-size pieces

Luting (sealing) paste

1 scant cup flour
5 tablespoons water
1 tablespoon cooking oil

The day before:

• Cut the meat into bite-size pieces and put them in a large non-reactive container with the pig's feet. Toss with the salt, pepper, herbs, garlic, celery leaves, and parsley. Moisten with the wine. Cover and refrigerate overnight.

Assembling and cooking:

• Preheat oven to 400°F. Select a large ovenproof casserole with a lid. Grease the bottom and sides with the butter or lard. Lay the pig's feet on the bottom and cover with half the potatoes, onions, leeks, and carrots. Remove the meat from the marinade and add, covering it with the remaining vegetables, ending with the potatoes. Strain the marinade through a sieve and pour the liquid over the contents of the pot. If necessary, add some extra wine or water to bring the liquid barely to the top of the vegetables.

• Work the sealing paste ingredients into a dough and roll this out into a rope long enough to wrap around the casserole. Press it firmly against the join between the lid and the casserole. Put the sealed pot into the oven and cook for 1 hour. At this point, reduce the heat to 350°F and continue cooking for 1 ½ hours more.

• For the most dramatic presentation, bring the casserole to the table, set it on a trivet, and break away the seal with the edge of a table knife. Otherwise, of course, this can be done in the kitchen and servings of the baeckeoffe brought to table in shallow bowls. Serve with a green salad, a loaf of crusty bread, and some of the same wine used for making the marinade.

COOK'S NOTE: **The pig's feet** provide a gelatinous cast to the baeckeoffe's juices. Oxtail is another traditional option, as is nothing at all. **The luting paste** is meant as much to keep the wine's vaporous aromas from escaping as it is to keep the cooking liquid from evaporating. A band of heavy aluminum foil will work almost as well.

Readers may smile at my describing this dish as easy to make, especially in contrast to Jean's casserole, with its single short paragraph of instruction. And they are probably right to do so, even though in Alsace *baeckeoffe* is considered the next step up from convenience food. The name means "baker's oven," and the dish is traditionally made on Mondays, the casserole being dropped off in the morning at the local bakery, to slowly cook in a corner of the bread oven while the housewife concentrates on getting the laundry done. This means that the prep work is all done early on and that no special bother need be spared to make it.

What it does require—and this goes a long way toward explaining the difference in recipe length—is that the cook take responsibility for the dish. The recipe only points the way. It has been shaped by many, many years of spirited input from a countless number of Alsatian cooks. They disagree about the kinds (and cuts) of meat—Le Baeckeoffe d'Alsace, a Strasbourg restaurant, offers several variations, including one made with duck, another with ox cheeks and calves' feet. Some add carrots to the marinade;

others, cloves. Some insist that a tablespoon of red wine vinegar pulls the flavors of the dish together; most don't mention it. An Alsatian Riesling is the wine most often used in the dish, but recipes can be found calling for Gewürtztraminer, Sylvaner, or Pinot Blanc (or even Alsatian beer). Some cooks use shallots instead of onions (small ones, peeled but left whole); others use only leeks. The addition of other vegetables apart from the leeks and potatoes is a matter of taste; some add none but most add something—carrots, celeriac, tiny turnips.

Over the years, Anne Willan has given us at least three recipes for *baeckeoffe,* in *French Regional Cooking* (Morrow, 1981), *La France Gastronomique* (Arcade, 1991), and *Château Cuisine* (Macmillan, 1992), each quarreling amicably with the others. Interestingly, the last recipe of the three is by far the simplest, as if suggesting that time eventually pares things down to the essentials: the meat, the potatoes, the wine, the onions, the garlic, the bouquet garni.

If you make the dish, you will ponder on these things yourself. In fact, if you make it more than once, that may well be because you want to resolve some questions that came up the first time around. Those who ate it might have found it simply delicious, but you want to know if it would taste better if you sautéed the leeks in a little lard or butter before adding them to the casserole; whether veal might go better with pork and lamb than stewing beef.

Such issues and their resolution continually sharpen its focus. Keep at it and the dish will eventually attain the melodic tautness of a well-tuned guitar. It will ring true, and that, to a cook, is an astonishingly satisfying thing. This explains why we collect so many recipes but end up making, over and over, the same familiar dishes. The other night, listening to the Be Good Tanyas (BLUE HORSE: Nettwerk America, 2001) singing "Oh Susanna," I thought how hard it was to wear out a good tune. You just keep making it new. Surely the same is true with recipes, dishes; it's why I like so much to cook.

Being lazy and liking to cook and to entertain, we struggled futilely for a long time over how to combine

these features pleasantly. Finally the thing came to us—
that thing being a casserole. Stews and other wrongly
demeaned dishes take on a dash of simplicity and
sophistication when prepared in a casserole.

—Marian Tracy,
Casserole Cookery (1942)

Since there could be no better characterization of me than as a lazy person in love with cooking, perhaps the reason that Marian Tracy and other casserole makers go one way and I the other can be found in the word "entertaining." This is something I rarely do—I'd much rather get together with friends and family at a restaurant, where we can all walk away from the dirty dishes together. I do understand, though, that entertaining must make a lot of people nervous, there being so many, many reassuring books on the subject.

Even so, earlier in my life I was innocent enough to often have people over, in couples and in groups, and it never occurred to me that they might turn up their noses at a good Irish stew (let alone *baeckeoffe*, had I known about it then). Nor have I ever read a food writer who argued to the contrary. Where then does the fear that such things are "not good enough for company"—or, more to the point, that guests might secretly sneer at their hostess for serving them—come from? Or, to put it another way, was Marian Tracy—who would go on to publish at least two further books on convenience-food-based casserole cookery—reading the mind of her public or planting in that mind a germinating seed of doubt?

Just as the invention of the personal deodorant transformed body odor, until then a mere fact of life, into a universal embarrassment, so could casserole cookery, which impressed cooks with its unthreatening easiness, make the uncertain work of preparing something pleasing from scratch seem rife with potential discomfiture.

Convenience food cookery frees the cook of responsibility for the dish, and freedom from responsibility is such a delicious experience that it becomes part of the deliciousness of the dish itself— just as it is part of the deliciousness of living in a tract house. The vinyl siding doesn't so much fool the eye as persuade it that what it sees is surely good enough if this means never having to scrape and paint the outside of a house again.

A bargain with the devil, yes, albeit one that's easy enough to ignore. (That's what's so nice about deals struck with Old Scratch.) But, nonetheless . . . it used to be that old houses, like old people, aged into increasingly fragile, complex collations of successes, failures, and compromises—which is to say surviving the consequences of what seemed like good ideas at the time. Today's houses, locked in a lackluster permanence, gather no such patina. The passage of time merely makes them increasingly boring.

And so it is with tuna noodle or poppy seed chicken or Jean's casserole. They will never again be as good as the first time you tasted them, however slowly the experience rolls downhill. In fact, Shirley can't remember the last time she made that casserole; she was as astonished as we were to find the recipe card, stained and brown with age, still in her file. When Matt first entertained, she served it to company herself. But the recipe card brought back less a rush of nostalgia than one of surprise. She remembered the casserole as being distinctly cosmopolitan for its time, which may indeed be true. Her astonishment, though, came from the fact that two key ingredients—the can of condensed soup, the slug of soy sauce—had completely vanished from her memory. As soon as she saw them, the recipe lost its sheen . . . and any interest she might have had in making it again.

We get tired, too, of dishes that demand more from us than to be just thrown together. But, most always, that says something more about us than about them. We've made them too often; we and they both need a rest. But if we return to them, even decades later, they often can spring instantly back to life. They need to be freshly tuned, it's true—the amount of olive oil cut back; the garlic actually added to the dish, not merely rubbed around the inside of the pot. They won't taste the same as they did back then, but, with luck, they'll taste just as good. They might even taste better—after all, you have learned a few things since, some tricks that, it turns out, this old dish is eager to learn. That, after all, is what keeps it—and us—feeling young.

Do Try This at Home

by Matt Lee and Ted Lee

from *The New York Times*

The Lee brothers are food writers who love to get elbow-deep in their research. Here they chronicle what happened when they set themselves a *tres haute* cooking challenge—with decidedly mixed results.

When friends come for dinner we tend to cook what we know. There is no sense attempting sea urchin napoleons when roast chicken and braised pork shoulder have proven to be crowd pleasers. But life gets dull without a challenge, so we decided to stir some risk and ambition into our routine, composing a spring dinner inspired by the new wave chefs, the ones turning culinary tradition on its head from suburban Barcelona to the Lower East Side of New York.

Even if you have never sampled their handiwork, you may have heard about such haute-cuisine iconoclasts as Heston Blumenthal, the chef at the Fat Duck in Bray, England, which recently earned three Michelin stars for a repertory that includes bacon-and-egg ice cream and sardine-on-toast sorbet (Carvel take note). There's Ferran Adria, the chef of El Bulli in Rosas, Spain, and the de facto dean of avant-garde chefs, who spends six months of every year in a Barcelona lab refining such inventions as wonton wrappers made from the "'skin" of scalded milk. On these shores are visionaries like Grant Achatz at Trio, who has introduced Evanston, Ill., diners to the pleasures of lobster slow-cooked with Thai iced tea.

They're the sort of chefs who consider themselves artists and philosophers more than fish grillers and asparagus poachers, testing the limits of a diner's trust (and often charging a king's ransom for the privilege), but succeeding far more often than they fail.

As for us, we had an agenda other than simply shaking off the winter doldrums with a night of kitchen gymnastics. We wanted to rifle through the chefs' high-concept tool bags for any techniques or tools that amateur cooks might take home. An encounter earlier this year with a bright red pixie dust at the Manhattan restaurant WD-50 had encouraged us: the powder had a fruity, exotic and deliciously intense pepper flavor. It was in fact a common bell pepper, Wylie Dufresne, WD-50's chef, revealed, dehydrated in a simple device you can buy on eBay for less than the price of a fancy cocktail, and then pulverized in a coffee grinder. If we could learn to tease sophisticated flavors from everyday sources, the exercise would be worth the risk.

So we ordered a dehydrator (rather than risk losing an eBay auction, we bought a brand-new Nesco/American Harvest dehydrator direct from the manufacturer, $59.95 at www.nesco.com) and went to work planning the menu. The cookbook *El Bulli 1998-2002*, the nearly 500-page, nine-pound volume by Mr. Adria and his associates seemed the ideal place to start, and fortunately a friend lent us a copy—it's about $200. Flipping through the book was an instant immersion in the new wave mindset, where sweet meets savory in alarming ways (olive and white chocolate, tuna and black currant), where hot and cold are transposed (barbecued corn sorbet, hot mayonnaise) and where textural expectations are upended wherever possible (cauliflower is couscouslike, almonds foamy).

Some of Mr. Adria's tools seemed out of reach—anybody got a Pacojet, the Swiss-made, 2,000 r.p.m. frozen-food processor? Or a Thermomix, the German steamer/food processor? And the photos of the superminimalist kitchen at El Bulli, with leagues of lab-coated chefs at attention, were intimidating. But the book got us thinking outside of the box.

These chefs' testimony was refreshingly plain. Culinary imagination at this level seems to spring from fairly simple insights, unbridled experimentation and a "what if?" playfulness familiar to the parent of any healthy teenager. Mr. Adria will forever be remembered for the time he put a vegetable puree in a whipped cream canister and transformed it into an ethereal foam. Countless chefs throughout the world have since repeated the trick, to the growing dismay of restaurant critics, as well as of Mr. Adria himself (who has moved on to "airs," even lighter foams).

But why not recreate the moment ourselves? In the back of our refrigerator, we found a leftover oxtail braising stock that had gelled in its Tupperware container; we spooned it into our own cream whipper ($35 at Zabar's), and when we pulled the trigger—fffffft!—out came the richest, beefiest and lightest "butter" we had ever tasted. The vegetable and herb flavors in the broth seemed to blossom, too, as the trapped air in the foam spread the stock over a larger surface area and diluted its saltiness.

Oxtail foam is no dinner, however, and we still needed a first course, so we called Jose Andres, a Spanish-born chef who trained with Mr. Adria at El Bulli, for some grounding. Online, we had seen a photo of the deconstructed New England clam chowder he serves at his six-seat Minibar in Washington, a shrine to avant-garde cooking. "It's simple," he told us, launching into the inspiration for his chowder. "I was tired of muddy, overcooked chowders. I wanted to create a clam chowder that had more of the pristine flavor of the sea."

Mr. Andres breaks the classic dish down into its component parts: cream, potatoes, clam, clam broth, onion, bacon and chives. From each of these elements, he creates a puree or sauce, thickening them to varying, and slightly unexpected, viscosities: the onion is a thick jam, the potatoes are a runny puree and the cream, flavored with smoky bacon, is lightly frothed. A nearly raw clam floats on top of the different components, lacquered with a clam-broth gel. A pinch of crushed potato chips scattered on top gives textural contrast to the goos and oozes. The diner's spoon provides the final stir that blends the ingredients and sets the "chowder" in motion.

Deconstructed clam chowder brought some focus to our menu. If we were going to take our guests for a wild ride, we reasoned, we had better stick to the road, making each dish on the menu familiar in idea, if not in design. So the menu would be steakhouse-straightforward: we would pass martinis and a crudites plate for the cocktail hour. Mr. Andres's chowder would be the first course, and a small serving of paella—a tribute to the Spaniards leading the charge—the second. New York strip steak with potatoes and a trio of seasonal vegetables would be the main course.

And then the fun began. The dehydrator arrived, and we made thin, crispy wafers of whatever we found in the larder: dill pickles, turnips, beets, kimchi. We created a palette of seasonings—not only Mr. Dufresne's red pepper powder, but green pepper powder and red onion powder (a pretty lavender color) that we found turned scrambled eggs into a respectable lunch or dinner. We made a lemon and a lime powder from pulverized, dehydrated zest that gave a refined citrus perfume to everything it touched: tomato soup, vanilla ice cream, iced tea. And we concocted a new wave snack of seasoned puffed rice by dehydrating and then frying in olive oil overcooked arborio rice (a technique Mr. Andres had described), and sprinkling the crispy rice with red pepper and onion powders.

We called up Mr. Achatz, who offered a couple of more dehydrator ideas: chips made from thinly sliced cured meats and a mango and mandarin orange fruit leather he makes in the dehydrator's liquid tray. Fruit leather got us thinking: why not vegetable leather? We pureed roasted peppers and poured them directly into the liquid tray, and in a couple of hours, we had turned out grown-up roll-ups to add to our crudites plate. The chorizo chips we made gave shape to the paella course. First, we imagined a paella napoleon, using the chips as "pastry," but that seemed a little pedestrian and too meaty, so we imagined the shrimp and saffron being a savory ice cream, the rice as puffed rice sprinkles adhering to the ice cream. Paella ice-cream sandwich!

In Mr. Adria's book, we had been introduced to agar-agar, a seaweed extract found at most health food stores and an ingredient in many commercial yogurts. When blended into liquids, agar-agar creates a gelatinlike texture that, unlike gelatin, doesn't melt when heated. But hot jelly hadn't seemed appealing until Mr. Achatz said that he makes quick dairy-free, egg-free "puddings" by setting liquids with agar-agar and then softening them to a puddinglike consistency in the blender. Virtually any liquid can be treated this way.

Our minds began to wander in ever-widening, lightbulb-popping loops—orange juice pudding, guava juice pudding, olive juice pudding, cola pudding, beer pudding, water pudding and the postmodern end-of-innocence: milk pudding. Mr. Achatz's red-wine pudding, served slightly warm, sounded like the natural accompaniment to a New York strip steak.

When we phoned Mr. Dufresne for some home-kitchen-friendly tips, he confessed to using an inexpensive home smoker in unconventional ways; for example, smoking mashed potatoes. The cheapest smoker we could find was a $55 stove-top model that was little more than a roasting pan, a rack, a cover and finely ground wood chips. We left the smoker behind, but bought the wood chips for $3 and fashioned our own smoker quite easily from what we had in our kitchen: a deep roasting pan, a metal rack and a couple of large sheets of aluminum foil. Our test results were phenomenal, and we felt confident in our main course: New York strip with oxtail foam, Rioja wine pudding and smoked mashed potatoes. The vegetables accompanying the main course would be three simple purees, served in shot glasses alongside the plate. We settled on parsley root, spinach and red beets—chosen for color as much as for seasonal flavor—and cooked each, seasoning them with a little salt and black pepper before pureeing them individually in a food processor.

When the unsuspecting guests arrived on a recent Saturday night, we passed around a small platter of martinis that were neither shaken nor stirred, they were quivering. On a tip from Mr. Dufresne's bartender, we had prepared a glass baking dish of gin gelatin (four packets of gelatin dissolved in two cups of hot gin), set firm in the fridge, and cut the solidified gin, which had turned a pearly white, into one-inch cubes. We skewered each cubic martini with an olive on top and squirted a drizzle of vermouth foam into the cavity of the pitted green olive. We didn't gain many converts from the traditional martini ("James Bond would be appalled," remarked one guest), but the bite-size format was easier to abide than a full glass and was surprisingly effective. After a couple of martinis, the guests seemed to become more open-minded about the meal ahead, though quicker with their criticisms.

The "dry crudites" were pounced upon, and clear favorites

emerged immediately. Briny, parchment-crisp strips of dehydrated dill pickle were gone in seconds. Not so the faintly sweet jicama chips that looked like suede: "I feel like a secret agent, eating her instructions," said one guest. Golden beet chips and turnip chips were a surprise hit, offering the sweetness of the jicama, but none of the toughness. Caper "nuts" didn't find many takers—the verdict: too salty, even though they had been soaked and rinsed for half an hour before being dehydrated—but the roasted red pepper leather was a nice nibble, hovering between sweet and savory in an appetizing way.

The clam chowder, with its layered whites and grays, its electric-green chive oil garnish, and the pinkish-orange clam on top, looked gorgeous, and it may have been the night's most popular course. Guests were sympathetic to Mr. Andres's frustration with conventional clam chowders. "Clam chowder is usually like wheat paste with potato nubbins lost in it," one told us. "Here, you can taste the potato and onion." To our tastes, it was an advantage that the clam flavor was pushed forward so vividly, in the salty, raw clam, but that nakedness might have been a degree too bold for a few guests. Still, all plates were polished clean.

The paella ice-cream sandwich had fans and detractors. On the plus side, the shrimp and saffron ice cream alone, according to one guest, "tasted like Barcelona." Others thought the flavors were muted by the coldness of the ice cream, and by the busy textural effects of the crispy rice and chorizo chip, the smooth ice cream and the unctuous disc of raw scallop that formed the base of the sandwich. The dish was a real show stopper, though, in terms of its nouvelle, "Clockwork Orange" design, and several of the guests, including the most conservative eater, asked for seconds.

The smoked mashed potatoes were the sleeper hit of the main course, with a suave smokiness that had a sweet, vanillalike edge. Everyone who tried the oxtail foam liked it, but some thought the turf-and-turf concept was a shade too rich. As for the Rioja pudding, we think we'll stick to the liquid form, or next time try to bring out more flavor by sweetening the wine first. The agar-agar, fortunately, doesn't impart any flavor of its own, but it does dilute the flavor and intensity of whatever it solidifies.

Perhaps the most shocking dish of the evening was dessert: each guest was served a single ripe Bartlett pear and a paring knife. The guests worked nearly as hard bending their minds around this dinner as the hosts had, so we felt they deserved a conclusion that was uncomplicated and utterly comfortable, so that the conversation could freely wander away from the subject of food.

Ultimately, a new wave dinner, with its manifold obsessions, turned out to be nearly as exhausting to discuss as it was to cook, and while the paella ice-cream sandwich won't soon displace our roast chicken, a few of the techniques did hit home—the smoked potatoes and the dehydrated pepper powder, especially. Even the solid martini is likely to work its way into our routine, when the time is right. But most of all, we were grateful to be able to tap into the new wave's spirit of invention, and to bring a few flashes of ambition back into our cooking. Who knows, we might even tackle that sea urchin napoleon.

⁓

New England Clam Chowder

Adapted from Jose Andres | Serves 6 | Time: 1 hour and 45 minutes

2 tablespoons kosher salt
12 cherrystone clams, rinsed clean
12 to 16 ice cubes
1 packet (¼ ounce) unflavored gelatin powder
½ cup extra virgin olive oil
½ cup minced chives (about 1 ounce)
½ pound russet potatoes (about 1 medium potato), peeled, cut into
   8 pieces
1 cup plus 2 tablespoons heavy cream
Crushed black pepper to taste
2 cups chopped white or yellow onion (about 1 large)
¼ pound thick-cut bacon, about 4 slices
6 potato chips, finely crushed.

1. For clams and clam-broth jelly, fill a 6-quart pot halfway with water, add 1 tablespoon salt, and boil over high heat. Immerse 4 clams for 15 to 20 seconds, and remove. Working over a small

bowl, shuck the 4 clams with a short sharp paring knife, reserving liquid they release. Reserve shelled clams in another small bowl. Return any stubborn clams to boiling water for a few seconds. Repeat, cooking 4 clams at a time, using all 12. Drain any accumulated clam juice into clam juice bowl, cover clams with plastic wrap, and chill in refrigerator for about 15 minutes.

2. Meanwhile, pour 1½ quarts cold water into a large bowl and add ice cubes. Strain clam juice into another small bowl. (You should have about 1 cup; add water if necessary.) Pour ¾ cup clam juice into small saucepan, and heat over medium-low heat until it simmers. Soften unflavored gelatin in remaining clam juice. Pour hot clam juice over gelatin, and whisk until it dissolves. Set bowl of clam juice and gelatin halfway into ice-water bath, whisking often, for about 5 minutes, as the gel begins to set. Remove bowl when juice is barely set, but not firm.

3. For chive oil, heat ¼ cup olive oil in a small saucepan until just smoking; remove from heat. Add minced chives and ¼ teaspoon salt, stirring to dissolve. Let cool for 10 minutes, puree in a blender, strain through a fine mesh strainer or coffee filter, and reserve.

4. For potato puree, boil 4 cups water in a small saucepan. Add 1 teaspoon salt and potatoes, and cook until fork-tender, about 15 minutes. Drain, reserving boiling water, and mash potatoes in medium bowl. Add 1 teaspoon olive oil, ½ teaspoon of salt and 6 tablespoons potato water, blending with an immersion blender or food processor until potatoes are a thick paste. Add 2 tablespoons cream, stirring, until potato is consistency of thickened cream. Thin further, if necessary, with potato water. Season to taste with salt and pepper. Keep warm, or warm before serving.

5. For onion jam, heat 2 tablespoons olive oil, ½ teaspoon salt and chopped onion in a medium skillet over medium-low heat and saute, stirring frequently, until onion is very soft, but not caramelized, about 15 minutes. Puree in a food processor with 1

tablespoon olive oil until smooth; season with salt to taste and reserve. Keep warm or warm before serving.

6. For bacon cream, lay bacon in a cold, medium skillet, and fry over medium-high heat, flipping several times, until crisp, about 5 minutes. Add 1 cup cream to pan with bacon still in it and turn off heat under pan. Allow to rest 5 minutes; remove and reserve bacon strips from pan. Chop bacon finely, for use as a garnish. Keep cream warm but not hot, whipping to a froth in a bowl just before serving.

7. Assemble servings in 6 small shallow bowls. Spoon 2 tablespoons warm potato puree into each bowl. Add 1 tablespoon of warm onion jam, slightly off-center. Spoon 1 tablespoon bacon cream around edge of purees. Place a room-temperature clam in center of bowl. If clam broth jelly has solidified, pulse it with an immersion blender or whisk it until it is a loose gel, and spoon 1 teaspoon directly over clam in each bowl. Drizzle chive oil over dish. Garnish with reserved diced bacon and with pinches of crushed potato chips.

Smoked Mashed Potatoes

Adapted from Wylie Dufresne | Serves 6 | Time: 1 hour

1 tablespoon plus 1 teaspoon kosher salt, more to taste
2 pounds russet potatoes, peeled and quartered
2 pounds Yukon Gold potatoes, peeled and quartered
3 tablespoons unsalted butter, cut into pieces
½ cup heavy cream, half-and-half or whole milk
Freshly ground black pepper.

1. Put 1 gallon of water in six-quart stockpot, add 1 tablespoon salt and bring to a boil over high heat. Add potatoes and cook until fork-tender, about 25 minutes. Drain, reserving 1 cup cooking water.

2. Smoke potatoes to taste in a smoker, according to manufacturer's

instructions. If you do not have a smoker, set a 13-by-16-inch aluminum roasting pan with a rack on the stove top so that it spans 2 burners. Scatter 2 tablespoons ground hickory, apple or cherry wood chips (designed for stove-top smokers) evenly in pan. Lay a double thickness of aluminum foil over rack, and crimp any over-hanging foil around edges. Arrange potatoes in a single layer on foil. Cover pan tightly with 2 sheets of aluminum foil laid side by side, if necessary. Turn both burners to medium-low, and smoke potatoes for 15 minutes.

3. Transfer potatoes to a large bowl, and mash them with a fork or pass them through a ricer or food mill. Add 1 teaspoon salt, butter, cream and ½ cup potato cooking water, whip until thoroughly combined. Add more cooking water, 2 tablespoons at a time, until potatoes reach a smooth, fluffy consistency. Season with salt and ground pepper to taste.

A Menu Marathon

by Julie Powell
from *The New York Times*

New Yorker Julie Powell launched herself into the food world this year with her weblog detailing the Julie/Julia Project—a lunatic one-year quest to cook everything from Julia Child's *Mastering the Art of French Cooking*. This subsequent *Times* piece gives a taste of her wry, outlandish style.

So maybe late spring in Long Island City is no April in Paris. But when the robins flit among the birches in front of the Citibank building and brief storms wash the diesel exhaust out of the air, a giddy spirit of renewal prevails even here. Spring fever rages, and from the pages of food magazines, recipes beckon.

One of the curious and welcome properties of food magazine recipe roundups is that they are capable of transforming a perfectly reasonable person into a delusional, drooling moron. Spend an afternoon flipping avidly through the May issues of *Bon Appétit*, *Gourmet* and *Food & Wine*, and you may come away convinced that any halfway respectable Memorial Day weekend dinner party must include two appetizers, a special cocktail, a fish course before a main dish or two, six or seven side dishes and two desserts.

Faced with a dazzling array of delectations, you may concoct a completely absurdist Thai-Scottish-Southern fusion menu requiring a shopping list longer than most divorce settlements. You may actually go shopping, and invite friends for dinner. I know. I did.

And it took a long time.

"Active cooking time" is the yardstick by which food magazines let you know how long it takes to make their recipes. And a remarkable yardstick it is. By the estimate of *Food & Wine* magazine, an Arkansan farm picnic bash takes up seven and a half hours of active cooking time. *Gourmet's* northern Thai menu clocks in at a daunting 13 hours and 35 minutes.

These figures, of course, do not allow for the cross-pollination of the menus, nor for shopping. Certainly they do not allow for parking. But when your shopping list includes such items as kaffir lime leaves, green tomatoes, imported Scottish oatcakes and a large granite mortar and pestle, park you will. Even I, creator of Thai-Scottish-Southern fusion cuisine, am not so daft as to suggest employing the New York City transit system to scurry all over town obtaining this load, much less to haul it back to a Queens apartment.

Active cooking time also does not include the time spent searching for 104 Mosco Street—pronounced MOS-kah, at least by the half-dozen police officers you will have to ask to find it— a one-block thoroughfare buried deep in Chinatown that seems to exist just to provide an address for the miraculous Bangkok Center Grocery. There, for roughly the price that Whole Foods demanded I spend in exchange for a parking validation, I bought three 24-ounce bottles of fishy Thai sauces, a jar of shrimp paste, a pound of banana leaves, a bunch of Thai basil, five pounds of sticky rice and a small glassine bag of fresh kaffir lime leaves, as well as the granite mortar and pestle I suppose some readers already have.

Yet more unaccounted-for time goes into the panicked errands you impress on put-upon family and friends—"It's spelled R-A-T-N-A, and it's the only mango purée that will do!"—as the active cooking time actually starts ticking on Friday night and spins into Saturday morning, spinning faster and faster toward dinner itself.

So. For the cocktail hour, Scotch eggs with fresh herbs, and smoked salmon on oatcakes, with Champagne. Then steamed catfish with red Thai curry paste, followed by Arrowhead Farms' fried chicken, Auntie Buck's dinner rolls, smoky black-eyed peas, green-tomato pickle, stir-fried Chinese broccoli, and thyme-roasted vegetables, all accompanied by watermelon coolers. A salad. Scottish cheeses. Pineapple and mango-coconut ice creams with lacy rice noodle crisps for dessert.

Totally doable—except for the pickle. My research indicates

that one cannot actually make the green-tomato pickle recipe that appears in *Food & Wine*'s May issue in May, for the simple reason that green tomatoes don't exist in May, at least not in Manhattan, Brooklyn or Queens.

A feast of this magnitude requires a battle plan. On Friday evening you can make the chicken stock, hard-boiled eggs, dough for the rolls and the custards for the ice creams. All of these go into the fridge to chill, except of course there's no way they'll fit. Naturally I would never suggest just leaving the stock out on the kitchen counter all night. This is where having two refrigerators would come in handy. Friday dinner will be, of course, takeout fare. Margaritas may sound like a good idea but probably aren't.

At 7:30 AM, you will begin your morning, as most Americans do, by starting up the ice cream maker. This will wake everyone else in the house, so maybe they can help. Once the ice cream is made, you can make the bed. And if you want to take a shower, honestly, this is going to be your last chance.

After about 11 AM, you have crossed the Rubicon. There are rolls to bake, chicken to marinate, black-eyed peas to soak and then cook in ham-hock broth. There are hard-boiled eggs—12 of them—to peel, dip in flour, wrap up in sausage meat, dunk in a mustard-egg wash, and coat with bread crumbs. This alone will take an astonishingly long time, all for something nobody's going to eat anyway.

You will think you're doing pretty well at this point. But there is still the Thai red curry paste—very, very much chopping, followed by very, very much pounding with a granite mortar and pestle. It does smell amazing, though.

And there is sticky rice to toast and lacy rice noodle crisps to deep fry, which sounds like a disaster waiting to happen, but is actually great fun—very Iron Chef. Meanwhile, like sands through the hourglass, so goes your afternoon.

By 5, you'll be frying the chicken. Frying chicken on a late May afternoon in an un-air-conditioned apartment is not much fun, and takes longer than you might think. Accept it and move on.

Food magazines seem to assume you have a spouse. Certainly, such a thing comes in handy. I sent mine off in search of oatcakes and stinky Scottish cheeses. Spouses are also good for chopping up parsnips and fennel for the thyme-roasted vegetables, rinsing salad greens, and dicing up catfish fillets. Keep the task of cutting up the banana leaves for yourself, though. It's fun, like being a botanist and a seamstress at the same time, and anyway, between batches of chicken and cooking the catfish, you've got nothing but time.

Another essential resource when you give an insane Scottish-Thai-Southern fusion dinner party is the Patient First Guest, who will, first, not mind when you come to the door hysterical and drenched in sweat, and will, second, prepare the smoked salmon on oatcakes for cocktail hour and the watermelon coolers you want to serve with the main dishes. And thanks be, because you are sure not going to get around to it anytime soon.

The next guests to arrive can crack open the Champagne and pass around the Scotch eggs you've just fried. These are either shockingly delicious or you are just very hungry.

One particularly idiotic thing food magazines may convince you to do is serve dinner in courses. Unless you have a maid or a caterer, this is just dumb; plus impossible to pull off.

That said, steamed catfish wrapped in banana-leaves makes for an exceedingly impressive first course. When your guests unwrap their little green packets tied with ribbon that is actually lengths of the banana leaves' ribs, and are greeted with a whoosh of spicy steam—well, this is what food magazine addicts live for. You will in one dizzying moment forget 24 hours of sweat and suppressed hysteria, the backaches, the groceries more expensive than some bargain flights to southeast Asia.

When on a high like this, you can ride out the rest of the evening on a wave of fried chicken and black-eyed peas and alcohol. Sautéing the Chinese broccoli you scoured Chinatown for will be the work of an instant. You'll slice radishes for the salad course as if in a dream. Slack Ma Girdle cheese will smell like ambrosia. And when, some three hours after dinner began, you dish out dainty scoops of two kinds of ice cream, topped by your triumphant lacy rice noodle crisps, and sip your South African red muscadet, you will perhaps feel that the good life is indeed, for this night anyway, yours.

Next time, maybe I'll splurge on a French maid's outfit. Or a kilt.

The Meat of the Matter

The Art of Carving

by Jeanne McManus

from *The Washington Post*

> Besides editing one of the country's best food sections, Jeanne McManus has a knack for getting to the heart of the matter in her own *Post* pieces. Though this piece appeared as part of the customary pre-Thanksgiving section, it mulls over a question. We face—or don't—year round.

It's a boneless, skinless, bite-size world, a world of tenders, cutlets, nuggets and morsels, where speed and convenience hold sway.

The magnificent prime rib with bones as thick as hammer heads has been ousted from the meat counter by a compliant rolled roast as soft as a cheese log. The stunning crown roast of pork, whose ribs arch into circles, the tips of its bones decked with frills, is missing in action, replaced in the vast refrigerated aisles of markets with pale, flabby blobs of vacuum-packed tenderloins. Even the mighty ham is now just a shaft around which are draped spiral-sliced and honey-glazed pieces, sawed by some machine so that no buffetgoer will ever have to struggle or encounter any resistance.

You can cut this world with a fork.

But it's a convenient world, a quick world, a less encumbered world. What's so wrong with that? Well, along come the holidays and into many lives a big slab of meat—the turkey for Thanksgiving, the prime rib for Christmas, the duck for New Year's Day—lands like an alien spacecraft on the carving board. Hmm, let's see: Knee bone connected to the thigh bone?

When Greg Preast first started to learn the art of butchering, more than two decades ago, the world was a different place. "The mother of the family would come in and shop, and the dinner table was a nightly gathering place. She would buy a roast, a pot roast or a bone-in sirloin for dinner, bring it home and cook it. When the family was assembled, father would carve."

Now, laments Preast, owner of Partlow's Market in Ashburn, "Today's society doesn't even know how to cook, let alone carve."

More has been lost than just a tableside skill. As a roast or a bird was artfully cut apart, ironically, the family came together. Dinner was not hastily assembled or a patchwork of takeout boxes. The roast gave weight and order to the table; family and friends were seated and attentive. The meal did not begin until the meat was carved.

It was an act that brought theater to the ritual of dinner. "Correct carving is an art, which, when mastered, is an accomplishment that adds greatly to the charm and grace of dining," wrote Duncan Hines in "Adventures in Good Cooking and the Art of Carving in the Home" in 1939. "It brings both genuine pleasure to the carver and an abundance of praise from the assembled guests."

It started as a guy thing. In Ethiopia's Afar desert, the bones of Australopithecus garhi were unearthed four years ago, and with him were stone implements that may indicate that 2.5 million years ago this was our first ancestor to carve meat. An antelope jaw and other animal bones found near the skeleton showed cut marks from the tools of a hungry creature perhaps in search of marrow.

Crude tools to satisfy a basic hunger evolved, and carving became a flourish, an honor. By 18th-century France, the ecuyer tranchant was a nobleman entrusted with cutting and serving the king's meats, a highly lucrative and prestigious position.

The carver wielded great power beyond the blade of his knife, often entrusted in parceling out the favored parts to the appropriate individual. So knowledge of etiquette on the carver's part was of key importance. Certainly, an honored guest would be given right of first refusal to dine on the head of an animal. And ears were great favorites, observes Margaret Visser in "The Rituals of Dinner" (Grove Weidenfeld, 1991), especially those of hares. In the mid-1800s it was "improper to give a woman a bird's leg," reported Visser; "legs were much too corporal and suggestive of what lay under skirts." (Breast meat was called "white meat," solving that delicate problem.) In contemporary times, the role of carver could be so critical that his actions might result in fodder for the psychiatrist's couch years later: Why did Junior always get the end cut?

Gradually, whether in the kitchen or at the dining room table, whether the scene of a special celebration or even a Sunday supper, women picked up the knife. By the late 1700s, "a thorough knowledge of carving was considered an important part of every young gentleman's and lady's education," according to "Sunday Roast" by Clarissa Dickson Wright and Johnny Scott (Headline, 2002). Almost 150 years later, Hines wrote, "Today in America many women are taking an active interest in carving; and what a thrill it is to watch a woman do an efficient and dainty job of it . . . We men had better be careful, or the first thing we know, we will be relegated to the kitchen to become experts in the realm of dishwashing."

In fact, the opposite proved true. Modern life took many a man and woman out of the kitchen, not farther into it. Smaller families, working parents, takeout and fast food and more casual entertaining changed not only the way families ate but also what they ate. In a consumer survey conducted this year by the National Chicken Council, 65.6 percent of the respondents said they purchased boneless, skinless chicken breasts; 33.6 percent bought whole chickens. The tasty flavor of roasts was lost, but in many cases it was compensated by convenience.

The changes showed up at holidays as well. According to Craig Kurz, CEO of The HoneyBaked Ham Company, the size of these festive gatherings are smaller, their frequency is decreasing and the entertaining is more casual: "The formality of the large dining room table and the Norman Rockwell holiday setting has passed," says Kurz.

Kurz's grandfather, Harry J. Hoenselaar, who founded the company in 1957, invented and patented the first spiral-slicing machine and process, a development that with one swift stroke sent the carving knife to the back of the drawer for many a holiday buffet. A presliced ham allows the host to be cut free from the moorings of a traditional table, to throw off the responsibility of having to grab a slippery, glazed ham shank and stand and slice.

It's a fine solution if ham is part of your holiday repertoire. But whether driven by the inevitability of serving turkey on Thanksgiving, or some primal memory of rib roasts of the past, the holiday cook eventually will be faced with a hunk of meat. And it won't be presliced.

"The calls start coming about this time of year," says Sara Reddington, director of the Culinary Center for the National Cattlemen's Beef Association. "We get telling feedback from retailers who are being asked by consumers: How do I cook this, how do I cut this?"

A cook who's done nothing more vigorous or deft all year than trim some fat off a sirloin is not going to be able to take a rack or a roast or a bird and dispatch it cleanly and evenly without practice, for the same reason that medical students go to teaching hospitals before they are allowed to remove a gall bladder. So how can a cook jump into the holiday carving ritual?

Preast likes to encourage his customers to establish a relationship with him, their butcher, the guy on the other side of the meat case. "The people who buy standing prime rib usually are those who remember growing up with it or who are preparing a traditional family holiday meal, such as Christmas dinner," he says. "About 80 percent will ask, 'What do I do with it?' Others are hardheaded enough not to ask and are ready for a fight when it comes time to carve it."

Is carving a lost art, one that could be recaptured with a bit of practice, even if it means test drives on $70 roasts? Reddington pauses: "My feeling is that people today never knew the art of carving. At my dad's table, my grandfather carved. My husband has no idea how to carve."

If carving and all of its attendant values of family and togetherness are ever to return, perhaps it's best to take things slowly. "If you're going to carve," says Preast, "if you're smart you're in the kitchen, not at the head of the table—you don't want to look like a complete fool."

The Butcher's Art

by Kathleen Brennan

from *Saveur*

Thanks to Atkins-inspired diet regimens, meat-eating is on the rise—but is it too late for the old-time butcher shop? Veteran food writer Brennan's richly detailed feature story not only profiles a pair of traditional artisans, it also sounds an alarm for saving this arm of the food-supply chain.

Yup, things sure have changed around here," mutters Joe Maresca as he drives his beat-up candy green Ford pickup past a sprawling housing development on Route 523 near Sergeantsville, the sleepy town in western New Jersey where he has worked for 56 of his 76 years. "For centuries, all this land was pastures and crops," he says, slowly motioning out the car window with a callused left hand. "Then, in the last 25 years, things went crazy."

But along with the plush new homes, the manicured lawns, the fancy tile and "country" furnishings shops, and the numerous transplanted Manhattanites, vestiges of the past do exist: stone farmhouses with dirt driveways, cows chewing contentedly in open fields, hand-painted signs announcing, DUCK EGGS 4 SALE.

And then there's S. Maresca & Sons, the butcher shop that Joe and his brother, Emil, inherited from their father, Salvatore, in 1973. Located in a plain ranch-style building whose interior is memorably decorated with a series of murals of animals frolicking amid smiling butchers, Maresca's, celebrating its 60th anniversary this year, is a local institution.

From the start, the shop has been as much a social hub as a place to buy expertly prepared quality meats—from freshly ground beef to a beautifully boned-out leg of lamb. Although Maresca's no longer has the only phone in town (people once used its number as their own), the bulletin board by the entrance is still crammed with flyers and business cards advertising everything from a community play to in-home care for pets. Like their father before them, Joe and Emil, who both officially joined the family business in 1954 after serving two years in the military, are on a first-name basis with most of their customers, quite a few of whom are the children or grandchildren of the shop's original patrons. Similarly, many of the customers know one another—all of which makes for a constant exchange of news, gossip, even recipes.

Much a part of the community as Maresca's may seem, though, remaining a fixture on this stretch of narrow country road has not been easy. While small, independently owned butcher shops used to thrive in practically every American town, they're disappearing at an alarming rate. According to the American Association of Meat Processors, roughly 5,000 such shops carry on across the country today; two decades ago, there were about 15,000. The decline can be attributed to several things, including the proliferation of large grocery chains and discount outlets like Wal-Mart—which offer the convenience of one-stop shopping, longer hours, and lower prices—and the simple reality that fewer people are interested in learning the butcher's trade. Indeed, these factors are also contributing to the death of the art of butchery itself, which takes years to master. It's a situation all too familiar to the Maresca brothers, who work alone and have no children or designated heirs.

Emil, two years Joe's junior, calls himself a "baloney man." Kielbasa, pepperoni, bangers, lamb sausage—if it comes in a casing at Maresca's, he made it. Most days, in fact, you can find him in the butcher shop's prep room, wrist deep in a plastic tub full of ground meats and seasonings. So it is on this frigid late-winter morning as he mixes a batch of liverwurst. Everything about his actions, from his rhythmic kneading of the filling to the way he stares off into the distance, indicates that he's done this countless times, that he could do it blindfolded if necessary.

Homemade liverwurst, however, along with items like smoked

chicken breasts and grill-ready marinated kebabs, are relatively recent additions at Maresca's, put on the board as a way of keeping old customers and attracting new ones. Back when Salvatore Maresca, who emigrated from Italy as a child in 1901, ran the business, butchers concentrated on one thing: transforming carcasses of meat into retail cuts. The elder Maresca learned the trade while apprenticing at various shops in New York, and after he bought his own place, he began teaching it to his two sons, then just teenagers.

But as Joe, who resembles a kindly, oversized gnome, points out, "these days, it's not about staying in the butcher business; it's about staying in business." People don't cook as much, families are smaller, and there is less demand now for big pieces of unprepared meat. So, the brothers are not only cutting more individual steaks and chops, but they've also had to expand their repertoire and embrace a broader definition of what it means to be an independent butcher.

As with many of the small butcher shops that have managed to hang on, dairy products, produce, and a variety of dry goods now line the shelves, too. The Marescas, who also used to do a lot of catering, have even hired someone to prepare soups, pies, and breads for them. But what's good for the bottom line isn't always good for the soul. "The other day I was putting soda in the cold case," Joe recalls, "and I said to Emil, 'It's kind of demeaning [to do this] after all these years.' But the customers want it."

After Emil, a self-effacing, soft-spoken man with a deceptively stern-looking face, finishes filling natural casings with the liverwurst mixture and poaching the resulting links—which have a coarser texture than commercial liverwurst and a cleaner, milder flavor—he checks on another house favorite, pâté Louise. With muscular hands that seem too big for his trim frame, he opens the left door of a double-oven Garland stove. A heady aroma of pork, garlic, and liver wafts out, but a quick look inside reveals that the pâtés, named for Louise Douglas, a late, beloved customer who shared the recipe with the Marescas more than 40 years ago, aren't quite ready.

The shop, which has been open for several hours now, is silent save for the buzzing of the fluorescent lights overhead. "Business falls off after the holidays," Emil explains, as he wipes down the grinder.

"But it's more stimulating to us when it's busy. You know, we're reactive. When people come in or the phone rings, it gets us going." Emil admits that for him, unlike for Joe, butchering was an acquired taste. "After graduating from school, I was in limbo," he recounts. "I didn't know what I wanted to be. And sometimes I think I still haven't gotten there. I think I wanted to be a baseball player. I was pretty good, too. But I didn't get any encouragement from my father to try anything else, 'cause he wanted me to come join him."

Out front, Joe is about to prepare some seasoned Boston butts, more commonly known as pork shoulder butts, for the display case. He slams the eight-inch-thick door of the meat locker shut and plunks down two butts on a maple butcher block whose dips have been decades in the making. ("You turn the block every week so it gets worn out evenly," says Joe.) After deftly running a boning knife across a sharpening steel, he begins to trim off the excess fat. "See, this is a lymph node," he says, pointing the knife tip at a small ovoid near the surface of one of the butts before carving it out. Next, he removes the blade bone from each butt, examines them, and notes that not only are both pieces of meat from the left side of a pig but, judging from the softness of the cartilage, the animals were probably about six months old when they were slaughtered. This autopsy report is undoubtedly accurate: the Marescas used to raise and slaughter much of the meat they sold, once common practice for rural butcher shops. The brothers had to stop in the mid-'80s when they found they could no longer handle the physical strain. (Most of the meat in America used to be slaughtered at small operations across the country; today 82 percent of the steers and 60 percent of the hogs are killed and processed by just four companies.)

Joe recommends that customers try slow-roasting the butts, which are naturally tough, in a heavy covered pot. "It breaks down the fibers, melts the fat, and makes them really tender and moist," he tells them. Before he trusses the two before him, which he's stuffed with garlic, parsley, salt, and pepper, he cuts a stray flap of meat off the end of one. "It just doesn't look nice," he says in his expressive, raspy voice. "It's a point of pride. You know, in the old days, when butchers would visit each other, they'd check out the display cases, and if something didn't look good, they'd say, 'Who the hell did that?' "

It is noon when Joe moves on to cutting strips of chicken for kebabs, and not a single customer has come in. "It's often either really slow or really busy," he comments. "People are like sheep. They come in flocks."

Several weeks later, Joe and Emil are running through their combined ailments—which include two stomach aneurysms, a bout of prostate cancer, cataract surgery, a few hernias, fractured hands, carpal tunnel syndrome, arthritis, and a complete hip replacement—when the bells attached to the leather pig cutouts on the front door signal the arrival of several customers. Joe, who underwent the hip replacement, uses a mahogany-colored cane to help push himself up from a workbench, where he's eating a late lunch of chorizo sautéed with onions, white beans, and tomatoes—what the brothers, both competent cooks, call "a quick butcher's meal". Emil, relatively spry by comparison, is already at the counter, tying up a specially ordered baked and sliced ham for a woman who's having a party. "Look how nice he prepared it," she says admiringly.

Filling his first order, Joe grabs a hacksaw to cut through the bone of a porterhouse steak: "Lots of people use the [electric] band saw 'cause it's simpler, but this makes a cleaner cut," he says, adding with a chuckle, "If you saw my right chest muscle compared to my left, you would see how much bigger it is from sawing." Meanwhile, two women waiting in line trade their favorite "time-consuming-but-worth-it recipes", while beeps and rings from the cash register punctuate their conversation. Joe begins pounding a flank steak, then scoring it so that it is a little more tender and doesn't curl when cooked.

"A pound of bacon, please," a customer says to Emil, who cuts a piece on the slicer and holds it up: "How's that?" "Uhh, a little thicker, please," the man responds, holding two fingers about an eighth of an inch apart. Emil cuts another slice. "Is this okay?" he asks without a trace of irritation. (Customized service, after all, is a chief reason people continue to patronize small butchers. "If people wanted precut meat," Emil says later, "they'd go to the supermarket.") When someone requests a five-pound leg of lamb, Joe instantly replies, "No problem," even though he has only ten-pound legs in the walk-in. He takes one out and proceeds to cut off the shank, followed by three one-inch chops, all of which he will hope to sell separately. After trimming some fat and membrane, he puts the leg on the scale: 5.62 pounds. "We can't manufacture a leg of lamb," he says, "but we can make up pretty much everything else. And that's what it's all about."

In addition to meat, people pick up broccoli, pears, a pie here and there. And everyone seems to pay by check. "Hi, Emil, hi, Joe!" someone calls out. Looking up, the brothers reply in unison, "Oh, hi, Joanne!" A resident of nearby Stockton, Joanne Kratzer has been coming here for 28 years, and, like most of the Marescas' customers, she realizes that the aging brothers probably won't be able to go on much longer. "I can't bear the thought of them closing," she says. "I really felt so privileged to live in such a beautiful area with a great butcher shop around the corner. It's depressing to see every town turning into the same thing— McDonald's, Linens 'n Things." The brothers pretend not to be listening, but their proud faces betray them.

At about 11 AM on an unseasonably cold spring day, a car crunches into the shop's gravel-strewn driveway. Emil, standing by a set of shelves stacked with dried herbs and spices as well as an odd mix of books—*Eminent Dogs, Dangerous Men; Meat Hygiene; The Prostate; Clean Your Clothes with Cheese Whiz; The Essential Italian Cookbook;* and *Mysteries of the Ancient Americas* among them—peers out a window and nods. It's Fred Herzer, their sales rep from R&R Provision in Easton, Pennsylvania, paying his weekly visit. The Marescas, who started buying from R&R about 12 years ago, used to order only hanging, or carcass, meat, but dwindling sales forced them to switch over to mainly primal cuts—shoulders, legs, and such. (Most of their meat is also high-end choice; see "The Ratings Game.") The change certainly made their jobs easier, but, as Joe says, it also "took a lot of the romance out of the business."

Even though recording the brothers' order takes only about 15 minutes, Herzer, whose clients include restaurants and supermarkets, spends almost an hour with the Marescas. "This is one of my favorite stops," he confides. "There's always something going on, and their all-around knowledge is incredible." After a brief discussion about the impact the use of pesticides on golf courses is having on the flavor of Canadian geese, the talk turns, as it does more and more lately, to the decline of the butcher's art. The advent in the 1970s of Cryovac'd, boxed meat, which is broken down into smaller cuts and vacuum-sealed at the packing house (this makes it cheaper and simpler to ship and gives it a longer shelf life), greatly reduced the need for skilled butchers in supermarkets, where 90 percent of the meat purchases in this country take place. The latest trend, "case ready" meat, which goes straight from the shipping crate onto store shelves, is expected to render most in-house butchers obsolete. Not only that, but "meat cutters" now perform the butchers' job. Generally speaking, these are not craftsmen but assembly-line workers, trained to make only a few cuts; hand them a whole carcass and they'd probably have little idea how to break it down, let alone produce an individually tailored piece of meat. "The customers are losing out in the end," laments Herzer. "But they really don't know any better."

At a certain point, say the Marescas, there won't be any of the old-school butchers left to pass on their art. But they also acknowledge that people aren't exactly beating down their door asking to be trained. (It takes about two years to acquire the basic skills. Traditionally, people learned the trade through apprenticeships; nowadays, certification programs at vocational schools are becoming the norm.) "We never could find anyone who wanted to stick it out and learn the business," says Emil. "It's one of the most dangerous professions, and it doesn't pay a lot." As for the shop's future, neither brother thinks it has much of one. "All my father had to have was an idea and some money," Joe says. "Today, with all the government restrictions and regulations, not to mention the fees and taxes, it's very different, and expensive."

"There isn't that much incentive to do it," adds Emil. "We've been approached by a big food chain about turning the place into a combination butcher shop and restaurant. But I don't know...."

It's 6:30 PM, quitting time, and the brothers are scraping down the butcher blocks, putting all the meat into the front locker, where the air is drier, and sweeping the floor. Like an old married couple, Joe and Emil find no reason to fill the silence. But before they remove their aprons, say good-night, and head off down Route 523 in opposite directions, there's one more question to answer: How much longer will they stick it out? "Well," says Joe, rubbing his white-stubbled chin, "we'll see how the end of the year goes. But we say that every year. We get through Easter, then Christmas, then all over again. Something will happen someday where we'll say 'the hell with it'. But we always feel a responsibility to our customers because they're the ones who will really be hollerin' when we're gone."

THE RATING GAME

While the inspecting of meat for wholesomeness is required by federal law, the grading of meat, begun in 1927, is voluntary. (Grades are essentially determined by the amount of marbling— the traces of fat in meat: the more, the better.) The USDA has quality grades for almost all types of meat, but at the retail level you most commonly find them for lamb and beef (about 96 percent of the beef raised here is graded). Beef is graded prime, choice, select, standard, commercial, utility, cutter, and canner. Only the first three, described below, are usually available to consumers; the others are sold to meat processors for making items like hot dogs. The retail lamb grades are prime, choice, and good. Meat grades are certainly useful, but it's important to note that there is a range of quality within each category and that the criteria have been altered many times over the years, in part to appease producers. So, for example, the prime steak you invest in today may once have been considered choice.

> PRIME: The top of the line. It has the most marbling, which contributes flavor, juiciness, and tenderness. Only 4 percent of the beef raised in the U.S. is graded prime; most goes to restaurants and hotels.

> CHOICE: The grade most widely sold at the retail level. It has less marbling than prime and is generally good, not great, meat.

> SELECT: Popular with those who like lean meat, it has very little marbling and is likely to be both tough and relatively flavorless.

Farm-Fresh Find

by Dara Moskowitz

from *CityPages*

Writing with a brash, colloquial voice and absurdist wit, Dara Moskowitz—a transplanted New Yorker—has become a mainstay of Minneapolis's alternative weekly paper. Her enthusiasms are as fierce as her criticisms; she insists that her readers care as much about good food as she does.

A few years ago, I found myself on a typical Minnesota night, cozy between quilt and feather bed, the cat curled in a dimple at my feet, the moonlight a glowing stripe above the curtains, peaceful as a dolly in a box. Except for one of those persistent, annoying little thoughts that sneak in on you sometimes: Just who exactly do you have to kill to get a fresh chicken in this town? Such are the night terrors of restaurant critics.

But really. Why exactly is it that to get great quality local lamb, you have to go to a restaurant, like Lucia's or Sapor? Doesn't it seem that in this rich city ringed by all this farmland, we should be wealthy beyond counting in products of the winter farm?

And yet, walk into almost every grocery store in town and the beef is from Colorado, the lamb is Australian, the chickens are *driven in from Indiana*. Even our fanciest grocery stores are like this. Especially, ashamedly, our fanciest grocery stores, and even some co-ops, are like this.

And you just know chickens, cows, hogs, and lambs are rambling all over the landscape by the zillion! And you just know our local family farmers are going broke out there selling their carefully raised animals on the commodity market, where their plump happy animals get mixed in with sick factory farm ones, and fetch the same price.

It's ridiculous, and it's been ridiculous for years. Here in the Twin Cities we have a bottomless pool of eager home cooks. Out past the suburbs we have a bottomless pool of family farmers making the tastiest products on earth. And there has been nearly no way for the two to meet. Water, water everywhere, and not a drop to buy!

Which is why when I saw the banner in front of the old Linden Hills butcher shop announcing Clancey's Meats & Fish, I thought the same thing I always think: Is it you? Has someone finally chiseled a door into the treasure chest?

Paint me pink and call me Bubbalicious, Sugar, they sure have.

I walked my little self in there one lazy afternoon, got to chatting with new owner Kristin Tombers, who bought the place last October, and then got to chatting with Greg Westergreen, who got to mentioning that they had just gotten some lamb in from Joe and Bonnie from the Hill and Vale Farm, and if I had a few minutes he'd go in the back and French a rack for me. Now, I never in my life have refused a gentleman offering to French me a rack, and neither has any other sensible Minnesota lass (as proved by the recent failures of the teen abstinence programs), and this was one of the wisest decisions of my life.

When I got home and unwrapped the rack of lamb, with each of the dear little handle-bones cut free and scrubbed clean of any meat or fat (that's a Frenched rack), I felt like I was behind the line in a four-star kitchen. Mere civilians rarely see meat this beautiful. When I cooked it (as simply as possible, just pan-searing it, then gently warming it in a low oven) and dug in, I truly thought I might collapse in joy: The meat was so tender, so good, it was certainly the best lamb I've had in my life. Little chops with a wee black raspberry edge to the meat, a bit of cedar, herbal mist, the kind of food that tricks the deep, core carnivore out of a girl and leaves you wilted in your chair, panting. That's why we needed a local butcher shop!

It turns out that the butcher, Greg Westergreen, is far more than a butcher: He's the former chef from the Nicollet Island Inn, and so anytime you go into the place you're likely to find some of the most high-level gourmet take-out imaginable. One day they had Pekin Duck Wild Rice Soup, an unspeakably rich, velvety concoction of little pearls of curled wild rice swimming through nut-brown luxury. He puts together cold salads made with white beans the size of baby fists, tossed with roasted red peppers and roasted artichokes. Only the top restaurants in the state serve antipasto this good.

Westergreen even managed to impress me with olives—and I am quite jaded with olives, you know. But he took olives beyond themselves: Quail's-egg-sized hondrolias were marinated with slices of garlic and shallots in a sherry vinegar, and were so rich, meaty, and vibrating with flavor that I could only think, yes, such olives do require a butcher! Meanwhile, in a nearby bowl, green, sharp little luques were tossed with angel-hair curls of orange peel and sprigs of fresh thyme. These olives were a salt-and-citrus confetti on the tongue. They had me thinking about sitting by the sea in Sicily, and if I run off with the next Sicilian who crosses my path you'll know who to blame.

Over a series of visits I tried other things from the simple black plates that line Clancey's modest (for now) refrigerated cases: A subtle garlic sausage which cried out for a surrounding cassoulet, but still cut quite a figure when paired with scrambled eggs. A fine, mushroomy, robust, and noble pork tenderloin from Elgin, Minnesota's Hidden Stream Farm. A perfect, Clancey's-made gelatinous veal demi-glace, so you can cook like a four-star chef without roasting bones all day. A fascinating grass-finished steak from Misty Meadows farm in Pine Island—fascinating because it was bright red, light tasting, and had a sort of musky sweetness to it, like a muskmelon does. It almost reminded me of sushi-grade tuna, not in terms of tasting like fish, but in the sense that the flavor was so light and clean and front-of-the-palate, not the classic rich thunder of beef. Think of the difference between a Beaujolais and a Burgundy. That pure, light taste is because the beef was grass-finished, which means that the cow put on at least its final 200 or 300 pounds living out of doors, eating pasture and hay.

Then I talked to Todd Lein, who works for a farmers' collective called the Southeast Minnesota Food Network, which represents a few dozen family farms located in the fertile lands that lie between us and Iowa, and he explained two interesting new things to me: First, that I'm not the only person who's been driven nuts by the separation between farmer and consumer; and second, that pasture-raised farm animals are the new hot thing for keeping the environment together.

More on that in a minute. For the time being, please know that the University of Minnesota Extension folks, the Land Stewardship folks, and local restaurant visionaries like Lucia Watson at Lucia's have been working for years now on ways to get local farmers' products into our hot little hands, and this is going to start being something you'll see more and more in metro-area grocery stores, including the co-ops, but also the various Kowalskis' and outstate chains like Coborn's.

For my money, one of the creepy things about the way the organic standards have finally played out is that it's been a lot easier for big agribusiness, especially out West, to jump through and finance all the certification hoops. And so in some instances the small, conscientious family farms organic shoppers mean to support are getting lost in a big-money organic game. If you find yourself someday soon confronted with officially organic things from far away versus unofficial local things that adhere to principles similar to the organic standards, I say local is far more important.

For instance, all of the farmers in that Southeast Minnesota Food Network *(www.localfoodnetwork.org)* are small family farms who don't use drugs or hormones and raise their animals in an environmentally safe way, meaning that the farm isn't creating run-off or pollution problems, the animals aren't crowded or confined to small areas and are given access to the outdoors, and all of the meat is processed in small, local USDA-inspected plants that allow close inspection of the meat and provide more local jobs. These are old fashioned meat processing plants where they process a few animals a day, not thousands, as in factory farms. (If you want a primer on why factory farms are bad, check out *www.themeatrix.com*.)

But what about this whole grass-finished thing? I have been reading a lot lately about how good it tastes. And when I talked to Lein, who used to work for Land Stewardship, he explained to me that having free-roaming herbivores on the hills and dales is exactly what we need. "Large herbivores, bison and elk, were a huge component in this ecosystem," he says. "There are two ways of managing grass, you can either cut it or burn it. Animals cut it, eat it, and transform it into nourishment for the soil. Their walking causes a disruption in the soil surface, which distributes seed. A crusted soil doesn't allow any seed penetration, their herding behavior works just like tilling."

In addition, animals raised outside are healthier and require fewer vet visits because they spend all day getting exercise and eating salad. Well, ground salad, anyway. "Farmers who go from a confinement situation to pasturing see all of their costs of production go down," explains Lein. "After years of careful study we have discovered that cows have legs. They are in fact capable of feeding themselves and distributing their own manure. You don't have to use energy to bring them their feed and take away their manure."

After years of careful study, at least one local woman has decided we are capable of understanding, and supporting, this difference. Kristin Tombers has a 20-year background in local restaurant kitchens and in fish wholesale, and after looking at the problems for a decade finally decided she'd be the one to do something about it—which is why she opened Clancey's. "Food and what we eat is such an important decision," explains Tombers. "Shopping at Sam's Club or eating at McDonald's versus purchasing something where you know the animals have been treated properly and you can see the families and the land your money is going to help support. I saw [opening Clancey's] as a huge opportunity to put in place some of my community-minded thinking. I got the nastiest letter the first week we opened. This lady wrote to say, 'Did you think you can charge these prices because of the neighborhood you're in?' And being a capitalist is about the farthest thing from my heart, we need to make money to stay open, sure, but it's more important that the idea of supporting local farmers catches on."

And that's why, when you walk in, Tombers or Westergreen will be happy to explain the provenance of each and every piece of meat in the case, and almost every piece comes from a place you've heard of, with a farm family you can call to thank, if you want to.

Imagine it yourself the next time it's a Minnesota night and you're cozy beneath your quilt: What would it be like if up here in town we could eat like kings, and out there, out under the moon there would be no manure lagoons, just farmers who could afford to keep their farms, and lambs who eat hillside salads. And the town and country feed each other, abandoning the previous era of mutual indifference? I'm sure you're all going to write me and tell me I'm naive, but I think there would be at least a few less night terrors, and a little more sleeping like dollies in boxes.

Barbecue? You Could Do It In Your Sleep

by Sam Sifton

from *The New York Times*

Sifton's profile of grillmeister Chris Schlesinger is not only a wonderful character portrayal, it's also a focused look at that most manly culinary endeavor—slapping meat on a hot grill. Which, of course, involves much more technique than your typical backyard barbecuer ever suspects.

C hris Schlesinger was snoring softly on the couch. This was in the living room of his sprawling ranch house here in southeastern Massachusetts, nestled high above a pebbly beach. A Bill Murray movie was playing on the television in the corner, and the cool breeze sliding off Buzzards Bay had dampened the room, covering the warmth of the day. Outside on the sweeping deck, in a giant ovoid kettle grill, three pork butts sat in the smoky braise of a small oak fire, glistening, ruddy, plump. It was well after midnight. Seven hours' cooking done. Seven hours to go.

The snoring came to an abrupt stop as someone in the room moved to open a sliding door and go check the fire.

"Barbecue Man may appear to be asleep," Mr. Schlesinger roared, climbing off the couch. "But Barbecue Man is always awake and in control!"

He padded barefoot to the deck and placed his palm on the covered grill. "Barbecue is such a typical guy thing to do," he said. "Much ado about nothing." He lifted the kettle top and a cloud of fragrant, oaky smoke engulfed him. He laughed from within it. "But it is intense."

The plan was to make an American holiday meal, or at least the part that could be made on a grill, overnight, for lunchtime celebration the following day. The menu: North Carolina-style pulled pork sandwiches, with their characteristic vinegary sauce, on cheap hamburger buns. You might accompany these with a simple preparation of coleslaw or some salad and a load of cut watermelon.

To make the sandwiches, you simply pull—or tear, really—shreds of meat from slow-roasted shoulder of hog, which is known among butchers and barbecue aficionados as pork butt, and place these on a bun with some sauce. (A hog's rear quarters are called, conversely and somewhat more attractively, hams.) The cooking time for the pork may exceed 12 hours, but you could start after work tomorrow and easily be done in time for a Fourth of July lunch with little effort beyond getting up a few times in the night to tend the fire. (For those leery of sleeping while fire burns bright, the meat could be cooked throughout the day and enjoyed as a late dinner about the same time the holiday fireworks wrap up, or even refrigerated until the following day, to be reheated in the oven.)

Mr. Schlesinger's fire started slowly. About 6 PM, he poured a pile of hardwood charcoal about the size of a large box of cereal into the front of the grill's firebox and added to it a generous, unapologetic spray of lighter fluid. "I don't have a problem with this stuff," he said. "I want to get my fire going." When gray ash began to appear on the edges of the charcoal, he placed on it a large piece of dry oak, which popped and crackled in the heat.

Mr. Schlesinger's grill is a Weber Ranch kettle a yard across. Behind the fire was almost two feet of open grill space, plenty for the three pork butts he planned to cook. (A conventional grill has less space, but plenty for a single butt.) The meat would cook slowly in heat that would not often, Mr. Schlesinger estimated, exceed 212 degrees. "You want to melt the fat into the meat," he said. "You don't want to incinerate it."

To protect the butts during the cooking, Mr. Schlesinger used a dry rub of spices that adhered to the pork and seized up in the heat, creating a flavorful crust. To make it, he mixed generous amounts of brown sugar, dry mustard, ground coriander, cumin, cayenne, paprika, chili pepper, freshly ground black pepper and sea salt in a bowl.

When he was finished he set the rub aside and pulled the pork from his refrigerator.

"There's no extra benefit in letting this meat come to room temperature before cooking it," he said. "I don't like to take chances with bacteria." He cut the butts out of their packaging with a small knife and rinsed the meat in the kitchen sink. "Likewise," he explained.

Outside, the charcoal fire was dying down and the oak smoking furiously. Mr. Schlesinger placed the three butts in a large disposable aluminum-foil pan on a table next to the grill and, using his hands, slathered them with the dry rub.

"It's O.K. if it's a little wet," he said. "It gets pasty, and that helps spread the rub around."

One by one he placed the butts on the grill, fatty side down, well away from the fire. "I'll turn them later," he said. "In about eight hours." He slid the kettle top onto the grill and adjusted the top vents. Smoke rose into the air from them in a steady stream.

"It's running a little hot," Mr. Schlesinger said. "But the one time you're not going to be overcooking a butt is now, at the beginning." He looked down at the smoke for a while, silently watching it rise.

"Let's get some dinner," he said.

Mr. Schlesinger checked his fire again at 9:30 PM, adding another piece of oak, and then retreated to the living room with a can of Pabst Blue Ribbon to watch television. "Groundhog Day," the 1993 movie in which Mr. Murray experiences the same day over and over, had started on TBS at 8 o'clock. This morphed, at 10:20, into "Ghostbusters" (1984), in which Mr. Murray plays a parapsychology professor with a ghost-removal business. (Mr. Schlesinger added another log to the fire at 11:40.) "Stripes," the 1981 movie in which an unemployed Mr. Murray joins the Army to meet girls and have a good time, got under way at 12:35 AM An hour later, Mr. Schlesinger reluctantly abandoned the narrative to add more charcoal to the fire, at which point he turned the butts over. More charcoal went on just after 3 AM On the television, "Ghostbusters" was playing again.

Between these chores, Mr. Schlesinger said, it only appeared that he was dozing.

At 8 AM, with the sun beginning to dry the dew that had gathered on the deck during the night, Mr. Schlesinger declared the cooking complete, 14 hours after it had begun. "Feel that," he said, pressing his finger into one of the butts. It felt like a ripe peach, or a late-summer tomato. "Done," he said.

With tongs in his left hand and using his right hand for balance, moving carefully so as not to tear the skin, he pulled the butts, which now had the color and texture of redwood logs, off the grill and placed them back in the disposable aluminum-foil pan, which he had cleaned the night before.

"We'll let those rest," he said, and went to the kitchen to get the sauce: a cup of white vinegar, a cup of cider vinegar, a tablespoon of sugar and a not inconsiderable dash of Tabasco sauce, mixed together in a bowl.

"We'll let those butts rest all morning," Mr. Schlesinger continued. "They'll be perfect for lunch."

But he soon pulled some hamburger buns out of a plastic bag and moved back to the porch. With his tongs, he picked up the largest of the butts by one end. It tore under its own weight, releasing a small cloud of steam. The smell was incomparable: sweet, smoky and fine.

He tore off a sliver of meat and tasted it, then smiled.

"I was a little nervous," Mr. Schlesinger said. "You always get nervous, even when you know it's going to be good."

He pulled some more meat off the butt and placed it on a bun. Breakfast was served.

~

Pulled Pork

Adapted from Chris Schlesinger | Serves 10 to 12
Time: 14 hours, largely unattended

4 tablespoons paprika
4 tablespoons brown sugar
2 tablespoons kosher salt

2 tablespoons cracked black pepper
2 tablespoons ground cumin
2 tablespoons chili powder
2 tablespoons dry mustard
2 tablespoons ground coriander
1 tablespoon cayenne pepper
1 pork butt, 5 to 6 pounds
Barbecue sauce (see recipe)

1. In a grill with a cover, build a small fire to one side, making sure all the wood or charcoal becomes engulfed in flame. (This dish should not be attempted on a gas grill.)

2. Mix dry ingredients together in bowl, using a fork to break down hunks of brown sugar. Apply this rub to pork butt with your hands, covering meat entirely.

3. When flames begin to die down, leaving flickering coals, place meat on grill on the side without fire. Do not let flames touch meat at any time.

4. Cover grill, vent slightly and cook, checking fire every 30 minutes or so, and adding a bit more fuel as necessary, for about 14 hours, until meat is soft to the touch.

5. Remove meat from grill with tongs, let rest 10 minutes, and pull meat apart with tongs. Serve on hamburger buns, drizzled with sauce.

~⊃

Barbecue Sauce

Adapted from Chris Schlesinger | Yield: About 1 cup.
Time: 10 minutes

½ cup white vinegar
½ cup cider vinegar

½ tablespoon sugar
½ tablespoon crushed red pepper flakes
½ tablespoon Tabasco sauce
Salt and freshly cracked black pepper to taste.

Whisk ingredients together in a bowl. Drizzle on barbecued meat.
Covered, sauce will keep about 2 months.

Meat Loaf Mania

by James Villas

from *Stalking the Green Fairy*

> Villas, whose distinguished career has taken him from *Town & Country* to *Esquire* and through a host of cookbooks (see John Thorne, above, for discussion of his casserole classic), champions in this essay the humblest form meat can take: ground up and patted into a loaf.

Most serious foodophiles in the United States are closet eaters when they're not indulging in all the fancy stuff. I've watched Julia Child demolish an entire bag of Pepperidge Farm Goldfish in less than an hour. Nobody can knock off a fat cheeseburger faster (and with greater relish) than Jacques Pépin. Paula Wolfert is addicted to Fritos throughout the day, even while testing her latest complex Moroccan or Sardinian recipe. Jeffrey Steingarten, I'm convinced, literally couldn't exist without a bottle of ketchup within immediate reach. And Jeremiah Tower's inordinate love of fresh beluga caviar is surpassed only by his spiritual need of greasy fish and chips and Häagen-Dazs ice cream. As for yours truly, I won't touch commercial cookies, cakes, or jams, but I'll kill for a heaping tablespoon of peanut butter (crunchy) or wedge of thick-crusted, gooey pepperoni pizza.

No doubt these disparate, furtive gratifications are as sensual to present-day *becs-fins* as spaghetti and meatballs was to Craig Claiborne, but if I had to name a single gustatory passion that unites all foodists but stubbornly remains on the back shelf of respectability, it would have to be all-American meat loaf. When Mimi Sheraton, for instance, gave up reviewing restaurants for the

New York Times, the first thing she announced ecstatically was how she was now free to slip over to a favorite hideaway in the bowels of Brooklyn for all the meat loaf with gravy she wanted. Wander into the unfashionable 72 Market Street Oyster Bar & Grill in Los Angeles any late night of the week, and you're likely to see at least a couple of the city's most cutting-edge chefs doing full justice to the hefty meat loaf and mash. One surveyor for the Zagat Guide to Chicago restaurants raves about the "classic" meat loaf at Ed Debevic's Short Orders Deluxe, but adds timidly that "loving this place is one of my guilty secrets." When I asked Georgia's star cooking teacher and television personality Natalie Dupree to recommend a restaurant in Atlanta where I could find some no-nonsense American food, she almost whispered that the veal meat loaf with celery mashed potatoes at the Buckhead Diner was not to be missed. And I'm never in Dallas that one savvy hostess, who normally entertains on a grand scale at the chichi Mansion on Turtle Creek, doesn't quietly suggest that one evening we steal over to the Dixie House for what has been pegged Mom's Meat Loaf for as long as anybody can remember.

It's not that the food snobs are exactly embarrassed over their craving for putatively humble meat loaf; the problem is that they've yet to perceive the dish as worthy of the same serious critical analysis, messianic discussion, and concerted experimentation as, say, pickled pigs' cheeks or braised monkfish liver. As a result, most simply don't understand meat loaf, and, as a result of this benign ignorance or indifference, most are not too fastidious about the loaves they ingest with such blissful abandon. Yes, a few professional chefs have had the courage and curiosity to include some imaginative version of meat loaf on their trendy menus, but more often than not, the concoction is so contrived that the whole idea of recreating their secret dream dish is utterly defeated—like transcribing a classic Bach fugue into a rap mode to such a radical degree that the integrity of the glorious original music is lost completely.

And here I part company with my peers, since I have nothing but unadulterated respect and concern for meat loaf and am proud to tout its lofty social status loudly and clearly whenever the dish warrants praise. Needless to say, there is meat loaf, and there is meat loaf, and the horror stories I could relate about meat loaf meals in cafeterias, highway diners and third-rate coffee shops, friends' houses, and a few snazzy restaurants are hairy. In a nutshell, for every Platonic meat loaf I've encountered, there are at least five that were best relegated to my beagle's bowl. And there's absolutely no excuse in this, none whatsoever. Any fool should be capable of turning out a superlative meat loaf, one that is so sublime, so special, and so personal that those at the table will leave wondering how in heavens name the dish ever acquired its questionable reputation and why it isn't featured in even the smartest American restaurants.

This by no means implies that you must search desperately for some exotic ingredient, since there are no exotic ingredients in a great meat loaf. Nor does it require purchasing any fancy equipment or practicing a certain cooking technique, since even a novice is fully capable of producing superior meat loaf with a minimum of expense and bother. Never in the annals of gastronomy has a dish demanded so little to be so good, and never has there been a preparation whose success depends so much more on love and respect than it does on culinary expertise.

Although there are not—and should never be—many rigid rules for making meat loaf, serious meat loafers like myself do agree on a few essential points that can make the difference between a mediocre loaf and one that truly stuns. First and foremost, a great meat loaf is moist and succulent, even when the surface is delectably crusty from being baked free-form in an uncovered shallow pan. Moisture is supplied and maintained mainly by an ample amount of fat in the ground meats used, so if you have a phobia about cholesterol, you might as well discount from the start the possibility of turning out a memorable loaf. Too much fat, on the other hand, can result in a soggy, unappealing loaf, which is one reason I personally prefer leaner cuts of meat with a little bulk sausage added for moisture (as well as for extra flavor). Other acceptable sources of moisture are small amounts of beef stock, tomato sauce or ketchup, chopped fresh vegetables, milk, and Worcestershire sauce. I've also discovered that bread crumbs soaked in heavy cream or half-and-half can provide an almost unctuous quality to the finished product.

Some fanatics like meat loaf made exclusively with beef. I don't, for the simple reason that such a loaf tastes more like well-seasoned hamburger than the more complex dish that great meat loaf should be. For my palate, an equal combination of ground beef, pork, and veal yields the ideal loaf in flavor and texture. I must say, however, that when ground veal (whose gelatinous properties add juiciness and enhance texture) has been difficult to obtain, I've turned out some pretty impressive examples with only beef, pork, and that sneaky sausage. I do know about meat loaves prepared with chicken, chicken livers, ham, tongue, lamb, and heaven knows what else, but as far as I'm concerned, that's more like some fancy pâté or terrine than meat loaf—and I won't hear of it.

Nor does authentic meat loaf contain such frivolous additions as curry, apples, anchovies, walnuts, cloves, horseradish, or other alien items that certain zealous young chefs might somehow feel add "character." Nonsense. Experimenting with various classic components (onions, mushrooms, bell peppers, Worcestershire and Tabasco, garlic, herbs, etc.) is one thing; changing the identity of the loaf beyond recognition is another. Forget also about trying to make a loaf that contains no filler or eggs unless, again, you want to end up with a heavy pâté. Small amounts of bread crumbs, crushed soda crackers, rolled oats, or the like help balance the texture, while eggs at once lighten the loaf and bind it for easy slicing.

There's one way, and one way only, to mix a meat loaf: with your hands. And don't be timid. Just dive in, blending the ingredients evenly with your fingers and scraping any stray mixture from the sides of the bowl. (But don't overmix, which will toughen the loaf.) Then, when you're satisfied with the feel, the look, and the aroma, you can always pack the mixture tightly into a loaf pan, which will yield a fairly crusty top but soft sides. On the other hand, you might prefer, as I do, to form it into a thick oval or a long rectangle or a square before positioning your creation in a wide, shallow baking vessel—for overall crustiness—and draping a few slices of smoky bacon over the top.

And, you ask, what about gravy? There is no gravy. There is no call for gravy. Great meat loaf would be utterly desecrated by gravy, just as great mashed potatoes need no gravy. Do not serve gravy.

Predictably, I think my ultimate meat loaf is indeed the best on earth, and I must say, I've had lots of compliments on it. Some overly sensitive fellow addicts, I regret to say, do not agree that my meat loaf is the finest on earth, and they've told me why. That's fine, for at least I know that their interest is genuine and that maybe they're just trying to overcome any dumb reservations over the supreme merits of a dish that should be right up there in popularity with seared fresh tuna steaks and braised rabbit legs. Besides, what I never fail to remember is that no matter how masterful I think my cooking is, no matter how high jubilant spirits may soar, and no matter how many thunderous plaudits may come my way after every delectable morsel on every plate has been devoured, I and my noble meat loaf must stand alone.

The Ultimate Meat Loaf

Serves 8

5 tablespoons butter
½ pound large fresh mushrooms, stems finely chopped and caps reserved
1 large onion, finely chopped
½ medium green bell pepper, seeded and finely chopped
2 celery ribs, finely chopped
3 garlic cloves, minced
½ teaspoon dried thyme, crumbled
½ teaspoon dried rosemary, crumbled
1 pound ground beef round
1 pound ground pork
1 pound ground veal
½ pound bulk pork sausage
1 tablespoon Dijon mustard
½ cup tomato ketchup
3 tablespoons Worcestershire sauce
½ teaspoon Tabasco
Salt and freshly ground pepper to taste

3 large eggs, beaten
1 cup breadcrumbs soaked in ½ cup heavy cream
3 strips bacon
Stuffed green olives, cut in half

In a medium skillet, melt 3 tablespoons of the butter over moderate heat, add the mushroom stems, and stir about 5 minutes or till most of their liquid has evaporated. Add the onion, bell pepper, celery, garlic, thyme, and rosemary, reduce the heat to low, cover, and simmer about 15 minutes or till the vegetables are soft and the liquid has evaporated.

Preheat the oven to 350°F.

Place the meats in a large mixing bowl, add the sautéed vegetables, and mix lightly. Add the mustard, ketchup, Worcestershire, Tabasco, salt and pepper, eggs, and breadcrumbs and mix with your hands till blended thoroughly. Shape the mixture into a firm thick oval loaf, place in a shallow baking or gratin dish, drape bacon over the top, and bake 1 hour in upper third of the oven. Remove the bacon strips and continue baking 15 to 20 minutes longer, depending on how thick the loaf is and how crusty you want the exterior to be.

Shortly before the meat loaf is removed from the oven, melt the remaining butter in a small skillet over moderate heat, add the reserved mushroom caps, and stir about 2 minutes or till nicely glazed. Transfer the meat loaf to a large, heated platter, arrange olives over the top, and garnish the edges with the mushroom caps.

Eating Out

La Carte

by Andrew Todhunter
from *A Meal Observed*

> Todhunter set out to describe minutely every detail of one superlative meal at Paris' Taillevent restaurant. Having worked in its kitchen, he had an insider's perspective on what went into the meal he was about to eat. But the view from the dining room is often vastly different.

*M*inestrone *d'Artichauts Poivrade au Pistou,* it begins, at the top of a column of *entrées,* or first courses. In France, of course, the *entrée,* or "entry" into the meal, is not a main dish, or *plat,* but an appetizer. How this became confused in translation into English is beyond me, but I'm sure there is the willful mischief of a seventeenth-century French diplomat to blame. The folded rectangular menus are large and elegant, printed on stiff, cream-colored paper. When closed, they are more than a foot and a half tall by a foot wide. On the front page, appetizers, fish, and meat and game are separated by engravings. The wine list occupies two facing pages within.

I know immediately that I did not come to Taillevent for anything resembling minestrone, however sublime or unorthodox, and jump ahead with mild irritation. As much as the thought of artichokes *à la poivrade* (typically a kind of pepper vinaigrette) coupled with the garlic and basil normally associated with *pistou,* a Provençale soup, might appeal to me, I feel surprised, even ambushed, by the word "minestrone" in a restaurant of this stature, in France. Although I may not have known it, the word "minestrone," or the host of images it conjured, was one of the innumerable things

I hoped to evade in moving to Europe. Not that my associations with the soup were in any overt way identifiably negative: stacks of blue cans on the shelves of the Grand Union in a suburban New York town, unprepossessing Italian restaurants, bowls of my mother's minestrone on our dinner table (and with the bowls come the woven blue and slightly rumpled cotton place mats, the small, chipped crystal bowls of salt and pepper, each furnished with a tarnished silver spoon no more substantial than a sparrow's rib, the silver napkin rings engraved with the initials of long-dead relatives, and the floating, ambient cat hair that somehow made its way into every dish served in that house).

When I recovered our car in Le Havre, on a drizzling January day six months before, having shipped it from the end of a New Jersey pier, and pulled finally onto the highway toward our rented apartment off the rue Lepic in Paris, I felt an immeasurable sense of lightness and renewal. Above all, I felt a sense of possibility more profound than any I had had since my early twenties—since the largely illusory promise of dawning adulthood. Illusory because, apart from attractive and vivacious company, nothing comes of youth and ambition without the sustained and patient effort that ambitious youth too often finds tedious. I had lived in France sporadically over the past decade, a year here, a year and a half there, each time returning to the States for ostensibly practical reasons—to finish my degree in the first case, and later to marry on family ground. But this move to Europe was potentially permanent. I shipped nearly everything we owned as an anchor, a dead weight to discourage retreat. Since the appearance of our daughter, two at the time of our move, this anchor had gained appreciably in mass. Let's start with a few years, I said to my wife, and then we'll see. I hoped she would agree to stay indefinitely. What *of* the smoke screens in the restaurants, the drifts of dog excrement, the bureaucrats, and the bleak, endless industrial winters? This is *France*. As I upshifted and changed lanes, gaining speed, scanning the highway—French pavings, French road signs, French license plates on French cars—a soaring buoyancy rushed through me. I felt like shouting, and did: I whooped in the car. Yes! I bellowed. Yes! I pounded the steering wheel, crushed it in my grip, pounded it again, and flew on. And though I did not at the time think in any such specifics, I knew that the minestrone, and the cat hair, and the napkin rings of dead and faceless relatives (I myself would be a dead and faceless relative soon enough, as I well knew) hadn't made it onto the boat.

Or so it first appeared. As I would ordinarily be quick to acknowledge, each of us is a Trojan Horse, packed with the Greeks of our pasts. But, for a moment, for a few exquisite months, I thought I had actually managed to cut loose and had left Troy to burn.

In any case, I did not come to Taillevent for a bowl of minestrone. I read on.

Royale de Champignons à l'Aigre-Doux
Crème de Cresson au Caviar Sevruga
Asperges vertes poêlées au Jus de Truffes

It goes without saying that we will try the asparagus. I believe there is no vegetable—indeed, no edible object of any kingdom—which rivals the asparagus properly cooked. When singing the praises of that green shoot, or defending its virtue against attacks of indifference, I might even be mistaken as a foodie. I owe this largely to my college adviser, an eclectic savant, misanthrope, and self-exiled inhabitant of the seventeenth century, who, while disabusing me of my misconceptions surrounding Virginia Woolf, Franz Schubert, and the student films of Roman Polanski over dinner, introduced me to asparagus properly steamed, and to a simple dipping sauce of mayonnaise, Dijon mustard, and dill. My debt for this recipe shall never fully be repaid. The list continues:

Escargots braisés, Sauce Poulette
Ballotine de Foie gras de Canard
Mousseline d'Oeufs aux Morilles et aux Asperges
Raviolis de Fromage de Chèvre à l'Armoricaine
Cannellonis de Tourteau, Sauce Ravigote
Boudin de Homard à la Nage

The main courses follow. The fish:

Daurade à la Tomate et au Basilic
Rougets en Filets aux Anchois et au Fenouil
Bar de Ligne au gros Sel
Sole en Filets au Cresson de Fontaine, Sauce Marinière
Darne de Turbot rôtie au Beurre fumé
Fricassée de Langoustines en Cassolette
Homard poêlé aux Châtaignes

Followed by the meat and game:

Pigeon rôti en Bécasse
Poulette de Bresse en Cocotte lutée (2 personnes)
Canette de Challans au Miel et au Citron (2 personnes)
Andouillette de Pied de Pore aux Truffes
Foie de Canard poêlé au Poivre torréfié
Selle d'Agneau farcie au Jus de Truffes (2 personnes)
Côte de Veau fermier à l'Oseille
Escalope de Ris de Veau aux Morilles
Cœur de Filet de Bœuf en Pissaladière
Côte de Bœuf grillée aux trois Sauces (2 personnes)

As we read the menu, unhurried, each of us is lost in a suc-
cession of oral fantasies engendered, one after another, by the
barrage of culinary flavors, aspects, and methods. I move down
the list, weighing choices, while saliva gradually pools in the well
beneath my tongue. Closely read, a good menu is an onslaught,
and, like the flickering response to an equivalent string of bodily
terms—lips, breasts, thighs, feet—each word or phrase on the
menu, particularly something like "sautéed in truffle juice," or
"roasted in smoked butter," thumps and shudders like a depth
charge in the animal mind. *Beurre, crème, fenouil, basilic, sauce, jus,*
poêlée. The impact of this verbal suggestion is heightened by con-
textual anticipation (I *know* we will be eating in this quarter-
hour), like erotic innuendo in a taxi home. The impact of such
language can attain an excruciating pitch if reflected upon in
times of forced abstinence.

In August of 1982, before my junior year in high school, a
friend and I took a month-long course in mountaineering and

wilderness survival through the National Outdoor Leadership School in Lander, Wyoming. At month's end, fit as Olympians but wraithlike, we hiked out of Wyoming's Wind River Range to the road head in small groups, a four- or five-day trek, fasting. The fast was a crowning indignity; we had survived the month on little more than dried fruit, bulgur, and Grape-Nuts. Our external-frame packs weighed more than seventy pounds, including climbing equipment, camping gear, and emergency rations, and we were hiking as much as thirteen miles a day, route-finding with map and compass through wilderness. The hollow pain in our bellies seemed to peak and subside on the second day, but by the last night, camped under a tarp in sight of the pickup zone, we were delirious, semihallucinatory, and the pain returned. As we had come down out of the mountains, into the arid foothills of Wyoming in late August, many of the springs on the map had proved dry. Despite conservation, we ran out of water near the middle of the last day, and added dehydration to our discomforts. Unable to sleep, we spent most of that last night writing lists of all the sweet and savory things we would consume, and in what order, on our return to civilization. One of us would call out an entry; after a silent moment of absorption would rise a chorus of oaths and moans.

"Philly cheese steak, covered in onions . . ."

"Don't say it."

"A big oily sausage-and-pepperoni pizza . . ."

"Ohhh, you bastard."

"A Double Whopper," rasped a parched voice in the darkness, "with bacon and cheese, large fries, and a Coke." The company groaned like dogs.

Other entries on my personal list of nearly a hundred items included Key lime pie, lobster rolls, jelly doughnuts, and Buffalo wings. Red meat and pizza reappeared in countless forms. Greasy substances, high in fat and protein, were the staples on everybody's list, the T & A of our culinary pornography. Around three in the morning, overcome with desperation, I ate a few inches of tooth-paste and gagged.

Soon after dawn, when the bus appeared in the distance, throwing up a rooster tail of dust, we ran down to the road like liberated POWs, braying for food and water. They gave us plastic bowls of cornflakes immediately, with sliced banana and skim milk—nothing too complex for our withered viscera. The sweet and milky taste was wondrous, but the *sensation* of something substantial—something that could be chewed and consumed— was so intense as to seem unprecedented, as if we had never before eaten solid food. Later, we learned that the other groups had broken into their emergency rations in the first two days. How we scorned them.

On our return to Lander, disregarding our instructors' warnings, we ate as much meat, fat, and candy as we could get our hands on. In a rural, Western American town, this amounted to a good deal. Alone and with others, I systematically combed the grid of downtown Lander, hitting every fast-food place and convenience store in my path. I scratched items, one after another, from my list. Double cheeseburgers, chocolate bars, steak sandwiches, vats of soda and lemonade, huge, loaded pizzas wolfed down alone in a corner booth.

The morning after our return, the very instant I awakened in our hotel room, I sprang out of bed with the intention of cleaning out the adjacent doughnut shop. I took one half-conscious bound down the staircase, missed the fifth step I had aimed for, and tumbled end over end to the next landing. Thirty seconds later, rubbing my elbows, I stood before the shop's glass cabinet, peering in. Glazed doughnuts, powdered doughnuts, chocolate doughnuts, cinnamon doughnuts, jelly doughnuts, old-fashioneds, crullers, twists, eclairs. Row upon row, illuminated, under glass.

This three-day orgy destroyed my digestion for months, and at the time I could feel it happening—all that heavy protein backing up in my intestines like wet sand. But I couldn't stop; the imperative to eat was too strong.

I have never sat down to a meal in quite the same way since, and for the first seven or eight years the sense memory and the fear of that hunger stayed near me. More often than I would have expected, as I set into something as simple as a cheese sandwich, I would remember that hunger—it would rush me like violence relived—and I would eat the sandwich like a dying man.

At Taillevent, our appetites enflamed, Erin and I consult

conspiratorially, in low tones. The importance of this moment is often overlooked. If the apéritif marks its nativity, pondering the menu is a meal's youth. Like that period in one's early life when one is regaled with unrealized choices, the short span of minutes just prior to declaring your order must be properly observed and appreciated. Then, and only then, everything on the menu is yours.

With the understanding that we can hardly err, we tentatively decide to split a bowl of the watercress soup, followed by the asparagus and the *mousseline*. Both the *crème de cresson* and the *mousseline* have been highly recommended by reliable sources. As a second course, we intend to move on to the *boudin de homard* and the *langoustines,* and conclude with the *daurade* and the *homard aux châtaignes.* You can never put away too much lobster.

Thus prepared, I merely glance up. The captain steps forward from his position, near the serving station, where he can observe all nine of his tables. He holds a small pad at the ready.

"Would it be possible . . . ," I begin in French.

"Yes," the captain breaks in politely. "Whatever it may be, it is possible."

He assures us that the soup, and any other course, may be divided in two. Because the *mousseline* has asparagus, however, he suggests that we omit the *asperges au jus de truffes.* I propose the escargots in its stead. The captain nods: first the soup, "as an *amuse-bouche,*" he adds, an indication that the soup will be on the house, followed by the escargots, followed by the *mousseline,* all divided in two. And if we would like the *daurade* and the *homard aux châtaignes,* the captain suggests foregoing, for reasons of volume, the *boudin* and the *langoustines.* What we have overlooked in our gluttony is that any plate divided in two in the kitchen is not truly one half of one serving. In fact, primarily for reasons of aesthetics, a *demi,* or "half," is much closer to a full serving. Each *demi* is prepared separately as a slightly smaller (or in some cases, like that of the *boudin,* no smaller) variation on a full plate. Thus, we will each be served three appetizers and a main course, to say nothing of the gougères, or of the cheese and the desserts to follow. An additional dish apiece, the captain knows, divided or no, would prove uncomfortable, if not physiologically improbable, to consume. No need to overdo it, he might say, but doesn't.

Indeed one must, objects the ghost of A. J. Liebling. In his 1959 classic *Between Meals,* Liebling recounts his apprenticeship in Paris in the 1920s. Lunch for the younger, lighter Liebling, a cub reporter, boxing aficionado, and "eater in training," might consist of *truite au bleu, daube provençale,* and young roasted guinea hens with asparagus, followed by cheese and dessert. With barefaced adulation, he presents numerous accounts of those prize heavy-weights of the table, capable of consuming, for example, two cas-soulets, a steak with beef marrow, and a dozen or more oysters at a sitting. He reports that the celebrated Yves Mirande, a playwright and gourmand to whom the book is dedicated, once lunched on "raw Bayonne ham and fresh figs, a hot sausage in crust, spindles of filleted pike in a rich rose *sauce Nantua,* a leg of lamb larded with anchovies, artichokes on a pedestal of *foie gras,* and four or five kinds of cheese, with a good bottle of Bordeaux and one of Champagne." Mirande, a small man then in his eighties, was only ramping up. For dinner a few hours hence, he dispatched "larks and ortolans (buntings) . . . with a few *langoustes* (crayfish) and a turbot—and of course, a fine *civet* (or stew) made from the *marcassin,* or young wild boar."

We accept the captain's counsel, and close the door, with regret, on the *boudin* and the *langoustines*. He returns to the serving sta-tion and gives a carbon copy of the order to a *commis,* or assistant, who will take it to the kitchen and place it directly into the hands of the chef. I lean back into the banquette with a sensation of relief. It is done. Out of our sight, a machine of near-legendary precision has been set in motion.

The Deal with Raw

by Joe Dolce
from *Gourmet*

When the new editor-in-chief of the tabloid-gone-glossy *Star Magazine* covers a food trend, you can bet it's hot—although, in the case of raw food, never over 118 degrees. No mere trend-spotter, however, Dolce has the foodie creds to take a good hard look at the raw food movement.

G o ahead, smell my trash." Juliano Brotman lifts the lid of his garbage can, sticks his head in, and inhales deeply. "Ohmigod. Dude, it smells so good! I have the best-smelling garbage in the world." It's true. He does. That's probably because there's no grease or grisly bones in it—there's nothing but grated vegetable skins and the leaves and stems of plants and flowers. Not that the smell of somebody's garbage will tell you anything about that person. Or even, for that matter, anything about the quality of the food he eats. Still, this is one example raw foodists cite when making the case for the supremacy of their way of life.

By now you've probably heard about the raw food movement. Among the world's most extreme dieters, raw proponents hold certain truths to be inalienable: First, that heating food above 118 degrees kills enzymes that are key to life; second, that starches create an unhealthy "acid" condition in the stomach; and third, that meat and fish—indeed, all proteins, which the raw diet notoriously lacks—are hugely overrated.

To anyone who has ever worried that man is moving too far from his natural state, there's a certain romantic appeal to this eating regimen. To others, it reeks of the crackpot.

Juliano embodies both points of view. A scallion of a man with long hair that he wears braided and twisted into a bun, the 33-year-old admits to bleaching his locks but says he hasn't touched shampoo for several years. His eyebrows are plucked into pointed arches, and his signature outfit is a midriff tank top and pants that hang as low as legally possible. He dresses like a girl but is an avowed heterosexual. (Within the span of the three days I spend with him, a dozen gorgeous young women approach him as he bounces down the street, grabbing his butt or locking his lips.)

Juliano goes out of his way not to wear leather or drive, and he prefers sleeping outdoors on his roof. ("Dude, I have the highest ceilings in the world.") His week consists of eight days, a calculation based on the fact that he sleeps only five hours a night (a much-vaunted benefit of eating raw). He has been neither sick nor depressed in the past decade. By preserving the chemical composition of food and keeping enzymes alive, he says, the raw diet not only adds years to your life but reclaims gray hair, eliminates wrinkles, and provides you with levels of energy previously unknown to humankind.

"We're cosmic lottery winners," Juliano says when asked to explain how this could possibly be. "We have laptops and cellphones, and now we have raw. I mean, do you know why people are unhappy in rotten jobs? Cooked food."

A little bit Liberace, a little bit Euell Gibbons, the man is an original. A gender-bending, good-humored cyclone of energy, he is also the major force behind a trend that shows no signs of slowing down.

The son of a Mongol (his dad, a chef) and a Sicilian, Juliano turned vegetarian at age 15. He was vegan four years later and "rawish" by 22. One day, laid up for a week after a skateboarding accident, he forgot entirely about the wheatgrass he'd begun growing in the kitchen. When he finally got to the jar, he saw the sprouts had formed a hard crust. "That's it!" he thought. The crust of the raw pizza he'd been searching for revealed!

"Guess what?" he told a friend in San Francisco. "I invented this new food and it's called raw, and I've been eating it for like three days and I've been sleeping like forty-five minutes a night." The

friend gently informed Juliano that there were already raw foodists out there, and then went on to tell him about one group that
held potluck dinners.

Juliano showed up with raw pizzas and burritos, and, he says,
the crowd went wild. "They had broccoli and olive oil dip and
Celtic sea salt. I mean, it was nice, but they were, like, going
crazy over hummus and wheatgrass," he recalls. "Once they ate
my pizzas, my friend was like, 'You know what! You did invent
raw food, dude.' "

That was 11 years ago.

With a $30,000 loan from his mother, Juliano went on to open
a restaurant, Raw, in San Francisco's Sunset district. It wasn't easy
convincing the masses to pay for food that had never seen a stove.
"They thought it was gonna be like a few lettuce leaves," he says.
"I had to build a customer base from, like, two people. I mean, a
restaurant looks really big when there's no one in it."

After the *San Francisco Chronicle* ran a rave review, though, and
he changed the restaurant's name to Organica, word spread. There's
this new diet. It's totally natural. It doesn't kill your enzymes. And
it makes you really, really skinny.

In 1997, Juliano relocated to Los Angeles. There, he began
hosting underground dinners in warehouses and soon learned that
where a new diet goes, celebrities inevitably follow. Alicia Silver-
stone and Lisa Bonet hosted events, and he "cooked" for David
Duchovny, Bill Cosby, Woody Harrelson, and Steve Jobs. Two years
later, he published *RAW*, his "UNcook Book" (ReganBooks).

After visiting Juliano's restaurant in 1999, restaurateur Dan Hoyt
was so inspired he went on to open three branches of Quintes-
sence raw restaurants in Manhattan. Meanwhile, in San Francisco,
a one-time pastry chef named Roxanne Klein got in touch with
Juliano and asked him to serve as her consultant. For $1,000 a day
(plus food and limo), Juliano says, he agreed to make the trip up
to Klein's mansion in Tiburon, where he schooled her in the ways
of raw. (Klein disputes the financial details of the arrangement.)

She, in turn, put together an entire menu of gussied-up recipes
and opened Roxanne's, a fine-dining restaurant in Larkspur, in
December of 2001. Outfitting the room with Bernardaud china

and solar-powered lighting, Klein elevated the raw idiom in a single stroke.

Juliano bears no malice. "The only time I ever feel ripped off is when people make bad raw food," he says, recalling the time he went to see a pal who was working at Oprah's Harpo Studios. "I go, 'Hi Oprah, I have this amazing food, it's called raw,' and she turned and said, 'I tried that stuff, I ain't eating it ever again.' And she ran away—not walked, ran. Someone got to her before me and they did a bad job."

It's 9 AM, and Juliano is zooming about, putting together several dishes in the tiny kitchen of Juliano's Raw, his gleaming, nine-month-old restaurant in Santa Monica. He's blending tomatoes, garlic, herbs, and strawberries to make a marinara sauce; dousing zucchini strands with oil and sea salt to turn them into "pasta"; and dehydrating a sheet of macerated nuts and seeds to create his trademark "bread."

The kitchen of a raw foodist doesn't look like yours or mine. Dehydrators replace ovens; $1,000 turbocharged Vita-Mix machines substitute for blenders. It doesn't smell like a kitchen, either: Instead of homey aromas, there's the drab odor of a new refrigerator. As for ingredients, in addition to the predictable vegetables, fruits, and nuts there are superfoods like chia seeds, ground ocean extract, and tocotrienols (said to have 5,000 times the antioxidant power of vitamins C and E).

Such a pantry requires a readjustment of expectations. In this world, for example, avocados double as butter; almonds are turned into "milk" and "ice cream"; macadamia nuts get whizzed and fermented into "cheese"; and seeds are pounded, dehydrated, and spiced to form "fish cakes" (to be served with a tartar sauce made from herbed nut cream). Preparing this food is a complicated, time-consuming endeavor—"breads" alone can dehydrate for up to 12 hours. It's a good thing these people sleep only 5 hours a night: They need the extra time just to make lunch.

The staff at Juliano's Raw is spacey and more luminously thin than those you'll find at other health-food restaurants. (They don't have normal names, either. Nala, the hostess, for example, is dating Atom—@+Om sign—a cook.) And like Brahmin priests who distinguish themselves by what they won't put into their mouths, they believe they are among a select few. When a customer complains about the skimpiness of her raw taco (guacamole in a cabbage leaf), the waitress snarls, "You should learn to eat less food."

Yoga mats, Birkenstocks, and Toyota Priuses are the favored accessories of most customers, but the place is also frequented by regular folks looking for something: a new taste sensation, better health, a skinny mate, or a personal way to help save the planet. Juliano's cuisine probably isn't for everyone—most dishes have more garlic than a pastrami sandwich—but you can't deny that it's clever.

"This is a whole new cuisine," he says, "and we didn't invent it. Mother Nature did. Raw isn't only new, it's perfect!"

Nutritionists, doctors, and scientists will likely tell you otherwise. "The theory is nonsense," says Robert L. Wolke, professor emeritus of chemistry at the University of Pittsburgh and author of *What Einstein Told His Cook: Kitchen Science Explained.* "The enzymes we need for human metabolism are not the same as the enzymes we take in with fruits and vegetables, which are in any case digested, rather than being absorbed unchanged."

Also, say the experts, the low calorie count is akin to starvation—bulimia without the vomiting. And the few studies available conclude that over time a raw diet causes women to lose bone density and interferes with menstruation.

Philosophically, the theory, which bucks the last 15,000 years of the history of civilization, also has its flaws. Rather than viewing fire as an evolutionary advantage, rawists see it as messing with the natural order of things. If whales and apes—who eat only raw vegetables—can grow so big without cooked protein, they argue, then why do we need it?

It's a ridiculous question, says Daphne Derven, an archaeologist and authority on the prehistoric pantry. Fire not only kick-started our evolutionary ascendance, she says, it contributed to the qualities that make us human. It bumped up the nutritional value of food by making more plant life available and by widening the field of digestible ingredients. "Cooking allowed infants, children, and the elderly to eat and digest more," she says, "and it kept them alive longer."

Ultimately, however, all these arguments may be moot. Because raw isn't only about food. It's about the way you think about food—and the way you view the universe as a whole.

Nala, the hostess, says she believes the man behind the movement is capable of conjuring virtually anything he wants. She mentions a test that rates people's optimism. "Imagine a stairway up to your ultimate goal," she says. "How many stairs would you have to climb to get there?" I imagine a few thousand. Juliano, she tells me, sees just one.

These days he's got reason to be cheerful—his message is being heard. There are now some 50 raw restaurants in this country. And, like yogurt, soy milk, and sushi—all once unapproachably foreign—raw food, or some variation thereof, will soon turn up in a mall (or at least in a Whole Foods in a mall) near you. *The New York Times* recently reported that a new Manhattan nightclub, Spirit, will feature "uplifting" house music, an aromatherapy spa, and a raw food bar.

There are raw personal trainers, raw support groups, raw sailing retreats, and raw dog food. At least three raw cookbooks will come out this year. Already on the shelves is one that Roxanne Klein coauthored with Charlie Trotter, who says he's convinced that raw offerings will soon appear on menus across the U.S. "Everyone's interested in health," he explains. "And everything that starts in the extreme eventually trickles down into the mainstream."

There's no doubt that raw is here to stay. The only question is what form it will likely take. For most, it will be another detour along the endless trail that includes Atkins, South Beach, and whatever other calorie-counting schemes are lurking in our future.

For true believers like Juliano and his ilk, though, it will remain a whole lot more. Right now, these folks will tell you, the world is undergoing a massive change—more radical than the Industrial Revolution. We've got cloned sheep, genetically modified food, weapons of mass destruction, and a planetary fever that our leaders prefer to ignore. The problems are huge, they say, too big to even fathom.

And so the rawists practice yoga, drive hybrid cars, and create a world around them that preserves something of the innocence of youth. Whether or not their diet is nutritionally sound is ultimately beside the point. Because as any anorexic teen will tell you, regulating what you put in your mouth isn't just about controlling weight. It's about combating the uncertainty around you. And if not cooking can help you overcome that fear, it seems like a small price to pay.

Raw Cream of Spinach Soup

From RAW: The UNcook Book | *Serves 4*
Active time: 1 hr Start to finish: 2 hr

This uncooked soup isn't for the timid—raw garlic, ginger, and shallot impart strong flavors. Unless you can get freshly made vegetable juice from your local juice bar, you will need an electric juicer to make the tomato or carrot juice.

2 cups fresh tomato and/or carrot juice (from about 1 lb vegetables)
2 cups chopped spinach leaves
2 tablespoons chopped escarole leaves (optional)
½ medium California avocado, pitted and peeled
½ cup olive oil
⅓ cup packed fresh cilantro, chopped
¼ cup Nama Shoyu (unpasteurized soy sauce) or
   1½ teaspoons sea salt (preferably Celtic)
¼ cup finely chopped shallot
2 tablespoons chopped scallion
2 tablespoons minced garlic
2 tablespoons dry white wine
1 tablespoon fresh lime juice
1 tablespoon chopped fresh mint
1 teaspoon minced fresh jalapeño, including seeds
1 teaspoon minced peeled fresh ginger

Garnish: 1 small portabella mushroom cap, halved and thinly sliced

Purée vegetable juice, spinach, and escarole (if using) in a blender until smooth. Add remaining ingredients and pulse to combine, leaving some texture.

Chill soup, covered, until cold, about 1 hour.

A Snail's Pace

by Jonathan Gold

from *Gourmet*

Gold's assigned food beats have ranged from L.A.'s ethnic foods to Manhattan's top restaurants; recently transplanted to the Italian countryside, he mines yet another rich vein of cuisine and comes up with some surprising winners. (It's a tough job but someone's got to do it. . . .)

In the heart of Emilia-Romagna, around eight miles east of Modena, the single best pasta restaurant in the world sits on a rutted drive that runs through a sea of Lambrusco grapes. It's a sagging building with a half dozen Lamborghini tractors parked out front and shaded picnic tables in back crowded with shirtsleeved businessmen who've downed too much homemade grappa to make it back to Modena without a cab. The hand-rolled *garganelli* in bolognese sauce, a fugue of slippery texture and long-simmered animal, is everything that pasta should be—supple, resilient, almost alive under your teeth. The paper-thin tagliatelle, the luxuriantly rich *tortelli* stuffed with homemade ricotta, and the tortellini in capon broth are hardly worse. This is the kind of pasta made by women who measure weeks in flour and seasons in egg yolks, and every fold and crevice of noodle can seem as eloquent as a sigh.

But it is not easy to navigate your way to Osteria di Rubbiara through the knotted skein of farm roads in the region, and once you get there, the proprietor, a gnarly cuss named Italo Pedroni, tends not to make things easier. If you have remembered to reserve, he will frisk you for your cellphone, which he will then ceremoniously place in a lockbox. Pedroni does not believe in

antipasti, so there is no track with boar *salame* or beakers of Pros-
ecco or any of the other gimmicks to which many Italian restaurateurs resort to put you into a good mood. There is also no menu,
so you eat precisely what Pedroni thinks you should be eating—
probably a couple of those transcendent pastas, some roast meat or
the kind of *coq au vin* that you may have tried to cook for company when you were in college, and a few leaves of lettuce drizzled with Pedroni's own balsamic vinegar, which Modenese regard
as one of the very best in the region, which is to say the world. It
is a safe bet that you will end up drinking a bottle or two of
Pedroni's own Lambrusco and a bit of his walnut liqueur.
Favored tables are rewarded with gelato flavored with 12-year-
old vinegar—the only ice cream I have ever tasted that could be
said to be spiritually rewarding—even if one's young daughter, say,
pines for chocolate chip. And there will be no cappuccino, no
matter how nicely you ask. Only *caffè*.

Pedroni has a culture to uphold. You are just eating lunch.

On my last visit to the osteria, on a trip from Parma with my
then-eight-year-old daughter, I had forgotten to make a reservation, and although I had been to the restaurant several times
before, Pedroni stood behind his locked gate, pretending not to
understand my fractured Italian. I said that we would like to eat
lunch. Pedroni responded that he did not sell office supplies. I
made a sort of pasta-twirling gesture. Pedroni denied that the
premises housed a restaurant, raising his voice to be heard over the
clatter of silverware. My daughter started to cry. I cursed him
under my breath—Italian is a most satisfying language in which to
mutter imprecations, as anybody who has ever watched the third
act of any Verdi opera knows—and slunk next door to buy some
of his vinegar, which I had promised to bring back for friends,
although at this point I would almost have preferred to purchase
the vinegar shelved next to the tanning lotion at the Autogrill.
Pedroni strolled into his store, greeted me as an old friend he
hadn't seen in years, and sold me 500 euros' worth of the *extravec-
chio*. There turned out to be a table for us after all.

The Italian countryside is, of course, simply lousy with places to
eat—shacks and grand dining rooms, pizzerias capable of wild

rabbit roasted with juniper or quail sizzled with grapes, and road-side lean-tos that serve platters of grilled porcini strewn with garlic and parsley. At trucks parked at the Tuscan equivalent of the kind of crossroads Robert Johnson used to sing about, cooks carve up whole roasted hogs stuffed with thyme and wild fennel and mountains of fresh garlic, then pile them into sandwiches. It is not uncommon to charge up a dirt road and find something like Castiglioncello del Trinoro, a medieval fortified town perched above Tuscany's Val d'Orcia, and a restaurant, La Rosa del Trinoro, where the magnificent gnocchi, truffle-stuffed rabbit, and roast pork with *cipolline* are eclipsed only by the fresh Pecorino with honey. The local wine happens to be Brunello.

Even dining rooms that seem ordinary in every way can turn out to harbor one or two dishes that are worth a journey by themselves. In the hill town where I rent a house in summer, the most basic of the village's three restaurants—the trattoria you might stop by for an omelet and a plate of spinach when you don't feel quite up to cooking that day—also happens to serve braised guinea hen on liver-saturated croutons that is yelpingly good. The trick is avoiding the somewhat overmatched restaurant down the road, which has linen tablecloths and a trilingual menu of generic Italian specialties that attracts an eccentric amount of customers from the Low Countries. The man who said that it was impossible to eat badly in Italy obviously never tasted spaghetti carbonara adjusted to please the Belgian palate.

I happened to find Pedroni's restaurant on the recommendation of a friend, but friends are not always available or reliable. Nor are guidebooks, really, although bookstore shelves in Rome sag with Italian-language guides put out by the television gourmand Luigi Veronelli, by the leftish culinary society Gambero Rosso, by the center-left magazine *L 'Espresso,* and by the Touring Club Italiano, which is what the triple-A might be if its booklets were devoted to things like truffle tourism instead of tire maintenance.

Michelin, the red-jacketed kaiser of European cuisine, publishes an annual guide to the restaurants of Italy, but outside of the biggest cities it tends to recommend what I have taken to calling *prego* restaurants, the kind of grand, hospitality-intensive villas where the proprietor spends so much time telling you where the squid was caught and how many cubic meters of tufa were dug out for the wine cellar that by the time you get around to eating—*prego, prego*— your food is already cold. And after a long, solemn *Michelin* meal of stodgy vegetable molds and roast beef and elaborately composed salads, followed perhaps by a panna cotta indistinguishable from the boccie balls being hurled on the courts across the street, it is hard to avoid gazing longingly at the guys gobbling *pici* with goose sauce outside the gnarly trattoria down the block.

Several years ago, I started to notice that a high percentage of my favorite restaurants in Italy seemed to have doorposts emblazoned with a cute little *chiocciola,* or "snail," the insignia of Slow Food, an organization whose tortured pronouncements and truly awful name had led me mostly to ignore it. But when I spotted a copy of Slow Food's *Osterie d'Italia* next to the motor oil section at the local *supermercato* (in the U.S. the guide is sold only through the Internet), I realized that at long last I had found a guide whose priorities coincided with my own: local cooking, local wines, fanatical owners, and a slightly eccentric pursuit of oddball ingredients.

If a rice-size bean, obscure sheep's-milk cheese, or mildly disturbing innards concoction can only be tasted in a certain mountainous patch of the Marches, *Osterie d'Italia* is there. If a wine list is excessively deep in the sort of small-production Friulian whites rarely seen outside Collio, the guide has probably noted that, too. Where *Michelin* rewards restaurants that have exquisite napery and bull moose-size flower arrangements, *Osterie d'Italia* seems to prefer a backdrop of rusted farm machinery and walls that aren't perpendicular to the ground. *Gambero Rosso,* although it began as a supplement to *Il Manifesto,* Rome's Communist daily, will always point you to the sort of posh hotel restaurant that pushes its minted lobster no matter how far it is from the sea. Slow Food extols that loud restaurant just off the main square, the one with sausages grilling in the window, a house wine grown within sloshing distance, and a long roster of the local specialties that will never make it to the next town, much less to the Upper East Side. *Osterie d'Italia* reads as if it were meant for the enthusiast who really wants to taste the differences between the traditional dishes of Norcia and those of nearby Visso.

Osteria di Rubbiara and La Rosa del Trinoro, it almost goes

without saying, are Slow Food restaurants. So are La Darsena, a trattoria by the Viareggio shipyards where I once had a rather obsessive antipasto that included seven different kinds of braised cuttlefish; Osteria La Solita Zuppa, in the ancient Etruscan strong-hold of Chiusi, where the owner's sense of propriety is such that ten of us once sat at a table laid with the proper number of table settings but with only nine chairs because that was the number of people for which we'd reserved; and Locanda del Principato, near the south shore of Lake Trasimeno in Umbria, which appears to be a crash pad the four days a week the restaurant is closed, and which is encrusted with enough Mussolini paraphernalia to make the place a sort of Hard Rock Cafe of Italian Fascism.

In Panicale, a beautiful medieval hill town high above Lake Trasimeno, *Osterie d'Italia* singles out Lillotatini, at the top of the steeply sloping main square. It's an ambitiously, almost stubbornly Umbrian osteria with an awe-inspiring antipasto of porcini and forest snails, a wine list that includes rare small-producer Sagran-tinos, and a handwritten menu in a local dialect so obscure that even natives have trouble parsing it out. The kitchen may try a little too hard—it splits the difference between the distinctive lake fish dishes of the Trasimeno region and the truffle-intensive rustic cooking of landlocked Umbria, and there is a truly peculiar appe-tizer that involves both panfried lake eels and stewed tripe—but when the potato *fonduta* comes out sizzling in its casserole, scenting the entire dining terrace with the fresh Umbrian truffles thickly strewn over its entire surface, it is difficult to care.

Near Montevarchi and the shopper's grail of the Prada outlet store, Hosteria Costachiara is an oddly located restaurant not far from the autostrada, an old manor house where chickens peck at your feet and the antipasto table is like some fever dream of inspired Tuscan hospitality—stuffed tomatoes and grilled zucchini and roasted peppers and a delicious sort of Etruscan couscous made with spelt, a school of marinated fishes that have clearly leaped out of the Mediterranean just in time to swim in garlic and oil, roasted prosciutto crusted with Tuscan spices, and fresh Pecorino weeping butterfat. Only then does the lunch proper appear, perhaps thick hand-rolled *pici* sauced with a ragout of wild boar or a bowl of *pappa al pomodoro* seasoned with basil, and then the proprietor himself, bloody-aproned and brandishing a knife not much smaller than a machete, carving up the giant Chianina beefsteaks that he has just grilled in a fireplace upstairs.

I don't blame *Osterie d'Italia,* I suppose, for once leading me to a shuttered restaurant so deep in the Umbrian countryside that it took me 45 minutes to turn my car around on the cliffside goat path that passed as a mountain road, but I do fault the compilers for the fact that it was impossible to determine whether the trattoria had collapsed in the most recent earthquake or was merely closed on Wednesdays.

In Italy, slow food has become big business since its birth in the 1980s, with its biennial conclaves in Turin, its roster of cookbooks and travel guides, and the well-regarded if cranky quarterly *Slow.* Recognition by *Osterie d'Italia* can vault a small restaurant into the big leagues of international cuisine, where *Michelin* stars await and the guide's rough 35-euro-per-person price average no longer applies.

In *Osterie d'Italia,* the restaurants Slow Food really likes carry the snail insignia, which I imagine indicates a particular fidelity to the ideals of the movement—often a stubborn rusticity or a devotion to local foodways rather than an absolute standard of food quality. At snail restaurants, as I've taken to calling them, you are likely to be served a liqueur made from wild forest cherries the proprietress has picked herself, or encounter a lost recipe that the chef found folded between the pages of an ancient library book. If you ask for a substitution at a regular restaurant, you only insult the skill of the chef; if you ask for a substitution at a Slow Food restaurant, you insult the memory of the chef's grandmother. Swords have been drawn over less.

Osterie d'Italia does have its limitations, as anybody who has used it will tell you. The guide restricts itself to relatively inexpensive places, so many wonderful, local, representative restaurants you might want to know about have been rigorously excluded from the book—Alfredo, Gran San Bernardo, in Milan, say, or Il Postale, in Citta di Castello. It is less reliable in big cities (where there is often an overemphasis on cheap eats) than it is in the countryside. And the guide seems rather weighted toward the selfconsciously folkloric (which is to say dishes not served since the days of Pliny the Elder) and exhibits an almost perverse dedication to ingredients and techniques that even the most tradition-obsessed locals haven't seen since the days right after World War II.

My best meal last summer was at Taverna Castelluccio, which is a beery bar-restaurant in the remotest corner of Umbria, in a hill town known, to the extent that it is known at all, for its shepherds, for its tiny organic lentils, and for the empty desolation of the broad valley, the Piano Grande, at its feet. In mid-June, the wildflowers and the blossoming lentil plants show as broad, delicate washes of color on the valley floor far below. To get to the taverna, you twist east out of Norcia, then over the precipitous front range of the Sibellini, and beneath hang gliders lazily circling through the valley.

Even in the context of Castelluccio, the taverna doesn't seem like an obvious place to have lunch. It must be the only establishment in town that doesn't have a sign out front advertising its lentils or its sheep's-milk ricotta, and a lot of the guys lounging out on the terrace don't look as if they have a lot more on their minds than Heineken. But then the food comes. Truffles are abundant enough in Umbria that they sometimes seem as common as grated cheese, but the *stringozzi* at the taverna can still make you gasp, a sharp, intensely fragrant slurry of minced black truffles so dense that the dish for a moment resembles a bowl of Cocoa Puffs, and the short, twisted noodles themselves are buried almost a fork's-width deep. Grilled chops of *castrato* (yearling lamb) are almost obscenely flavorful. The minuscule lentils, cooked with plump Norcia sausage, are creamy yet distinct, sweetly earthy, popping like caviar under the teeth—like no other lentils on earth. And as you sit there, picking at the last of the musky local Pecorino and draining the last drops of Sagrantino wine from your glass, the slow road through Italy seems like exactly the right place to be.

Osteria Di Rubbiara *Via Risaia 2, Rubbiara, just south of Nonantola (059-549019).*
La Rosa Del Trinoro *Via di Mezzo 3, Castiglioncello del Trinoro (0578-265529).*
La Darsena *Via Virgilio 150, Viareggio (0584-392785).*

Osteria La Solita Zuppa *Via Porsenna 21, Chiusi (0578-21006).*

Locanda Del Principato *Località Badiali 34, Pani-carola (075-9680220).*

Lillotatini *Piazza Umberto I 13-14, Panicale (075-837771).*

Hosteria Costachiara *Via Santa Maria 129, Badiola (055-944318).*

Taverna Castelluccio *Via Dietro la Torre 8, Castelluccio (0743-821100).*

Bright Lights, Pig City

by Kathleen Purvis

from *The Charlotte Observer*

> A journalist for over 25 years and a Southerner her entire life, Kathleen Purvis takes a break from editing the *Observer*'s food section to judge barbecue contests all over the place, and claims to be completely non-partisan in the subject of Eastern- versus Lexington-style 'cue.

B arbecue in New York. It sounds like an oxymoron, like a jumbo shrimp or a fat-free french fry. Something that can't, maybe shouldn't, be. And yet. Scan the New York restaurant news and you come away with barbecue sauce on your fingers:

The owner of top spots like Gramercy Tavern and Union Square Café opens his next big thing, and it's barbecue.

A restaurateur moves to the Upper East Side and spends $36,000 on a rooftop gizmo so the neighbors won't smell pit smoke.

Young chefs in Hell's Kitchen and Brooklyn get the chance to do what they want, and what they want is pulled pork and sauce.

Even in the neon glitz of Times Square, a flame-red sign glows "BBQ."

And through it all, a Southerner wonders: Why does New York need barbecue? It has bagels and lox, and pastrami on rye; it has four-star foie gras and tuna tartare. It couldn't leave us this one thing?

Maybe the city that proclaims itself the capital of everything just can't stand to miss anything.

Here in the Carolinas, we have a few claims of our own. We may not have Broadway, but by golly, we have pulled pork. When it comes to barbecue, I have a few opinions. Georgian by birth and Tar Heel by raising, I come from a family of outdoor cooking fanatics. I've eaten barbecue, even judged it, from Mississippi to Miami, from Kansas City to Wilson. On styles, I'm strictly nonpartisan. As long as it's cooked well, my favorite barbecue is the one in front of me.

So on a recent trip to New York, I set out to answer the question: Has New York bitten off more than it can chew?

SCOUTING FOR PIG

Hitting the city on a Thursday afternoon, I headed for Hell's Kitchen and Daisy May's BBQ USA.

Chef Adam Perry Lang has attracted attention for his food and his story: Offered the job as chef at an executive men's club (read "high-class topless"), he was allowed to do what he wanted with a small space next door. So Lang opened a barbecue joint. It's tiny, just a service line and a ledge where you can lean if you want your take-out eat-in.

Opening my $8 Carolina Pulled Pork Sandwich with Cole Slaw, I had to count the little things that weren't right:

The sandwich is served on a wide kaiser roll, a fancier choice than you'd find in the South. The meat is chunky, not minced or shredded, and the extra sauce I requested on the side is thick and orange with a Southwestern tang.

Then I counted what was right: The roll is a very good roll, with a flaky crust and soft interior made for soaking up juice. The meat is tender and moist, not too smoky. And the slaw, while not a vinegar slaw, is on the sandwich where it belongs.

Licking my fingers, I hailed a cab and crossed Central Park, to Pearson's Texas Barbecue on East 81st Street. A stroke of bad luck: Pearson's is closed at 2:30 PM. A city that never sleeps does need an afternoon nap. I headed down Second Avenue, trusting to serendipity. Stopping for a manicure—a girl's got to have luxuries—I was holding out my fingers when I spotted a sign: Nancy Lee's Pig Heaven. It wasn't on my list, but it sounded

Southern. Wrong—Nancy Lee's is Chinese. But the stylish pink restaurant takes pork so seriously, the menu is divided by "Cold Pig," "Cold No Pig," "Hot Pig" and "Hot No Pig."

Skipping the Tangy Shredded Pig's Ears, I ordered "BBQ Pork Butt." It was chewy sliced pork similar to thick-cut country ham, served with a salty/sweet juice. Delicious, although it was no more barbecue than chop suey is Chinese.

A few blocks south, I reached Brother Jimmy's. Homesick Carolinians should keep it in mind for the atmosphere, like a well-worn campus hangout. The menu brags, "If God were a man, he'd be a Tar Heel," and Long Island Ice Tea is called "Charlotte Tea."

A $7.95 pulled pork sandwich with two sides brought very peppery Lexington-style pork, with a roast-pork flavor. Despite my request, the slaw came on the side, which was a good thing. It was heavy with mayonnaise, more at home next to a corned beef sandwich. The sauces included a vinegar style close to the real deal, but Brother Jimmy's left me hungry for more.

CLOSEST THING TO HOME

I waded back into the fray Saturday morning, catching the F train for Brooklyn's Park Slope. Joining a friend, Kaly Soto, who now works for the *New York Times,* we hurried to Flatbush Avenue and a small, funky place called Biscuit.

Brooklyn native Josh Cohen lives in the same house where he was born, but his cooking has wandered far. After training at Johnson & Wales University in Providence, R.I., Cohen cooked and traveled, trying barbecue styles.

"Carolina, hands down, that's my favorite," Cohen told me, showing off the smoke box, custom-made in Chinatown, where he slow-cooks pork shoulders until "they fall off da spikes."

His earnestness has paid off. We ate our way through double-dipped fried chicken (Kaly's choice, and a good one: Extra-crispy outside, moist and steamy inside), rich braised greens, and fork-tender pork ribs covered with a dark sauce.

A $7 order of pulled pork brought a small pile on sliced bread with two sides. Tender and moist, the pork was delicious, the closest thing to home I'd had yet.

Leaving Kaly at 42nd Street to head for work, I changed trains and rushed uptown to give Pearson's another try.

For years, New York barbecue fans raved about Pearson's Texas Barbecue in Brooklyn and Queens. When the original closed, owner Robert Pearson headed to Manhattan to bring smoked brisket and pulled pork to his fans.

Conquering the problems of making wood-smoke barbecue on the densely populated Upper East Side, the new restaurant opened four months ago, with a special filter on the roof to handle the smells. You can still get just a whiff as you near the red-and-white awning.

The N.C.-style chopped pork plate for $14.95 had the most smoke of any I'd had. While the meat was chunky rather than minced or shredded, it had a definite vinegar-sauce taste and reminded me of barbecue at competitions, where the meat is cosseted and babied. There may be a reason for that: Pearson has cooked at contests such as Memphis in May. Tall and handsome with white hair, Pearson stopped by my table and ended up sitting down to talk. A native of London, he was a fashionable hair stylist in the 1960s. How did he get from bobs to barbecue?

"Young women like you don't want old men like me cutting their hair," he said, smiling. In the early 1980s, Pearson switched careers and went into food, looking for a niche he could learn.

As a stylist, he used to go to Texas to teach the latest New York cuts, and people would take him to barbecue joints. He liked the atmosphere. "I thought, 'New York really doesn't have that.' "

To pick which kind of barbecue to make, he first traveled around the Carolinas. Although he found a recipe, from a barbecue stand in Boone, he still had trouble sorting the many styles of Carolina barbecue. "I couldn't get a consensus (on barbecue) in a town, let alone across the road. I got so baffled, I kept going until I got to Texas."

WITH CHAMPAGNE?

If you want to know what's heated up New York barbecue, even Pearson points to Danny Meyer, the owner of Gramercy Tavern, Union Square Cafe, Eleven Madison Park and Tabla.

"Danny Meyer and Blue Smoke raised the level," says Pearson.

Just before 6 PM, I reached Meyer's Blue Smoke on East 27th Street. Not able to get a reservation, I had been told to get there early. Minutes after I settled in at the last open table, people were stacked up at the door. Although Blue Smoke took hits from critics after it opened, it adjusted and has hit a fast-walking, downtown stride. Even early, the bar and two-level dining room were packed.

The menu is wide, covering Kansas City, St. Louis, Texas and Carolina styles. I grabbed the chance to answer the age-old question, "Does champagne go with barbecue?" ordering a glass of Billecart-Salmon. (Answer: Yes, but it will make you feel as shameful as Martha Stewart.) Happily spotting big bottles of North Carolina's Texas Pete on the table and "Mount Olive, N.C., salt peanuts" on the menu, I settled in for a fun meal.

Even at $14.95 for pulled pork, beans, slaw and Tom Cat White sliced bread, this barbecue was a treat. Finely shredded with just a hint of smoke and a soft, pillowy texture, it even had a little of the real Eastern Carolina whole-pig flavor.

Skipping the lackluster slaw and only picking at the beans, I still ate more than a sane person should and I had one more stop. So I did calorie penance with a 20-block walk to Times Square for an 8:30 reservation at Virgil's.

If Virgil's isn't the best barbecue in New York, it's certainly the most visible. The red neon sign glows over Times Square at 44th Street. On a Saturday night, it's as packed as Myrtle Beach on Memorial Day.

Joining Kaly again, we made our way upstairs, past tables packed with out-of-towners and businessmen on expense accounts. They'll need them: The prices hit a new high, $17.50 for a pulled pork plate with two sides, $20.50 for Memphis pork ribs.

Spreading our laps with Virgil's "napkins"—thick, red hand towels—we prepared to dig in. Well, Kaly dug. After four meals, the best I could do was pick.

Even after all I had eaten, I could still work up a little enthusiasm. Virgil's pulled pork is finely shredded with a light smokiness, even though it's mixed with a red, tomato-y sauce. The meaty ribs were the dry style, rubbed with spices.

Leaving most of it to Kaly, along with the banana pudding for dessert, I finally threw in the hand towel. While I never found a sandwich that tasted exactly like Lexington or Shelby, I did find some well-cooked pork, handled by people who show it respect.

Yes, New York, you can take the barbecue out of the South. Lucky for us, we never need to.

Barbecue, Jamaica Style

by Rand Richards Cooper
from *Bon Appétit*

> Travel pieces studded with food raves are a dime a dozen (after all, a fella's got to pay for all those freebie meals); it's the rare travel writer who makes a trip just for the food. Rand Richards Cooper's account of his jerk chicken pilgrimage is so focused on the eats, he makes you hungry too.

I smelled the place before I saw it, and heard the music, too: a tantalizing waft of roasting meat and spices, a pulsing blast of reggae. The road turned, disclosing cinder-block buildings and tin roofs in a haze of smoke. I had finally arrived at Boston beach, Jamaica, the world capital of jerk barbecue.

For years I've been passionately devoted to jerk, seeking it out in various cities where Jamaicans live: in Philadelphia, at a hole-in-the-wall next to an incense and palm-reading shop; in East London, at a stall at the Ridley Road Market; and in Manhattan, at a restaurant named Maroons.

It was at Maroons, during my bachelor party a year ago, that my dozen best buddies commanded me to order . . . well, you get it. The joke was lame, but the jerk lavish. So good, in fact, that a few days later I called Maroons's owner, Arlene Weston. I wanted to go where that taste came from, I told her.

"Then you have to go to Jamaica, to Boston beach," she said.

Boston jerk is the authentic thing, she told me—peppers right off the bush, pimento wood coals that add an earthy smoke flavor, powerful Jamaican spices. She added a warning: The jerk chicken I'd had at Maroons was a cooled-down version of the original.

"What we do down in Jamaica, it would blow people away up here," she said, laughing. "It's different when you're sitting on the beach, and it's hot out, and you have your beer."

That was what I wanted—to sit on the beach and be blown away. For years I'd been praying at far-flung temples. Now I wanted to make a pilgrimage to the center, to the Mecca, the Jerusalem of jerk.

The search for jerk takes you to a Jamaica well off the beaten path—not to the polished resorts of Montego or Negril or the cruise-ship clamor of Ocho Rios, but far east, to the Blue Mountains and Portland parish, a landscape of jungly hills and ruggedly beautiful coastline.

My base was Port Antonio, the former center of Jamaica's once-mighty banana trade and a destination for celebrities and the wealthy during the 1950s. But this cachet is now barely a memory.

Today Port Antonio exudes the kind of fantastic dilapidation that guidebooks might call "faded glamour." Victorian houses are outlined with decaying gingerbread, goats canter along the harbor road, and vendors at an open-air market sell goods from the backs of rusting trucks. Even a popular bar called Woody's Low Bridge Place—where Woody (aka Charles Cousins) serves homemade ginger beer—appears charmingly battered. I found the town alluring, in a rough-edged way, but it couldn't keep me from my ultimate destination for long.

Soon after settling into my hotel, I drove east from Port Antonio along a coastline rich with lagoons (including the Blue Lagoon of kitsch movie fame). Several minutes and many road bumps later, I landed in Boston beach, a small village on Boston Bay where beat-up Volkswagen Beetles dispense surfers, kids play soccer—and jerk stands abound.

As I parked, jerk touts vied for my attention. I made my way to the place Weston had suggested, Mickey Burke's Number One Jerk Center, a row of open-sided huts with a bar in back serving the coldest Red Stripe beer in town.

It was a rowdy scene. The main hut was packed with people shouting orders to pitmasters, who tonged slabs of pork from the pit onto the counter, then chopped away with cleavers. Smoke wafted, acrid with pepper and the smoldering hardwood stakes that make up the grill, or patter. (One aspect of authentic jerk barbecue is that wood serves as not only the fuel but also the cooking surface; the equipment itself is a flavoring element.)

While I waited to order, I chatted with Joel Martin, a frequent visitor from Brooklyn. "Nobody cooks like they do here in Boston," he enthused. "And Mickey, he is the wickedest of the wicked."

I took a table in the eating hut next to a group of college-age Italians making helpless fanning gestures in front of their mouths. My own ample sampler plate came, and sure enough, it was wickedly good: chicken and pork, grilled lobster, and red snapper smothered in onion, okra, and fresh thyme.

The heat of jerk smacks you at first, then deepens as you eat, the flavors mingling in your mouth in intricate balances: Scotch bonnet peppers, intense but light and almost orangy; rich Jamaican allspice; strong undertones of garlic; hints of ginger and cinnamon. I ate it with roasted breadfruit and an oversize hush puppy called a festival. Both were bland and slightly sweet and calmed my mouth, providing little silences in the opera of jerk.

Afterward I grabbed a last Red Stripe and wandered to the beach. A surfing competition was under way, and a crowd looked on from bamboo benches built into rock outcroppings. A Rasta emcee manned the mike: "He lookin' for more, but de wave is not cooperatin'." Then out in the bay, the surfer pulled a stunt, standing on his head on the board. "Oooh, now, what is that?" shrieked the emcee as the spectators roared approval.

I was back at Mickey's at just past dawn the next morning. Roosters crowed and the sun came up for the last time on six grill-bound pigs snuffling underneath the trees. I'd arranged with Burke to take a look behind the scenes, and as the crew arrived, drifting in one by one, people set to work sweeping up the previous day's ashes, scrubbing the chopping boards, and trimming branches for the patter.

One of the last to arrive was Burke himself, a wiry guy with a cigarette and Red Stripe in hand. In his early 40s, he has been turning out jerk at Boston beach for more than 20 years; before he took over, the business was his grandfather's. He buys his pigs from a nearby farmer, and concocts his jerk paste in big batches in a nearby kitchen. "We mill it," he told me, making a cranking gesture. He ticked off ingredients: Scotch bonnet peppers, tomatoes, onions, garlic, celery, paprika, allspice, rosemary, green onions, wild cinnamon, ginger. Plus a few ingredients he said were his, and his alone.

"It got *everyting*," he said, grinning, as he sharpened the knife he would soon use to butcher the pigs.

In the pit area, other team members were cutting chicken and sifting cornmeal, everyone working hard but joking nonstop. Discussions of last night's cricket matches were interspersed with bantering refrains of "Now, ya buy me a beer!" and "Got no money, mon." Eventually, Burke's brother-in-law, Wayne Morgan, showed up with a bucket of milled paste, and as spices were added, the boss came over now and then to adjust the taste.

By eight-thirty, things were heating up in the pit, where the wood burned in a corner fire; later, the hot coals would be shoveled under the patter. Finally, the jerk was ready—a thick mortar that Burke and his crew rubbed into the meat. Sides of pork were spread out on the hardwood grill, where they would slow-cook for three hours to produce that steeped-in taste. By noon, the first surfers would drift in, the wall of roadside speakers would crank out the vibe, and Boston beach's daily food party would begin all over again.

"Jerk," writes grill guru Steven Raichlen in *The Barbecue! Bible*, "is simultaneously a dish, a cooking method, and a way of life." It is history, too. This fiery food traces to a fiery period of Jamaica's past, when former slaves known as Maroons—the name comes from *cimarrón*, Spanish for "fugitive"—waged guerrilla war against the British. They hunted wild boar from strongholds in the Blue Mountains, where their descendants still live today.

One overcast afternoon I drove up the Rio Grande Valley into the heart of Maroon territory. In the remote village of Moore Town, I met Wallace Sterling, a smiling, quick-witted man in his 40s who serves as the elected colonel—the mayor, more or less—of the present-day Maroons. We sat on his porch amid intermittent bursts of rain and talked local history. "Our forefathers were living in the hills," Sterling said. "When they were far from home on the hunt, they would cook the meat they caught over a slow fire and cover it with palm leaves to smoke it. This was the beginning of jerk."

The choice of wood was crucial to traditional jerk, he told me. People knew the different hardwoods for the flavors they imparted. As for seasoning, the original Maroons favored a pepper called a bird pepper, smaller and hotter than the Scotch bonnet, today's standard. Hunters would crush these peppers and mix them with salt to make a dry seasoning.

"They would keep this spice mix with them in the forest," Sterling said. "Of course, over time they added more ingredients." From his pocket he pulled a piece of cinnamon bark and passed it to me. It had a sharp aroma. "Wild cinnamon," he said. "Very pepperish."

There are still wild pigs in these hills, Sterling told me, and people still hunt them. Barbecuing is a deep tradition in this lonely, lovely valley. So deep that when I asked Sterling about the etymology of jerk—did the word reflect how the meat is flipped on the grill, or did it derive, as I'd read somewhere, from the patois expression for spearing an animal?—he was perplexed. "*Jerk* is an original word," he said, shrugging.

Later, we hiked up into the forest. It's a forbiddingly beautiful landscape, with clouds hanging low over steep hills, and a path diving among shaggy monsters of bamboo and giant tree-ferns; you could imagine someone who knows this landscape escaping into it without a trace.

During my last few days in Jamaica, I escaped into these mountains, too, staying at Strawberry Hill. The resort, one of the island's most elegant, is a heaven of tropical gardens and cottages with majestic porch views.

This lush area is coffee country, where the dry morning trade wind, known as the "doctor breeze," and the cold, wet night air, the "undertaker breeze," provide prime growing conditions. At Craighton Coffee Estate, near Strawberry Hill, I climbed the hillside with Alton Bedward, a coffee roaster, and watched pickers fill sacks with ripe Blue Mountain coffee cherries. Then I stopped at the 1805 manor house for a cup of the estate's premium roast—its scent intense, its taste sweet and nutty.

For me, the jerk trail ended at a patio dinner table at Strawberry Hill, the lights of Kingston glittering below as I tucked into a feast: crab gnocchi, plantain soup, mashed potatoes with avocado, and, of course, jerk chicken. This was a preparation mellower than I'd had down at Boston beach. It had the same tantalizing melody, but was played in a lower key. I'd had Jamaica loud, and now I had it quiet.

It isn't always true that the flavor of a place mirrors that of its food. But sometimes it does. "The heat of jerk can be intense at first," says Catherine Peplowski, Strawberry Hill's executive chef. "But then the taste dangles on your palate. It stays there for a long while."

Breakfast

by Tim Morris
from *Gastronomica*

A creative writing professor from the University of Texas, Morris gets inside the scene at his local diner with a masterly touch for describing the place and its people. What he also captures is the meaning the place holds for him—and the sacramental power of certain meals.

I t has to be the same thing every day, but the waitress isn't always the same. So I order in a way that's clear, alert, and respectful. "I'd like the number two, with eggs over easy, sausage, and whole wheat toast [spacing my requests neatly so she can write it all down, then pausing]. And I'd like grits instead of hashbrowns, *if I could*." That conditional tag is very important. I mean, I'm ordering, but I'm not *ordering*. I'm making allowance for the kitchen being out of something, for the short-order cook to exert some discretion, for the waitress to tire of my routine and interject some substitution. Nobody ever interjects. There are always grits aplenty to fill in for the hashbrowns.

Once I get the food (with water, please, *just water*, not coffee, though they always put 95 cents for coffee on the check, so that every day I have to explain to the man at the register that I haven't had coffee, and it's the same man every day, so he knows, but the situation never fails to perplex him, so it needs a fresh explanation every morning)—once I get the food, I don't have to deal with social niceties anymore. I'm in the most intimate of intimate situations, in self-communion.

Eggs first, with a little salt. Two yolks to be mopped up with the whole wheat toast. Since there are two whole slices of toast, there's usually a half-slice left over, to be eaten with honey or mixed-fruit jelly—never strawberry or apple, and Concord grape only at a pinch. I keep track of which tiny jelly tubs are in stock at which tables, and though I've never actually made the decision to sit at one table rather than another on account of its supply of jelly, it's always there in the back of my mind.

After the toast is gone, I match the sausages (three patties, though some days they only bring two, which is better for my cholesterol, so I don't complain) with the grits. The grits come in a little bowl on top of the main plate, unbuttered, unsalted. I parse the sausage into bite-sizes with my fork and put the right amount of grits on top of each piece. I try to end up with the perfect ratio, so that I have no sausageless grits and no gritless sausage.

The sausage course is not a labor-intensive, two-handed business like the egg portion of the meal, so I can go back to the book I was reading before they brought my food. I prop it up on the plastic box that holds Sweet'N Low, which, since I don't have coffee, I don't need. I'm following Bobby Thomson's baseball across the continent with Don DeLillo, or sledging the ice shelf with Shackleton, when I run out of grits and sausage, sip the last of my water (with a lemon slice today, for a blessing), leave a dollar as tip, and pick up the greasy check. It's $5.60, and after I knock off the 95 cents I don't owe for coffee, my total with tax is five dollars and one cent, exact change, except Tuesdays when the two-egg breakfast is the special at $3.25 and I never can remember the tax on $3.25. Every weekday, every week of the school year, August to May.

I caught the breakfast habit young. My grandfather started every day with a bowl of Kellogg's Corn Flakes in half-and-half. He'd eat them at the snack bar in his house. Like other 1940s houses, my grandfather's had some traditional living areas and other areas that reminded one of diners or taverns, which is where he'd rather have been spending his time anyway. Brought up in the house of a cereal-eater, my mother set me on a cereal path. Every morning, I had the same thing: cereal in whole milk, poured into one of the shatterproof beige Melmac bowls that endured my whole childhood. I had more milk on the side in a rubbery plastic cup that was similarly indestructible. I ate with a silver-plated spoon representing one of three Presidents of the United States—Washington, Adams, or Jefferson, we never got the rest of the set—on the handle, with one of that President's great achievements pictured in the bowl. When I drew the spoon out of my mouth, leftover milk would pool into the Louisiana Purchase or the Farewell to the Troops.

I say I had the same thing, but I certainly did not. I covered the whole cereal waterfront. I went from tasteless tufts of shredded wheat and cindery Grape-Nuts all the way over to Cocoa Puffs that left the milk dark brown, Apple Jacks that left it a vomity pastel pink, and a defunct cereal that I still long for called Stars, that left the milk a deep caramel, good enough to drink for dessert. I ate representational Crispy Critters and abstract Sugar Smacks. I listened to Rice Krispies and smelled Froot Loops and felt the texture of Honeycomb and gazed on Stax, that marvelous 1970s polygonal cereal that filled with milk in unpredictable stochastic ways. I fell for an ad campaign that suggested that Wheat Chex were an R-rated cereal for adult audiences. I felt very grown-up eating them. Then the next week I'd go back and eat childish Quisp and Quake, two cereals that promoted themselves as bitter rivals when in fact they were the exact same stuff in different shapes. I liked every kind of cereal except Life, which had a disagreeable saccharine aftertaste. I still won't eat Life. The hell with Mikey.

Now I can't take milk any more. Intolerant, they call it, a cranky middle-aged word. On weekends I struggle to get down a bowl or two of organic six-grain Heritage Bites with lite soy milk, but it just isn't any fun. What gets me out of bed in the morning during the week, what fortifies me for a nine-thirty class I cringe at the thought of (though it's always OK when I get there), is the two-egg breakfast at the local meat market.

It's literally a meat market. This is not some metaphor for a pickup joint. You really don't want to pick up singles at breakfast, not these ones, anyway. These ones are either in tracksuits and haven't showered, or they're just out of the shower, letting their hair dry, smelling unevenly of cologne and chlorine. Or they're eighty years old, the modal age in this meat market each

Thursday, when emeritus professors from my university assemble to tell stories and set back their diet regimens a whole week— after which they'll converge on the meat market again and resume the process.

Until last year, you ate at tables right in front of the meat counters. You put away your sausage and eggs while staring at oozing tenderloins and splayed fryers. I can't imagine this wasn't a code violation. Ultimately they built a thin wall between the meat and the eaters. The top half is glass, so if you rear up out of your chair you can still see the butcher cases on the other side.

Meat is a prominent theme in breakfast at the market. It's not quite that there are no plant foods at all—they do have those grits—but you really would rather not be forced to eat there with vegetarian friends from out of town. This is Texas, after all, where an alfalfa sprout is something that grows up and gets fed to a steer.

It's legitimately unhealthy, all this animal food, all these animal fats. (One thing free of animal fat is the butter, which is totally ersatz.) Hour after hour, the waitresses come out of the kitchen, balancing plates on their grease-stained sleeves. The plates are full of sausage, bacon, eggs, ham, Canadian bacon, breakfast steak, pork roll, chicken-fried steak, chicken-fried chicken, hashbrowns. The food is salty, oily, fatty, greasy, gummy, and overprocessed. Pools of yellow oil float on top of the eggs, draining off to mingle with the artificial butter that melts off the toast. Plate after plate is served to people who really don't look like they should be ordering this stuff. I'm overweight; my fellow diners are excessively so. Most are AARP-eligible. Several are wheezy in that distressing way that indicates congestive disorders of the whole system. They start to cough after the third flapjack. One old gent is connected by tubing to an oxygen tank. He wheels his tank in on a little handtruck, sits down, and orders biscuits with sausage gravy.

The meat market has a Texas decor to match its Texas cuisine. It starts with a stenciled cactus design around the top of the walls. Half of the dining room is devoted to dead animals in perky poses. You eat beneath a duck startled permanently into flight. A fish opens its gills wide as it jumps. These trophies are standard-issue Texas-diner highlights. They'd look more at home out west of Sweetwater in a cinderblock jerky shed on some farm-to-market road. There hasn't been a fish that size caught here in Arlington in years, if ever. There was a possum in our yard once. My wife killed it with a shovel. We didn't think to stuff and mount it. Maybe we should have.

The other half of the place is paneled in rustic wood, and its central feature is a big photo of the Three Stooges. Larry and Moe are holding Curly's mouth open and spooning mashed potatoes into him. I like that one. The other wall candy consists of old license plates and bits of barbed wire. The license plates say things like "1 TEXAN" and "AH NUTS." One reads "NO AL G." An item from the Bush 2000 campaign, it seems, but it was up there long before anyone ever heard of Al Gore. It must have belonged to someone who owned a pool-cleaning business.

Across from the Three Stooges are tennis-ball cans on the register counter with coin-slots cut in the lid so you can give pennies to palsied children. Near the register they've taped a *Fort Worth Star-Telegram* review of the place from 1985 which praises its home-cookin' atmosphere. The tape has dried out completely but somehow the review stays on the wall. I wouldn't have bothered to put up the review; the place only got a star-and-a-half to begin with and I can't imagine it's improved.

You can buy extra things near the register. Not condoms, thank God, but useless things like gumballs, short handfuls of redskin peanuts, and 75-cent capsules of Tic-Tacs, orange flavor only, everybody bought all the mint ones a long time ago. Near the vending machines, people leave business cards in a broken-handled mug. Better Tree Service. Kate-Lynn Psychic Readings. Concealed Handgun Classes by Bruce. Once I put my own card in the mug: Director of Graduate Studies / Literature and Rhetoric Ph.D. Programs / University of Texas at Arlington. I never got any calls from people who had seen the card at the meat market, at least I don't think I did.

There's a pretty stable group of regulars, as far as I can tell. I get there at 8:05, after I drop my son at school, so I can only speak for the 8-8:30 crowd. One woman is always there before I arrive and after I leave. She seems to run a business from her table, which is always covered with invoices. She talks on a cell phone while she eats. One guy, very cleanly dressed, holds court all morning at another table, with another cell phone. Different people eat with him every day. Cops eat here, and firemen, and two guys from the local burger shop on busman's holiday. Another guy, immense, with brick-red neck and forearms, wearing a ball cap, takes business calls at his table, too. He has a tiny purple phone clipped to his belt. It looks like one of those toy phones that come filled with fruit-flavored candy. Instead of ringing, it plays the first four bars of the "Barney" theme.

I never meet anyone I know at the meat market. That's odd, because it's a half-mile from my house. Is this an indicator of how many people I know? Sometimes someone will come in and I'm sure I recognize them. I rack my brains trying to figure out who it is. A county judge who's been in the papers lately? A wanted criminal? Maybe they just remind me of some obscure character actor in old movies. It can't *be* Woodrow Parfrey, it just looks like him.

One day I look up at the next table and know immediately who it is. It's a former pro athlete who has faded from star to backup to broadcaster to celebrity hanger-on. He plays at pro-am golf tournaments and hosts occasional Teens Against Drugs marathons on the cable access channel. Now, from the indiscreet conversation I truly can't help but overhear, he seems to be working full-time for an evangelical group that is trying to interject some Bible-based living into Dallas boardrooms.

The new job isn't going well, from what I can gather. Unlike the locker rooms he grew up in, his new office features women: women who file, women who make calls and copies, women who bring coffee, women who run departments, and a woman who supervises him from the next cube over. Between mouthfuls of bacon, the old star explains that he has always had a hard time working alongside women he's physically attracted to. They smell better than ballplayers, and they wear filmy sweaters that they take off and drape over their desk chairs by mid-day, so he can see their bra straps peeking out from beneath their tops. He has been praying a lot about this.

"I had it all," he asserts, not real modestly. "I was a college All-American, and a high draft pick, and I made twelve All-Star teams, and I was a starter on a World Championship team. But now at work I talk to Amy, or Dawn, or Melissa, and they don't really know that. They are not attracted to me. I've always had women attracted to me. Now it's the other way round. I'm attracted to them. I've just had to put things into the Lord's hands." I finish my grits, hoping for his sake that the Lord doesn't feel like writing this guy some weird erotic scenario.

The waitresses are regulars too, of course, in a sense. The meat market must pay well enough, because even in an economic boom the same women who have worked there for years are still at the same jobs. I know which ones work which tables, and when most tables are free (and they usually are), I try to spread myself around from day to day. I like the gentle Mexican woman who calls everyone "Hon." She sees me reading and tells me that she's had to stop reading books.

"That's too bad," I say.

"Yeah, but I had to. I was reading all these romances. And they were taking over my life. That's what my doctor said. You start reading these books, and then you want to do what's in them, and you want your life to go like that. So I'm not supposed to read books any more."

I look down at my book. *Lolita.* I cover it with my napkin. "Over easy, right Hon?" she asks over her shoulder as she walks away.

One waitress abuses all the customers. She's popular with the old professors. They flirt with her and she tells them they're gonna need a whole lot of Viagra to make good on their promises. I'm getting the last grit out of the bowl with my spoon when she comes up. "You didn't like that at all, did you? Hell, I think I'll take that plate right back and put someone else's food on it. Won't even have to wash it."

Another waitress doesn't like me, but I sit at her table every few days to show my disinterestedness. She's tall and blonde and built like a *Sports Illustrated* swimsuit model. Every other middle-aged overweight guy in the place (a large selection) tries to hit on her. I can understand why she might not be overjoyed to see me. I forced myself not to look at her for six months, even when she was serving my eggs. She eventually started talking to me and even smiled once. This is the extent of my feminist praxis. Think globally, act locally.

Another waitress cries when she goes behind the kitchen partition. Since the partition is just a frame of two-by-fours, it doesn't offer much privacy. It's as soundproof as any other eight feet of air. The waitress details her life to the short-order cook. Her first husband, father of the child she's trying to get in her custody suit, never kissed her after the wedding. "And he only did it then cause everybody was taking our picture." Her second husband owes her a boat, or at least the payments she made on it before he divorced her and took the boat away with him. Her boyfriend doesn't like the kid, so she's going to move out after she gets custody. My problem with my eggs—they're a little hard this morning—loses its gravity.

She walks out, composed, and gets my plate. She says to me, "You're finished, you're done. I'm always done but I'm never finished." She laughs.

I'm not sure why I eat here every day. The food isn't good for me. It's not particularly cheap. I belong to no community here. Nobody even knows my name. *Cheers,* it isn't.

When I was ten, my father would take us all—my mom, my brother, and me—to a diner for supper once a week. I always had the same thing, fried filet of flounder. Lemon, no tartar sauce. The waitresses were named Connie and Maxine. We lived through Maxine's cancer as if she were a soap character. When she was out doing chemo, Connie kept up the narrative. On my birthday Connie would lean over and kiss me—I say "would" because it happened two years in a row. She knew everything my father was up to. She knew what he was doing at work and what movies he liked, to say nothing of the way he liked his steak. She was nice to my mom, too. There wasn't anything going on. At least I don't think so. Connie was fifteen years older than my dad, and men didn't go in for that sort of affair in the 1960s, did they? They slept with students or secretaries, not with fifty-year-old waitresses—unless, like my grandfather, they were sixty themselves. We always kept Grandpa away from Connie.

Connie was family, family in a starched apron with precise mannerisms. She made sure that my brother didn't get any parsley on his plate and that his meat didn't touch his french fries. She looked like Marjorie Main in *The Harvey Girls,* only pretty.

Then one day I was at the strip mall, going into the K-Mart. Leaving the store was Connie, obviously Connie—I knew her better than most people in that town—but very hard to place *as* Connie, because she was in shorts and a halter top, wrinkled, her hair down out of its neat waitress bun. She was pushing a stroller with two kids in it that I'd never heard of. A fat short woman at her side—the kids' mom, who was Connie's daughter, it seemed— was trying to persuade her that they should have bought whatever they should have bought. Connie looked at me in terrible pain, and I didn't say hello. Next Saturday, she brought my flounder like nothing happened. She was family again, but I didn't know her at all.

I don't want an extended family at the meat market. I just want my food, and I want it to be the same food every day, so that I don't have to think, so that I can take completely for granted one part of my daily battle for survival. (I exaggerate, you say, but you are not neurotic. Meals and commutes and housework are a snap for you, just part of that wonderful style that nobody does quite the way you do. Provided you are a character in a TV commercial.)

Nor do I want to eat breakfast at home. I feed my son a bowl of cereal every day. He's still young, still tolerant. My wife rarely eats breakfast. When she does it's different every day: a bagel, some yogurt, *huevos rancheros,* Weetabix, a kipper. Weetabix or kippers because she is not Texan or even American, but Irish. Irish people hate routine. If my wife had to have two eggs with sausage, toast, and grits every morning, it would blight her life. Yet oddly enough, breakfast in Ireland is the most predictable part of one's day.

The Irish breakfast: first, people get up and have a chat. About half an hour into the chat, someone suggests the idea of a nice cup of tea. It seems to be the first cup of tea ever suggested on the island. Well, what should we do? Put the kettle on. Will you have milk with that? Four million cups of tea are consumed every morning in Ireland, every one with milk, but the option is always considered and discussed.

And after we are intent on our tea for a good while, the thought of food occurs to someone, who, with a vacant and puzzled expression, suggests that one might eat to stave off hunger. Right then, what'll we do? I'll do—what do you think now—an egg? Now an egg would be lovely. An egg is just the man, first thing. But now, on its own, wouldn't an egg be a lonely sight? Shall we have a rasher with that? Do we have rashers in? (Every house in Ireland has rashers in, every morning.) Now while that rasher's on the grill, what do you say to some black and white pudding? Just the job.

And then, as the inevitable meal assembles itself, it occurs spontaneously to everybody in the room that what this breakfast lacks, what would distinguish it from all other breakfasts, what would, in fact, top it off as the masterpiece of morning meals, the veritable dog's dinner of breakfasts, would be *a grilled tomato*. "Ah," says everyone, with the indrawn breath that means "Yes" in Dublin, "a tomato, that would be perfect. That would be just the thing, that would set it off, sure that would be something *different*." Different from the last six hundred breakfasts principally in that it will be a different tomato, the last six hundred tomatoes being unavailable because they have already been eaten. And so it goes.

Everyone has their morning routine. It would be too hard to come back to reality without it. Some of us like to conceal routine behind theatrics. Me, I'm blunt. I like to go where nobody knows my name, but they know, when they see me darkening the door, "over easy, sausage, whole wheat toast." And could I, *could* I, have the grits?

Appetite

by Louise DeSalvo

from *Crazy in the Kitchen*

Literary scholar DeSalvo's often searing memoir depicts how food expressed her family's dysfunctional dynamic, and how that played out into her own adulthood. Luckily, by the time in her life this excerpt covers, she'd learned to deal with all her food issues—more or less.

On our last trip to Italy, to the South, to find my ancestors' villages, Ernie and I have eaten a lot of splendid pizza topped with the finest and freshest ingredients, cooked in wood-burning ovens. We have eaten pizza every day. Pizza marinara, with tomatoes, garlic, oregano—the original pizza; pizza *canzone del mare* (song-of-the-sea pizza), with cherry tomatoes, basil, garlic; pizza *verdi,* pizza with buffalo milk mozzarella, anchovy fillets, fresh parsley, capers, garlic, arugula; pizza *alla melanzana* (with eggplant); pizza *con cardofi* (with artichokes) and *con cipolle* (with onions). And, of course, pizza Margherita.

In a bookstore, I have discovered the cookbook *La Pizza: The True Story from Naples.* This is my fifth pizza cookbook. But it is definitive, because it relates the origin of pizza, tells how it is cooked in the finest pizzerias in Naples.

I have read it, underlined it, taken notes from it, especially on the chapter "Pizza Taboos," listing the rules for pizza laid out by the Associazione Vera Pizza Napoletana. Yes, there are rules for making an authentic pizza, and strict ones. You can't use any kind of fat in the dough, including olive oil; you must knead the dough by hand, although you can use a special pizza-kneading device approved by the Association; you can't use a rolling pin to flatten the dough; you can't use a baking tin; you can't use an electric oven—only a wood-fueled, bell-shaped oven.

The aim is to produce a pizza that will be "supple, perfectly cooked, fragrant and framed by a high, soft border."

Pizza is taken very seriously in the land of my ancestors. People argue about it. People come to blows about it. You would stand a chance of getting away with disrespecting someone's mother sooner than you would of getting away with disrespecting someone's favorite pizza. I take pizza very seriously too, and when we arrive home, I begin what my family calls my Pizza Period.

Before this, there have been the Risotto Period; the Tagine Period; the Paella Period; the High-Heat Roasting Period; the Slow Cooker Period; the Stir-fried Period; the Artisan Baker Period; the Homemade Pasta Period; the Lasagna Period; the Creative Salad Period; the Panini Period; the Homemade Yogurt Period, the Homemade Ricotta Period (a very short period, because making ricotta is such a pain in the ass and the result doesn't taste as good as the ricotta from my favorite Italian market); the Homemade Ice Cream and Homemade Waffle Cone Period; the *Minestra* Period; the Tuscan Period; the Ligurian Period; the Pugliese Period.

During each of these periods, I have purchased cookbooks, special ingredients, special equipment. I have so much kitchen equipment, so many cookbooks, so many special ingredients that any thief who comes to our house should avoid the jewelry box and head straight for the cupboards.

I *love* all my cooking equipment. I talk to my appliances. I praise them for jobs well done. And I don't yell at them if something doesn't go right; I just give them some time off. I don't want to get into a power struggle with my equipment.

I love my kitchen. It's not a gorgeously decorated, high-end, industrial-stove, giant refrigerator, handmade-tile-and-back-splashes kind of kitchen. It's an ordinary serviceable kitchen, with a small prep area, but it's a cheerful kitchen, and it's right next to my study, so I can run back and forth all day long, from writing to cooking, from cooking to writing. And I do. My kitchen is my refuge. My cooking makes my writing possible.

When we travel, we look for equipment and ingredients to lug home from wherever we've been—an authentic mortar and pestle (from Genoa, very heavy, carried by Ernie); salted capers (from Sicily, bought in Taormina); bottles of tuna (from Liguria, caught in the waters off Camogli); dried wild marjoram (from the area near San Rocco di Camogli in Liguria); dried wild mushrooms (from Varese Ligure); peperoncini and sun-dried tomatoes (from Albero-bello, bought from an extraordinarily handsome young man who looks like one of my sons); wild honey and handmade pasta, estate-bottled olive oils and wine, and bottles of aged balsamic vinegar (from Don Alfonso's in Sant' Agata sui Due Golfi on the Sorrento peninsula). And whenever we visit Liguria, we always bring back dried wild herbs—marjoram, basil, and oregano (all from the forest on the Portofino peninsula; gathered and dried by monks).

Sometimes we return with food you're not supposed to bring into the country: fresh wild fennel, scamorza cheese, an amazing salami made on a farm we visit. With every excellent meal I make using my special ingredients, I drive away the phantom of my mother's kitchen, try to obliterate the want of my ancestors.

My husband and I don't go out to many restaurants; like many Italians, we prefer to eat at home. But when I order something in a restaurant, on the rare occasions when we go out, I am in an agony of waiting. I do not make good dinner table conversation. I am not a chit-chatter. I might be seated next to a Pulitzer Prize winner, and I don't give a shit about whether the book was hard to write. All I care about is *When will the food come? When will the food come? When will the fucking food come?*

I am not good company in a restaurant. I like to have complete control of my food. Which means cooking what I like just the way I like it, and serving it attractively, but certainly not in little piles or towers. At home, there's none of this waiting around for someone to bring you your food.

Restaurants. I don't understand them, don't understand giving a stranger control over what you eat. If my own mother fucked up my food, why should I trust a stranger?

But in Italy—first in Tuscany, then in Liguria, all over Sicily, and, most recently, in Puglia and Campania—I have learned to enter restaurants with joyful anticipation; learned to love eating in restaurants; learned to love choosing my food; learned to trust the chef and the staff; learned to trust the pace of the meal; learned to visit kitchens at the invitation of the chef with a feeling akin to the intense love you had for someone when you were in high school. (Though I still hate eating out in the United States.)

Why? Because in Italy, even in small, unprepossessing places, people care about food. Really care. They get teary eyed over little tomatoes grown close enough to the sea so their flavor intensifies. They caress eggplants the way a mother caresses a baby's bottom. They sniff melons before they buy them, the way an elegant woman chooses the finest perfume. They care about food in a way my mother never cared about food. And they want you to care, too. They want to please you, for they know that food is about pleasure. About appetite, and its satisfaction.

Once, while we are savoring wine and a small meal in an *enoteca* in Chiavari in Liguria, we see the owner at a table in the back, cleaning fresh porcini for the next day's service. He's doing this while we're eating our dinner.

On the table is a huge wicker basket containing the porcini. He has his tools—a knife for paring away imperfections, a brush for cleaning, some immaculate napkins for wiping off the dirt— lined up beside him. He cleans the porcini where we can see him work, to show the care he takes, to show how it should be done, to show the respect he accords this magnificent fungus, but also to show the respect he accords his patrons.

For all the time we're there, he scrapes and brushes and cleans and holds each mushroom close to his eyes to examine it. Each takes a long time to clean, and I watch in fascination, learning the meaning of patience and care. As he works, he smiles. His work is satisfying, and he's doing it as if there is nothing more important to do in all this world.

At La Cucina di Nonna Nina in San Rocco di Camogli in Liguria, for the first time in my life, I eat *corzetti,* a pasta made with wine, rolled out, cut into circles, then stamped between two pieces of hand-carved wood. At Nonna Nina, one side of the *corzetti* bears the restaurant's name; the other, the rays of the sun. The indentations and raised surfaces of the pasta introduce subtle differences in the texture of each bite. Tears come to my eyes as I taste. I am happy. I am in the moment.

The owner's wife notices my pleasure. She introduces herself—Signora Rosalia Dalpian—and she invites me into the kitchen to meet her husband, the chef, Signore Paolo Dalpian. He shows me the *corzetti* stamp, which has been in his family for generations.

La Cucina di Nonna Nina specializes in traditional dishes made in the old way from heirloom family recipes. Over the years, my husband and I eat there a score of times. Each time, there is something new to savor; the menu changes with the seasons, and with available ingredients.

One spring, Signore Dalpian presents a ricotta torte he makes at the beginning of the season when the grass is at its sweetest, which means that the cheese will be at its sweetest. We travel back the following autumn, and there is no ricotta torte: ricotta torte is made only in spring, Signore Dalpian says. So we travel back the following spring to have it again. And yes, it's worth the journey.

In Recco, in Liguria, we eat at Da ö Vittorio because we want to savor their famed focaccia *col formaggio,* made with Crescenza or Invernizzina cheese made nearby. Only certain restaurants can advertise that they make this specialty; in Recco, famous for this focaccia, its production is scrutinized and regulated to make sure the approved restaurants serving it meet stringent standards. It is a huge focaccia, its dough is flaky and extremely thin, its melted cheese tangy and unctuous. The food writer Fred Plotkin calls it "the most addictive food on the planet." It is served in wedges, one huge focaccia shared among several diners. After our meal, we talk to the proprietors, the brothers Gianni and Vittorio Bisso, about how the focaccia is made. Back home, it is something we dream about. And when we return to Liguria, one of our first stops is to this restaurant.

On our second trip, after our meal, we talk to the brothers for over an hour. They remember us from our last visit; they're glad we've come back. During our conversation, we mention we would like to make our own *corzetti.* So Gianni gets a map, shows us a village—Varese Ligure—in the mountains, where we can buy a stamp for embossing *corzetti*. He takes the time to make sure we understand his directions. We travel there, buy two, make *corzetti* all year long.

On our most recent trip, when we arrive at Da ö Vittorio, we feel as if we've come home. After our focaccia, we're taken to see the special ovens; shown a model of the wagon that delivered focaccia through the streets of Recco during the Bisso brothers' grandfather's time; and on a tour through the restaurant's archive to see photos taken during the World War II bombardment of Recco, which nearly obliterated the village. The restaurant was one of the few buildings left standing.

In Sicily, in Aci Trezza, north of Catania, at a restaurant over-looking lemon groves and the Ionian Sea, I am eating pasta *ca Norma* (pasta *alla Norma,* in Italian)—pasta with sautéed egg-plant, tomatoes, basil, and ricotta salata. This is the third time in a week we are dining here, the third time I've had this traditional Sicilian pasta.

The pasta is homemade; it is in the shape of an elongated tube pierced with a very small hole. I want to learn how it is made; I want to reproduce it back home.

I summon the courage to ask the owner. He obliges me by giving me his recipe for the dough, and telling me the strands are shaped by wrapping strips of dough around a knitting needle. No special tools are used; just the knitting needle any Sicilian house-hold would have.

The owner tells me what kind of flour to use. I tell him I doubt I'll be able to find it back home. So he goes into the kitchen and comes out with a packet for me. And tells me if I can't find it, to write him, he'll send it. He wants me to make this at home; he's happy I care enough about this food to want to make it myself. When we leave, we say we'll come back the next time we come to Sicily, and we mean it.

In the Panificio Maccarini in San Rocco in Liguria, I am buying packages of pasta, ones I can't get in the United States—*troffiette, corzetti,* special small oblongs of lasagna—and, of course, Ligurian olive oil. (In the Milan airport, my husband will complain as he trundles fifteen pounds of pasta and several liters of olive oil, all too precious to be stowed, from one end of the airport to the other. But he's used to it. This is the way we always return home: our bags stuffed with delicacies.)

The owner of the *panificio,* Anna Maccarini, notices my excitement. Even though there are many people waiting for her to serve them, she stops and calls someone from the kitchen to help so she can teach me recipes for what I buy. She teaches me to use the lasagna noodles to make a recipe that's not baked: you use a low pan, she says, and you layer the pasta with a tomato sauce (with carrot, celery, and onion, the vegetables removed, macerated, and returned to the sauce). She teaches me her recipe for pesto. I complain about the basil in the United States.

She asks me what I'll do with the aniseed. I give her my recipe for a bread I make with orange rind, almonds, and ground aniseed, a family favorite. She writes down the ingredients.

I speak almost no Italian, but from years of living with my grandmother, I can understand everything Anna Maccarini says. Using gestures, helped along by my husband's meager Italian, we exchange a score of recipes before it's time to leave.

Signora Maccarini comes out from behind the counter. Hugs me. Kisses me. For a moment, though I am in my fifties, I want her to be my mother. I have found a food friend. A woman I return to each time we visit Liguria.

It is here, in a land that starved my grandparents until they were forced to leave for America, that I truly learn the pleasures of the Italian table.

Way to Go

by Jason Sheehan

From *WestWord*

> Denver's alternative newsweekly gives the prolific Jason Sheehan lots of room for his discursive restaurant reviews, each a mini-novel in its own right. Even though you may never dine at this same restaurant, anyone who truly loves food has had a night like this.

People who say you can never have too much of a good thing just haven't tried hard enough.

It's Saturday night—technically Sunday morning, but not by much—and I am lying on my back in the middle of my living room, all the lights out, with my arms and legs splayed like a man carelessly run down and left for dead by an out-of-control mathematical proof that one person most certainly *can* have too much of a good thing. My belly is bloated over the top of my favorite party jeans. And I smell *bad,* like something a pig found buried in an alley behind a wine bar, like overpriced Italian Chianti, cigarettes and the intoxicating, powerful and dirty funk of truffles.

White truffles, specifically. Good ones. Not quite as strong and a little less delicate than their black cousins, but still powerful stuff. If a mushroom junkie were to break into my house right now and sniff me, he could probably tell exactly what variety of truffles I'd overindulged in—white Piedmont, black Umbrian, you name it—because the stink is oozing from my pores and rolling off me in waves. But I live in a good neighborhood now, not the kind of place where roving gangs of unemployed fungologists go around breaking into people's houses, so I am confident that I'll be left alone with my misery.

It was the "rabbit, three ways" at Luca d'Italia that did this to me.

No, that's not fair. It was me that did this to me. It was me eating at least part of each of the eleven courses that came my way previous to the rabbit that did it. But it was the rabbit that put me over the edge. Had chef/owner Frank Bonanno and his team of white-coated pushers in the kitchen chosen to serve rabbit just one way, I would have been fine. Two ways? I still might have made my way to bed without collapsing into a moaning, evil-smelling lump in the middle of the living room. But three ways was simply one way too many.

The game had been to get my mom to eat three weird things—three things she'd never eaten before and would probably never even consider eating under normal circumstances—before the dessert menus hit the table. It would be fun, I figured. My folks are not reckless eaters. Never have been, probably never will be. They are solid, upstanding suburban omnivores, fully satisfied for years with the classic meat-and-potatoes American diet before recently giving that up for on-again/off-again vegetarianism. And even this was a radical departure for them, so when we talk on the phone, they are sometimes justifiably confused and horrified by the things that I eat. And even more so that someone pays me to do it. *Well, he didn't learn it from us,* I can sometimes hear my mom telling her friends when I write about eating fish eyes or deer penis. I had no intention of having them eat anything that strange, just something new. Something different. This was their vacation—their first trip out to Denver to visit me, the prodigal son now made good as a restaurant critic—and I wanted them to have a memorable meal.

Which was why I chose the seven-month-old Luca for our big dinner out: Frank Bonanno doesn't cook anything that's *not* memorable.

Bonanno is obsessed. We've spent hours on the phone gabbing about nothing but fish. Or liver. We like a lot of the same restaurants, are pissed off by a lot of the same chefs. He cooked for me (while I was disguised in a rubber Nixon mask and blaze-orange tuxedo) earlier this year at a Steel Chef competition, laughing maniacally as he put out plate after plate of stunning grub and soundly trouncing his challenger. Bonanno is one of the good guys—a serious, old-school restaurant lifer not made for doing anything else, totally mad for ingredients, bonkers over high-quality product, and crazy for prep and recipes that showcase these at their best.

What's more, he's fearless. Unafraid to take risks and put things he loves on his menus that maybe no one in his right mind would pay money to eat.

Lucky for him, there are plenty of diners in Denver these days fully in their wrong minds. Luckier still, I'm one of them. Even luckier than that, I'd brought guests.

Luca's menu is designed for gluttonous abandon, arranged for wild flights of pairing and sharing, set up in an attempt to make people eat the way the Italians do—with several courses of small plates leading up to the entrees. The portions are small, the plating simple, the combinations divine. If you absolutely refuse to eat the way they want you to, they will do it your way, right away, just like Burger King. But the house won't be happy about it.

To begin, an *amuse* from the kitchen that set the tone for the night and gave us—my parents, my wife and me—something to nibble on while we perused the short, compact wine list and sprawling menu. At first look, the amuse was just an open-faced egg-salad sandwich. Only it wasn't, because egg-salad sandwiches are soggy things that moms make on chewy white bread with the crusts cut off. This, on the other hand, was egg and truffled mayonnaise mounded up on a crusty, toasted piece of bruschetta. It was not the kind of thing you give your kid to eat while he sits on the couch watching *Thundar the Barbarian* cartoons on TV, but it was exactly what you want brought to your table by a young, well-educated waiter (okay, he pronounced bruschetta as "broosketti," but that's forgivable in a restaurant where almost every menu description has at least one misspelling) while you sit in an abstractedly hip dining room burning under the nuclear glow of the orange-on-orange walls, hung with orange-on-orange art (courtesy of Bonanno's partner, Doug Fleischmann, who died in a car accident this summer), trying to eavesdrop on all of the conversations around you as the two- and four-tops crowding the joint swoon over some dishes, puzzle over others. It was grown-up comfort food, done simply and with a weird sense of humor. It was Bonanno through and through.

Antipasti arrived with a flourish and a quick juggling of plates, glasses and silver. This was when I got my mother to eat octopus. Although she'd tried calamari before, octopus was something new, and Luca's braised, marinated and grilled octopus had about as much in common with some strip-mall trattoria calamari as a scallop does with a marshmallow. Here, this straight Sicilian plate came with two meaty tentacles, suckers still attached, that had been beaten ("I saw it on *Iron Chef*," says Bonanno), bruised, braised in white wine with Italian *mirepoix* and cork, then marinated for two days before being flash-grilled and curled lovingly over a pile of white beans drizzled in lemon verbena vinaigrette. Octopi are all muscle (which means they're almost totally edible), but our guy must have been the Schwarzenegger of his peer group, because the fat ends of his tentacles were bigger around than my thumb. They were a little springy on the teeth, sure, but a bite that included bean, oil and tender octopus all together had a wonderful texture and a taste as non-threatening as the mildest white fish. The only trouble was that the tips of the tentacles had gotten overdone in the process of cooking the rest perfectly. They were pleasantly crunchy at first, but once the crunch was gone it was like chewing a mouthful of erasers.

We passed the octopus around, pushing the overcooked bits off to one side, then chased that plate with some of Luca's house-cured bresaola—paper-thin slices of dark, meaty, salted filet mounded up with baby spinach, split black figs sweet as candy and sparks of bright, bittersweet balsamic vinaigrette. After that, there were meatballs—a light mix of veal, pork and beef cut with fresh bread and cooked rare, then bathed in a thin red tomato gravy and topped with two or three fine slivers of Peccorino romano—and *prosciutto di San Daniele*, which arrived as a wonderful mess of wispy prosciutto dampened with extra-virgin olive oil, fresh mozzarella that the kitchen makes itself, chiffonade basil and strips of roasted-by-hand red pepper that were so much better than the greasy little worms of red bell you get out of the can that they made me want to find the closest pepper canner and punch him in the neck. *See? This is what peppers are supposed to taste like!*

And when the waiter came around to clear our plates and reached for the prosciutto, I felt an almost uncontrollable urge to poke him in the hand with my fork. We'd left some scraps and squid ends on the other plates, and I had no problem with those being taken away—but my prosciutto wasn't going anywhere. I kept it next to me like a close friend for the rest of the meal, picking at it and running my finger through the oil whenever there was nothing else in front of me to eat.

My mother had never tasted wild boar before. Now she has, and I hope she flaunts it to her friends back home, because while being an adventurous eater might get you strange looks in the McCarthyian suburbs where I grew up, it's a badge of honor in the world where I live now. And I'm proud of her, because the only comment she had on Luca's wild boar *pappardelle Bolognese* was that it wasn't strange *enough*.

"I don't know, Jay," she said (and to get the full effect, you have to imagine this coming from a tiny woman with a sweet voice, but an accent just a little more nasal than the sort you hear in Minnesota). "I don't know, but I just expected more, ya know? You eat something like wild boar and you expect it to be kinda *different*."

But it's not, really. Wild boar is a bit gamier than regular pork, but pork itself is generally so mild that a so-called wild pig's meat is more deeply flavored only by degrees. Plus, this wild boar was leg meat, ground, seared off, then stewed with a tomato mirepoix, garlic, fennel and red wine, thickened with cream and juiced with butter, which conspired to further mute its essential oddness.

Following the wild boar around the table were three more tasting portions of pasta. The first, a spaghetti carbonara, was disappointing. The noodles swam in a simple yolk-thickened Peccorino romano-butter sauce that lacked any definition other than the minute, crackly pieces of pork-cheek *guanciale* pancetta that studded it like fatty, salted Rice Crispies. It wasn't bad, but there wasn't a lot to it. The spicy lobster *fra diavola,* on the other hand, was truly great, with a sweet red sauce kicked up sharply by crushed red-chile flakes, fat chunks of stewed tomato, and big pieces of buttery lobster-claw meat twisted up in a bed of angel-hair pasta (one of the few pastas in the house that come from DiCecco, and not from the hands of the cooks). The only thing missing was an East Coast address and that ineffable something that comes with it.

The potato gnocchi with crabmeat and lobster sauce was fantastic regardless of address, all my Big Apple bias aside. I used to spend three hours every day hand-making and fork-crimping thousands of gnocchi for one of those New York restaurants I'm always on about, and I can honestly say that this kitchen could've whipped my ass without even trying. The gnocchi were perfect—tender and mushy, but with just enough integrity to stay solid in a rich, velvety brown sauce that was made with absolutely criminal amounts of butter. Add to that a generous portion of flaked back-fin crabmeat so sweet and fresh and gently handled that it tasted like the crabs had been pulled fresh from the ocean and delivered to the kitchen by time warp five minutes before we ordered, and this was a matchless dish, a plate without equal anywhere in town. (As a matter of fact, if you happen to be reading this review from death row and are stuck for what to order as a last meal, tell the guards to call Luca and have a double order sent over right away. That's what I'd do, anyhow.)

We had salads next, most notably a plate of warm artichoke hearts, shaved parmesan and field greens dressed in truffle oil that played nicely with the nutty taste of the 'chokes, the hard sourness of the cheese and the slightly bitter fresh-cut-lawn flavor of the greens but quickly became overpowering. With each successive bite, it seemed that a dark, woody, oily fog was growing around our table. It smelled like fresh rain in a thick forest and what the earth's armpits would smell like if the earth had armpits.

We survived the salad, though, and moved on to our entrees: a plate of massive fresh-water Thai prawns in an emulsion of white wine, white vinegar, garlic, oil and (you guessed it) even more butter. Each crustacean was roughly the size of something that would attack Cleveland in a Saturday-afternoon monster movie. That was followed by a castrated version of chicken picatta that had the strange effect of leaving us feeling incomplete after each bite. The egg batter was soft and silky, the chicken supple and sweetened by the lemon-heavy sauce, and the capers added a sharp, salty tang to the mix. But just when you expected the tastes to go further, they stopped. Something was missing: The flavor was all top-note, all high, singing melody, with no bass line to keep it in check. It was the boy band of the chicken-picatta universe.

But then the rabbit entered the picture, and the flavors got deep. Very deep.

The truffle is some powerful line-cook hoodoo, the uranium of the culinary world. Like atomic energy, once its power is harnessed, it must be used with monkish discretion—rarely, delicately and never without a damn good reason. Luca's kitchen had a damn good reason for using truffles: I'd ordered the rabbit, three ways, off the entree menu, and nothing goes with rabbit quite the way truffle does. It gives life back to the lowly *lapin*, lends the mellow flavor of bunny a deep and earthy context, and can put such a kick in a dish that you might still be tasting it two or three days later. And here the kitchen used the truffle with all necessary discretion, adding it with a light hand to the tiny confit foreleg and big, tender, juicy back thigh; using it to jack up the slivers of cremini, shiitake and porcini mushroom mixed into the small pile of braised and shredded rabbit meat in the center of the plate; blending the truffle oil into the reduced braising liquid that made the rabbit gravy, then leaving the thin, sweet, fanned slices of grilled loin mercifully untouched.

The rabbit was excellent in all of its three ways, the true star of the table. I got my mom to try some, too, and though she took only a dainty, reluctant nibble of her third new thing of the night, she did it. Game over, and good for her. I kept eating it, though, and I would pay for my excesses later. As I said, the effect of truffle is cumulative. It builds until you reach a point where all you can taste and all you can smell is the musky perfume. Like durian fruit, it gets into your hair and clothes. It works its way into your pores. It hangs with you like Superglue.

Lying here on the floor, surrounded by the stink of voracious consumption, I accept that I've had more truffle in one night than any human should consume in a year, maybe a lifetime, and have crammed myself to the larynx with more heavy, wonderful Italian food than can possibly be healthy. The room is heaving a little. I'm finding it difficult to take deep breaths, and I wonder if I may yet become the first-ever victim of terminal, truffle-induced narcosis.

In this line of work, I have many friends. There's Pepto and there's Pepcid; there's Advil for the hangovers and Tums for my tummy. At times, there's been Compazine. Antibiotics. Imodium and ipecac syrup. But my best friend of all is a little bag of *ting ting jahe* ginger bonbons that I picked up at the Japanese grocery. For times like this—times when I have exceeded my gross physical volume by dangerous levels and indulged too fervently in what would, in smaller doses, be considered a very good thing—the ginger candies are the only things that get me through the night. They settle the stomach marvelously, can cut through nearly any aftertaste, and while they're not going to do anything about the smell of truffles and rabbit and bloat still lingering around me, at least my breath will be sweet when my wife finds me dead in the morning.

But you know what? I don't regret a bite. This world is full of fence-sitters, middle-of-the-roaders, abstentious temperate fellows for whom a little is always enough, and I will not go down as one of their number. I say everything in excess. I say moderation is for pussies and Mormons. You can never really have too much of a good thing.

And I think Bonanno and I are on the same page with that.

The Inside Scoop

Something from the Oven

by Laura Shapiro

from *Something from the Oven*

Laura Shapiro pries the lid off of the "happy homemaker" myths of the 1950s and '60s in this fascinating social history, picking up where her earlier *Perfection Salad* left off. Read it and you'll never again take Betty Crocker or the Pillsbury Doughboy at face value.

Few products emerging from the American kitchen have the sentimental heft of the classic frosted layer cake, universally recognized as a triumph of love as much as skill. "Can you think of anything more symbolic of the loving comfort and security of home than the fragrance of good things baking in the kitchen?" Marjorie Husted asked a conference of gas company salesmen in 1948. They couldn't, and neither could the editors of *McCall's* when they made publishing history in 1950 by becoming the first major women's magazine to put food on the cover—a picture of a cake. Since colonial days women had been marking holidays and festivities with the best cakes their households could afford. Many of these celebratory cakes were rich, fruit-studded yeast breads, but by the early 1800s pound cakes and sponge cakes had moved to center stage, with special reverence attending those that rose majestically into the air thanks to quantities of eggs and hours of hard beating. With the invention of baking powder in the mid-nineteenth century, it finally became possible to achieve light, handsome layer cakes with fewer eggs and far less kitchen labor, and the American cake sailed into its heyday. "Cakes from every land have been introduced to America—but none is so glamorous as the typically American cake developed in this country—the gorgeous concoction of richly tender layers, crowned with luscious creamy icing!" wrote Betty Crocker in a 1942 recipe booklet, and she went on to brandish one sentiment-laden symbol after another: "The beautiful cake for the announcement party . . . the triumphantly towering wedding cake . . . children's birthday cakes, blazing with candles . . . the proud cake celebrating the silver or golden wedding. . . ." It was rare for Betty Crocker to indulge in such rhapsodic prose. Even when she evoked the homemade bread of yesteryear in the same booklet ("the full wheaty flavor of the buttered slice!"), she wasn't able to summon the angel voices that soared when the subject was cake. But cake had a grip on the heart that bread simply couldn't match.

Betty Crocker had another motive for polishing her adjectives when she talked about cake: At General Mills and all the other flour companies, sales of flour for home use had been declining since the late 1920s. Despite what everyone felt about homemade bread, baking sufficient quantities for the family's needs all week was a major chore; and as white, airy loaves became more widely available in stores, fewer and fewer women baked their own every week. Eating patterns were changing, too, with rising incomes and a greater popular awareness of the role of vitamins. Americans were consuming less bread and fewer potatoes, and more fruits, vegetables, and meats, than they had at the turn of the century. The crowning indignity, as far as the flour companies were concerned, was that bread was getting a bad reputation: Women thought it was fattening. For all these reasons, by the 1940s families were keeping much less flour on hand. As a Pillsbury executive put it, "The era of the hundred-pound sack was drawing to a close." The flour companies didn't try to revive home bread-baking, its day seemed so definitively over, but instead put their hopes in the other baked goods that traditionally came from home kitchens—biscuits, muffins, cookies, pies, and cakes.

The first great instrument designed to spur homemade biscuits and muffins was Bisquick, which General Mills introduced in 1931. Like pancake mixes, which had been on the market since Aunt Jemima launched hers in 1889, Bisquick was based on self-rising flour; the innovation was that it was already mixed with short-ening. All the homemaker had to do to make biscuits was add water or milk; and she could make a host of more elaborate baked goods by adding eggs, sugar, or other ingredients. But the eventual success of Bisquick did not automatically blaze a trail for cake mix. Cake was different. It was never just dessert. "*Betty Crocker says*: A gift you bake is a gift from the heart," ran a typical flour ad from General Mills. At General Foods it was "*Remember,* men love Swans Down cakes (and the girls who bake them!)." To sell Calumet baking powder:"Love and Kisses to the gal who bakes this luscious cake!" Or Swift-ning, shortening: "He'll think he married an angel! Can you blame him? One taste of this homemade beauty is enough to convince any man he's in heaven!" Or as Pillsbury summed it up, "Nothing says lovin' like something from the oven." Cake was love, femininity, happiness, and a man around the house. Not that the women who glanced at the ads in newspapers and magazines needed much reminding. "When my beloved husband reached home this evening, he as usual gave me a big hug and kiss and asked: 'Did you make a cake or pie today?' " confided a reader of *The Boston Globe* in a letter to the "Confidential Chat." Luckily, she had just taken a two-egg cake from the oven.

Cake recipes sent in by readers who wanted to share them with their Chat sisters ran constantly in the *Globe*. In 1959, when the paper's food editor invited readers to submit their very favorite recipes out of all those they had ever clipped from the *Globe,* nearly half were for cakes. "What recipes do women ask for most fre-quently? Cakes!" announced Mary Meade in the *Chicago Tribune,* introducing a "Cake of the Week" recipe feature in 1948. The response was so enthusiastic that even she was taken aback."My staff and I have known for a long time that women love cakes, but we were somewhat surprised at the popularity of this weekly cake pres-entation,"she wrote when the feature had run for nearly a year.The plan was to move on to a "Dessert of the Week," but some readers still begged for cakes. Two hundred women—Meade called them "cake addicts"—telephoned the paper in a fury the day a recipe for Orange Lemon Sunshine Cake appeared too blurry to read.

But cakes could be as treacherous as they were powerful. Baking was a precarious enterprise; much could go wrong even in an oft-used recipe, depending on such factors as the weather, the size of the eggs, or the freshness of the baking powder. When a 1953 Gallup poll asked respondents to name the dish providing "the real test of a woman's ability to cook," both men and women put apple pie in first place, showing a healthy respect for the demanding nature of pastry. In second place men put "roasts," while women—who did most of the baking and knew very well what could befall them—put "cake." Whenever homemakers were offered the chance to ask a cooking expert for help with their kitchen problems, questions about cake were paramount. *Household* magazine, published in Topeka, Kansas, for a largely midwestern readership—that is, for America's prototypical home bakers—ran an advice column called "Kitchen Questions" that featured cake problems more regularly than any other aspect of cooking. "Before my sponge cake is cold, it falls out of the pan." "Why does the brown coating around my angel food cakes always stick to the pan?" "Here is my recipe for Milk Chocolate Cake which is much darker than it should be." Irma S. Rombauer, the personable author whose beloved *Joy of Cooking* went into its fifth edition in 1951, attracted a great deal of mail from women who used the book, and many of them wrote to her about cake. A Connecticut woman couldn't manage to make the Velvet Spice Cake properly; it came out "thick and horrid." A San Francisco woman loved Rombauer's pound cake, but the fruit kept settling on the bottom. A Cincinnati woman wondered about baking fruit cakes in small pans. And a woman from the Bronx mailed Rombauer a family member's recipe for walnut torte, wanting to know why it always fell. (Rombauer scribbled her analysis in a quick note to herself: "recipe no good.")

The stakes were high and the journey was perilous; no wonder the food industry sensed a market for cake mixes. Such a product might make up for the languishing sales of home flour and of course could be sold for a higher price. Duff cake mixes were the first to appear, starting with gingerbread in 1931 and later including white, spice, and devil's food cake. Other manufacturers followed—more than two hundred of them by 1947—but most of these rudimentary products were distributed only regionally. The concept itself didn't begin to take root until the two biggest players, General Mills and Pillsbury, launched cake mixes after the war. General Mills was first out of the gate with Betty Crocker Ginger*cake*—so named, complete with italics, because it was made with Softasilk cake flour and was a lighter product than the term *gingerbread* would have implied. Pillsbury was right on Betty Crocker's heels with white cake and chocolate cake mixes, both introduced in 1948. That same year General Mills came out with devil's food and a product called Party Cake, a mix that became white, yellow, or spice cake depending on what the homemaker added in the way of eggs and spices. The possibilities didn't end there: By following the frosting recipes that came with each package, the homemaker could actually make sixty-four different combinations of cake and frosting.

With the power of national distribution and advertising, especially TV advertising, three giant companies—Pillsbury, General Mills, and General Foods—quickly swamped or bought their smaller competitors. Pillsbury launched the first angel food cake mix in 1951; Swans Down followed, and General Mills jumped in two years later. Meanwhile, Nebraska Consolidated Mills, an Omaha flour company, had been experimenting with cake mixes, and in 1951 it launched its own, packaged under the Duncan Hines label. Thanks to the power of Duncan Hines's name—Hines was a homey food writer who published a popular series of restaurant guides—the company gained 10 percent of the cake-mix market within a year despite limited distribution. Throughout the '50s these four industry leaders battled furiously for the affection and loyalty of homemakers.

As far as most home cooks were concerned, cake mixes were still quite new in the late 1940s and early 1950s, but to the food industry this brief span of time was the product's golden age. The prototypes on the market in the 1930s had mysteriously failed to take hold among consumers. Now at last women were waking up, and so were sales. In 1947, just before the big companies introduced their first mixes, shoppers spent about $79 million on cake mixes. By 1953 they were spending more than twice that amount. "These were the days when cake mixes were miracles; when using them was like having the essence of the modern world in your own kitchen," a Pillsbury executive remembered fondly in 1960. His nostalgia was understandable, for after the initial excitement, the rate of increase dropped significantly, with only a 5 percent gain between 1956 and 1960. Worse, the industry wasn't attracting new buyers. Through the latter years of the 1950s, the number of home cooks using cake mixes hardly budged, not even reflecting population increases.

Cake mixes had definitely arrived, but the industry had no clear picture of the extent to which they were supplementing or replacing traditional baking. Published estimates ranged wildly: In 1953, General Mills decided that 20 percent of homemade cakes came from mixes; two years later, the company raised the estimate to 50 percent, and that same year Pillsbury claimed that 70 to 80 percent of families were using mixes. More plausible numbers, albeit gathered from a very small survey, appeared in the 1958 study referred to earlier in which a doctoral student interviewed 210 Pennsylvania homemakers and asked about their meal-planning habits. She found that 68 percent of them baked cakes from scratch. She also found that nearly all the women, including the scratch bakers, kept a variety of mixes on hand—cake mix, Bisquick, muffin mix, piecrust mix, and more—and used them from time to time.

Plainly, baking mixes of all sorts had a permanent place in the American pantry by the late 1950s, but when it came to cake mixes a lot of women seemed to be balking. They made use of cake mixes but were still distinguishing between cake-mix cakes and real cakes. The flour companies preferred to talk about great leaps in the sales figures, but they knew their customer base was stagnant. In fact, they had been puzzling over women's reluctance to discard traditional baking ever since Duff's first gingerbread mix made its debut. Back then, despite the tremendous sentiment that surrounded a homemade cake and the attendant nervous frenzy about baking one, the prospect of serving a cake that took no skill just wasn't very alluring. Good cooks were proud of their handiwork. And struggling cooks had enough problems coming to terms with their inadequacy in a world where food is love without being forced to deal with what looked like guilt in a box. There were women, of course, who latched on to cake mixes with enthusiasm, but they weren't always the consumers that the industry had expected to reach right away—namely, novice cooks, brides, and working wives in the city. The homemakers who were buying cake mixes disproportionately were farmwives—women who had to put big meals on the table for hungry men, including family members and farmhands, two or three times a day.

Homemakers who weren't producing meals under such pressure all day long might not have been particularly impressed by the amount of time they saved using a cake mix. When home economics students at Hood College conducted a study in 1950 comparing cake-mix cakes with traditionally made cakes, they found that mixes saved only three to fifteen minutes per cake. In 1954 a study at Michigan State College pinpointed the time saved at exactly thirteen minutes and made a point of noting that apart from measuring out the ingredients, similar work was required for both kinds of cake. Other studies (these projects were very popular in college home ec classes) tended to find that cakes baked the old-fashioned way were more "palatable" than the ones that came from a box. Too much sugar and too much artificial vanilla doomed the cake-mix cakes in the Michigan State study. In the long run, quality would prove to be an imprecise measure of cake-mix acceptability, but at least in the early years women seemed to feel that the extra minutes they put into their own scratch baking paid off.

Looking for reasons why so many women who could benefit from cake mixes seemed to be ignoring them, advertisers and consumer experts chose to embrace the egg theory. Ernest Dichter had come up with this analysis in the course of a study he was carrying out for General Mills. After interviewing women and exploring the emotions that surrounded cakes and baking, Dichter reported that the very simplicity of mixes—just add water and stir—made women feel self-indulgent for using them. There wasn't enough work involved. In order to enjoy the emotional rewards of presenting a homemade cake, they had to be persuaded that they had really baked it, and such an illusion was impossible to maintain if they did virtually nothing. "This is typical of what the average housewife said: 'Yes, I'm using a cake mix; it saves me a lot of trouble but I really shouldn't,' " Dichter wrote later. His advice was to leave the homemaker something to do—for instance, add the eggs—whenever she made a cake from a mix.

She would feel she had contributed something of herself, and the mindless nature of the task would no longer plague her.

According to Dichter, his client—and, by implication, the other manufacturers—seized on this wisdom and promptly reformulated their mixes, leaving out the dried eggs. Women started adding their own fresh eggs, stopped feeling guilty, and cake mixes became a success. Over the years this story came to be a favorite among other consumer experts, who often rounded up more psychological studies to reinforce Dichter's analysis. The egg theory, with its emphasis on the homemaker's personal investment in the cake, set the tone for much subsequent advertising ("You and Ann Pillsbury can make a great team") and has been widely acknowledged as the insight that saved cake mixes.

But while Dichter's work was influential, its precise role in the success of the cake mix is unclear. It's true that the earliest mixes were what the industry called "complete"; the box included dried eggs and everything else except water or milk. And these were the mixes that failed to catch on, prompting Dichter's study. But manufacturers did not quickly or unanimously fall in line behind him. When Pillsbury and the other big companies were working to develop their cake mixes in the 1940s, the question of whether or not to include dried eggs was a major in-house debate. Paul Gerot, the CEO at Pillsbury in this period, called it "the hottest controversy we had over the product," and he noted that even after the mixes made their debut, the arguing went on for years.

For the industry, the problem wasn't so much that dried eggs deprived the housewife of her contribution, it was that dried eggs produced inferior cakes. They stuck to the pan, the texture was poor, the shelf life was shorter, and they sometimes tasted too prominently of eggs. General Mills, which conducted a great deal of technical research on dried and fresh eggs as well as commissioning Dichter's study, staked its fortunes squarely on fresh-egg mixes and made a point of saying so. "Unlike most cake mixes, there are *No dried egg whites, no dried egg yolks, no dried eggs of any kind in* Betty Crocker Cake Mixes," announced a 1952 ad in *Life*. Three years later, on a Betty Crocker radio show, Betty Crocker told her listeners about a recent trip to Alaska, where she chatted with the wife of the Barrow Airport manager. This Arctic home cook preferred Betty Crocker cake mixes to all others, and why? "Because she can add fresh eggs to the mix," Betty Crocker said firmly.

Pillsbury conducted extensive research as well, including surveys of consumers to gauge their preferences, for either complete mixes or fresh-egg mixes. The company found that people tasting both kinds said they preferred the fresh-egg mixes but indicated they would be more likely to buy the complete mixes. Rather than try to decode this particular message, Pillsbury simply made the decision to go with complete mixes. By 1955, General Mills and Pillsbury shared most of the cake-mix market between them despite wholly contradictory egg philosophies.

Chances are, if adding eggs persuaded some women to overcome their aversion to cake mixes, it was at least partly because fresh eggs made for better cakes. But Dichter rightly perceived the overwhelming weight of the moral and emotional imperative to bake cakes from scratch. His research spurred countless ads and magazine articles aimed at persuading women to differentiate between the plain cake layers—"merely step number one," according to *Living*—and the finished masterpiece. "Now, success in cakemaking is packaged right along with the precision ingredients," Myrna Johnston assured readers of *Better Homes & Gardens* in 1953. "You can put your effort into glorifying your cake with frosting, dreaming up an exciting trim that puts your own label on it." For modern women, these authorities proclaimed, the real art of baking began after the cake emerged from the oven.

This perspective changed the nature of the traditional challenges facing home bakers. Flavor and texture were no longer at issue, and they had little importance anyway in a cake that was destined for a great deal of imaginative frosting. Cover a quick angel food cake with apricot glaze and icing, and surround it with ladyfingers cut to size, the experts suggested. Or split the cake, fill it with buttercream, border it with chocolate, and top it with chocolate-dipped cherries. Fill and frost layers of yellow cake with butterscotch pudding, dot the top with salted pecans, and call it a torte. Cover an oblong cake with chocolate frosting and sprinkle it with green decorating sugar—that's the football field. Use white frosting for the lines, and stick candy for the goalposts. A piece of banana covered with melted chocolate is the football. Cut a hole in the center of an angel food cake, fill it with partially jelled orange gelatin and canned peaches, frost the whole thing with whipped cream, and cover that with toasted coconut. *McCall's* gave directions for making a Humpty-Dumpty cake—there were thirteen steps to it, including making three different frostings, painting the cake with food coloring, and assembling the various parts with wooden skewers and drinking straws. It took about twelve hours, though much of the time was spent waiting for various layers to dry. The thirteen steps didn't include making the cake itself from two boxes of mix.

A huge, lavishly frosted layer cake, opened up wide so the viewer could gaze at the tenderness inside, became the presiding image in cake iconography. Ads for flour and cake mix, as well as for baking powder, shortening, chocolate, and coconut, invariably displayed a cake in this posture. Like models whose mesmerizing, inescapable faces define beauty in their time, these cakes set the standard for perfect festivity and made most others look humble by comparison. The standard itself was purely visual. Flavor would never count for much in an industrially produced cake, because simple sweetness was so easily achieved in the factory and so widely acceptable. But the distinguishing attributes of the iconic cake—its height and lightness— were just the qualities that technology could achieve with ease. Cake mixes never completely lost their aura of being second best or their near-indelible association with cheating. To this day, guilt follows many of those boxes home from the supermarket the way Jiminy Cricket followed Pinocchio—his conscience always with him. But the promise of a foolproof cake became more and more tempting, especially for a housewife who didn't trust her own hands. At *McCall's* Congress on Better Living, the forum staged for advertisers in 1958 at which homemakers offered their views of household products, one of the few delegates who voiced no compunctions about opening a box instead of baking from scratch was a woman who said forth-rightly, "I really don't know how to bake, and I wish I did." She told the group that she had finally worked up the nerve to try baking a cake and had deliberately started with a mix. The whole procedure delighted her. "I never enjoyed anything so much as knowing I couldn't make a mistake," she reported, "and at least it would come out being a cake."

Stone-Ground Revival

by John T. Edge

from *Saveur*

Warmth and thoughtfulness shine through John T. Edge's ongoing explorations of the byways of Southern folks and their food. His upcoming book is the definitive *Fried Chicken: An American Story*; here he investigates another iconic Dixie dish, the often-misunderstood grits.

I grew up in Clinton, a hamlet in rural middle Georgia. But I was reared on grits milled by the Quaker Oats company of Cedar Rapids, Iowa. As a child, I learned that grits—the archetypal ground-corn porridge popular south of the divide mapped by Mason and Dixon—were not supposed to actually taste of corn, were not expected to be flavorful. Back then, I knew grits to be prized for their blandness, their function as a vehicle for the conveyance of other tastes, like cheddar cheese or redeye gravy.

By the time I was a teenager—say, about 1976, the year our country elected Georgian Jimmy Carter president and Minnesotan Walter Mondale vice president on the strength of a campaign that urged voters to choose Grits and Fritz—grits were teetering on the brink of culinary irrelevance. Sure, they served as a cultural marker: Southerners were thought to relish grits, while Yankees were said to consider them fodder for fattening cattle. More often, grits served as a punch line, as in the time singer Bette Midler told a Charleston, South Carolina, audience that, though she dearly loved their region, she thought their grits resembled "buttered Kitty Litter".

For years, I savored gussied-up grits swimming in redeye gravy, capped with stewed river shrimp and sweet onions, or, on special occasions, studded with smoked oysters fished from a golden tin. The idea of eating them with nothing save butter and salt was anathema. Then, when I was nearly 30 years old, a friend turned me on to the grits sold by Charlestonian John Martin Taylor (also known as "Hoppin' John"), the cookbook author, former cookbook store owner, and artisanal-food purveyor. The grocery store grits I had always known were made of processed corn that had been soaked in a lye solution that removed its hulls, bleached the nutritive tissue within its seeds, and pulverized it by way of steel rollers, so when cooked they tasted, in effect, like Dixie-fied Cream of Wheat. Taylor's whole grain, stone-ground grits, however, were a revelation. These tasted like cracked corn—sweet, but with a bass note that bespoke the dank earth in which the ears had grown to maturity. I quickly developed a half-sack-a-month habit that to this day shows no signs of abating.

"Grits have always been with us," says Stan Woodward, director of the 1980 documentary It's Grits! "It's just that we tend to be fickle in our relationship with grits. We neglect them; then all of a sudden we realize we're missing them. It's sort of like the Lord. When you turn around and find Him there, you're surprised. But He has never left you."

Indeed, while American Indians have consumed hominy (originally treated with the ash from campfires) for more than five millennia, the past 30-odd years have proven especially interesting for grits eaters. In the late 1960s, when the national media were struggling to make sense of soul food, grits were often touted as a distinctly African-American dish, born of privation. In 1968, bluesman Little Milton sang, "If grits ain't grocery / Eggs ain't poultry / And Mona Lisa was a man." Less than ten years later, when president-elect Carter took office, grits came to be viewed as a totem of rural identity for Southerners of all races. By the mid-1980s, grits were beginning to reclaim a place on the better Southern tables. Renowned regional chefs—among them the late Bill Neal, author of the seminal Southern cookbook Southern Cooking (University of North Carolina Press, 1989) and chef at Crook's Corner in Chapel Hill, North Carolina, and Frank Stitt, chef and owner of Highlands Bar and Grill and two other restaurants in Birmingham, Alabama (and a *Saveur* consulting editor)—cultivated relationships with small millers and began offering on the menus of their establishments such sophisticated dishes as (in Stitt's case) grits soufflé with fresh thyme and country ham.

During the 1990s, smaller producers of grits, such as Old Mill of Guilford (North Carolina), Falls Mill (Tennessee), Logan Turnpike Mill (Georgia), Adam's Mill (Alabama), and War Eagle Mill (Arkansas)—staffed oftentimes by refugees from white-collar corporate America—grew from weekend diversions into thriving businesses. Given time and enough whole grain stone-ground grits, consumers came to appreciate a taste that harked back to the years preceding World War II, when most towns of substance in the South boasted a mill and fresh ground corn was a commodity, not a luxury.

If Taylor is the alpha grits grinder whose goods lit the fire behind this new movement, then Glenn Roberts, reared in La Jolla, California, and now milling corn in Columbia, South Carolina, is the insurgent fire-and-brimstone fundamentalist of the ongoing grits revival. Inspired in part by Taylor, Roberts has taken the production of grits to its logical—some might say fanatical—ends.

In a derelict warehouse set behind a car wash, Roberts manages his Anson Mills company. The millstones he uses are quarried, balanced, and dressed by the Meadows mills of Wilkesboro, North Carolina. (Just a mile away, Adluh Flour Mills, a Columbia mainstay since 1900, uses the same blue-granite stones to grind its grits.) But Roberts, who has been milling in earnest only since 1998, has accessorized his mill with all manner of sleeves and spouts that call to mind the bells and whistles of a Rube Goldberg device as engineered by Dr. Seuss. In order to ensure that the fragile flavors of the milled corn are not muted by the inhospitable local climate or the frictional heat generated by the stones, he chills his organically grown corn to -10 degrees. He then grinds it in an oxygen-free environment and ships it the same day it is packed. The super-coarse ground grits Roberts sells to chefs and dedicated home cooks are among the best you will ever taste—sweet as a fresh-picked ear of corn, with a pronounced floral nose.

"For me, it's all about the quality of the corn," says Roberts. "We work with only viable seed corn—Carolina Gourdseed White, John

Haulk Yellow Dent, Bloody Butcher Red Dent. This stuff is alive, and we work to see that the grits emerge from the mill tasting of corn. I've spent a lot of time on the road, in search of the best corn I can find. Early on, we learned that some of the best varieties were in the possession of families who had previously distilled corn liquor. They had a need to preserve the best, to grow their own corn from their own seed rather than risk notice of the law. As you might imagine, it's not an easy task to gain the confidence of old moonshiners."

Roberts is an unapologetic wonk, willing and able to hold forth on such subjects as, for example, the efficacy of a carbon dioxide envelope to prevent oxidation of the ground product and a maneuver called shatter milling that is performed to guarantee the optimal facet exposure of the grain to the grinder. But to his credit, he's also a student of the old ways of doing things and the old truths of those practices. "If I do the job right, my grits should taste like corn tasted 100, 200 years ago," explains Roberts. "This is not about culinary one-upmanship; this is all about breathing new life into traditional foodways."

With any luck, Glenn Roberts and his like-minded compatriots will succeed in this revival. My two-year-old son, Jess, has never tasted anemic grocery store grits. I figure that binds him with his great-grandfather and name giver, of the last generation of my family born and reared eating stone-ground grits. By the time Jess is shopping for his own breakfast provisions, I hope, our local grocery will stock the kind of grits that Roberts and other disciples of John Martin Taylor are grinding. Until then I'll keep my pantry stocked with the good stuff—and pray that my son won't backslide and call for smoked oysters.

⁓

Basic Grits

Serves 4–6

1 cup stone-ground grits
Salt
2 tbsp. butter

1. Put grits into a medium bowl, cover with cold water, and stir until chaff floats to the surface. Skim off chaff, then drain grits in a fine-mesh strainer and set aside.

2. Bring 5 cups water to a boil in a medium enameled cast-iron or other heavy-bottomed pot over high heat. Stir in grits and ½ tsp. salt. Reduce heat to medium-low and cook grits, stirring often to prevent a skin from forming on surface and to keep them from sticking to the bottom of the pot, until soft and creamy, 1½ to 2 hours. Add ¼ to ½ cup water as needed during cooking if grits become too dry. Stir in butter and season to taste with salt.

VARIATION—CROCK-POT GRITS: *Set Crock-Pot temperature indicator to high. Follow step 1 above. Put drained grits, 5 cups room-temperature water, butter, and ½ tsp. salt into Crock-Pot and stir to combine. Reduce temperature to low on indicator, cover, and cook until grits are soft and creamy, about 8 hours. Adjust seasonings. Serves 4–6.*

YOU SAY POLENTA, I SAY GRITS

What's the difference between grits and that other popular cornmeal mush, polenta? It turns out that the best answer is based on particle size: grits are of a coarser grind than polenta. Glenn Roberts, maker of artisanal grits and polenta (he's even ground the latter for Marcella Hazan), pegs the particle size of grits at ⅙ inch to ¹⁄₂₀ inch and of polenta at ¹⁄₁₂ inch to ¹⁄₈₀ inch. To complicate matters further, Roberts explains, both grits and polenta come in white and yellow varieties, depending on the type of corn used to make them. In general, he says, white grits are preferred by those who live near coastal port cities (such as Charleston), while yellow are traditional for inlanders. In some parts of Georgia, they even mix white and yellow grits together. In terms of polenta, yellow is ubiquitous, but Roberts also makes white, which he says is the color preferred in Italy's Veneto region. Either way, Roberts assures us, grits and polenta (and, for that matter, Romania's cornmeal mush, mamaliga) may be used interchangeably in recipes, even though their respective genealogies and heritages are quite different (and their cooking times vary). "It's a continuous stream of the same kind of corn cookery, only seen through different cookways," Roberts says.

Sex, Death and Oysters

by Robb Walsh

from *The Houston Press*

The title of Robb Walsh's most recent book, *Are You Really Going to Eat That?*, should clue you in that this is one adventurous eater. His regular restaurant reviews for *The Houston Press* profit from his bold palate; this feature story allowed his journalistic curiosity even more scope.

Eating raw oysters is exquisitely perverse. If they're freshly shucked, as they ought to be, you're putting the mollusk into your mouth while it's still alive. The wonderfully slick texture, delicate briny flavor and beachfront aroma make it easy to understand how oysters came to be associated with the tenderest portion of the female anatomy and thus considered an aphrodisiac.

But since a bacterium called *Vibrio vulnificus* found in raw Gulf Coast oysters poisons a few people every year, I also find myself contemplating my mortality as I eat a dozen on the half shell. It's a heady appetizer, each pale oyster so languid and vulnerable, brimming with images of sex and death.

The local oysters are incredibly sweet this year—so sweet that such famous Louisiana oyster restaurants as Drago's Seafood in Metairie are serving Texas oysters alongside the Louisiana shellfish. "Texas oysters are the best right now," Croatian-American oysterman Drago Cvitanovich told me when I stopped by his Louisiana restaurant last December.

I always assumed Texas oysters came from a distant and pristine lagoon down past Corpus Christi somewhere. Given the heavy tanker traffic and the refineries hugging the coast along Texas City, you don't think of seafood thriving near the Ship Channel. I've always figured if there were any fish under there, they probably had three eyes.

So I was more than a little surprised to learn that, right now, acre for underwater acre, the most productive oyster reefs in North America are in Galveston Bay.

The waters of the bay are calm, the sky is blue, and the water temperature is hovering at 60 degrees—perfect oyster weather. The *Trpanj* is a typical oyster boat, wide across the middle with a huge foredeck; it looks like a barge with an upturned nose. When the boat's dredge, a five-foot-long metal rake and net contraption, is hauled up, oysters and debris are tipped over onto the work table. The Mexican deckhands sort the "keepers" out of the gray jumble of empty shells and undersized oysters, throwing the legal ones into a growing pile on deck. Then they shove the empty shells and too-small oysters overboard.

The oysters are plentiful, and spirits are high. But things suddenly turn somber when a Texas Parks and Wildlife patrol boat pulls up alongside the *Trpanj* and two uniformed game wardens jump aboard. Warden Bobby Kana comes forward wearing wraparound sunglasses and a tough-guy frown.

The Texas Parks and Wildlife Department, which publishes a map showing where it's legal to harvest oysters, polices the oyster-fishing business. There's a large public oyster reef in the middle of the bay where anyone with a license can harvest oysters. Then there are four "conditional" zones, all of which are closed today because of excessive rainfall. (Runoff after a big rain is a major source of pollution in the bay.)

Oyster leases are areas leased from the state by private companies; marked by buoys, they're off-limits except to permitted boats. Areas close to shore and most of the upper bay are closed for oystering at all times.

Everybody in the business knows the rules. But the unprecedented number of oyster boats working Galveston Bay this year is putting tremendous pressure on the system. Nerves are frayed, and there's tension between the locals and boats from other waters.

"Who is the captain here?" Kana asks. Captain Rene Rivas introduces himself.

"Captain, you are working a leased area. Do you have a permit to be on this lease?" Rivas doesn't have the right paperwork. The other game warden accompanies the captain while he goes to get the boat's oyster license. Meanwhile, Kana produces a strange, square, C-shaped contraption and starts using it to measure the oysters in the pile on deck.

The *Trpanj*, which is named after a village in Croatia, is owned by the same Croatian-American family that owns Misho's Oyster Company, the largest oyster processor on Galveston Bay. They also own the oyster lease. So I'm confused by what the game wardens are doing here.

"It's Misho's boat and Misho's oyster lease, right?" I ask Kana.

"Yeah, but the permit hasn't been filed," he says. "And the lease is not properly marked."

"Are the oysters the right size?" I ask.

"Most of them are okay," he says. He holds up an offender that slips through the measuring device. "Two-and-a-half-inch oysters are very popular for oysters on the half shell," Kana says. "But anything under three inches is illegal in Texas."

"You must be having a busy day," I say, looking out over the bay. "I've heard that there are 430 oyster boats working on Galveston Bay this year."

"That's about right," says the game warden. There were 170 oyster boats on Galveston Bay last year. The huge jump is due to the perfect conditions.

In Louisiana, they might make 30 or 40 bags in a day's dredging. In Galveston Bay, boats have been topping out at 150 bags for most of the season. Texas oysters are being shipped to Florida and the Carolinas, where they're resold to other seafood concerns. Few of the end consumers on the East Coast ever realize they're eating Texas oysters.

Kana ordered all of the *Trpanj*'s oysters dumped overboard and fined the boat more than $250, Misho Ivic tells me later.

"Why wasn't the lease properly marked?" I ask him.

"The thieves cut your markers first," Ivic fumes, "so they don't get caught stealing your oysters."

It was last December when I first encountered burly Croatian-American oysterman Misho Ivic and his son Michael (English for Misho). The Ivies brought their oyster boats to Galveston 30 years ago from Louisiana, where Ivic's wife's Croatian-American family also works in the oyster business.

We met for lunch at the popular oysterman hangout Gilhooley's in San Leon, where we were joined by a marine biologist named Dr. Sammy Ray. An animated 85-year-old with wispy white hair and glasses that seem too big for his face, Ray, a professor emeritus at Texas A&M at Galveston, is one of the foremost authorities on Gulf oysters. He had a bowl of gumbo, and Ivic had "oysters Gilhooley," which are smoked oysters on the half shell with shrimp on top. I had a dozen on the half shell.

I'd arrived with a few misconceptions. As far as I understood it, pollution had wiped out most of America's native oyster reefs around mid-century. For example, at its height in the mid-1800s, the annual harvest of Virginia's Chesapeake Bay was measured in the millions of bushels. Today it produces about 1 percent of its historic peak production.

Conservationists and the states that border Chesapeake Bay are now attempting to rebuild the oyster fishery through tougher controls on pollution, strict limits on oystermen, and the possible introduction of an oyster species from Asia. I'd asked the Texas oyster experts to meet me so I could learn what kind of conservation projects were going on here.

"When was the peak harvest of the Galveston Bay oyster fishery?" I ask the marine biologist.

"Right now," Ray says with a wide grin. "I predict this will be the biggest season we've ever seen. Misho's Oyster Company alone will outproduce the entire Chesapeake Bay this year." I look at the oysterman in puzzlement.

"I agree," says Ivic. "And it's going to keep getting better. In the 1950s, there were boats dredging the oyster reefs and hauling off the oyster shells to build highways. Since they threw those guys out of Galveston Bay, the oyster reefs have grown 40 percent."

"But what about the pollution?" I ask.

"Pollution isn't a problem for oysters," says Ray. In fact, oysters eat the algae that sewage produces, filtering the water and making it cleaner. You just don't want to eat oysters that come from areas near pollution sources.

None of this is making any sense to me.

"I'll tell you a story," Ray begins. "In 1947, the oil companies were being sued for $30 million to 40 million for damage to the Louisiana oyster beds. We were told that Gulf oysters would soon disappear. The supposition at the time was the oil drilling was killing the oysters." Two teams of scientists set to work, one for each side of the lawsuit.

After two years, both sides came to the same conclusion, he says. If there was oil in the water and the water was salty, the oysters died. If there was oil in the water and the water wasn't salty, the oysters did fine. It wasn't oil or pollution that was killing the oysters; it was too much saltwater.

A hundred years ago, the Mississippi River broke into a lot of little distributaries that flowed into the salt marshes of western Louisiana. There were oyster reefs all over the Gulf in those days. But then a federal flood-control project built levees on the Mississippi River. The levees succeeded in controlling flooding, but they also cut off the flow of freshwater to the marshes and to the offshore oyster reefs.

Oysters can tolerate fairly high salinity, Ray explains, but their predators, mainly oyster drills, starfish and a disease called dermo, all thrive in saltwater. So you need a steady supply of freshwater flowing in to keep the salinity down and the pests away. Oyster reefs locate themselves where freshwater and saltwater meet. If you have a drought year, the oysters can survive. But after three years or so of high salinity, the oyster population gets wiped out.

The perfect scenario for oyster growth, Ray tells me, is a dry spring, which gives the oyster larvae the slightly elevated salinity they need, followed by a wet summer and fall, which drops the salinity and keeps the oyster's predators away. And that's part of the reason for Galveston Bay's remarkable oyster harvest this year. Not only have the oyster reefs benefited from years of recovery and better water quality, but last year we had the ideal weather pattern.

At a holiday party in a Montrose apartment, two women, both of them new to Houston, are talking about the disgusting waters of the Gulf of Mexico. One is from San Francisco and the other is from Cleveland. How could anybody swim in the oil blobs and flotsam of that ugly brown water? the San Franciscan asks. I smile and shake my head amiably. Personally, I swim in that water every summer, and I have marinated my children in it for most of their lives. But if Galveston is too unsightly for the newcomers' beach-going tastes, well, then "bless their hearts," as we say in Texas.

I don't bother pointing out to Miss San Francisco that only blub-bery seals and surfers in wet suits are insulated enough to venture into the icy waters of the Pacific around the Bay Area. Nor do I bother reminding Miss Cleveland that the Cuyahoga River is legendary among pollution watchers for its tendency to burst into flames.

"And who would eat oysters that come out of that water?" the San Franciscan continues. Suddenly, I feel my jaw muscles tighten. Newly informed about Texas oysters, I feel a strange need to defend them.

"I would," I say. "But actually, the oysters don't come from the Gulf, they come from Galveston Bay. In fact, it's one of the last great oyster reefs in America. And the oysters are fabulous this year."

"Where is Galveston Bay?" the lady from San Francisco wants to know.

"It's between Kemah and San Leon on the west and Anahuac on the east," I say, but she has no idea where I'm talking about. "You know where the ships enter the Houston Ship Channel?" I ask.

"Oh, gross," says a vegetarian woman who's listening in on the edge of the conversation. "So you think all those chemicals spewing out of the oil tankers give the oysters a special flavor?" Cornered now by skeptics, I feel the adrenaline beginning to flow.

I have a Texas Parks and Wildlife oyster map out in my car that shows how big the bay really is and how far the oyster reefs are from the pollution. I consider going out to get it.

"What I resent is that I can't get good oysters in Houston because they have so many cheap ones here," the San Franciscan says. "The Gulf oysters are big and tough. I don't want to chew on an oyster. I would never eat an oyster any bigger than this," she says, making a silver dollar–sized circle with her fingers. "I like blue points and Kumamoto oysters."

"How much do they cost?" I ask.

"I think the last time I had them, it was like $8.95 for three . . ."

"I like cultivated oysters, too," I admit. "They're delicious. But three little bitty oysters for $9? You live in the last place in America where you can get a dozen oysters for a couple of bucks—and you want to import $36-a-dozen cultivated oysters from California?"

"That's right," she says.

"You're an oyster snob," I say.

"Okay," she says. "I have no problem with that."

I try to put things in a cultural perspective. "You know, there were once oyster houses all over the country—California, New England, Chesapeake Bay—but those places are all gone. The native oysters are all fished out in most of the United States. The Gulf Coast is the last place where you can still sit down in an old-fashioned oyster saloon. This is the last of the old American oyster culture," I say. But it's no use. The conversation has turned to other topics.

The first oyster saloon in America opened in New York in 1763. For more than 100 years, oysters were popular among the rich and poor alike. In the 1800s, even landlocked cities such as St. Louis and Denver had oysters delivered in iced barrels by stagecoach.

Top-end restaurants like Delmonico's in New York sold oysters to wealthy patrons like Diamond Jim Brady (he liked at least three dozen before dinner). And outdoor oyster counters on New York's Canal Street sold poor folks all the oysters they could eat for six cents.

Americans got their oyster-eating traditions from the British, who in turn learned about oysters from the ancient Romans, who believed British oysters to be the finest in the world. And in fact, there was a good reason why the oysters got better as the Romans ventured farther north. In cold water, oysters "fatten up" to protect themselves. But instead of fat, they lay down a sugar compound called glycogen. The colder the water, the more of this sugarcoating they produce. That's why, even here in Texas, oysters taste best during the coldest part of the winter.

By the late 1700s, the once seemingly endless supply of oysters in Europe began to dwindle, and they became more expensive. The principles of oyster cultivation, which had been developed by the Greeks, spread throughout the empire to increase the oyster harvest.

The French system of oyster cultivation is the most sophisticated in the world. Oysters are bred on frames in one part of the sea and matured for several years in government-owned "oyster parks" along the coast. The oysters, called *claires,* are then fattened in tidal pools. But while French oysters may be the world's best, they're so expensive that they've become a rich man's treat.

The European gourmet oyster culture is now taking over in the United States. In the early 1980s, marine-biologist-turned-fish-monger Bill Marinelli popularized the tiny Kumamoto oysters, which were imported from Japan and grown in California's Humboldt Bay, by selling them to cutting-edge Berkeley restaurants like Chez Panisse, Fourth Street Grill and Zuni Café.

Unfortunately, some overzealous cultivated-oyster salesmen go overboard in trying to justify the high price of their product by belittling America's native oysters and the long culinary tradition they represent.

There's no doubt that expensive gourmet oysters are the wave of the future. Oregon, Washington and Massachusetts, along with Vancouver, Nova Scotia and Prince Edward Island in Canada, are all producing delicious farm-raised oysters these days. And contrary to the San Franciscan's protests, it's easy enough to find pricey cultivated oysters in Houston.

One night, I asked the lady from Cleveland and a Texas oyster lover to join me in an oyster tasting. We started in the funky turquoise and navy dining room of Joyce's Seafood and Steaks, where we polished off three-dozen Gulf oysters and a bottle of New Zealand Sauvignon Blanc.

Then we headed over to the tony environs of McCormick & Schmick's, where we were shown to a white linen-covered table. "We're just here to eat oysters," we told the waiter.

"We have Houston's best oysters," the waiter said.

They had 12 varieties of cultivated oysters available. So we got two dozen—three each of eight different kinds—and a bottle of French Muscadet. The standouts were the Malpeque oysters from Prince Edward Island, which were extremely salty with a strong fish flavor that harmonized beautifully with the lemony Muscadet. The tiny Kumamoto oysters were delectable, but they were so small you could barely tell you had anything in your mouth. We also sampled salty Imperial Eagle oysters from Vancouver, Fanny Bay oysters and several others.

"The difference between some of these is pretty subtle," I observed.

"With an accent on the 'b' in subtle," the Texas oyster lover said. When we'd finished the oysters and wine, he insisted on a nightcap at Willie G's, a seafood restaurant nearby. There we polished off another two dozen big, fat, watery Gulf oysters. I ate mine with a glass of Fat Tire beer.

"So what's your verdict?" I asked my fellow oyster lovers.

We all had to agree that the cultivated oysters really have more concentrated flavors than Gulf oysters. But a dozen tiny oysters at McCormick & Schmick's sell for $21.65. A dozen fat Gulf oysters at Joyce's go for $6.95.

"I have to admit, quantity does count," the lady from Cleveland said. "It's one thing to eat oysters as a delicacy, but it's another thing to chow down on them."

"I think there's gourmet oyster eaters and then there's oyster eaters," said the Texan.

The notion that oysters are an aphrodisiac seems rather quaint to modern minds. But then again, we don't eat oysters like they used to. Casanova had 50 with his nightcap every evening, and his libido was legendary.

In 1989, the Food and Drug Administration issued a report stating that the powers of most so-called aphrodisiacs were based in folklore, not fact. The scientists' explanation of why oysters are considered an aphrodisiac was particularly interesting.

"Many ancient peoples believed in the so-called 'law of similarity,' reasoning that an object resembling genitalia may possess sexual powers. Ginseng, rhinoceros horn, and oysters are three classical examples . . ." But according to the report, there might be some scientific basis for the idea that oysters were aphrodisiacs: "Oysters are particularly esteemed as sex aids, possibly gaining their reputation at a time when their contribution of zinc to the nutritionally deficient diets of the day could improve overall health and so lead to an increased sex drive."

But it's difficult to test aphrodisiacs, mainly because of the placebo effect. "The mind is the most potent aphrodisiac there is," says John Renner, founder of the Consumer Health Information Research Institute. In short, if you believe that oysters are an aphrodisiac, they're likely to have that effect. The FDA laments that there's been a shortage of studies on the subject. You can contribute to the cause of science by conducting your own experiments at home.

But while exploring the connection between sex and oysters promises hours of fun, the subject of oyster fatalities is not at all amusing.

On July 9, 2001, the Center for Science in the Public Interest, joined by Roger Berkowitz, president of Boston's Legal Sea Foods, held a press conference in Washington to announce the Serving Safer Shellfish campaign. The campaign urges oyster lovers not to eat raw, untreated Gulf Coast oysters. It also calls for restaurants, retailers and seafood wholesalers to sell shellfish harvested in the colder waters of New England or the Pacific Northwest, or Gulf oysters that have been sterilized. The group released a report, "Death on the Half Shell," that blamed government inaction for the more than 135 deaths from contaminated oysters since 1989.

So why would anybody in their right mind keep eating Gulf Coast oysters after a warning like that? Well, it helps to remember that Michael Jacobson, the head of the Center for Science in the Public Interest, has also spoken out against beer, coffee, Mexican food and buttered popcorn. The teetotaling vegetarian microbiologist, who once worked with Ralph Nader, also favors the enactment of the "Twinkie Tax," a special added tax on unhealthy food, and reportedly has said that instead of neighborhood taverns, "They should develop an alternative for people to socialize—a real fun coffeehouse. Maybe a carrot-juice house."

It's not very difficult to figure out why Jacobson should be joined in his condemnation of Gulf Coast seafood by the New England and Pacific Northwest seafood industries. If they can scare people out of eating cheap native Gulf Coast oysters, they stand to sell a lot more of their expensive farm-raised ones.

Efforts of the FDA's Interstate Shellfish Sanitation Conference, a group of federal and state regulators and shellfish industry representatives, to reduce the number of *V. vulnificus* cases haven't made much progress. Some members want to mandate postharvest treatment of Gulf Coast oysters by freezing, flash sterilization or washing to reduce the disease during the high-risk time of year. Others favor increasing the supply of treated oysters to provide more consumers with a less risky option. Unfortunately, the treated oysters don't taste all that great raw.

The Gulf Coast oyster industry argues that the education of the "at-risk consumer" is the best way to combat *V. vulnificus* infections. The vast majority of consumers have nothing to worry about and shouldn't be deprived of their right to eat regular raw oysters, they argue.

But educating consumers has proved difficult, as so little is known. The first reported case of *V. vulnificus* illness was in 1979. And some misunderstandings about the bacterium have been spread by the media. In "The Perpetual Oyster," a five-part series of articles about oysters in *Forbes,* Charles Dubow writes, "Although it is fairly easy to spot a 'bad' oyster—not only do they look dry and shriveled but usually smell something like rotten eggs—too many people over time have wished they had paid just a little more attention to what they were eating. Bad oysters are full of bacteria (*Vibrio Vulnificus* for those who care) . . ."

Before the invention of refrigeration, Dubow goes on to say, it was best not to eat oysters in months without an "r." He concludes, "Well, these days that is no longer a problem and one can eat oysters with impunity 12 months a year—but just be sure to smell them first."

I wonder if Charles Dubow is still alive. If so, it's not because of his knowledge of oysters. The stinky, shriveled oyster he describes is more likely one that has died in transit. In fact, *V. vulnificus* is an odorless, tasteless and completely undetectable marine organism that thrives in shallow coastal waters in warm weather, and it's present in both good oysters and ones that have gone "bad." Nor does *V. vulnificus* have anything to do with pollution or red tide, as many people seem to believe.

It may be safe to eat raw oysters all year long if you don't have a compromised immune system. The problem is, few people know exactly what shape their immune systems are in. And other factors can have an effect. For example, while stomach acids usually kill much of *V. vulnificus,* some common medications, such as antacids, allow the bacteria to multiply. Antacid users are now considered "at risk" and are urged to avoid raw oysters.

So where does an enlightened food lover draw the risk-and-reward line when it comes to raw Gulf Coast oysters?

On the two extremes, there are the oyster guys who want to sell you oysters all year round regardless of the increased bacterium levels and the fact that summer oysters don't taste very good. And then there's the Center for Science in the Public Interest, which insists that all Gulf Coast oysters should be sterilized. The truth probably lies somewhere in the middle. And this is the time of year to make up your mind. "We see a cluster of cases every year in late March and early April, when the water heats up again," says Gary Heideman, who mans the Seafood Safety Desk at the Texas Department of Health.

Heideman has some good advice on the subject of raw oysters. "Even though *Vibrio vulnificus* has no effect on most healthy people, there is always some risk," he says. "But you can improve your odds." Heideman suggests that if you want to eat raw oysters with a minimum of risk, then keep an eye on the water temperature. Little or no *V. vulnificus* is detectable when the water temperature at the point of collection is below 65 degrees. Generally, that happens between the beginning of December and the middle of March. (You can check the exact temperature in the marine forecast at www.weatherunderground.com.)

Based on Heideman's advice, I've decided to treat oysters as a seasonal food. I'll eat raw oysters in the winter, when the glycogen makes them sweet and the bacteria are scarce. When the water warms up in the spring and the bacteria start to swarm, I'll switch to cooked oysters. In the summer, after the oyster has spawned, it has little flavor or substance left. And that's also when the bacteria are the highest. So I might as well observe the "never eat oysters in months without an 'r' " rule.

But it's good to remember that even among the at-risk population, very few people die from eating oysters. Just to put the odds in perspective, Florida health officials and the USDA state: "In 1992, an estimated 71,000 Floridians with liver damage consumed raw oysters and nine died from *Vulnificus* infections. Four of the victims suffered from cirrhosis and a fifth had a history of heavy drinking."

The odds of dying from eating an oyster are around a million to one.

"People are constantly climbing a wall of worry," says Ray in exasperation as he eats another bowl of gumbo. "First they worried about pollution. Now that there's no pollution, they're worried about eating the fish."

It's three months later, and I've asked Ray and Ivic to meet me at Gilhooley's for lunch again. I want to ask them a few more questions about the future of the Texas oyster industry. It's the middle of March, and when I checked the water temperature this morning, it was hovering at 65 degrees. So I skip the raw oysters and order the oysters Gilhooley.

Before I dismiss the subject of pollution, I want to be sure I understand the condition of Galveston Bay. "When I arrived here in the 1970s, there weren't any crabs or fish north of Barbour's Cut," Ivic says. "It was dead water. Today there are crabs and fish all the way up the Ship Channel."

"There are fish and crabs all the way up to the port of Houston," says Ray.

"Would you eat fish that came from the Ship Channel?" I ask him.

"Sure, I would," he says, citing the Department of Health's fishing advisories that do allow limited consumption of fish from some parts of the Ship Channel despite continuing evidence of dioxin and PCBs.

"People would have you believe that Galveston Bay is a polluted cesspool," says Ray. "But that's a lot of nonsense."

"Galveston Bay is the cleanest it's been in 30 years," says Ivic.

He's right—and the reduced pollution is due to improved wastewater treatment facilities and changes in the rules regarding discharge, thanks in large part to the Clean Water Act of 1970. Scott Jones, water and sediment quality coordinator for the Galveston Bay Estuary Program, notes that dissolved oxygen rates, which were at unhealthy levels (below four milligrams per liter) back in 1969, had increased to healthy levels (six milligrams per liter) by the late '90s.

"We always fight the perception that the bay is polluted, but the reality is that the water quality overall is good," says Jones. "There are still problems with dioxin and PCBs in the Ship Channel, but there are people working on that, too."

"Galveston Bay covers 600 square miles," says Heideman. "About 10 percent of the upper bay is under fishing advisories." The culprit is mainly rainwater runoff contaminated with automotive fluids and excess fertilizer from residential areas. "There are problems," Heideman agrees, "but putting an area under a fishing advisory when you never even had fish there before is a good problem."

"The vast majority of Galveston Bay meets our criteria," he says. "And the oyster reefs are definitely improving. It's a very healthy situation."

No one is really sure exactly what happened to the native oyster reefs of Europe and the rest of the United States. Nor is there a consensus about what we should be doing to protect the oyster reefs of the Gulf Coast.

"People worry that dredging is damaging the reef," Ray says, "but it's not. It's creating new surfaces for oyster sprats to cling to." People worry that we're overfishing, he says, but that's not a problem either. There are a lot of oysters in areas that can't be harvested, and each oyster lays millions and millions of eggs, so there are always plenty of oyster larvae in the water. People worry about pollution, but that's under control, too.

"The real threat to the oyster reefs in Galveston Bay is the diversion of freshwater for flood-control projects," Ray says. "If you want to save the oysters, people in Houston need to stop building houses in the floodplain."

But Ray is the first to point out that the fate of the oyster reefs is mainly dependent upon nature itself. If we get three consecutive years of drought, the oysters will be wiped out no matter what we do. And if we get a couple more years of the same kind of weather we had this season, Galveston Bay could become one of the most famous oyster reefs in North America.

The Way of the Knife

by Chad Ward
from eGullet.com

A freelancer based in Wichita, Kansas, Chad Ward publishes work in magazines from *Aviation International News* to *Flatpicking Guitar*. He loves food and wine, but his greatest fascination is, not surprisingly, with kitchen gadgets and gear. Particularly knives—very sharp knives.

Knives are primal. Like fire. Knives have an exotic allure, a tidal pull that every cook feels. A chef's knife is an extension of his hands. It is his paintbrush, his assault weapon. A chef has got to have a good knife. And the ultimate in chef chic is a custom made knife.

We've all seen the standard heavy iron from Solingen. A big, meaty Henckels or Wusthof will get you a nod of respect, but only a small one. Too easy. Too pedestrian. Too Williams-Sonoma for a serious knife lover. An old school carbon Sabatler chef's knife will earn you extra points for style, or at least recognition that you're an independent thinker. Flash a Mac or Global chef's knife and you've announced to the world that you're progressive, high-tech and slick. Someone in the know.

But if you burn for a knife that makes your palms itch to hold it, a knife that makes you feel like you are conducting a symphony every time you dice an onion, you've got to go custom.

I went through four or five custom chef's knives before I found the right one. I've julienned with a shimmery art knife. I've sliced salmon with a hand forged Japanese gyotou. I've split chicken breasts with a tactical chef's knife armored in carbon fiber and titanium. I've butchered leg joints with a monstrous, cleaver-like knife more suited for bludgeoning oxen than fine dicing a brunoise. That one actually frightened my children. They wouldn't come in the kitchen when I was using it. If you ever need to gut a T-Rex, I've got the knife for you.

As excited as I was every time the Brown Truck of Joy brought me a new knife, I always found something wrong. They were too pretty, too thick, too uncomfortable, too . . . something. It was my fault. I was impatient and couldn't stand the lengthy wait to have a full-blown custom knife made to my specifications. At the time I couldn't have even said what those specifications should be. So I ordered knives that the makers had in stock. Custom, yes, but not *my* custom. Each knife was sold to another hopeful cook or knife lover within months of receiving it. I kept looking.

I got lucky. I opened the box from Steve Mullin at Pack River Knives and found a simple, functional knife—eight inches of *uber-steel* sweeping in a gentle arc from the oval cocobolo handle. It had heft, but not too much. It was blade-heavy, just the way I like it, with a wide blade for scooping. But it was thin—$\frac{3}{32}$" at the thickest point—for fine work. It had a simple flat grind with plunge lines that put a thicker chunk of spine between your thumb and fore-finger when held in a chef's pinch grip. The dropped blade style eliminated the blocky bolster that only gets in the way and makes sharpening a nightmare. Nice. And a bargain, too. I paid about the same for this knife as I would for any of the brand name chef's knives at the local kitchen store.

After using the knife for a month or so I began finding little flaws. The spine was sharp-edged and square. It cut into the base of my forefinger after dicing a couple dozen carrots. The edge, while sharp, wasn't as thin as I wanted. The back of the handle poked into the meaty part of my palm.

It was starting again, the dissatisfaction. But I wasn't going to let this one go. I liked this knife. I liked it a lot. I spent some time pondering all the chef's knives I'd owned, taking some-thing, some idea or design element, from each of them. I got out the power tools.

I'm not good with tools, so I started slowly, remembering every single one of my botched birdhouses, failed Boy Scout craft projects and home repair disasters. My wife hovered nearby with her finger poised over the speed dial button for the local emergency room. A gentle shoeshine motion with some high grit sandpaper broke the edges of the spine, sanding off the sharp corners. This was easy—certainly easier than my last plumbing adventure. Why hadn't I done this before? Courage increasing, I ditched the sandpaper and cranked up the Dremel tool rounding the spine into a smooth curve that wouldn't bite into my hand. I snapped a different sanding disc into the Dremel and reshaped the back of the handle to bevel the corners and grind off the poky parts. Anyone with even rudimentary skill would have sneered at my efforts, but in my own clumsy way I was *making* the knife I always thought I could buy.

Next I took on the edge. I started with a simple double bevel to thin the steel behind the edge. No power tools required, just a simple sharpening rig and some patience. That was better, but I was driven to experiment. I decided to see how far I could go, thinning it a little more each time, testing the knife in the kitchen for weeks before deciding if I could tease out just a little more thinness. I got it down to less than eight degrees per side before the knife became too fussy to work with. At that level of sharpness you don't even feel it when you cut yourself. You simply notice a sudden pool of blood on the cutting board. Slice yourself too deeply and there is only a buzzy tingle to let you know you've got potential nerve damage.

The pristine chef's knife delivered to my doorstep has been left behind in a pile of metal shavings and wood dust. The maker's stamp has nearly disappeared, which is fitting because this has become more my knife than his. I've hot-rodded the edge to glassy sharpness. I've molded the handle to my grip and worn it smooth with sweat. And, over time, I've molded my hand to the knife. I can feel through my knife. I'm intimately aware of the striations in a flank steak and know every pore in a potato. This is my custom knife, my paintbrush. Bring me an onion and I feel like Rembrandt.

It is not pretty. My knife has all the sex appeal of a bowling shoe. The acid from dozens of tomatoes and hundreds of onions has stained the battle-scarred blade. A friend broke the tip, not understanding that my knife, for all its industrial menace, is a delicate thing. It is not pretty, but it is *mine*. Even when I'm not cooking, I take it out just to feel it in my hands, thumb the brutal edge and grin with manic glee.

Tuscany's Soul Food

by Frances Mayes
from *Town & Country Travel*

Perhaps best known for *Under the Tuscan Sun*, Frances Mayes knows her adopted Tuscany intimately, yet never loses sight of what makes it most charming to outsiders. Which, of course, has to include the local *cucina rustica* and its soul-satisfying cornerstone, pasta.

My husband, Ed, has the ambition to try every pasta in Italy. Our local mom-and-pop-sized grocery store in Cortona, the Tuscan hill town where we have lived for fourteen years, sells fifty-odd shapes of dried pasta. The Bottega della Pasta Fresca, just inside the Porta Colonia, turns out the fresh version in wheels and Mexican hats and pillows and snail shells. The varieties of pasta in all of Italy must be impossible to count.

Everywhere we go we collect a new *orecchiette,* the ear-shaped pasta that is so delicious with broccoli florets; or *conchiglioni,* giant conch shells for stuffing; or *strozzapreti,* "priest stranglers," strands once fed to priests at Sunday dinner so they'd be too full to eat much of the expensive meat served after the pasta course.

We like the fanciful figurative language of pasta. There's a pleasure in buying something with a name that makes you smile— dinner is already getting off to a good start. *Farfalle,* "butterflies," remind us of our garden, swarming with white and purple wings in summer. The sounds in *fusilli* twist like the curly pasta itself. *Mezze maniche,* "half sleeves," look exactly like sections of a sleeve for a fat little arm. Hail is much feared locally because it can destroy the olive flowers at a critical moment; even so, a Tuscan pasta has been christened *grandinine,* "tiny hail balls." *Occhidi pernice,* the miniature rings used in soups, do resemble the eyes of a partridge. Lilies, stars, cocks' combs, radiators, elbows—all the good nouns of everyday life seem to have adhered to pasta.

Despite our fascination with names and shapes, Ed's progress toward eating all the pastas in Italy is distinctly hampered. After scanning a trattoria menu, he often says, as though it were a discovery, "I think I'll have the *pici.*" And I usually respond, "Yes, that sounds good."

True Tuscan soul food, *pici* is the most robust of the region's pastas. Oddly, no one seems to know the meaning of the word, though the De Mauro unabridged dictionary says it came into the language in 1891. I think that in these hills *pici* has been around for eons, as endemic as gnarly olive roots. Especially in Tuscany's Siena and Arezzo provinces, *pici* appears on almost every menu.

In correct Italian, one says "PEE-chee," but our local dialect slushes the "ch" sound into "sh." Around Cortona, you hear "PEE-shee," just as you hear "cap-pu-SHEE-no." *Pici,* a plural, has no singular in the dictionary, though people in these parts offer a *picio* to a baby or pick up a dropped one from the floor. Usually not included in cookbooks or seen on American menus, *pici* is the pasta nearest the Tuscan heart. The only thing that comes close is the simple soup *tortellini in brodo.* Every Christmas we've spent at our neighbor's bountiful table, we've had Fiorella's herbed-chicken *tortelloni*—double the size of *tortellini,* those little meat- or cheese-stuffed nubbins of pasta whose shape was inspired by the navel of Venus—floating in the hearty broth of an old hen. It's a dish that warms us all.

Pici is chewy and substantial. Size and length vary, but a hand-made strand is at least a foot long and about as thick as spaghetti enlarged three times. I've seen it almost pencil-thick. Most dried *pici,* available at every *gastronomia,* is quite scrawny by local standards, and although it can be tasty, fresh is definitely better. A good bowl of it brings you to the ample bosom of the signora who devised fabulous things to eat when the larder was almost bare. *Cucina povera,* the "poor kitchen," is the source of *pici,* as it is of countless other inventions in the repertoire of Italian cuisine. I imagine that the first *pici* maker had field-workers to feed at the end of winter, when the prosciutto and salami were gone. The thickness of this pasta makes it seem almost like a meat. It stokes the energy of wheat gatherers and olive pickers, as well as those of us now climbing steep streets to see a painting by Signorelli.

Ed and I visit Maria and Vitaliano's fresh pasta shop early on Liberation Day, Italy's memorial to the end of World War II, and look in the kitchen, where Maria is lifting off the long ropes of pasta as they extrude from the machine. A small line has formed at the counter. "We've sold almost 400 pounds of *pici* this morning," Vitaliano tells us. We order a quarter of a pound, plus a few *ravioli* stuffed with borage. Later we see him in his white coat crossing the piazza, tray aloft, making his deliveries to the trattorias for the *pranzo* rush—a scene from a Balthus painting, a visitor might observe, but to us it's just *normale*. By one o'clock, the rich aromas of chefs' special sauces are drifting from the doorways, and we head for Santino Cenci's place, suddenly starving.

Cortona's Trattoria Toscana, only three years old, has become one of our favorites. Santino's son, Massimo, and daughter, Sara, juggle the tables while papa mans the kitchen. Every day he offers a homey specialty, such as veal shank, beef stew or his version of *polpettone,* meat loaf, which banishes forever my old dorm-food association with the dish. He makes terrific *pici* with a classic duck sauce. He also makes a leek sauce, which I've never seen elsewhere.

Santino always comes out to say hello and to make sure that everyone is eating-well. "Do Americans order *pici*?" I ask him.

"Yes—always with the duck sauce. There's not a *picio* left on the plate." Ah, there's the singular again, which doesn't legally exist.

My favorite *pici* sauce here is the basic *contadina* (peasant-style) tomato sauce that has spent the afternoon on the back burner. During hunting season, Ed prefers hare or boar sauce. Obviously, the local wines go well with *pici*. Cortona's hills have been attracting a lot of attention among wine-makers recently. Of course, this area always had wine—from someone's Uncle Anselmo's to the vintages of the prestigious vineyards Avignonesi and Poliziano, between here and Montepulciano. Now we have several wines with the official DOC classification. Cortona's excellent Enoteca Molesini offers a well-curated selection of bottles from all over Italy. Marco

Molesini, the young owner, constantly tempts us and our guests to ship cases of Brunello and Vino Nobile back to America.

With my *pici* on Liberation Day, however, I tell Massimo I don't want any wine. Only water. I have work to do. He rolls his eyes and throws up his hands. In a few minutes he brings over two glasses of wine anyway, and we drink them.

Just down the street, our favorite late-night trattoria, Taverna Pane e Vino, serves *pici alle molliche,* also a simple recipe: anchovies, bread crumbs and a hint of hot peppers. Ed is wild for that. Owned by Debora and Arnaldo Rossi, a young couple expecting their first baby, Pane e Vino attracts a youthful clientele, drawn by the simple food and the inspired wine list. With this *pici* we drink a Tenuta Sette Ponti Crognolo, from a rising-star vineyard in Tuscany's rural Val d'Arno area, north of Arezzo. Ed says, "Why don't we start making *pici*?" He already makes the flat, wide *pappardelle* he likes with wild boar sauce, and flat sheets for *lasagne* and *cannelloni*. As we leave, he takes out his phone. "Let's call Silvia."

Our friends Silvia and Riccardo Baracchi own the pastoral dream of a hotel Il Falconiere, just outside Cortona. Riccardo inherited the property, and together they have transformed the 17th-century villa and lemon house. Silvia is one of the most brilliant chefs in Tuscany. I was flattered that she named her culinary school, Cooking Under the Tuscan Sun, after my first memoir. She's the only chef I know who manages to make *pici* light, with her sauce of cherry tomatoes, fava beans and a few dabs of pesto thinned with extra olive oil. A beauty who dazzles with a sense of style that permeates every aspect of her life, Silvia comes from a local family of women who can flat-out cook. Her mother owns La Locanda del Molino, a small inn on a stream, with a cozy restaurant where the tablecloths are angled layers of checked fabrics in cheerful colors. Her aunt owns Azienda Fontelunga, a complex of farmhouses for rent, with dinner served in her home; needless to say, *pici* is on the menu, sometimes with goose sauce, along with *farro* (spelt) soup, veal roasts and cheeses from a local shepherd.

"Will you teach us to make *pici*?" I ask Silvia. Before we can set a date, Riccardo is on the line, too, planning a feast after our lesson.

"Bring friends," he insists. "We'll have three kinds of *pici,* then a leg of lamb roasted in a crust."

A serene kitchen is a good sign of a fine meal to come. At Il Falconiere, the kitchen is blue-and-white tile, a wall of copper pots and gleaming counters brightened with baskets of vegetables. *Pici,* I soon learn, is easy to make. One of Silvia's assistants, Nulvia, forms the flour into a volcano shape, works an egg into the well, adds enough water to make the dough pliable but not sticky, then mounds it into a dome and covers it with a towel. This is the part of pasta—and bread—making that I love. There, done: the soft loaf resting under a white towel.

We move to the stove. The kitchen fills with robust aromas of garlic; duck pieces cooking with celery, carrots and onions; and handfuls of basil torn into a pot of quartered cherry tomatoes. Three sauces going at once. For the *pici all'aglione,* with garlic, toasted bread crumbs and, of course, a liberal amount of olive oil, Silvia simmers chopped garlic in milk, then throws away the milk. The bread crumbs she stirs into the garlic are quite fine. When she prepares the *pici* with tomatoes, fava beans and pecorino, I learn a trick. "The cheese is stirred into the just-drained pasta before the sauce is added," Silvia explains. "This makes the cheese cling to the pasta instead of melting into the sauce."

Once the pasta has rested, Nulvia cuts a slice from the loaf and quickly rolls it out. She then cuts the flattened circle into strands with a knife. This is where the fun begins. She and Silvia show us how to roll each piece with our hands until it is a yard long. Nulvia works on the board, pulling to lengthen as she rolls. Silvia prefers to roll in the air, letting gravity extend the length. Memories of Play-Doh! Ed and I have a good time looping the strands onto a tray, seeing how their *pici* has achieved more uniformity than ours. The result is a distinctly artisanal pasta with a bonus: the excitement of actually creating something previously produced only by the hands (or machines) of others. We're big proponents of the Slow Food movement. Making *pici* by hand is so nicely slow. The motion is meditative, and the result delicious.

Dinner in Il Falconiere's garden after our lesson lasts five hours. Iron arches twined with roses frame night views of the valley as the musical sound of water falling into a deep cistern floats up from the end of the garden. Each of the three pasta dishes is served separately, with a wine to match. With the lightest *pici,* the one with tomatoes and fava beans, we drink a Capannelle Chardonnay. With the garlic *pici*—my favorite of the day—we have a red wine from the coastal Maremma area of Tuscany, a Morellino di Scansano. With the duck-sauced *pici,* Riccardo pours one of his own estate wines, a 2001 Rosso Smeriglio Baracchi. The sauce is *magnifico.* After the duck was sautéed with the vegetables, ground veal and pork were added with fresh tomato sauce. The simmered result is incomparably rich and savory. I resolve to take the time to peel my tomatoes this summer.

As promised, the dinner proceeds to three-month-old lamb, butterflied and spread with herbs, then wrapped in bread dough and baked. To accompany this piece de resistance, Riccardo honors us with the unveiling of his big-lipped, mellow-voiced 2001 Baracchi Ardito. This is an exciting moment. We were there when he planted the vines, when the grapes were picked and when the juice went into barrels. Now the wine pours. We rejoice that such a blissful thing came from the hills spreading out below us, then rising to the noble profile of Cortona in the distance.

Candyfreak

by Steve Almond
from *Candyfreak*

Granted, Steve Almond (yes, that's his real name) has a thing about candy. But what makes this book a compelling read is not just the hysterically funny riffs, it's also the depth of his investigation into the science and commerce of candy bars.

THERE ARE MEN UPON THIS EARTH
THAT READ LIKE GODS

A friend of mine brought me two candy bars that I had never seen before. They were called Five Star Bars and the reason I had never seen them before is because they are sold primarily at Bread & Circus, an upscale grocery chain (that is, one I do not frequent). The bars were slightly larger than snack size, but they had a queer and pleasing heft. Indeed, they weighed nearly as much as a full-size Snickers. I tend to steer away from gourmet candy—at least from the *purchase* of gourmet candy—but here they were, gifts, and didn't they look pretty? Yes, they looked so pretty in their embossed wrappers that I was actually a little frightened to open them.

My friend had no such compunction. She unwrapped the Caramel Bar and took a bite. It was clear, simply from the way her mouth addressed the bar, that we were dealing with a different grade of freak. Her bite was smooth and concerted—there was an obvious density at play here—though interrupted by two muted snaps, both of which caused her a quarter-moment of anguish, followed by a twinge of delight, registered as a flushing upon her cheeks. She moaned. It was a lovely thing to hear.

268 | Best Food Writing 2004

This reaction was, in my view, restrained. I had never tasted anything like the Five Star. Fancy chocolates, truffles and so forth, are one thing. But this was a fancy candy *bar,* a complex and nuanced marriage of ingredients. There was caramel, obviously, but also roasted almonds and nuggets of dark chocolate. It was draped in a thin layer of milk chocolate. The interplay of tastes and textures was remarkable: the teeth broke through the milky chocolate shell, sailed through the mild caramel, only to encounter the smoky crunch of the almonds, and finally, the rich tumescence of the dark chocolate. You almost never see milk and dark chocolate commingled, but the effect in this bar was striking: The sweetness of the milk chocolate rushed across the tongue, played against the musky crunch of the nut, then faded. The bite finished with an intense burst of dark chocolate, softened by the buttery dissolution of caramel. What I mean here: there was a temporal aspect to the bar, a sense of evanescence and persistence. Because of the random placement of the almonds and dark chocolate, each bite offered a distinct combination. It was like eating several different bars at once.

The Hazelnut Bar was so: milk chocolate around a hazelnut paste (by which I really mean a rich hazelnut mousse) interspersed with crushed hazelnuts. If the bar had stopped here, well, as we Jews say: *Dianu.* It would have been enough. But there was something else going on with the bar, an ineluctable grittiness that conveyed a tang of vanilla.

"What is that?" I said. "It's like, what, a cookie?"

"More granular," my friend said. "Like tiny planes of sugar."

Yes, that was it. Planes. The geometric sort. Little vanilla-infused planes.

It will go without saying that I broke my long-standing boycott of gourmet groceries in order to seek out additional Five Star Bars. The ingredient list for the Five Star Peanut Bar was simple enough: peanuts, peanut butter, and crisped rice, enrobed in milk chocolate. But the taste was richer, more chocolaty, than expected. And for good reason: the peanut butter contained chunks of white chocolate. (The author is at a loss to explain how the otherwise loathsome white chocolate works in this confection, but it does.) The net effect was a bar at once crunchy and dense, a Whatchamacallit squared or, perhaps, cubed.

But it was the Hazelnut Bar that tweaked my heart. And specifically, that mysterious texture. So I tracked down the manufacturer, Lake Champlain Chocolates, and called their headquarters in Burlington, Vermont, and spoke to their PR guy, Chris Middings. He knew exactly what I was talking about. ("That very fine crunchiness, yes, absolutely.") But he didn't know what accounted for it. He was elaborately apologetic for this, explaining that he'd just taken the job, and promised to e-mail me an answer.

A day later I received a brief note: "The ingredient in question is called feuilletine. It's actually a crushed pastry, frequently used in European candies." Feuilletine is best known to Americans in its uncrushed form, those thin, pie slice-shaped cookies that are placed in ice cream sundaes.

Chris also invited me to visit the factory any time I was in the area. "You can talk to Dave Bolton," he said. "Our chocolate engineer."

I suppose I was aware, in an abstract way, that there were men and women upon this earth who served in this capacity, as *chocolate engineers*. In the same way that I was aware that there are job titles out there such as bacon taster and sex surrogate, which is to say, job titles that made me want to weep over my own appointed lot in life. But I had never considered the prospect of visiting a chocolate engineer. I could think of nothing else for days.

I arrived at the factory at nine in the morning, alongside a bus full of seniors from Mount Kisco, New York. Chris appeared and led me to a small room tucked away in the back of the factory. This was Dave Bolton's lab. It looked very much like your basic junior high science lab, except that the counters were littered with bags of recent work product—chocolate-covered toffees and cocoa nibs—along with jugs of flavoring and a tiny panning machine that resembled a space helmet.

Dave himself was hunched over a counter, scrutinizing what looked like an overgrown Junior Mint. He looked up when we came in and, almost reflexively, held the piece out to me. The dark chocolate shell gave way to an intense burst of sweet, chewy fruit. The texture was soft enough to yield to the teeth, yet firm enough to absorb the musky undertones of the chocolate.

"What you're eating," Dave said, "is a dried cherry, infused with raspberry and covered in a Select Origin 75 percent dark chocolate." He held out the bag. "Have another."

Here is what I wanted to say to Dave Bolton at that precise moment: *Take me home and love me long time, GI.*

"This is what I do back here," he explained. "Sales comes to me and says: 'Dave: think cherries.' I research what's out there on the market already and what ingredients are available. The whole idea with this piece was to get away from canned cherries, but to retain an intense cherry flavor. Then, of course, I had to find a chocolate with high fruit overtones, because I wanted the marriage of a fruity chocolate to a piece of fruit."

Dave had a neatly trimmed beard and a beaked nose and powerful, low-hanging arms that swung as he trudged about his lab. He looked like a rabbi. Or a navy cook. I couldn't decide. "People tend to think of chocolate in simplistic terms," he said. "But there's a tremendous variation based on where it's grown." He turned and grabbed a few boxes from the shelf behind him. These were his Select Origin chocolates, each from a different part of the world. They came in disks about the size of dimes. Dave's favorite, at the moment, was Tanzania. He was also a big fan of Cuba. "My first question, when I come up with a new piece, is always: What sort of chocolate makes the most sense?" He reached for the Santo Domingo and popped a few pieces into his mouth. "This has such an intense, smoky flavor. It would be best for a pastry. And it would be wonderful with figs or a fruit like that. A brown fruit."

It was now clear I was in the presence of freak genius.

FEUILLETINE, REVEALED

Dave came to Lake Champlain fifteen years ago. At the time, he signed on as a part-time truffle maker to help out his friend, owner Jim Lampman, during the Christmas rush. But he fell in love with the manufacturing process. As the business grew, he agreed to become chief of new product development. This, of course, included the Five Star Bars, which have become the company's signature product line.

"Those are all recipes we created," Dave said. "The Caramel Bar took us two years to figure out how to produce. Now, the Fruit and Nut Bar came much faster. I know it sounds silly, but I literally dreamed that candy bar. I dreamed of putting those precise ingredients together and came into the lab and made the bar in one or two tries. I'd read about Janduja chocolate, which is a very soft chocolate, the 'chocolate of love' according to the Italians. I figured it would go well with dried fruit and nuts."

When I told Dave that I'd never tried the Fruit and Nut Bar, he looked stricken and sent Chris to fetch one. With a delicacy any mohel would envy, he sliced the bar into thin slabs. The chocolate had a creaminess I associated with ganache, against which rose the chewier textures of raisins and pecans.

"The bar has a great finish," Dave noted, "because the nuts and fruit last a little longer than the chocolate. They clean the palate."

"What about the Hazelnut Bar?" I said.

Hazelnut, it turned out, had been especially tricky to devise. Dave spent months attempting to find the perfect ratio of feuilletine to chocolate. This was simple enough for a small batch. But somehow, moving to a large batch, there'd be too much chocolate, not enough crunch, or the other way around, and he'd have to start from scratch again. By the end, he was up to 50 percent feuilletine by volume, about 15 to 18 percent by weight. "This process is literally what we've built the company on," Dave said, "finding the proper proportion of flavors and textures."

He, too, had a healthy fascination with feuilletine. The Europeans, he informed me, call it a cereal, though it's really just the scrap from a patisserie cookie. It had become so popular as an ingredient that it was now mass produced. I imagined a whole army of men in puffy white hats and sterilized sneakers stomping on a sea of helpless patisseries and yelling curses in French, a sort of anger management thing for pastry chefs. Dave pulled a box from the shelf and pulled back the flap. I was alarmed to discover that feuilletine looked a lot like fish food. (In the interests of fairness, I should mention that Lindt makes a spectacular dark chocolate bar filled with feuilletine and hazelnut cream, which, thank God, is virtually impossible to find in this country, and which I know about only because my father/enabler recently sent me a bar from Switzerland.)

"Let me tell you a story," Dave said. "I was on a plane flying back from Baltimore and the guy next to me pulled out a Five Star

Peanut Bar and put it down on the tray table thing and cut it in half and said: 'Would you like to try the best piece of candy you've ever eaten?' I just looked at the guy and said: 'I *invented* that bar.' "

This was the glory of his job. But Dave assured me there was a fair bit of grunt work, as well. A good example: the raspberry truffle debacle. A few years ago, he used a raspberry filling that consisted of canned raspberries cooked in vodka and strained through cheesecloth. Then Lake Champlain decided to get certified as kosher and the rabbi wouldn't accept that process because of the alcohol. Dave had to invent a filling similar enough that the public wouldn't know he'd modified the recipe. This took well over a year of trial and error. Lampman would walk by his lab and snarl, "Where's that raspberry truffle?" He finally came up with a combination of all-natural raspberry concentrate and raspberry jam.

The rabbis weren't the only ones Dave had to please. Lake Champlain also had a group of tasters who gathered twice a year to sample new products. Dave had created a whole series of creams recently. Only one made it to market. "It can be pretty unnerving," he said. "I'll present a piece I think is marvelous and they'll say, 'This is crap!' I had a lemon-ginger cream I was pretty excited about, but they said it was too over-the-top. I have to keep my ego out of it."

Naturally, I asked Dave what cream got approved.

Mango, he told me. He suggested we go try one. This meant heading out to the production floor, which was just fine with me. Every candy bar factory smells like chocolate. But the scent at Lake Champlain was intoxicating. This was because they used a chocolate made for them by a Belgian company, one that I would grade as—to use the technical term—*totally ass-kicking*. The factory was impeccably clean. It was not only the cleanest factory I'd ever visited, it may have been the cleanest *room* I'd ever visited. A few of the twisting, overhead pipes had been painted in bright primary colors, which lent the operation a Yellow Submarineish feel.

We arrived just as the chilled hazelnut bars were being popped from their molds and lined up on a conveyor belt to be run through the enrober. A few feet away, a machine shaped like a pommel horse was spinning a series of specially designed molds to create hollowed-out Santas. Nor were these your average Santas: they had detailed beards and white chocolate trim on their coats and hats, which had been painted into the molds. Round and round they spun, with slightly dazed expressions.

Dave hurried past the enrober to a sleek, new machine. It featured a set of pistons, which shot various liquid fillings into molds of chocolate with a sharp pop. They were still figuring out what products could be made with the machine. They could do inclusions, anything that wouldn't jam up in the pistons. But the viscosity had to be just right. Lake Champlain had gotten big enough, as a company, that Dave now had to worry about whether they could mass-produce a piece. "Years ago," he said, "all I had to do was figure out the flavor. Now we're into flavor and technology." Dave gazed at the machine, a little morosely. The machine hissed and popped.

"Mango cream," I said.

"Right," said Dave.

We spent the next few minutes trying to locate a mango cream. Dave kept opening all these hidden doors. There were scraps of chocolate everywhere, little mutant truffles and Five Star Bars that had failed to pass muster, which I wanted very badly to snatch and stick in one of my pockets, as I feared otherwise they would be thrown away. Chris assured me he was having a selection of seconds put together for me.

The mango cream proved to be a milk chocolate piece, slightly larger than a gum ball, filled with a sweet, yellowish cream. "I would have liked a thicker center," Dave muttered. "But there were viscosity issues."

He made his way over to a large plastic bucket, which was filled with a moist white substance. "Smell," he said.

The aroma of coconut was overpowering. It was like I'd stuck my head inside a giant Thai food sauna.

"You know we'd like to have a fifth Five Star Bar," he said. "So I've been playing around with the idea of a Coconut Bar."

I told Dave, as politely as I could, that I thought this was a *very* bad idea, not least of all because of the creepy dead-skin texture of shredded coconut.

He nodded. "Try a little bit of this." To my shock, the substance had all the tropical wallop of coconut but a mouthfeel that was smooth and buttery.

Dave had found a company to manufacture this ingredient for him, all natural and kosher for Passover. He was well into considering the elements that might make up the rest of the bar: chocolate chips, dried fruit, possibly the cherries he'd been working with, and a dark chocolate, to balance the sweetness of the coconut. He was not about to introduce a fifth Five Star Bar unless it stood up to the other four. He was adamant about this point and I did not, for a moment, doubt him.

We headed back to the quiet of the lab. Dave plainly felt most comfortable here, amid his various ingredients, where he was free to improvise, to mix and melt and create. He had me sample some of his recent creations, including a dark chocolate-covered almond which tasted (curiously enough) a lot like the chocolate-covered graham crackers I had worshipped as a kid.

I confessed that I'd sort of hoped the fifth Five Star Bar would showcase coffee. Dave told me that he'd been working on a bar infused with coffee. He'd already tried sixteen or seventeen different extracts, none of which passed muster. Not long ago, Lampman had come to him with what he described as the perfect coffee flavor. He and Dave then set about trying to figure out how this extract had been made. Lampman felt certain that cocoa butter was somehow involved. "So what we did," Dave said, "was we got some good French roast and brewed it in cocoa butter and let it steep and strained it out and there it was. The exact same product. A lot of my knowledge has come that way: eating something and then trying to figure out what it is I'm eating."

"Do you ever get sick of chocolate?" I asked.

"Sure," Dave said. "Sometimes after I leave here I've got to go eat a head of cauliflower. Then again, I get to eat some of the best chocolate in the world. And I'm a chocolate snob, personally. I can't even eat a Hershey's bar. It's got maybe 22 percent chocolate liqueur, and that sour milk flavor. I mean, it's like baby vomit to me." It turned out that Dave had been born in England. His parents had immigrated to America, but much of his family had stayed in England, and he'd grown up eating European chocolate.

I had now taken two hours of Dave's time, and it was clear he had work to do. The idea of leaving his lab, however, made me a little panicky. I wanted to stay. I wanted, in some sense, never to leave. It occurred to me that Dave might need an apprentice. He indicated that he was not really in the market for an apprentice. He did promise to put in a good word for me when it came time to select a new member for the tasting panel.

This was certainly a kind gesture. But what I really wanted was this: for Lake Champlain—with its exquisite attention to intricacies of flavor and texture—to open a can of whoopass on the mainstream candy market. I asked Dave, as a kind of desperate parting shot, if this could ever happen. He shook his head. The company was toying with the idea of introducing a product in the impulse buy market, like the Ferrero Rocher, a German gourmet candy that had managed to fight its way onto the grocery racks. But that was as far as they could go.

So I headed out of the lab feeling a bit deflated. Most Americans, I knew, would never taste the glories of the Five Star Bar. They would continue to chomp through their PayDays and Fast Breaks, unaware of these deeper pleasures. A second tour group of seniors, this one from Maine, was milling about the retail store at the front of the factory, fretting over prices. This was certainly a bummer. But then, before I could launch into one of my self-thwarting diatribes, Chris the PR guy appeared and handed me a large bag of seconds—which included a raft of mango creams—and I felt much better.

Someone's in the Kitchen

Aboard Spaceship Adria

by Anthony Bourdain

from *Food Arts*

> Or, in other words, That *Kitchen Confidential* Guy meets The Spanish Chef Who Cooks With Foam. Except that Tony Bourdain actually is a worthy reporter, and this deft profile proves that Adria is no mere novelty act.

I t's the most magnificent book you can find," says Eric Ripert (Le Bernardin, NYC). He's talking about Spanish chef Ferran Adrià's mammoth cookbook, *El Bulli 1998–2002,* the first of a three volume set that tracks backward the development of recipes and procedures at the Michelin three-star restaurant in the Mediterranean beachside village of Cala Montjoi outside Roses, close to 100 miles north of Barcelona. Still available only in Spanish and Catalan, costing about 175 euros and weighing in at nearly 10 pounds, including an accompanying guidebook and CD-ROM, the tome looms more like the mysterious black monolith in the film *2001: A Space Odyssey* than a conventional cookbook. It's also the most talked about, sought after, wildly impressive, and imposingly intimidating collectible in the world of professional chefs and cookbook wonks. If you're a hotshot chef, even if you can't read it, every minute without it is misery.

Science fiction and space travel metaphors come up frequently when chefs discuss the book. "There's no cookbook like it. I love the fact that it's like Star Wars," says Wylie Dufresne, an uabashed Adrià acolyte whose menu at WD-50, his new Manhattan restaurant, was unapologetically created under the influence of an Adrià high. "He's going *backward*! [The next volume will cover the years 1993 to 1997.] We're all looking at Spain. And Adrià is ground zero."

For years now, I've been hearing from chef friends about their experiences at El Bulli. Some, like Tetsuya Wakuda (Tetsuya, Sydney, Australia), had life-changing experiences there. Wakuda immediately set about designing an upstairs laboratory/workshop along the lines of Adrià's El Taller in Barcelona. Others, like Scott Bryan (Veritas, NYC), were dazzled but confused by their meal. "I ate *seawater sorbet!*" Bryan gasps.

I'd been gaping with a mixture of fear and longing at The Book for some months when I finally decided that I had to cross the chasm in my culinary education. There were things I needed to know. It was time to investigate the matter.

Adrià sits at a small table in the closet-sized back room of Jamonisimo, an Ibérico ham shop in Barcelona. He's nearly vibrating with enthusiasm as he holds a thin slice of Salamanca ham in his hands and rubs it slowly on his lips. At exactly blood temperature, the wide layer of white fat around the lean meat turns translucent, then melts to liquid. "See! See!" he exclaims. We had already polished off a bottle of *cava,* several glasses of Sherry, a plate of tiny, unbelievably good tinned Galician clams, some buttery, also straight-from-the-can, sushi-quality tuna from the Basque country, some anchovies, and numerous slices of hand-cut Extremadura and Salamanca ham. The man generally thought of as the most innovative and influential chef in the world isn't turning out to be the detached, clinical, mad scientist I'd expected. This guy likes food. He likes to eat. And he neatly links the "scientific" approach of some of his cooking to simple pleasure.

"What's wrong with science?" Adrià asks. "What's wrong with transforming food?" He holds up another slice of ham between his fingers. "The making of ham is a process; you transform pork. Ibérico ham is better than pork. Good Sherry is better than the grapes it's made from."

At El Taller, metal shutters roll up at the touch of a button to unveil an otherworldly display of gadgets and utensils. A worktable slides back to uncover an induction stovetop. Cabinets open, revealing an impressive hyperorganized array of backlit ingredients, all in identical clear glass jars. The place looks more like Dr. No's sanctum sanctorum than a kitchen. But the subject here is always food.

"Which is better?" asks Adrià, holding up a small, lovely looking pear. "A pear? Or a white truffle? Is a white truffle better because it's more expensive? Because it's rare?" He doesn't know, he confesses. But he wants to find out.

El Taller is where questions are posed about the physical properties of food—"Can we do this? Can we do that? Can we make a caramel that doesn't break down in humid conditions? Can we make a cappuccino froth that tastes of the essence of carrot? Can we make a hot jellied consommé?" At El Taller, Adrià conducts inquiries into the fundamental nature of cuisine and gastronomy. For six months a year, Adrià closes his restaurant and, along with his brother, Albert, El Bulli's pastry chef; Pere Castells, a chemist; Luki Huber, an industrial designer; and Oriol Castro, El Bulli's chef de cuisine, he plays with food, scrupulously documenting every permutation. And the questions—some of which are clearly threatening, even heretical to the gastronomic status quo—never stop: What is a meal? What is dinner? What is a chef?

As I watch, Adrià and his crew are wondering whether a thick slab of ripe peach could be caramelized so that it mimics the appearance and consistency of pan-seared foie gras. (Apparently, yes.) Could a fresh anchovy be cooked, yet still appear raw, with its skin looking as sleek and glistening as it does in the ocean? (Seems like it.) Could one make "caviar" from fresh mango purée? (Again, yes.) Of five or six experiments—each conducted in various ways—during the course of the day, generally positive results are recorded.

"If I can come up with two or three important ideas a year, that's a very good year," says Adrià. Many of you have no doubt seen the ripple effects of some earlier successfully executed ideas on menus near you: foam (which he no longer makes), hot jellied consommé, pasta made from squid, jellied cheese, and frozen foie gras "powder." Say what you will about him, but many of the same chefs who sneer at Adrià shamelessly crib his ideas, peeling off the more applicable concepts to apply to their more conventional menus.

At his invitation, I join Adrià for dinner in El Bulli's kitchen, where I bear witness to, by turns, a shattering, wondrous, confusing, delightful, strangely comforting, constantly surprising, and always marvelous meal—30 dishes long, a four hour culinary performance. The kitchen itself defies convention—cool, quiet, elegant, and modern, with large picture windows and works of sculpture placed throughout. A crew of 35 to 55 cooks serves one seating per night to an equal number of customers. It's a serious, relatively serene—even clinical—environment, light-years away from the fiery mosh pits and sweaty submarine-like spaces most cooks inhabit.

The chef and I dine at a plain, white-covered table devoid of elaborate setups or floral arrangements. Whether the procession that follows is more of an experience and less of a dinner, or vice versa, will probably take me the rest of my life to figure out. The evening is a long gastro-thriller, ranging from the farthest reaches of chemistry class—a single raw egg yolk shellacked in caramel and encased in gold leaf—to the stunningly simple—two pristine prawns cooked in their own juices. Adrià, who claims he can tell everything important about a person by watching him eat, sets the pace, eating every course along with me (and in some cases ahead of me), explaining which striking looking object to eat first, which second, and in what manner each should be consumed. "Eat in one bite! Quickly!" he commands. Pace and rhythm are important, he insists. "One mustn't eat too slowly or one gets sluggish and tired."

Snacks arrive first: green "pine frappé cocktail," artichoke crisps, and an austere black plate with toasts, sea salt, finely chopped peanuts, and a white toothpaste tube of peanut butter hit the table at the same time as "raspberry lily pads," hazelnut in "textures," lemon tempura with licorice, rhubarb with black pepper, a terrifically tasty row of salty sea cucumber "cracklings" arranged on a tiny black rack, and large puffs of pork cracklings with a yogurt dipping sauce.

"Jamón de toro" comes next. A pun on the word toro (bull), it's fatty tuna belly cured like Ibérico ham, served with silver pincers that can pick up the ethereally thin slices without bunching or tearing them. The pincers look (intentionally) like a surgical implement.

Adrià studies me as I eat each course, his face lighting up again and again as my expression registers surprise. "Cherries with ham" looks like cherries covered with fondant but, in fact, is cherries glazed entirely in ham fat. A tiny "Parmesan ice cream sandwich" is an extreme example of a play on comfort food—a salty/sweet remembrance of a childhood that never happened—one of many thoroughly delicious practical jokes. Apple "caviar"—tiny globules of unearthly apple essence—is served in a faux Petrossian tin. Two courses of crêpes—one made with chicken skin, the other made, improbably, entirely of milk—are a pleasure. Pea "ravioli" is a seemingly impossible concoction in which the bright green liquid essence of baby peas is wrapped only in itself, with no pasta or outer shell to contain it, a ravioli filling miraculously suspended in space. Carrot "air" is an intensely flavored, truly lighter-than-air froth of carrot and tangerine served in a cut-glass bowl.

The inconceivable sounding iced "powder" of foie gras with foie gras consommé is one of those revelatory concepts for which Adrià is famous—a hot, perfectly clear consommé of foie gras sharing a bowl with a just-fallen snow of foie gras "powder." Instructed to eat from one side of the dish, then the other, alternating between hot and cold, I'm awestruck by the fact that the frozen, finely ground "powder" somehow maintains its structural integrity in a bowl of hot broth. It defies physics. And it tastes as good as anything else cooked anywhere else—a direct rebuke to centuries of classical cooking. This dish alone is the strongest argument for Adrià's ethos. "Every night is like opening night," he says. "It has to be magic."

"Oysters with oysters and yogurt, rolled with macadamia nuts" is another astonishing success: two perfect oysters in an essence of liquefied oysters, a dot of lemon relish, and then a macadamia/yogurt cream. When eaten precisely in sequence, the components take my tongue on a wild yet strangely familiar ride around the world—and then right back to my very first oyster. A shimmering, clear globe of raw tuna marrow topped with a few beads of caviar is so good that Adrià says he won't serve it to his Japanese customers because "if the Japanese find out about this, the price for tuna bones will go up!" He has a point. The otherworldly, substance tastes like top quality Edo style sushi—from another planet. Like nearly everything else I eat, it has a carefully calibrated progression of clean, precise flavors and a pleasurable aftertaste that doesn't intrude on the course to follow.

Cuttlefish/coconut "ravioli" are two tight pillows of cuttlefish that explode unexpectedly (and disturbingly) in the mouth, flooding it with liquid. When I recover my senses, I look up to see Adrià doubled over in delighted hysterics. Summer truffle "cannelloni" with veal bone marrow and rabbit brains is rich, over-the-top, sumptuous, and buttery flavored—and the most traditional "entrée" of many.

"2M of Parmesan cheese spaghetto" is a two-meter-long glassine strand of cheese-flavored consommé suspended in agar-agar. Coiled in a bowl like a small portion of spaghetti carbonara, with a dot of black pepper, it's meant to be slurped in one long sucking movement, as Adrià noisily demonstrates. A single rack of fried anchovy—just crispy head and bones—arrives in a funereal cloud of a cotton candy-like substance. Once again, a dish frightening to behold tastes wonderful.

The horrifying-looking "chocolate soil," which resembles a bowl full of playground dirt and pebbles, turns out to be a conventional tasting chocolate/hazelnut frozen dessert. A "morphing" course of "English bread"—a Wonder bread–looking loaf that virtually disappears on the tongue, leaving no trace of its ever having been there—is followed by a freebie take-home "surprise." A bag with what seems to be a baguette protruding from it is placed in front of me. Adrià lunges across the table and pounds it with his fist, scattering brittle shards of fennel-scented pastry.

Is the meal good? I don't know whether that's a word that applies in a description of the El Bulli experience. It can be more comfortably called "great," meaning hugely enjoyable, challenging to the world order, innovative, revolutionary. For an old-school cook like me, who always thinks that food should be composed of equal parts *terroir* and tradition, it's an uncomfortably revelatory experience.

"He's a phenomenon," Ripert notes. "But we need one Ferran Adrià, not five. I don't see anyone succeeding in emulating him."

The next day, Adrià and I eat lunch at his "favorite restaurant in the world," Rafa's, a simple, 20 seat eatery in Roses. The restaurant serves impeccably fresh seafood, almost always cooked with only a little sea salt and olive oil. Rafa, the proprietor, and his wife cook on a single stovetop and a tiny grill behind a glass front counter displaying seafood landed only a few hours earlier. After tucking into a few slices of grilled sea cucumber, Adrià attacks a plate of screamingly fresh local prawns, greedily sucking the brain and juice from each head. "Magic!" he proclaims, his eyes wild, his hands gesticulating with epileptic fervor. "It's magic! When we make prawns, we dream of Rafa's prawns. *This* is what I want! To find my way to this."

In his own strange and transgressive way, that's exactly what he's done.

A Tiger Tames New York

by Brett Anderson

from *The New Orleans Times-Picayune*

> When Anderson wrote this profile of a Baton Rouge-born chef working in Manhattan, little did he know it would become a sort of eulogy for La Caravelle, which closed on the heels of Lutece and La Cote Basque in 2004, spelling the end of a culinary epoch.

One afternoon this past March, Troy Dupuy arrived to work at La Caravelle, the legendary restaurant in midtown Manhattan where he's executive chef, to find that the daily shipment of cheese was not to his liking. "I was shocked," he told the cheese supplier on the other end of the telephone, referring to what he felt were unsportsmanlike prices to be charging "a very devoted customer."

Dupuy, a Louisiana native and LSU grad, is firm but proper, both on the phone to the supplier and in person, which befits the setting, a jackets-required, banquette-lined dining room that has served as one of New York's great social stages since its opening in 1960.

It's mid-afternoon, so the restaurant is empty, but Dupuy, 39, is highly presentable. He wears his chef's whites—spotless and pressed—buttoned to the top, and his voice is striking, a twang smoothed over to the point where it sounds almost British. It's a Southern accent that's well on its way to becoming something else.

"Something else" is a phrase that describes a lot about Dupuy, including his cuisine, a kind of French-Asian amalgamation that sparkles with imagination. "He's beyond chef material," says Rita Jammet, co-owner, along with her husband Andre, of La Caravelle. "You've met him, so you know what I mean."

He grew up in Baton Rouge and Port Allen allergic to, as he puts it, "basically everything known to man," including crawfish. Somewhat inexplicably, he overcame his allergies and went on to work in the kitchens of Jack Sabin's in Baton Rouge, the Sazerac Room in New Orleans' Fairmont Hotel and, after that, some of the most sophisticated restaurants in New York City. Last fall, a year after Dupuy took over the kitchen at La Caravelle, the restaurant received a three star review from the *New York Times*.

Dupuy's list of mentors includes some of the brightest culinary stars of the last twenty years, most notably Daniel Boulud, Jean-Georges Vongerichten and Gray Kunz, the four-star culinary mystic under whom Dupuy served as executive sous chef (or second in command) for five years at Lespinasse in New York.

But Jammet isn't only referring to Dupuy's resume when she calls him "beyond chef material." His meticulousness does not end with keeping a close eye on the cheese bill. When he came to La Caravelle, he insisted on bringing in his own team of devoted chefs, many of whom were on his staff at Lespinasse in Washington, D.C., a location he was dispatched to open in 1996. The shelves of his cramped office just off La Caravelle's basement kitchen hold ornate souffle molds he has had custom made in France, stout jars of mango chutney awaiting his approval and bags of loose curry leaf. In the two years between leaving D.C. and joining La Caravelle in 2001, Dupuy taught himself how to use AutoCAD, a complicated drafting software, and started up a kitchen design consultancy; the Manhattan restaurants Town and Citarella were among his clients. His office computer contains plans for his own dream kitchen, complete with exact measurements for counter space. "It's all in the details," he says, marveling at the computer screen.

Dupuy's cooking is similarly exacting and, by his own admission, uncategorizable. He calls the marinated tuna and gravlax with seaweed salad and mango dressing "the best example" of the "balancing act," the way his kitchen team marries "the spices with the oils. How we season the items. How we take the seaweed, the hikiki and everything else and bring it all together."

When Dupuy and his team first arrived at La Caravelle, they noticed a vinegar that they like to use in the tuna tasted "different." Dupuy alerted the supplier to the problem, who in turn alerted the producer, a Japanese company, who in turn dispatched a representative to La Caravelle's kitchen to analyze the vinegar. "And in fact, something sure was different with it," Dupuy says. "And they rectified it."

Dupuy is a product of Louisiana, but he's also a product of leaving it. His respect for its culinary traditions runs deep, even if they're not immediately evident in the food at La Caravelle.

His cooking brims with detail. Perfectly round cucumber pellets adorn his steamed black bass, cool bits of natural crunch interspersed with just-larger shrimp balls in fragrant shrimp broth. He seasons foie gras with a special powder comprised of 14 spices that tastes like a single, highly developed flavor, a kind of Creole seasoning with a decidedly Asian accent. The powder is something Dupuy developed years ago with Wang-Kay Fung, his cooking partner of a dozen years and La Caravelle's chef de cuisine. It's food that bears the mark of an open-minded, highly skilled perfectionist. "He's the kind of person who would never allow something that's close to perfect go out in the dining room," Fung said of Dupuy.

The most obvious cultural touchstones in Dupuy's cooking are French, which is evident in the versatility and sharpness of his technique, and, judging from his spice preferences, Asian. When asked where Louisiana fits into all of this, Dupuy mentions cooking red beans and rice, a dish that he's almost certain never to be asked to make in a professional capacity. "You season it with the basil, with the oregano, with the thyme, with the cayenne pepper, the black pepper, the white pepper, the salt," he says, sipping tea in the break room at La Caravelle, pausing after each mention of ingredient. "When you have that food in your mouth you want it to hit every area in your palate. That aspect of Louisiana I think is directly reflected in our cooking here. How it excites your mouth.

"I don't think that there is a better regional cuisine in America," he continues, "because the people of Louisiana"—he breaks for a moment to laugh—"south of Alexandria—know how to use spice."

His first real "eureka" moment as a professional chef came when he was a 15-year-old server at the Sherwood Country Club in

Baton Rouge, where the late chef John Boyd offered him the choice of eating a stuffed mushroom or being fired. Dupuy's experiences with food to that point in his life were hemmed in by allergy shots and strict dietary restrictions. Eating the mushroom, and not ending up in the hospital, took the fear out of eating for Dupuy, and soon he was trying to cook Boyd's recipes at home.

At Jack Sabin's, Dupuy was taken under the wing of Oliver Paige, one of the old kitchen hands in the now-shuttered restaurant. "I came into Jack Sabin's, and I didn't know the first thing about nothing," Dupuy remembers. Paige "took me in. He said 'Troy, I'm going to teach you.' The first thing we did was fry a chicken. There was a way to season a chicken. And that had meaning."

"He was always looking to learn something," Paige said of the young Dupuy, with whom he still talks frequently. "If he put out something, he'd want to know if people liked it, or what was wrong with it so he could straighten it out the next time."

The Sabin's experience compelled Dupuy to enroll at the Culinary Institute of America, in Hyde Park, New York. After working at the Fairmont, he set off for the big city and sought out employers whose drive matched his own.

Dupuy can speak at length and in detail about that lasting impact of each of his jobs, but he says his most profound experience by far was working under Kunz at Lespinasse. The Swiss-born Kunz was renowned for his high-concept, multi-cultural approach at Lespinasse, which just recently closed. "I've never worked in a more impressive environment," Dupuy said of Lespinasse. "It was a commitment to pure excellence. You lived and breathed that every day that you went in the establishment."

Dupuy said that there were 37 different nationalities represented in Lespinasse's 62 employees. In Washington, he says, "I was not quite as fortunate." He had only 22 nationalities represented on his staff there. "I think one learns from interaction with people of different cultures," he says.

Dupuy's cooking doesn't so much represent a commitment to diversity as it does his drive to use everything at his disposal to put the shock of the new into his food, to provide the excitement of tasting something for the first time. Just don't go looking for any updated etouffees at La Caravelle.

"I like to maintain the cuisine that I grew up with in its own element," Dupuy says. "I don't like to modify it." After a moment of thought, he amends the statement. "That's not entirely true. When I make a jambalaya at home, I use the andouille and the tasso from Bellue's (a Baton Rouge supplier). And if this is heresy, I apologize, but I use basmati rice."

Dupuy has worked in some of the most heralded restaurants in New York. But by joining La Caravelle, he landed near the source of American upscale dining as it exists today. The restaurant's roots extend to Le Pavilion, the French restaurant that grew out of an exhibit at New York's World's Fair in 1939. Staffed almost entirely by French immigrants trained in that country's professional kitchens, Le Pavilion was arguably the first restaurant in America that could meet the high standards of a stuffy Parisian. It was among the seeds that allowed New York to bloom into an internationally recognized culinary capital.

Le Pavilion was also a hotbed for social drama, much of it expertly curated by its French owner, Henri Soule. Soule was famously aloof, perhaps by design. In his book "Dining at the Pavilion," the late New Yorker writer Joseph Wechsberg explained Soule's coolness: "In the complicated relationship between restaurateur and his guests, familiarity breeds too many dangers." Soule often quarreled with his staff—in his recently released memoir, Jacques Pepin, a Le Pavilion alum, calls Soule "a bombastic tyrant"—and, in some instances, "club members," Wechsberg's term for the restaurant's preferred customers. Joseph P. Kennedy was one such customer. Soule so offended the political patriarch that he boycotted the restaurant in favor of La Caravelle, a restaurant opened by refugees from Le Pavilion who walked out amid a salary dispute with Soule.

La Caravelle far outlived Le Pavilion and in essence carried on its tradition. For its first several decades, it was a citadel of classic haute French cuisine with all the trappings, and in many ways it still is. Its wine cellar holds more than 15,000 bottles, and its menu still offers, under the heading "Les Classiques de La Caravelle," war-horses such as pike quenelles with lobster cream sauce and grilled Dover sole.

When the Jammets took over La Caravelle in the mid–1980s, they sought to, as Rita explained it, update the restaurant "without losing its cachet." The changes they imposed were by turns subtle, and of the type that would cause Henri Soule to turn in his grave. They started printing the menu in English, not French, and gave the dining room an understated facelift. More drastically, they hired the restaurant's first non-French chef, the American Michael Romano, who began a tradition of free-wheeling self-expression in the old restaurant's kitchen. With Romano (who's now at Union Square Cafe, one of New York's most popular restaurants) the restaurant also began to build a reputation as an incubator of creative young talent.

Today, La Caravelle's menu is a two-headed beast of chocolate soufflés and crisped soft shell crabs with pickled ramps and opal basil, and Jammet makes no apologies for the collision of the old with the new. Its history is still very much in evidence, and not just in the old-school caviar service. The erudite staff includes a maitre d', Andre Ihuellou, who has been at the restaurant for over 25 years, and a bartender, Adalberto Alonso, who has been there more than 40. And Jammet feels that Dupuy is, in his way, keeping La Caravelle's tradition alive as much as anyone. "I'm not talking for Troy, but I believe that if he had his own restaurant, he would want to be cooking all his own dishes," she said. "But I think that there is a classicism in his food. There is a lot of restraint there. It's very distinguished."

As a rule, Dupuy doesn't live more than a 20-minute walk from work, which is where he spends most of his time anyway. He doesn't get much of a chance to eat out in New York's more celebrated restaurants, but he does delve into his food culture. There was a Turkish restaurant in midtown that he used to like, save for the owner's devotion to Uncle Ben's rice. Dupuy brought him a bag of his favorite basmati, and when the owner returned to Uncle Ben's, Troy quit going.

"Troy doesn't like the food in our neighborhood very much," says his wife Nancy Leung, and Dupuy doesn't dispute this. The couple is riding in a cab to Chinatown en route to their ritual Sunday morning dim sum meal. Dupuy's trip to Chinatown is one of the non-work related highlights of his week. The destination is the Golden Unicorn, a sprawling Chinese restaurant in an office building on East Broadway. Earlier this year, the restaurant was the site of Dupuy's and Leung's wedding reception, and they seem to know most of the staff. The room is packed, with a long waiting list for tables.

Over the meal, Dupuy talks about the wedding and his love for Chinatown restaurants and Asian food in general. He brings up the mango in coconut milk that he ate once on a trip to Bangkok. "It was like nothing I'd ever tasted before," he says. "The coconuts were picked from the garden out back. The mangos were pure, fresh. You just can't get those kinds of ingredients here."

The topic zigzags from Lee's in Lecompte, Louisiana, a place Dupuy's grandmother swears is "the last outpost of good food before you hit the north," to the farmers he had to coach to grow him acceptable baby bok choy ("I kept telling them, 'Grow it tighter!' "), to, ultimately, home.

"When you come to the dinner table in Louisiana, everybody's on equal ground," he says. "Everyone loves a good fish fry or craw-fish boil, no matter what background they're from."

And with that, Dupuy orders some sharkfin dumplings in what, to the untrained ear, sounds like perfect Chinese.

Alice in Italy

by Thomas McNamee
from *Saveur*

What happens when the famous Alice Waters faces a banquetful of Slow Food activists? McNamee's behind-the-scenes story, a taste of his upcoming Waters bio, shows not only the Chez Panisse ethic in action, but also that seat-of-the-pants challenge that gets chefs' adrenaline pumping.

Hotel Victoria, Turin, Italy, October 27, 2002. Enter Alice at high speed. "Good morning," I offer, "and how are you today?" "Good morning, Tom." Effortful smile—nervous system zizzing. "Fine," meaning not. Exit Alice at high speed.

Cristina Salas-Porras, Alice's assistant—*assistant* is hardly the word; let's say chief of Alice operations, the one who must be hard when Alice is soft, diplomatic when Alice skins noses, strategic when Alice spins dreams—touches her hair as she does when troubled and says, "We've got problems."

Alice and a team from Chez Panisse who have just flown in are going to make dinner tonight at the Ristorante Real Castello di Verduno, 42 miles from Turin, as part of the Salone del Gusto, staged biennially by Slow Food, an organization founded in 1986 in horrified reaction to the appearance of a McDonald's in Rome's Piazza di Spagna. The Salone comprises hundreds of tastings, exhibits, seminars, field trips, and superlative meals—foremost among them some 65 blowout lunches and dinners at restaurants scattered across the nearby Piedmontese countryside.

Most of these feasts are being prepared by the restaurants' own staffs and are based on familiar local ingredients and feature classic local dishes. The Chez Panisse chefs, on the other hand, have seen the Castello kitchen for the first time only this morning and—except for the bread and the vegetables—have not been able to buy their own provisions. Hence, problems. The fish isn't good enough, and it's Sunday, so all the fish markets are closed. Alice wants the squab legs grilled, but there's no grill or firewood. The pears are hard as bricks. The porcini are full of worms. The stock-pots are too small. . . .

Al Qaeda prowls the overheating world, top-soil is blowing away, half the plants on the planet are going extinct, the oceans are dying—but Alice is focused on Verduno, on a smaller, clearer out-come: a nonwormy wild mushroom or an exquisite soupe de pois-sons might conjure from among the diners tonight a (wealthy, influential) recruit to the cause of organic farming, enlightened consumption, better European agriculture policies, healthy oceans. This is how Alice does what she does. Her route to virtue is via pleasure. Eating, she says, is a political act.

Meanwhile, we're still in Turin. The car isn't here, and besides our own bags and briefcases and other impedimenta, we are also supposed to be delivering the mountain of stuff now heaped in the Victoria's foyer—chefs' luggage, bags of goodies, boxes of Chez Panisse party favors, backpacks, shoes—and Cristina has no idea whether the car's going to be big enough, and anyway it was sup-posed to be here half an hour ago. The hotel is trying to find a driver with a minivan, but it's Sunday, you understand. . . .

At last the car arrives, and we all fit in. The route to Verduno testifies to the easy victories of profit over landscape and beauty. Cheesy furniture outlets, plumbing-supply dealers, and gas sta-tions line the road. In time they give way to gold and crimson vineyards, low green hills, a winding lane to the castle, a misted view across the valley of the Tanaro River.

When we arrive, the kitchen is at work in the Chez Panisse way, quiet, intent, unhurried, and amply staffed. Two chefs from the establishment are here—Christopher Lee and Russell Moore—along with cook Amy Dencler and a crew of Chez Panisse alumni now working in Europe.

Conferring with Alice, Chris looks every inch the CEO—

six-two, mild-spoken in the manner that betokens restrained authority, neither smiling nor frowning, all let's-get-it-done. Towering over Alice, who stands five-two tops, Chris reports that after one look at the mass of pre-chopped sea glop meant to be the base for the fish stock—including salmon, a fish of northern seas, hardly in keeping with Alice's inveterate decree that everything be local—Russ has thrown the whole mess out. Of what remains, there's no fish meaty enough to serve in small portions surrounded by a complex broth, as intended. If they can only find some good small Mediterranean reef fish, though, they may be able to make a decent passato—a thick soup passed through a food mill.

And then there are—voices drop low—the Burlottos. These are the owners of the castle, the three sisters Gabriella, Elisa, and Liliana Burlotto, plus Elisa's daughter Alessandra Buglioni di Monale, who is the chef. The Burlottos are annoyed, and no wonder. The sisters waited up last night to welcome the Chez Panisse brigade, who were expected by midnight but pulled in at two in the morning. (They'd stopped at Elena Rovera's Cascina del Cornale—an all-organic co-op, which has supplied the beautiful vegetables and bread for tonight's feast—and Elena had insisted that they stay for dinner; then they got lost on the way to Verduno.) Alessandra is now in her office with the door closed. "Cristina?" whispers Alice worriedly. "You've got to talk to her." With a long intake of breath, Cristina knocks, enters the lioness's den, and closes the door behind her.

Alessandra had curtly informed the Chez Panisse chefs that the only remaining possibility for fish was the supermarket. But Russ is now beaming at a just-arrived box of fat pink Mediterranean lobsters. Tall, wide-eyed, with a nearly constant thin, bemused smile and a shock of brown hair standing straight up at the summit, Russ moves deliberately, with the meditative tranquillity of a man who loves what he's doing. His idea of the fish passato undergoes a transformation: with the shells of these fantastic lobsters, some saffron, and some Pernod, he can make a rich, clear, bouillabaisse-scented broth. He'll cook the stock on an open fire of oak and vine cuttings that one of the cooks has scrounged up in the village, and the smoke will almost imperceptibly rusticate the aroma of the soup.

As activity accelerates, the kitchen remains cool and quiet. Leeks, onions, and fennel lie cut up in neat piles, ready for Russ's broth. Squab stock is simmering. And Alessandra Buglioni di Monale and Cristina Salas-Porras (nicely matched in double-barreled grandeur of name), having emerged from the office, face each other across a gulf of some ten feet and exchange elaborate compliments.

The number of guests tonight is supposed to be limited strictly to 55, but another 15—Slow Food officials and their friends—want to come too, at the last minute. "Can we fit them in?" Cristina asks Alessandra. "Alice wants there to be a particular spirit in the room." She adds, "We're very happy to be in this beautiful place." "We also are very happy to have you here," replies Alessandra in lilting English, "but overbooking is a problem." She has turned away friends and regulars of her own, she explains. The restaurant has a capacity of 55 and no more.

Alice sniffs a pear and frowns, watched closely by Chris, Russ, and Amy. Amy is tall, broad shouldered, with wide-set, watchful eyes, short salt-and-pepper hair, and a quiet manner that may be self-contained or merely shy. Others in the kitchen break into lively chat from time to time, but Amy has kept silent. The pears are her dish for tonight. They don't have much of a perfume, and they seem awfully hard, but Alice wanted pears and these were the best to be found. Is Alice about to have one of her . . . ideas? She is given to sudden inspirations, which may or may not be practicable. "She'll just say, 'Wouldn't it be nice this way . . . ,' " says Russ, "and it's up to us to figure out how to do it. I try not to say no unless it's truly impossible." But no inspiration comes to Alice this time. Chris's and Russ's shoulders visibly soften.

"Now," proclaims Alice, slipping into an apron, "I'm going to do the one little thing that I really like to do"—prep. In this case that means washing and drying the salad greens. A stillness comes over Alice's features as she works. Something uneasy and hurried is flowing out of her hands into the cold water. But something is still bothering her. "If we had our usual network of sources," she says, "none of this would be a problem."

While the kitchen works, I wander the dining rooms. Umberto I, king of Italy from 1878 to 1900, glowers down from a print on the wall, staring fiercely out the window at some of the best vineyard land in the world. On the sideboard below Umberto are arrayed eight bottles of the Castello's best wines—including barolo, barbaresco, dolcetto d'alba, barbera d'alba, and Verduno's own Basadone (whose name in Piedmontese dialect means "Kiss the ladies"), made from an ancient and genetically unique grape variety native to Verduno known as pelaverga piccolo, which was saved from extinction on this very estate.

Gabriella Burlotto materializes behind me. She is small, blue-eyed, elegantly dressed à l'anglaise in tweed and suede. These wines are her creations; she is the first woman in four generations of winemaking Burlottos. Would I care to come down to the cellar for a little tasting? Would I! The wines are sensational—the barolo brooding and earthy, the barbaresco like velvet, the dolcetto cherry red and cherry fragrant, the barbera spicy and pungent, the Basadone pure, juicy "Drink me", like nothing else I've ever tasted. Back upstairs, I report all this to Alice, eliciting a pained wince. "We're not serving them," she groans. "The wines for tonight are from Tuscany. We haven't even tasted them. They were donated."

She turns back to her work, assembling a trial version of the squab dish, the separated breasts and legs arranged just so on the salad—not architectural, just balanced. She and Chris study the plate, shifting a leg here, a leaf there. "I thought about julienning the greens," says Alice, "but then I thought, No, the hot squab might wilt them too fast, and anyway I like the colors like this. It's lovely, Christopher, don't you think?" She moves the squabs' ankles an eighth of an inch closer together, then puts them back as they were.

Russ has set up camp on the gravel courtyard in front of the castle, carefully crisscrossing oven racks across uneven stacks of bricks to create a rather unsteady-looking grill. "It's going to be dark out here," I point out helpfully, indicating the complete absence of lighting on the castle façade. He asks a helper to find him some flashlights. Alice appears, smiling contentedly at the makeshift barbecue apparatus. "I'm going to skewer the legs," Russ explains. "It shouldn't be too bad." "Can you use rosemary skewers?" asks Alice. "I love those."

The helper is back, holding his hands out palms up, empty. No flashlights. "It's going to be pitch-dark," says Russ. "Oh, well," says Alice. She holds my arm for a second, for no good reason but howdy. She touches everybody, and as far as I can tell, everybody likes it. She has coppery spikes newly dyed into her hair, and I keep expecting them to stand up or wilt with her mood, like a cock's comb, but before I can look she's off to whatever wants checking on next. Gabriella has found enough firewood for Russ to get started, and soon the fish stock is boiling away, lobster legs and shell poking out haphazardly. "Pot's too small," Russ explains, "so I've got to make the stock extra strong and then dilute it."

Russ's girlfriend, Allison Hopelain, appears bringing him two gifts: a glass of wine and a penlight—his sole source of illumination.

In the kitchen Alice is cutting yard-long strips of focaccia for the grill. Soon a test pear comes out of the oven. Doesn't look so good to me—kind of brown and shriveled and dull skinned. Amy Dencler spoons an ivory sauce around a pear half. She, Chris, and Alice all take a taste. Alice pronounces the crème anglaise too sweet. She doesn't like the almond stuffing, either. Amy nods and goes back to work.

The kitchen door flies open, hard enough to bang against the wall. It's Alessandra, catching nobody's eye. She cruises between the tables and ranges, looking at this, looking at that, then cruises out without a word. Alice and Chris share a quick "Who knows?" shrug. The numbers issue is still not settled.

Alice half-trips over a paper bag of potatoes. She takes a potato in her hand, holds it under her nose, holds it up in the light, turning it slowly around. Chris moves toward her warily. There are no potatoes on the menu. "Ahhh," she sighs, inhaling the loamy scent. "Let's split them and boil them and roast them." "We could grill them," Chris suggests. "Let's grill them!" cries Alice.

So now Russ's teetering crisscross of oven racks will be giving us fish soup, grilled focaccia, grilled squab legs, and grilled potatoes— in the dark. "How is this possible?" I ask. "This is my job," answers Russ. And the darkness? "I can do it by feel."

An experimental assembly of the first course, a cardoon salad with anchovies, is ready. The cardoons taste curiously nondescript, though the anchovies, fresh from the Mediterranean this morning and marinated all day in garlic and olive oil, are sublime. Amy fiddles with the dressing: lemon juice, taste; shallots, taste again; now a little finely chopped anchovy. More lemon.

Christopher tastes the dressing. "Some parsley would be good," he says. "And there are beautiful chives in the garden." Alice grabs a basket.

Russ, just in out of the dark, calls, "Alice, plus, while you're out there, we need herbs for the soup. Whatever looks good." She returns, aglow, with a huge bouquet, spilling out of the basket—chives, parsley, lovage, rosemary, mint.

Seven o'clock. The dining-room staff pours into the kitchen, all women, white blouses, black skirts, all business. Out in the halls of the castle, everything is still, in the strange prestorm calm of seamless preparedness. Alice and Cristina descend from upstairs in impeccable dresses and makeup, Alice's newly multicolored hair perfectly tousled. Mikhail Baryshnikov, one of Alice's friends, is the first to arrive. Soon the halls are thronged with the few devoted and the many curious. A consul arrives, gleaming-haired, with entourage. He waits on the threshold to be welcomed, then gives up and moves inside. A restaurateur from New York is here, quite sure that it's all a fraud and that the food is going to be lousy. Film people, Slow Foodies, gourmets from half a continent away, a contingent of Alice's friends—it is a jolly and good-looking crowd.

When the first course, cardoons and anchovies, is served, there are some sniffs of consternation. This is it? Well, yes, that's it. Is it great? No. Is it yummy? Yes. Pure essence of cardoon, a sparkling anchovy, some mild green oil, period. The fish soup, with chunks of lobster floating on a raft of focaccia, is deep and mysterious and almost fancy.

In the dark out front, Russ is picking up squab legs with his fingers, tossing one here, another there, over the waning coals. There's no more firewood. But the squab legs are crisp and juicy—in fact, just right, as are the pink seared breasts they're reunited with in the kitchen—and the sauce of reduced stock is subtle but potent. The pears have never really softened, but their flavor is intense, and the créme anglaise wraps them in satin smoothness. With the exception of the New York restaurateur, whose negative expectations have apparently been met, the diners appear quite blissful. The flavors have been pure and clear; the weight in the belly is satisfying but not heavy; people have talked, laughed, made new friends. Maybe a few are revising their notions of what great food is.

Alice, who has, of course, won the seating battle, makes sure that Alessandra shares in the bows. The crowd leans forward, silent, to catch Alice's little soft voice, which is telling them that everything tonight was organic and local, that virtuous farming means better-tasting food, that how we eat can change the world.

Clean Plate Club

by Dan Barber
from *Food & Wine*

> Chef/co-owner of Manhattan's Blue Hill restaurant, Barber is unusually articulate about the psychological drive that impels him to feed strangers night after night— not only that, but to care how they enjoyed the meal. The empty plate is his badge of honor.

Clean plates don't lie. That's what I say when waiters at my restaurant, Blue Hill, ask me why I insist on examining every plate that returns to the kitchen with the slightest bit of food on it. The waiters think I'm intrusive. They also think I'm neurotic and insecure, but like most neurotic and insecure chefs, I don't quite agree. I tell them that a clean plate is proof of a perfect meal—a lesson I learned on a trip my father and I took to Nice in 1982, when I was 12 years old.

As our taxi passed the famed Hotel Negresco on the way to the Nice airport, my father (a businessman and passionate food lover) smacked his forehead. How, he wondered aloud, could he have neglected to take me to the restaurant there? The Chantecler, with the brilliant (and manic) chef Jacques Maximin at the stove, was one of the most celebrated restaurants in the world. My father yelled at our cab driver to stop. He jumped from the taxi, then motioned for the driver to join us.

As I sat between the two men, I quickly became aware of a cultural divide. My father told the waiter, "No menus; bring whatever comes out of the kitchen," rolling his fists quickly around each other like a turbine. To my left, my father represented the all-American assumption that memorable experiences are always in reach, like apples, and that one simply needs to be bold enough to grab them. He fidgeted and worried about missing the flight but beamed with pleasure as I swallowed my seafood ravioli with obvious joy—small, soft clouds of briny sweetness in impossibly thin pasta. To my right, the cab driver looked around the room in awe, blinking with bemusement at the vagaries of fate. He poked his nose within inches of his baby lamb loin. He smiled, took a bite, and savored its flavor. But he wasn't even halfway finished when my dad waved for the bill.

"He's still eating," I cried.

"We have to go now," my father replied. Anticipating a confrontation, I bolted for the men's room. I passed the swinging kitchen doors and caught a glimpse of chef Maximin bent over a plate ready to be sauced, eyes at the edge of the rim.

When I returned to the table, the cab driver had lowered his head again so that his lips nearly touched the dish. He dabbed his thick, crusty bread into what was left of the sauce, then looked up and nodded. The waiter removed the empty plate.

Plates cleared, check signed, my father jumped up to go and I followed. Just then, small bowls of sorbet arrived, palate cleansers. There must have been miscommunication about whether we wanted dessert.

"Thank you, but we're running very late," said my dad. The cab driver, who had remained seated, picked up his spoon and carefully, intently, began eating. My father ran back to the table.

"Unacceptable!" my father said, banging his forefinger on his watch. "The flight leaves in an hour." The cab driver wiped his mouth and feigned departure by putting his napkin down and swigging the last of his wine. My father retreated. The cab driver went back to the sorbet.

"No, no," my father said. "Time to leave." Again, the cab driver playacted, pushing his chair out slightly with one hand as if he were about to leave, but scooping sorbet into his mouth with the other.

I left to wait in the taxi, but I will not forget what I saw through the window of the Negresco. The cab driver kept looking around the dining room, as if to taste the place itself. Hovering over the bowl, he scraped the bottom rapidly until it was clean.

It was a picture of defiance, but that's not all. I recognized in the cab driver a deliberate, maybe innate, understanding of the care that goes into a meal. He did not have to see the chef laboring over the plate to know the meaning behind the food.

I wish all the diners at Blue Hill were like the cab driver. Is it arrogant of me to look for that kind of reverence? If there's food left uneaten on a plate, I want to know what went wrong. I know it's uncomfortable to confront the diner—I've done it myself. More excuses have accompanied a half-eaten salmon fillet on its return to the kitchen than I've ever even given for overcooking it on the way out. "Late lunch" and "Saving room for dessert" are popular. No excuse rings true to me. I look at plates the way people look at themselves in the mirror. Love handles gotten a little smaller? The diet and exercise are working. Plates empty? I've cooked the food well.

Not long ago an experience with a customer shook the foundation of this belief. A writer I admire greatly visited the restaurant for the first time. Unfortunately, our newest waiter, Craig, had been assigned to the writer's section.

"He's incredibly excited about the tasting menu. No restrictions, no time constraints, Puligny-Montrachet to start," Craig assured me as he handed in the order.

I began simply: marinated Maine sea scallops with mussel juice and olive oil. The plates returned five minutes later. The writer had barely touched the scallops; his companion had finished hers completely.

"You told me no restrictions," I yelled.

"That's what he said," Craig responded. "I'm clearing the plates and he tells me this is the only way he likes scallops."

"You misheard him."

"No, chef, I heard it clearly. He said it's a great dish."

I cooked their next course—a sea bass roasted with pink peppercorns and lemon thyme—with incredible care, leaving the writer's piece in the pan an extra minute. He clearly did not care for raw seafood. The plates returned with his fish essentially untouched, except for a half-inch bite from the corner; his date had again cleaned her plate.

Craig started trying to placate me right away: "No worries, chef, he's cool. Adored it. Saving room for dessert."

"Adored it?" Remembering this was Craig's first night, I forgot for a moment about the writer. My shock, my embarrassment really, was for a moment less about the writer than about our newest waiter, who must have been thinking I couldn't cook.

"When was the last time you ate something perfectly cooked, Craig, like that piece of center-cut bass?" I asked. "Something that was your ideal—tastefully seasoned and thoughtfully plated, something so delicious you were amazed to be eating it—and then halfway through this wonder of a dish you threw up your arms and said: No more! Too good! The best damn bass I've ever had, and I'm throwing away half!"

Three more courses, I said to myself, no more than three—all of them perfect. I batted a pencil against my temple: trout, foie, steak. Hot smoked trout to start, fish that I'd picked out myself that morning. Pink, wholesome and beautiful to look at—a component I thought could have been missing from the first two courses. Emboldened, I declared the trout impossible to be left uneaten.

And then it was. The fish resembled a cartoon image of a piece of cheese with the corner nibbled off by a mouse. Otherwise the plate was undisturbed; the fillet's flesh seemed to blush at me. This took effort: It was as if, in a shocking role reversal, the writer had carefully considered how the dish should look when it returned to me.

"Really loved the smokiness," Craig told me.

Confused, I feigned calm as the kitchen swirled around me. "Okay, foie gras, sautéed, with pineapple," I said, to no one in particular. Who could refuse velvety foie gras with sweet fruit?

Craig returned with the plates of foie gras, one empty, one nearly identical to how it looked leaving me. "He said he wants to speak to you about the foie gras," Craig said cryptically as he left the kitchen. And then I saw him. The writer was standing in the kitchen. I went over to shake his hand. He grabbed it, then wrapped his arms around me in a bear hug. I realized that all this rooting around trying to figure the guy out was ridiculous. Letting me go, he pointed at me: "That was the best foie gras of my life, man."

The writer returns to the restaurant every few weeks. I've tried giving him a vegetable tasting menu. I've tried a long menu with extremely small portions, and a two-course tasting with mountains of food. I've tried grilling, deep-frying and cedar planking. He eats the exact same amount with admirable consistency.

So I've learned that a person's appetite is not necessarily proportionate to my cooking abilities. Or have I? There's no glory in offending a chef, so when I go out to eat I clean my plate—sometimes in less conventional ways. I recently traveled to London for the first time to cater a dinner party and had all of Saturday to myself before my late-night flight home. There were several restaurants I wanted try, so I ate two lunches. I was stuffed, but I still wanted to make it to my 5:30 reservation at Richard Corrigan at Lindsay House.

I was looking for fresh ideas and bold flavors. Instead, I found tuxedoed waiters offering tasting menus that included dishes like a game terrine with three inches of aspic. As the maitre d' led me to my table, I remembered that a new restaurant, Sketch, had just opened to incredible reviews—and that it was on the way to the airport. I couldn't think of an excuse not to be seated, though, so I decided to get what I could from the experience.

When I saw a pigeon and foie gras appetizer on the menu, I felt compelled to order it. A dish like that was a strong statement, I thought, and could be a chef's way of saying, You can trust me not to overwhelm you. But the dish was flat and gratuitously fatty. I stared at my plate. If I finished everything on it quickly, I would still have time to get to Sketch.

I wrapped the leftovers in my napkin and stuffed it into my bag. I used my roll to mop up the sauce. I might not have enjoyed the food, but why ruin the chef's night too? I know the heat, the exhausting hours, the frustration and mindless repetition of what chefs do. I am loath to inflict any more pain on another chef, even a bad one.

I got up to use the phone. Sketch had an open table; I promised to be there in 45 minutes. I sat back down to an enormous lamb loin, cooked extremely rare and looking thoroughly tough. It was. I played with the potato cake and eyed the waiters. No one in sight, the loin and most of the potato cake went into the bag. And when the waiter approached to clear the plate I stopped him suddenly. Giving in to an impulse, I grabbed the bread and wiped the sauce from the plate.

I shot across town. Sketch is restaurant-as-performance-art, with buzzing neon signs, flickering video installations and a pair of hostesses each six-and-a-half feet tall. I barely looked up. The menu was fascinating. There were spices and cooking techniques I had never heard of. But I had only 30 minutes to eat.

"Look," I explained to the waiter, "I've got a flight to catch, and I don't know when I'll be in London again. I hate to pressure the kitchen, but I want to try several dishes and, in the interests of time, I'd like to have them all come out together."

"All at once?" asked the waiter with pursed lips.

"That's right, yes," I said. "The artichoke with marinated and pickled vegetables, the foie gras and charcuterie, the lobster and the sea bass with conch fritters. And the check." I sounded just like my father, I thought.

The meal was incredible. Each dish was full of flavor and intricately prepared. With the exception of the chunks of charcuterie—which again went into my carry-on bag—I happily cleaned all the plates and raced to make my plane.

"Bag check," the airport security guard said. I went to a side table, where she unzipped my carry-on and started to open it. That's when it hit me. The food—the lamb loin, the pigeon and foie gras, the charcuterie—all of it was loosely wrapped in sauce-soaked napkins, sitting on top of my clothes. "I don't really know how to explain this," I said.

I am my father, rushing around grabbing at experiences and trying to fit everything in. But I'm the French cab driver, too, who knew how to savor a meal. There is a lot of satisfaction in the business of cooking, but there are few real pleasures. One of them is having the plates from a table of six return entirely empty. When the waiters reluctantly hold them up for inspection, it's as if I can see my reflection.

The Family Meal

Manning the Stove

by Andy Borowitz

from *Food & Wine*

Borowitz's main line is political satire—
very topical, very pointed, very *very*
funny political satire, as read in *The New
Yorker,* as heard on CNN. Here he tackles
another sort of political issue: Who gets
to be the family cook, and what power
does that convey?

C all me a sexist (you won't be the first,) but even in this
enlightened age I think it's unusual for the man of the house
to cook dinner every night. When I tell people that I've performed
this task for the last 14 years, they're invariably surprised—not just
because I'm a man, but also because I don't seem the type. I
didn't go to some fancy cooking school in France, and I've
never worn a toque—in fact, until a minute ago, I wasn't exactly
sure how to spell *toque.* I'm not a sensitive New Age house-
husband, either, nor am I married to a hapless, can't-boil-an-egg
spouse. In fact, my wife is a wizard in the kitchen who tackles
recipes that would have stumped the collective brain trust of the
Manhattan Project.

So if I'm not a gourmet and I'm not trying to make some sort
of statement about traditional sex roles and I'm married to a
woman who could easily take down Emeril (a somewhat frightening image, actually), why do I cook? It's a long story, but I
promise you, it has a happy ending.

Before my children were born, I never so much as picked up a
slotted spoon. Every evening when my wife and I got home from
work, I'd sit on the living room sofa with a magazine while she

searched her collection of cookbooks for a recipe with a degree of difficulty that was scary enough to be of interest to her. Additionally, it had to contain at least one obscure ingredient that we were unlikely to have on hand. On any given evening, I would hear her voice wafting from the kitchen, inquiring without any trace of irony, "Do we have . . . oyster mushrooms?"

A sumptuous feast was usually served around 10 PM, and at 11 we forced ourselves to confront a kitchen that invariably resembled a crime scene—the work of a perpetrator with a marked aversion to using the same knife twice. On most nights, we would finish tidying up as the clock struck midnight—and the next evening, for reasons probably best left to the realm of psychiatry, we would do the same thing all over again.

When my wife became pregnant, however, the culinary balance of power in our home suddenly shifted. The mere notion of cooking made her feel ill. I had no choice but to put down my magazine and strap on an apron. I was cooking for three now.

In those pioneering days, I was something of a tabula rasa in the kitchen, unless you count my knack for toasting a flawless Pop-Tart. Given my limited store of knowledge, I began cooking with what might be considered a serious handicap: a deeply ingrained distrust of recipes, which I found gratuitously, even intentionally, confusing. Nevertheless, I embarked on my new career as the family chef with unbridled (and very male) optimism, following no directions and never asking for help.

Going with what I considered my likely strengths, I relied heavily in my first meals on that most manly branch of the culinary arts, grilling. I discovered that all it took to grill a chicken breast was some store-bought marinade, a grill pan, a few sprays of Pam and a willingness to keep an eye on the meat and take it off the heat before it burst into flames. (This being 1989, "blackening" was considered chic—a vogue that, more often than not, worked in my favor.) I found steaming vegetables unexpectedly doable, and I could make a box of instant rice without incident. Before long, I was putting together meals that were fit, if not for a king, then at least for a pregnant woman suddenly averse to cooking. My wife was eating splendidly, and periodic ultrasound exams indicated that the baby was steadily gaining weight. Consequently,

I felt like The Man, even though I was wearing daisy-patterned oven mitts.

> Five tips for the novice male cook
> 1. Do not attempt any dish involving yeast.
> 2. Never try to make a dish that originates from another hemisphere.
> 3. Opt for slow-cooking stews that won't suffer if you leave them on the stove for an hour or two longer than you meant to.
> 4. Don't try anything "impressive"; go for "edible."
> 5. Leave adequate time to order pizza.

When my daughter was born, my wife was too exhausted from late-night feedings to resume her kitchen duties, but by this time I had acquired a repertoire of eight or nine meals and was on a roll. Once I'd learned to grill rainbow trout, I discovered, it was also possible to subject bluefish, mackerel and almost anything else with gills to the same punishment. No sooner had I mastered the art of boiling dry pasta than I boldly explored the possibilities of boiling fresh pasta, adding gnocchi and ravioli to my dinnertime arsenal.

By this point, I was enjoying my new virtuosity and finding the process of preparing dinner shockingly relaxing. Because of the straightforward nature of my meals, we were now eating by 7 PM and, thanks to my innovative technique of washing pots and utensils immediately after using them, were done cleaning up by 8:30. Suddenly, I had gobs of free time, exactly the opposite of what is supposed to happen when you have kids.

As the years wore on and our son was born, I gradually expanded my repertoire. I learned how to poach salmon, mash potatoes and roast chicken. (This last dish I generally reserved for Sunday afternoons; there's nothing like basting a bird every 20 minutes or so to give the impression that you're applying yourself to a serious purpose when what you're really doing is logging hours of football-viewing on the kitchen television.) I improvised coq au vin and beef Stroganoff, and just to prove I wasn't in a rut, I introduced venison and quail into my burgeoning rotation. Even my children began to notice my evolution into a culinary daredevil; once, upon seeing a Cornish hen defrosting on the counter, my then 3-year-old daughter asked, "Are we having that owl?"

Over time, my embargo against recipes became something less than total. I found the *Joy of Cooking* helpful, especially for learning crucial details like how hot the oven should be before you put something in it. But I still eschewed any recipe that had even a hint of complexity. If it advocated the use of cheesecloth or included the dreaded words *then set aside,* I turned the page.

Cooking has been such a positive experience that I have only one regret: that I didn't learn how to do it earlier, say, when I was single. In those days, my ability to make dinner would have multiplied my attractiveness to women by a factor of 10, easily, and the fact that I cleaned up afterward would have sent it off the chart. As a married guy, I'll never know what kind of raw power I might have had—so I have to content myself with smaller satisfactions, like telling my sister-in-law about my cooking and thereby making my brother look bad.

How long will I continue to be my family's nightly chef? It's hard to tell. My wife recently cast a covetous eye toward the kitchen and expressed a desire to make dinner every now and then. Acknowledging that our children could not be expected to dine at 10 PM, she theorized that if she started cooking earlier she could get her Herculean meals on the table in a timely fashion. She's tried it, and with astounding success: Now when she cooks, we eat at 7:30, 8 at the latest. Indeed, the happy result of my cooking dinner for 14 years may very well be that I will never have to cook again.

My Dinner with Rian

by Natalie MacLean
from nataliemaclean.com

When Canadian wine writer Natalie MacLean, who won this year's M.F.K. Fisher Award from the James Beard Foundation, dines out, she faces a not-so-uncommon dilemma: Is it possible to include your child in your life as a gastronome?

Ever since my son was born, I dreamed about taking him to a fine restaurant for his first formal meal. I imagined that Rian, now five, would wear a crisp white shirt, pleated black pants and a small tartan bow-tie. He and the maître d' would shake hands as equals. The haughty waiter François would melt when Rian made careful selections using the French acquired from reading his Caillou books.

When our meals arrived and Rian had his first taste of foie gras, his face would be pleasure made flesh; he'd devour his caviar with a lust usually reserved for Kraft dinner. My husband Andrew and I would sip our wine and wonder how we had managed to raise such a cultured, well-behaved child. We'd acknowledge the compliments from other diners with happy shrugs, as if to say, "Guess we just got lucky with this one."

It's nice to dream.

"Let's take Rian to Signatures," I suggest to Andrew one evening, after several glasses of port. Signatures is the local French restaurant that serves trés haute cuisine in the city's Cordon Bleu Culinary Institute, where chefs train to work in Michelin–starred restaurants. Andrew winces, and counters by suggesting our favourite burger joint.

"No, that's too child-friendly," I retort.

"You're designing trouble again aren't you?" Andrew accuses. That's how my husband unjustly characterizes the creative conflict that innocently bubbles up in our lives' situational dramas that just happen to provide the basis for a good story.

"But what if we see people we know?" Andrew asks limply. "What if we want to go back there again? Can't we do this in a city where we don't live?"

I stay firm and finally he gives in with a final pout: "Well, I'm going to drink a lot of wine."

His resistance may be futile, but it makes me pause. Should parents even take young children to good restaurants? Shouldn't they be kid-free zones, like executive class in airplanes and couples–only resorts? Shouldn't they be havens for parents who've hired a babysitter to escape somewhere for grown-up conversations that won't be interrupted? Are we just trying to make children into mini-adults?

And can kids even appreciate fine tastes? Most young animals are repelled by strange flavours, especially strong ones; it's a built-in survival instinct. A child's taste buds are sensitive because they haven't been broadened (and blunted) by years of hot, spicy foods. For adults, the rush of a bold curry is a pleasant perversion of our palate: it actually triggers our pain receptors. Not so for most children.

If it's an effort for parents to keep their offspring civilized when dining out, it's often twice as much work for the restaurant. Not only are children messy, prone to spills and crumbs, but requests for sixteen substitutions and bland food can frazzle even the most patient chef.

The flip side is if we wait too long to introduce children to the pleasures of a good restaurant, they may grow up on a diet that never moves beyond fast and frozen, unless we have the time and talent to cook great meals at home. For parents, good restaurants are a relief from house arrest; for kids, they can be another way to learn about the world. Children have many teachers outside of school: the dentist who explains the chemistry of sugar, the butcher who shows them weights and measures, the librarian who reads them stories and the waiter who brings the abundance of the earth to their plate.

After wrestling with these issues, I finally settle on the fact that dining out has become our family sport. I've recently abandoned the longing for us to be one of those outdoorsy families on the cover of the L.L. Bean catalogue, canoeing on a lake or hiking in the mountains. The down-filled vests I bought, which flutter like beautiful fall leaves in our closet, still have the price tags still attached.

So I make a reservation at Signatures for Saturday evening. I want Rian's first experience of fine cuisine to be a sensory awakening for him, one that will be both shield and sword for the onslaught of pizza joints in adolescence.

At 4 PM on Saturday, my anxiety surfaces. I'm beginning to think this is a big mistake. But just as Odysseus strapped himself to the mast before he heard the sirens sing, I too had a plan. When I called the restaurant, I asked for a bottle of Château Gruaud-Larose, an expensive bordeaux, to be decanted several hours before we arrived. So it's breathing peacefully right now, even though I am not.

There's little hope for the white shirt, black pants and bow-tie. Rian dislikes collars, Velcro, zippers, buttons or snaps—essentially everything except t-shirts and sweatpants. But the restaurant's dress code requires jackets for gentlemen. As we stand in front of his emptied dresser, all seems lost until Rian spies his Peter Pan outfit hanging out of his dress-up trunk. The forest green jacket has a crest with crossed swords, giving it the appearance of a private school blazer. Topped off with a green hat and orange feather, Rian looks like the heir to a Bavarian beer-making dynasty.

"Com'on Tink, we're off to Neverland!" Rian crows, jumping around the bedroom with plastic dagger drawn. I'm relieved that he's entered into his favourite story—perhaps I can even convince Mr. Darling upstairs to join in the fun.

When we get to the restaurant, Rian stares up in awe at the building's grey-stone turrets. "A castle," he whispers under his breath. Inside, he's enchanted with the soaring ceilings, the tinkling piano, the rich colours, the folded fabrics, the polished silver, the feeling of period graciousness. He responds serenely to a decorum that is such a contrast to the sensory assault of a fast-food joint.

The maître d' is Brian Donahue, a tall man in a dark suit. As he greets us, he gives Rian a conspiratorial wink. But Rian eyes him suspiciously: he knows only one other man who dresses mostly in black. When Donahue offers to take Rian's outer coat, he recoils. "This time Hook, you've gone too far!"

We convince Rian that Donahue is one of the good pirates and sit down at our table, Rian between Andrew and me. "This is how we've always sat," he tells Donahue with a five-year-old's sense of complete history.

I ask Rian to take off his hat. "Is that a manner for fancy places?" he asks. I nod, and he removes it. As he does so, our server Diane France-Vallière appears from behind him with a small stool to put it on.

"She poofed me!" Rian says delighted with both the stool and France-Vallière's invisible service act. Her gentility and graceful steps around our table make me feel as though we're dining in Stendhal's Paris. She gently unfolds the crisp linen napkins and places them on our laps. Their weight is comforting. Rian brings it to his face and breathes in, "Mmmm—summer."

France-Vallière addresses Rian with a small bow, "Good evening monsieur. And what is your name?"

"Shhh!" Rian says. I look at him horrified.

"That's what my parents always call me in places like this, so I'm changing my name to Shhh!" Rian explains matter-of-factly.

France-Vallière smiles playfully and hands us leather-bound menus.

"I can't read this, I just turned five," Rian tells her, slightly exasperated as he hands it to me. Browsing through the selections, we eliminate those that remind him of cartoon characters. This rules out venison (Bambi), duck (Daffy), beef (Daisy) and chicken (too close to a plucky little rooster named Ruddy). That leaves the unadorable halibut and potatoes.

"Are potatoes part of the Bread Society?" Rian asks. Like many five-year-olds, he would like to survive on bread alone; he'd just as soon form a club against vegetables. So when I ask him which ones he'd like with dinner, he gives me his dark cherub look. "I want to 'gotiate," he says. Rian can make the haggling over vegetables and dessert into a back-and-forth fiercer than Wimbledon. He never misses a weak moment, which in this case arrives with the champagne for Andrew and me, and France-Vallière's offer of a virgin crantini of cranberry and orange juice to Rian.

"What's a virgin Mommy?"

"A very good, ummm, drink."

Andrew and I toast that we've lasted this long, and relax into a whatever-happens-happens acceptance. On the table, our flute glasses glow against the candlelight like flaming tulips.

Rian asks for the lime garnishing Andrew's glass of water and puts it in his mouth to make a smiley face, as he does at home with orange slices. His face crumples at its sour taste and he exclaims, "Pucker!" Unfortunately, Rian is still working on the phonetic distinction between "p" and "f" and a few diners turn and stare. But they've already become charcoal smudges in my side vision.

A junior waiter brings five types of bread in a large silver basket. Rian is about to reach into the basket, when I gently catch his arm and ask him to allow the server to place the bread on the plate with his tongs.

"Spank-you very much," Rian says, with rakish, immoderate laughter. Fortunately, the server doesn't distinguish the word and nods at the polite, happy child. Rian drills out the centre of his baguette and eats it, leaving behind an onion-ring-style crust.

He lifts the tiny silver dome covering the butter with a flourish, proclaiming, "And now for my final finale, I present—the table-cloth!" Like most children, he's always ready for magic. The bread man is a sorcerer, trolls lurk in the fiery kitchen, there's pixie dust on the curtains. He reminds me to look at a world filled with enchantment.

When France-Vallière returns for our orders, Rian carves large slices with his arms. "I would like big chocolate for dessert please," he says.

"We have a chocolate pyramid that I think you'll love," she says.

"I'm one hundred excited!" Rian declares.

"And what would the gentleman like to start?" she asks.

"I'm a carnivore," Rian says, repeating the new word from last night's dinosaur book. "I'll have bare fish, sort of mushy, and potatoes."

"Perhaps a little steamed asparagus?"

"I will never, ever eat asparagus," Rian says. I give him The Look and he adds glumly, "One carrot please . . . I'll happy up when I see dessert."

Our amuse-bouches arrive: demitasses of diced oxtail meat set in a potato and celery root cream sauce. I tell Rian it's like chicken soup. He loves the doll-sized bowl and tries to get his spoon into it. "You can pick it up to drink," I tell him. His eyes shine with happiness. "Yum!"

After we finish, Rian stares dreamily at my necklace and says, "Mommy you look as beautiful as an editor." In our home, editors are elusive, mythical creatures who can never be pinned down.

Next come our appetizers. Andrew's is a sliver of roast deer in a dark cognac-and-juniper-berry sauce. Rian, ever the soaring bird of prey, eyes it across the table and asks if it's chocolate sauce. I have the lobster bisque, and he watches in wonder as the waiter pours the soup around the delicate piece of lobster in my bowl. Rian ploughs his appetizer of scallops around his plate bulldozer-style before eating them.

For a while we eat in silence, broken only by the soft clink of the silverware. Hunger is the most reflective of our bodily appetites, so perhaps that's why dining out has such a civilizing effect—even on untamed offspring.

As France-Vallière clears our dishes, she asks Rian if he liked his appetizer.

"My taste buds loved it," he says. "They're saying, 'More, more, more!'"

But dining at a good restaurant isn't just about food; it's also about abundance and connection, with the earth and with each other. Dinner has its own calm from goal-oriented lunch: there's no meeting to rush back to and no Victorian inhibition about alcohol and enjoyment. We sit in each other's company as we slowly sate one layer of hunger and then the next.

As we start drinking the bordeaux, Andrew and I reach that point of giving-over; the moment where the warmth flows through the tops of your hands and over your thighs, when the crease between your brows smoothes out as you let go of small irritations.

I wonder if we're imprinting on Rian with this experience—as wildebeests do when they take their young away from the herd. Will he spend his life searching for the tastes, smells and sounds that remind him of when his parents seemed the most relaxed and happy and expansive? In making him hungry for the world, we are also giving him the desires that will eventually lead him away from us. But perhaps it's not a bad gift for a child—Escoffier once said that gustatory pleasure remains when all others have left us.

As we wait for our next course, Rian becomes fascinated with the pepper grinder. He investigates its mechanics and admires how its dark-mottled contents contrast with the tablecloth, his plate and his lap, until I gently move it to the other side of the table.

Our entrées are delivered under big silver domes and the servers uncover them in choreographed unison. "Do it again!" Rian says clapping. And they do.

His face lights up as he bites into the tender halibut, a tribute to the first fish that swam free—it needs heavy sauce like Eve needed Revlon. He eats with a feral hunger, like a crouching bobcat. While I eat my own dinner, I devour his expression, an early vocabulary of my own, and envy him the joy of discovering his gustatory pleasures: to feel for the first time a deeply savoury taste glide across your tongue or the heat against the inside of your cheeks.

His face is soft and pink, a chick down illumined by the candle. His eyes hold only what is in front of him, but I can see the thousands of wonderful meals ahead of him, a banquet of possibilities stretching into the future.

But at this moment, Rian picks at his three carrots like a bomb disposal expert, then asks France-Vallière for a "free refill of the virgin."

"Certainly monsieur, it's on the house."

Rian looks up at the ceiling with interest. "Where?"

When she cleans the table with a silver wand, Rian says admiringly, "She's got a snowplow for crumbs." His bliss crests when she brings dessert, the promised chocolate pyramid. He does a happy wiggle-dance in his seat. "Deeelicious!"

With chocolate smears across his face and his eyes aflame with sugar and cocoa, Rian looks like a swarthy preschool pirate. He eats slowly with seraphic equanimity, almost purring. His fist rests on the table like a small satin cushion. We hold our gaze in a flickering shaft of silent thoughts over the candlelight.

I wonder if he'll remember this dinner when he is my age and tonight is a fading photograph with ragged edges. Perhaps some sensations are strong enough to be salted into memory. And perhaps we know when they're not and start to miss some moments even as we are in them.

Donahue returns to ask how our meal was. "It was super-duper!" Rian says. "Do you ask everyone that or just us 'cause there's a kid at the table?"

"We want everyone to have a super-duper meal," Donahue replies. "But I'm especially pleased that you did."

As we get ready to leave, I ask Rian how he feels. He searches in his mind for the right phrase the way he rummages through his dress-up trunk, knowing that what he wants is probably at the bottom. "I'm a speck sad to go," he finally says quietly.

A whitecap of crazy love for him washes over my heart. We walk out of the restaurant into the dark blue night, light-limbed, warm and full. Then Rian clutches my hand and points excitedly to two blinking street lights about a mile down the road.

"Look mommy," he exclaims. "It's the second star to the right—Neverland!"

Devil with A Red Apron On

by David Leite

from *Ridgefield Magazine*

Wry, self-deprecating humor leavens David Leite's food writing, both in his magazine articles and the features on his website, leitesculinaria.com. He's not the first cookbook writer to try to worm recipes out of a traditional home cook, but his mother seems a force to be reckoned with.

Enter my mother's kitchen, a domain she has ruled with benign autocracy for more than 45 years, and all physical laws and culinary edicts cease to exist. It's like finding yourself in the loony world of a Warner Brothers cartoon, where pain is comical, gravity acts as if it never heard of Sir Isaac Newton, and time and space are elastic. For example, when making garnish for a dish, my mother will grab a gargantuan bunch of parsley and, with the ferocity of the Tasmanian Devil, buzz through it in seconds, leaving a thimble-size pile of green flecks. She is a human Ginsu knife.

Apparently, in her kitchen short tempers cause short cooking times, too. Proof: She can fill a pot with water, dump in three fistfuls of dried fava beans, add a 10-ounce link of Portuguese sausage, called *chouriço,* and crank the flame to high. If she's had a rough day, she'll give the pot a hooded glance, and the soup is roiling in minutes. Whoever said a watched pot never boils never knew my mother.

On her "Me Days," though—peaceful afternoons when all she has to do is write several dozen e-mails, wash and iron my father's underwear, vacuum the drapes, and reorganize the silverware drawer—she'll go through the identical process of soup making. Yet the pot, even though set over the same high heat, will only burble, never boil, no matter how long it's been on the stove. Considering her preternatural ways in the kitchen, it's no wonder that until the age of 12 I was terrified that I was a real-life Damien, as depicted in the film *The Omen*, a prepubescent possessor of dark and supernatural powers.

But despite her ample gifts at the stove, she has one of the worst *batterie de cuisine* in New England. Search her cupboards and cabinets, and there's not a cookbook, measuring cup (save the one she got from Weight Watchers in 1964), or measuring spoon to be found. The one knife she does have is older than me, and every so often my father trundles to the basement, puts on his protective goggles, flicks on the rotary grinder, and files off another sixteenth of an inch in the name of sharpness.

It was into this anarchic and wacky kitchen that I walked to learn our family's repertoire of Portuguese dishes.

I began by pestering my mother for recipes, which proved futile because I soon discovered she didn't cook with any. Sure, tucked away in a bedroom drawer was a green leather-bound telephone directory (circa 1958) filled with a sizable collection of recipes that she had carefully transcribed onto its gray pages—under the correct alphabetical tab, of course. But these recipes were so lackluster and ordinary, nothing like the dishes she makes nowadays, that my only recourse was to cook with her.

So there we stood, side by side, weekend after weekend: her chopping, dicing, poking, and pounding, and me frantically scooping ingredients into measuring cups or weighing them on a scale that I had brought from home before she could elbow her way to the stove and toss it all in a big pan.

"Measuring cups are for wimps," she warned, pointing her knife at me. Then she held out her cupped hand: "*This* is all you need." I put my hand alongside hers; it was three times the size.

"But Ma," I tried to explain, "measuring is the only way to standardize a recipe. To know exactly what you do."

"You really want to know what I do?" she asked tenderly.

"Yes, I do," I said. "I really do."

"Then stand here for the next 43 years, and you'll get the hang of it," she said. "How do you like them bananas!" And with that she directed her superhuman energies to sawing through five pounds of onions—all without shedding a tear.

Out of desperation, I hit upon the idea of videotaping her cooking. That way she could tear about and improvise as much as she wished, and all I'd have to do was keep rewinding the tape until I deciphered the recipes.

And improvise she did. If a three-pound pork shoulder wasn't available for a dish, in went a four-pound chuck roast.

"When will it be done?" I asked of the unusual substitution.

"When it's done," was the standard-issue answer.

If a trip to the local fishmonger for two dozen littlenecks was a bust, she'd make a quick calculation then swap out a dozen quahogs or two quarts of Ipswich clams.

"We'll keep the extras for chowder," she'd say, taking a deep whiff of the briny, sandy bag. "How's that, kiddo?"

Vegetables were the worst, though. For the past 25 years, the entire family—all 66 of them—assumed long before I was baptized that the 15,000 square feet of land beyond my parents' yard would be given to me when I turned 21, so I could build a house. That's what you do when you're Portuguese: cook and bequeath land. Sensing my reluctance, for I had my heart set on New York City from the time I was 10 years old, my father commandeered the plot and turned it into one of the most astonishingly fecund gardens in the Northeast.

That meant that armfuls of corn, fava beans, potatoes, cabbage, kale, tomatoes, onions, squash, and carrots were added to my mother's nightly improv. So what if her *carne assada* (roasted beef) calls for potatoes? The carrots were perfect that day, so in they went instead. Her New England boiled dinner looked a little anemic? No problem. A half head of cabbage, a few turnips, and a splash of my father's homemade white wine were added for good measure. By this time I had gone through more footage than Quentin Tarantino did while filming *Kill Bill*.

But after five years of skirmishes, I triumphed. I finally cobbled together a reasonable facsimile of our beloved family dishes, some of which my mother even approves.

Not long ago, I was in my kitchen making a decidedly

unPortuguese meal—marinated flank steak, thyme-and-rosemary-flecked potato wedges, and honey-lavender salad dressing. And although I had two cookbooks and a magazine sprawled open over the counter and table, I barely took a look. While my measuring cups and spoons sat on a shelf, I found myself freelancing at the stove, tossing in a handful of herbs, sprinkling a good four-finger pinch of *fleur de sel,* turning the balsamic vinegar and soy sauce bottles upside down to let the liquid glug into the Pyrex dish until it felt right. *Bastante,* I heard my mother say. Enough.

Remarkably, the dinner was wonderful. A guest asked for the recipes and as I got up to get them, I realized there really were none. After all those years of cooking (read: battling) with my mother, she had taught me to rely upon my senses instead of a book to make something out nothing. Maybe I am Damien after all.

A Flowering of Appetite

by Mei Chin

from *Saveur*

Food customs can bind a family together, even the customs that a younger generation think they have shed. In this poignant essay, Mei Chin—a New York-based culture reporter and novelist—limned the emotions submerged in her Chinese-American grandmother's funeral feast.

Those about to die often develop a tremendous appetite. People have been known to get out of bed, help themselves to the contents of the fridge, and then expire.

One September day in 2001, at two in the morning, my maternal grandmother, Tung-yun Chin, clutched at her second daughter Yen's sleeve and whispered, "Go and cook yi tiao yu for me." By "yi tiao yu", she meant a whole fish—skin, bones, and all—the kind of fish that is meltingly sweet when steamed, crisp on the tongue when fried. At two in the morning, in the New Jersey suburb where Tung-yun lay dying, you'd be lucky if you could get some Gorton's fish sticks from the A&P. Within hours, Tung-yun slipped into a coma, and by 10 AM, when the local fish store was laying out sea bass and red snapper on beds of ice, her heart had stopped.

For the last decade of her life, living in Boston with her youngest daughter, Shoping, Tung-yun was a health-conscious woman, shunning butter, red meat, and cream. Cancer changed her. A few days on an IV was enough to make her hungry as an ox. Food, in her conversation, took poetic flight. She described the texture of cheese, the sensation of rice porridge in her throat, the oil oozing from a pork chop. She rhapsodized about things she had never even cared for, like pizza and yogurt. At one point she said, "I dreamed that I was painting again, but all I could paint was shrimp, chicken, all kinds of squash. Your grandfather came in and said, 'Why do you want to draw that stuff?' " My grandfather had been deceased for almost 20 years, and like many families, ours believes it doesn't bode well to dream of the dead, because it means they are calling you. Dreaming of him used to make my grandmother frightened. Now he only made her chuckle. "Your grandfather and I were squabbling last night about the last piece of steak. Then I woke, and you know what? I never got to eat the steak."

Early in her illness, she craved everything: seafood pâtés, triple-cream cheeses, pastas, petits fours. But toward the end, all she wanted was Chinese. Her extended family, so proficient in American, Italian, and Frenchified Pan-Asian cooking, found themselves crimping dumplings, stewing spareribs in vinegar, braising meatballs and cabbage in rice wine. We pitched camp in the New Jersey kitchen of my eldest aunt, Sha, with whom my grandmother lived for the last month of her life. During this period, I had my own culinary triumph: I poached a chicken with dried black mushrooms and plenty of ginger (for both its healing properties and its sharp, floral flavor) to make granddaughter's chicken soup; for days, she ate nothing but. Sometimes I dressed the broth with udon noodles; other times I poured it over cubes of deep-fried tofu and floated scallions on top, enriched it with beaten egg, or added zucchini ribbons. "You know, the last time I went to China," Tungyun, who was born in Manchuria and moved to America from Taiwan in 1961, told me, "I went to Yangzhou and they had this marvelous braised pork shoulder. Can you believe I actually refused it? Yangzhou pork shoulder!"

The woman at the Chinese restaurant near Shoping's Boston home asks Shoping why she's ordering so much food. Is there an occasion? "It's for a funeral. My mother passed away," she explains. "Your mother? Oh, I'm so sorry," says the woman, who begins to weep. "I'll include this dish for free, and this and this. Have you eaten? You have to eat. Anything you want, it's on the house. Our curried beef today is really good." Shoping, who does not eat beef, feels tears spring up. So it is that on a sunlit day in Chinatown, two women cry while customers eat fried rice and Shoping is tempted to take her first bite of beef in 20 years.

Two days later, Tung-yun's grandchildren, slumbering on the floor, wake at dawn with suspicions that Shoping's Chinatown restaurant has taken up residence in the living room overnight. The air is thick with the smell of soy sauce and of oil heating. As her family prepares foods for Tung-yun's burial ceremony, the matriarch reigns in her urn in the hallway, next to the vessel containing my grandfather's ashes. Yen is in her mother's kitchen frying up Tung-yun's last request. She has chosen huang yu (yellowfish), beloved by the Chinese for its fresh taste and delicate flesh, and coats it with cilantro and red pepper flakes. Meanwhile, in Shoping's own kitchen upstairs, fans hum. Tung-yun's only son, Yo, watches scallion pancakes sizzle. Next to him is a crock of braised beef tendon—sticky and chewy with a glassy sheen—my grandmother's favorite part of the cow.

Sha makes jiaozi (dumplings). The filling is meat interspersed with plenty of green, everything from chopped green beans to fennel fronds; cooked, it becomes moist and full of perfume. Rolling jiaozi pastry is an art, one that in our family only Sha and Yo have learned. You twist a knob of dough with one hand and work your rolling pin with the other until the thinnest, smoothest circle is achieved. My grandfather was a master at this: his wrappers were always perfectly round, translucent, and humped slightly in the center.

Meanwhile, my mother, Annping, slides a pork shoulder, which has been simmering for hours in a dark, faintly sweet star anise–spiked sauce, under the broiler. The skin, covering fork-tender meat, glistens and crackles.

By 8 AM we're ready, and we cart platters, chopsticks, and my grandparents' ashes (it was their wish to be buried together) to the chapel—a beautiful Boston relic—in which we are holding our quasi-Asian nondenominational service. There are many guests. Yo remarks, "It's like a *Godfather* film, only with an Asian cast." Chinese musicians are playing with somber faces. My grandmother loved Chinese music; to me, it sounds like squawking. Shivering, we gather behind the pulpit and spoon out still-warm pork shoulder, pile dumplings high, arrange flowers, prop up photographs, funeral tablets, and an incense burner. The table is so full, there almost isn't room for both of my grandparents' urns.

The dishes we are offering are wonderful but pungent. We brought the incense burner but forgot the incense, so as we each step to the pulpit to deliver our eulogies and, later, to make our bows of respect, we are greeted by the smell of pork and vinegar. By this time, our shivering has turned to shaking, but it is not until we are at the cemetery that we realize why. We want lunch.

Still, we are the hosts, and back at the house we are expected to serve before we can eat. So we lay out silverware and arrange the food we ordered from the Chinese restaurant—at the same time munching on spring rolls and swilling champagne, reveling in the magical mix of bubbles and grease. My grandmother's American friends are appalled when the grandchildren hand out napkins as they chew. The grandchildren, on the other hand, are appalled to find their parents nibbling at the foods we brought back from the chapel.

"Aren't you damning yourselves to hell or something?" asks my cousin Jay. "It's okay," says my mother, "You're supposed to eat the offering." "Well, you teach Confucianism," he says, taking a forkful. "I guess you'd know."

Later, after the guests have gone, we remove the pork shoulder from the fridge and strip it to the bone. There is a lot of food left, but we set out slabs of cheese, too, which we demolish in a twinkle. While Tung-yun was dying, we cooked for her but had no appetite ourselves. Now that we've buried her, we are hungry once again.

⁓

Granddaughter's Chicken Soup with Egg

Serves 4

15 Chinese dried black (shiitake) mushrooms, rinsed
1 3½- to 4-lb. chicken, rinsed
6 scallions, trimmed

4" piece ginger, peeled, sliced, and crushed
¼ cup Chinese rice wine
Salt and freshly ground white pepper
1 egg
4 tbsp. soy sauce
1 tsp. Asian sesame oil

1. Soak mushrooms in 1 cup hot water in a small bowl. Meanwhile, put chicken into a large pot and cover with cold water. Bring to a boil over high heat, cook for 1 minute, then drain. Return chicken to pot and add mushrooms and their soaking liquid, 5 of the scallions, ginger, rice wine, salt and pepper to taste, and 16 cups cold water. Bring to a boil over medium-high heat, skimming foam as it rises to the surface. Reduce heat to medium-low and simmer until chicken is cooked through, 40–45 minutes.

2. Transfer chicken to a bowl and set aside until just cool enough to handle. Remove breast and thigh meat from chicken and return carcass to pot, reserving meat for another use. Bring stock to a boil over high heat, then reduce heat to medium-low and simmer, skimming any foam as it rises to the surface, for 1½ hours. Strain stock through a fine sieve, discarding solids.

3. Bring 4 cups of the stock (save remaining stock for another use) just to a simmer in a medium pot over medium heat. Beat egg well with a fork in a small bowl, then gradually add to pot, stirring stock constantly with the fork until ribbons form. Remove pot from heat.

4. Thinly slice the remaining scallion and set aside. Put 1 tbsp. soy sauce and ¼ tsp. oil into each of 4 warm soup bowls. Divide soup between bowls and garnish each with scallions.

If This Is Wednesday, It Must Be Liver Loaf

by Will Pritchard
from *Gastronomica*

While Julie Powell (see *A Menu Marathon*, page 131) may have set herself this year's most daunting culinary challenge, English lit professor Pritchard does pretty well with his own experimental cooking project: Replicating his grandmother's menus from the 1930s.

The last time I saw my grandmother was after her one-hundredth birthday party. Despite having been briefly hospitalized earlier that weekend, she presided triumphantly at this event, attended by all her relatives and friends. Not being one to rest on her laurels, or even to rest much at all, she was (when I left later that evening) re-arranging the furniture in her apartment in preparation for the next morning's family breakfast.

Two months later, a fatal stroke finally persuaded my grandmother to slow down a little, and we gathered again in Florida to remember her and divide her things. I came away with some old photographs and a small cache of cookbooks. Most intriguing among these was a silver-and-black volume from 1930: *My Better Homes and Gardens Cookbook*. My grandmother apparently acquired it in 1936, when it was in its eighteenth printing. She was then thirty-five, and so was I when I inherited it.

I don't remember ever seeing her use this, or any, cookbook. The foods she served—hamburgers, ham, noodles, mashed potatoes, beans, peas—were truths held to be self-evident: all men are created equal, all meat is served well-done, all vegetables can be canned or frozen, all plates must be cleaned before dessert. This cookbook was not the source of these beliefs, but it seems to have held her attention at one point. She dutifully clipped "Endorsed Recipes" from *Better Homes and Gardens* magazine—recipes that passed "tests of actual goodness of taste and family usefulness"—and added them to the loose-leaf cookbook. The authors optimistically describe their book as "still young, with plenty of room to grow," but my grandmother stunted its growth. After the berry desserts of July, 1938, there are no further insertions. But if the book did not expand, neither did it languish. Its stained and taped condition signaled repeated use. The foreword bills this as "truly a *lifetime* cookbook," and so it turned out to be. Even when, at the age of ninety-one, my grandmother moved to a world where she would no longer cook dinner, she brought along her *Better Homes and Gardens Cookbook*.

What most intrigued me was the book's series of menus. "Every homemaker," it explains, "likes concrete examples in the form of menus to help her." There were menus for every season, each menu covering a full week's meals. Wouldn't it be fun, I thought, to follow one of these menus for a week? It would teach a lesson in old-fashioned homemaking, helping me to "bring the efficiency of a well-organized business into [my] job as home director." It would also be a tribute of sorts to my grandmother, a way of walking a week in her shoes. The book seemed to have anticipated my scheme, billing itself as "your starting point for a whole new adventure in meal-making."

I wondered, though, if the other half of my family would join in this adventure. As the cookbook rightly notes, "Providing the right foods—serving a perfect meal, for that matter—would be of no avail, if we could not get our family to eat it." My wife, Mo, has tastes that run towards the organic and the vegetarian. What would happen if she came home to find me carrying out this savage recipe for "Stuffed Heart?"

> Wash the heart thoroly [sic] in cold water and cut out veins and arteries, being sure heart is freed of blood. Fill the heart with poultry stuffing and sew up . . . Brown the heart in a little fat and then add a little water to the kettle or pan. Cover and allow to simmer

either in the oven or on top of the stove to become
tender (3 to 4 hours).

Somewhat to my surprise, however, Mo gave her consent. She is a
professor of history and appreciated the spirit of the undertaking.
As I was already on summer vacation, I could devote myself fully
to this enterprise. And so, without going into too many of the
specifics, we agreed to try a "Late Spring" menu from 1930.

MONDAY

Breakfast was a pleasure. We shared a shirred egg, and sliced
oranges and bacon made welcome additions to the more familiar
coffee and toast. Mo headed off to work, and I stayed home to
work on lunch. The menu was plausible, if somewhat unusual:
macaroni and cheese, beet greens, rhubarb conserve, saltines, tea,
milk. I was a little dismayed to find that the cookbook contained
no recipes for macaroni and cheese and beet greens. This may be
a lifetime cookbook, but it's not for babies.

I quickly turned to Mark Bittman's *How to Cook Everything*
(1998) for remedial help. Bittman assumes nothing. His directions
are fussily explicit: heat the milk until small bubbles appear along
the sides, melt the butter until it is foamy, etc. I knew I was cheating
a bit, here; the *Better Homes* folks back in Des Moines would not
have allowed me to give the macaroni and cheese a pleasing sharpness by folding in ½ cup of freshly grated Parmesan. I cheated, too,
by omitting the rhubarb conserve. (Any item from Chapter 6
["Canning & Preserving"] or Chapter 10 ["Pickles"] was beyond
the scope of this short-term experiment.) We didn't drink milk or
tea, either, and the saltines were actually Stoned Wheat Thins. We
were following the spirit, not the letter, of the lunch.

The same could not be said of dinner, whose main course—
creamed sweetbreads—posed a number of difficulties. We live in a
town, nay, in a world without butchers. Where to find the thymus
gland of a calf? The meat manager at the Safeway could recall the
days when they used to stock a bin full of innards and outards:
hooves, ears, kidneys, spleens. One could still special order a heart,
but he wasn't sure about sweetbreads. "I'm not sure what they do
with them," he said.

I considered substituting tofu (texturally similar, ethically simpler), but the revised recipe did not tempt:

> Parboil tofu and break into small pieces. Add to a white sauce and season well, adding extra butter. Serve on toast points.

Better to focus on the remainder of the meal: vegetable soup, French fried potatoes, cucumber pickles, lettuce and radish salad, rolls, strawberry preserves, lemon tapioca, "Top Milk" and coffee. Sadly, the vegetable soup, though vegetarian and well within my means as a cook, sounded wretched. The only vegetables in sight were two tablespoons of onion, two cups of stewed tomatoes and a cup of canned corn. The onions were to be sautéed in butter, and after the addition of a little flour, the tomatoes and corn were to be added, along with a tablespoon of sugar and two cups of water. After cooking this mess for thirty minutes, I was expected to rub it through a sieve, and then add a half cup of cream beaten stiff with an egg yolk. I decided to pass on the soup as well.

The book, as I had begun to anticipate, gave no recipe for French fries, so I took this opportunity to renew my acquaintance with the Ore-Ida family of frozen potato products. But when dinnertime rolled around, I was diverted and defeated by the ample leftovers from our lunch. Why was no provision made for these? Don't these people know that we're in the middle of The Great Depression? How are we supposed to enjoy an entirely new meal while Okies are trudging their way across the Dust Bowl? Instead, our dinner was comprised of leftover macaroni and cheese, leftover beet greens, and—the only "official" dinner item—a delicious lettuce and radish salad. For dessert, we had the prescribed lemon tapioca pudding, but I botched it somehow, producing a runny, lemony tapioca with unincorporated meringue on top and within. "You know," I told Mo, "if you ordered 'Molten Lemon Tapioca' in a restaurant and they served you this, you'd think it was delicious." Unpersuaded, she demanded to be taken to Baskin-Robbins for a properly executed dessert.

TUESDAY

Once again, breakfast was delightful: French toast à la Bittman, maple syrup, fresh strawberries, and coffee. During breakfast, we peeked at the lunch menu (Ham Omelet, Horseradish sauce) and decided to skip it entirely. Even after thus scaling back the experiment, however, I encountered serious familial resistance that afternoon. "Are you not appalled," Mo asked, when she returned home, "at the amount of food being produced and consumed in this household?" I allowed as how we had been rather busy, but that I was not yet ready to abandon the adventure. For her part, Mo declared that she would not be participating in any sort of evening meal. I was unconcerned, since I had hardly expected her to join me in tonight's Irish Stew. And when the time came, I thought, she might be persuaded by Asparagus Salad.

The absence of an official recipe, I expected, would free me to do something *au courant* with the organic asparagus I had purchased at our local food co-op. But, alas, under "Gelatine Salads—Vegetable" I found a most unwelcome recipe for Asparagus Salad. This would have me heat butter, flour, lemon juice, salt, softened gelatin, and beaten eggs. Into this, I was to add whipped cream and my lovely asparagus. I would then chill it overnight and serve squares of it on lettuce with mayonnaise and a sprinkling of paprika. Happily, I came across this abomination too late to gelatinize or refrigerate. Instead, I pan-roasted the asparagus with a little lemon juice and dressed it with sesame oil. Mo ate this dish and some radishes for dinner, while I set to work on my Irish Stew: beef, water, a turnip, two carrots, an onion, a potato, some flour to thicken, salt and pepper to season. It was simple and delicious, a useful reminder that one can cook without wine, garlic, bay leaves, thyme, etc. For dessert, I had the remaining Lemon Tapioca Dream-Cloud, and went to bed quite pleased with the day, yet anxious for the morrow.

WEDNESDAY

It wasn't breakfast that worried me; I happily made the prescribed "Pancakes Delicious." Nor was lunch a concern, since, with plenty of Irish Stew remaining, I wouldn't need to scallop corn or measure a half peck of spinach. My concern was the evening's main course: Baked Liver Loaf. Liver loaf was a bold challenge to my commitment and dedication: How far would I go? The name seemed intentionally unappetizing, and yet the dish might prove delicious, a meatloaf with the richness of a pâté. Even Mo the Vegetarian was intrigued and dared me to attempt it.

I got a little fancy, replacing the stipulated pound of beef liver with milder-tasting calves' liver, available frozen, sliced, skinned and deveined at the Safeway. I defrosted the liver slices, boiled them in salted water and threw them into the food processor until I had, well, chopped liver. To this I added bread crumbs, ½ cup of ground pork, chopped onion, ketchup, a raw egg, salt, pepper and (exotic!) paprika. I pressed it into a loaf pan and it baked for an hour, during which time no subtle alchemy occurred. What came out of the oven was exactly what you'd expect: a meatloaf with a dark secret it was powerless to conceal. With each funky bite, I was forced to ask—and unable to determine—whether the liver improved this loaf. Was this comfort food or discomfort food? Mo and our guest, Sarah, were unable to help me decide, as they dined solely on green peas, buttered carrots, and cabbage salad. The peas (stir-fried) and the carrots (quick-braised) were modernized. The cabbage salad ("Delicious Cabbage Salad") was vintage: raw cabbage, apples, and raisins with a peculiar dressing of mashed bananas and orange juice. It tasted like coleslaw with a smoothie spilled on it.

The odors and oddities of dinner were forgotten, however, when we reached dessert: sponge cake, fresh strawberries, whipped cream. The cookbook offered both " 'Old Reliable' Sponge Cake" and "The Perfect Sponge Cake," and I chose the former. It turned out truly spongy, with a toughness that marked it as reliable rather than perfect. But no matter; with this dinner, I felt I had finally tasted the 1930s.

THURSDAY

Pride goeth before a fall. Instead of stewed fresh rhubarb, cooked cereal, and muffins, we had sponge cake with raspberry jam and whipped cream for breakfast. After thus indulging ourselves, we proceeded to feed our dog liver loaf for his breakfast. Unlike his owners, he had no qualms about it. Heartened by this vote of confidence, I made myself (when the time came) a tasty lunch of cold liver loaf, Ore-Ida crispers, and cold asparagus. I gave not a thought to the canned baked bean salad I ought to have been preparing. And when dinnertime rolled around, I just didn't have the stamina to cook another damn meal, even this lovely-sounding one:

Breaded Veal Cutlets
Scalloped Potatoes and Carrots
Buttered Beets
Wilted Lettuce Salad
Baked Apples, Whipped Cream
Cookies

Breaded, scalloped, buttered, wilted, baked, whipped: these are a few of my favorite participles, but I was worn out. Mo was working late, and so for dinner I got some Kentucky Fried Chicken, which I ate while watching basketball and drinking beer. I don't even know what she had for dinner, if anything.

FRIDAY

Like a backsliding alcoholic, I awoke awash in self-loathing. How could I have fed myself without accounting for the needs of the rest of the family? Why couldn't I follow a simple menu for one short week? *What kind of home-director am I?* Having fallen off the wagon, or rather, having taken the wagon to the drive-thru, I resolved to get back on track. One step at a time, I told myself. Breakfast was a pretty close approximation of the official menu. Lunch, we customarily avoided, even though its dessert, "Prune Whip," had already become, like Liver Loaf, a term of endearment in the household. I was unable to make the entrée, however, and (to paraphrase Pink Floyd) if you don't eat your creamed dried beef on toast, you can't have any prune whip; how can you have any prune whip if you don't eat your creamed dried beef on toast?

On to dinner, then. It began with a simple cream of asparagus soup: a bunch of asparagus boiled and pureed, added to a quart of milk, thickened with butter and flour, and seasoned with salt and pepper. It occurred to me, while making this soup, that these dishes were originally made without the help of electric appliances. I tried at first to "press the tough stalks thru a colander or sieve" as directed, but only generated about a tablespoon of asparagus puree. I felt morally and physically weak as I tossed it into the Cuisinart.

The main course, it being Friday, was fish. I was relieved to read that "a certain amount of iodine, furnished us agreeably by fish and shellfish, is a help in preventing goiter and other ills." That's one less thing to worry about. The menu called for Fried Fish Fillets, but gave no further guidance. I bought some red snapper and made, instead, Mark Bittman's "Oven-Fried" fish fillets. The peas and carrots I kept on the menu; the hot potato salad I dropped like a hot potato. For dessert, we polished off the sponge cake with strawberries and whipped cream. It was a lovely meal, made more so by the knowledge that it was likely to be the last.

SATURDAY AND SUNDAY

We were leaving for the summer on Monday, and Mo made it clear that it was time for me to "bring the efficiency of a well-organized business" into other aspects of my job as home director. Instead of Cabbage and Pineapple Salad, how about cleaning and packing suitcases? Frankly, I was ready for the change. The only thing I lamented from the lost meal was Sunday's traditional midday dinner: Baked Ham, Creamed New Potatoes, Buttered String Beans, Celery, Rolls, Jelly, Head Lettuce Salad, Sponge Cake à la Mode, Coffee, Milk. I had enjoyed this meal, or something very much like it, several times at my grandmother's house on Master Sundays. It is the meeting point of my culinary tastes and hers, and I was sorry not to revisit it.

On the way out of town, I purchased a copy of *Better Home and Gardens* magazine, curious about the current state of the "home-business woman." I was pleased to discover that BHG, as it calls itself, still solicits, tests, and prints readers' recipes, and that other readers are still invited to add these recipes to their *Better Homes and Garden New Cook Book*. But the more I read of the insouciant prose and permissive attitude of the new BHG ("dig out your blender, mix a fruity smidge of this and a tart dash of that, and blend away"), the more I appreciated the stark, inflexible tone of the old cookbook.

After a week of trying be a thirties housewife, I had a new

appreciation for those who prepare three meals a day. "Set aside some time each day to cook dinner," writes Mark Bittman, "and you will find it becomes a rewarding, energy-giving routine." Fine, but set aside all day every day to cook three meals, and you will find it becomes an exhausting, insupportable burden. I had a clearer sense, too, of how far we have come, and how low we have sunk. I'm glad for modern conveniences and exotic spices, for hot peppers and hand blenders. I'm glad that we homemakers don't have to work as hard as our grandmothers did, starting every meal from scratch with only our pickles and preserves to help us. But when I see BHG soliciting recipes for "Best Bread Machine Loaves," I can't help but feel that maybe it's all too easy now.

For me, though, the real lesson of the original *My Better and Homes and Gardens Cookbook* is the importance of naming. Whenever my grandmother, visiting, would catch me stir-frying some garlicky pile of vegetables and noodles, she would always ask derisively, "What do you call that?" To her, a dish without a name was like a person without a social security card: suspicious and probably foreign. The *Better Homes* cookbook adheres stringently to the principle that every dish should bear a name, an elegant one ("Mushroom Supreme"), or a whimsical one ("Kentucky Corn Dodgers"), or a plain one ("Shortcake"). The liver loaf taught me that a catchy name can go a long way towards making an odd dish palatable. So if I ever cook from this cookbook again, I will begin with this glorious menu:

Planked Smelts
Cheese Monkey
Lazy Woman's Chow-Chow
Okra Savory
Nippy Rolls
Quince Compote
Prune Pie
Philadelphia Ice Cream

Like they say, "This book is your starting point for a whole new adventure in meal-making."

Hearth Strings

by Jason Epstein

from *The New York Times Magazine*

Renowned publishing executive Jason Epstein, a passionate home cook, has turned to his kitchen lately as an outlet for his literary sensibilities. It isn't just what he creates there that matters—it's the room itself, as a gathering place, as a haven. And now he realizes why.

I have two kitchens, one in Manhattan, the other on Long Island. Each has a table that seats six. The one in the city is made of stainless steel and was built by a shop on Grand Street that does sheet-metal work for Chinese restaurants. Normally the shop doesn't bother with individuals, but one of the owners had a young son named Jason and made an exception in my case. The table in the country is an old, somewhat battered reproduction of a round-topped table that might have been in use when the house was built in 1790 and was left behind by the previous owner when I bought the place in the 1960's. Until I was asked some years ago by a food magazine to write something about my kitchen I hadn't noticed what has since become obvious to me: these two kitchens bear a strong family resemblance, despite the different tabletops. It was as if I had designed them with a common ancestor in mind.

For years, between marriages, I seldom visited the other rooms in my Long Island house, spending most of my time in the kitchen reading in a comfortable blue chair beside an old brick fireplace. I had what, in retrospect, seems to have been an aversion to the bedrooms upstairs to which, I imagined, foolishly, my grown children might someday return. I slept in a room off the kitchen. Only when more than six people came to dinner did I use the dining room, reluctantly, and still do. The same is true in the city. I prefer to read and write in the kitchen and almost never sit in the living room. This part of the apartment has always seemed off limits to me, like the front parlors of Victorian houses with their rubber plants, stuffed birds and antimacassars. Only on the grandest occasions do we use the dining room with its gleaming Louis XV table surrounded by crammed bookshelves and old silver candlesticks made into pink-shaded lamps.

When I sat down in my city kitchen to write the article and looked toward the ceiling for inspiration, I noticed for the first time that the varnish that had been applied 10 years previously to the wainscoted walls and ceiling had by now turned the color of honey. I wondered how long it would be before these walls acquired the look of the ancient pumpkin pine of which the cabinets and counter-tops in my country kitchen were made. It was then, in a flash of memory, that I saw with sudden clarity the ancestor from which these two kitchens with their paneled walls and utilitarian Garland stoves derived: it was my grandmother Ida's kitchen in Maine, where I spent my most vivid, most pleasant and perhaps most formative childhood years.

My grandparents lived atop a steep hill in what seems to me in memory to have been a very large house whose rooms ran one into the other. There was very little central heating, so in winter, when frost formed sharp peaks on the heavy storm windows, everyone sat in the kitchen, warmed by the big wood stove with nickel trim and the words Model Home Fireside above a temperature gauge on the oven door. My own perch was to the left of the stove, atop a wood box painted robin's-egg blue, from which I could observe the activity around me: my grandmother in a faded apron and oxford glasses removing a towering apple pie from the oven; an aunt at the sewing machine between the windows, beyond which I could see the wind-whipped snow swirling against the blackness of the open barn doors and my friend Raymond, who would grow up to be a priest in Canada, trudging uphill on his wooden skis. Pete, the old English bulldog who once rescued me unnecessarily from a snowdrift by tugging at my sleeve, growling softly, was asleep on a blanket beneath the oven door. The walls were wainscoted from floor to ceiling like the walls of my present kitchen, but the varnish was older and mellower. The copper plumbing at the black slate sink must have been added later, since it was bracketed to the walls and groaned and rattled whenever the faucet was opened.

On summer days when the kitchen became uncomfortably warm and the fumes of melting tar on the road clutched at our throats, I would retreat to read in a large, cool pantry—called the shed—off the passageway that led to the barn. It was in this shed, with its remnant of winter cold, that my grandmother kept her preserves: shelves of peaches and green tomatoes, figs in syrup, pears, rhubarb and purple plums, eggplant, applesauce, cucumbers and peppers in shiny jars, which in memory I have conflated with my grandmother's gleaming oxford glasses and their gold chain. Old patchwork quilts were piled in a corner where Pete spent the night.

Whether my grandmother was a good cook I can't say, but she was said to be, and mealtimes, when the family gathered around the large oak table, were always a joy. I remember in summertime bowls of coleslaw, pickled cucumbers and green tomatoes, beet soup, platters of fried or roasted chicken, apple pies and, in winter, double brisket and braised root vegetables, breast of veal stuffed with Swiss chard, lamb braised slowly for hours.

My grandparents were immigrants from the Crimea who joined other family members who had already settled in Maine to become peddlers and later shopkeepers. They were not religious, but on holidays my grandmother, as a matter of pride, cooked and baked for the synagogue, and the family, most of whom were strictly nonobservant, shared her ethnic menu at home: chicken soup with dumplings, pickled fish, stuffed cabbage and so on. When the chickens she fattened were ready to be killed, it was my job to carry them in a burlap sack down the hill to the ritual butcher who cut their throats and I turned them over to a weakminded nephew who sat in a dark corner and plucked their feathers. When he had finished, I put the chickens, wrapped in the Yiddish newspaper, into the burlap sack and trudged back up the hill. Next door to the butcher's shop was a secondhand bookstore, where a studious cousin, then in college, found a five-volume edition of Macaulay's "History of England" and asked me to help carry it up the hill. Though these books probably weighed no more than the chickens, they felt much heavier in the summer heat. I remember gasping for breath as I finally reached the summit of Prospect Hill. To this day, I cannot think of Macaulay without recalling the ritual butchery and his speechless nephew pulling feathers in the darkened corner.

I have never taken much stock in psychoanalysis, with its emphasis on repressed memory. It has always seemed to me that the important roots of human suffering are to be found within the shared failings of the species itself, modified by personal genetic determinants, and not primarily amid the accidental encounters of one's childhood. Nevertheless, I am grateful for the occasion to have uncovered the source of my affection for varnished wainscoting, for the robin's-egg-blue kitchen armchair where I like to read and my preference for the kitchen as a place in which not only to cook and eat but also to read, write and contemplate the world, and of course my habit of bracketing England's great Whig historian with a plucked chicken wrapped in a Yiddish newspaper.

My grandmother's chicken potpie was a family favorite, but I didn't like her crust, which, no matter how shiny on top, was gummy underneath. When I began to make my own chicken pies I saw that an obvious way to avoid this was to bake a puff-pastry crust separately and serve it in a wedge, like a gaufrette, atop the contents of the pie.

Chicken Potpie

Serves 6

3 tablespoons vegetable oil
4 8-ounce skinless and boneless chicken-breast halves, cut into
    1-inch cubes
8 tablespoons butter, plus extra for greasing parchment
20 pearl onions, blanched and peeled
3 carrots, cut in ½-inch rounds
1 celery heart in ½-inch dice

20 button mushroom caps or ½ pound porcini mushrooms, stems
cut off, cut into 1-inch pieces
4 cups strong homemade chicken stock or 5 cups of organic
chicken broth from a carton, reduced to 4, plus extra if needed
½ cup all-purpose flour
1½ cups half-and-half or heavy cream
1 sprig fresh rosemary, leaves finely chopped, plus extra for garnish
1 tablespoon chopped thyme leaves
1 tablespoon chopped Italian parsley
3 tablespoons dry sherry
Salt and freshly ground black pepper to taste
3 tablespoons lemon juice
1 pound homemade puff pastry (or Dufour brand ready made)
Egg wash (1 egg yolk beaten with 2 teaspoons heavy cream)

1. In a Dutch oven, heat oil over medium heat and sauté the
chicken, in batches, until lightly golden but not cooked through.
Set aside.

2. In the same, cleaned pan, melt 2 tablespoons butter. Sauté the
onions until golden brown, about 5 minutes. Remove to bowl
with the chicken. Repeat with carrots and celery and then mushrooms. In a separate pan, heat stock to boiling.

3. Clean Dutch oven again. Melt remaining butter over medium
heat. Whisk in flour and cook until pale gold, 2 minutes. Whisk in
boiling stock, half-and-half, herbs, sherry and salt and pepper and
heat to a slow boil. Reduce heat and simmer 5 minutes or until
thick enough to coat a spoon. (If too thick, add more stock.) Stir
in 2 tablespoons lemon juice, the chicken and vegetables. Cover
with buttered parchment. (Pie can be prepared ahead to this point
and refrigerated until 1 hour before cooking.)

4. Preheat oven to 425 degrees. Roll out the pastry into a square
just less than ½ inch thick and, using a very sharp knife, cut a round
the size of the pot. Line a rimmed baking sheet with parchment
and invert the round on top. (Sprinkle the scraps with sugar, twist

them into corkscrew shapes and bake them as cookies.) If using Dufour, follow package directions.

5. Brush pastry with egg wash, without letting any drip down the sides, which will prevent it from rising evenly. Prick all over with a fork. (For a flatter, denser crust, omit the wash, cover pastry with a second sheet of parchment paper and a second sheet pan on top, forming a sandwich. This keeps the puff pastry from rising and provides a crunchy, buttery pastry.)

6. Bake pastry until puffed, browned and crisp, 15 to 20 minutes. Reduce heat to 350 degrees and bake until cooked through, 15 to 20 minutes longer.

7. Reduce oven temperature to 275 degrees. Bake chicken mixture until sauce is bubbly around edges and chicken is just cooked through, about 30 minutes. Place baking sheet with pastry in oven to reheat the last 10 minutes of cooking.

8. To serve: Remove parchment from Dutch oven and taste sauce. Adjust seasoning and stir in remaining lemon juice if needed. Slide pastry onto chicken mixture and display your pie. Back in the kitchen, cut the crust into wedges with a serrated knife. Spoon chicken onto warmed plates, stick a corner of a wedge into each serving and garnish with rosemary.

NOTE: Reheat chicken in a microwave or double boiler—it may scorch over direct heat.

Appetites

Forming a Palate

by Greg Atkinson

from *Pacific Northwest Magazine*

Like other food writers who've been professional chefs, Greg Atkinson has the how and what of cooking at his fingertips. Where he excels is in also pondering the why of cooking—which, as he muses here, is inextricably connected to the who and where of one's life.

Through sharing and experience, we find the 'good' in food. One evening last summer, as the season drew to a close, I played host to a "Dinner in the Barn" at the home of my friend Jerilyn Brusseau on Bainbridge Island. On a whim, we scrubbed her old sheep barn from top to bottom and invited in the angels of air and light and water. Then we invited a bunch of friends to join us.

Jerilyn and my wife Betsy set a table for 18 and covered it with linen tablecloths, old silverware, bowls of flowers and polished brass candlesticks with beeswax tapers. When they lit the candles, afternoon sun still streamed in through open doors and windows, and through gaps between the boards of the barn itself. Before we were seated, a wreath of whole-wheat bread on a board piled with goat cheeses was brought forth, and as we spread the soft, white goat cheese over the warm, brown bread, I wondered if anything had ever tasted so good.

I suppose that given the setting, almost anything would have tasted good.

That gathering of friends in the barn constituted a charmed and magical moment. But it's also fair to say that the food itself was inherently good. The cheese, handmade by Beverly and Steve

Phillips of Port Madison Farm on Bainbridge Island, was no ordinary cheese, and the bread was baked with considerable care by Brusseau herself, a world-class baker who created the original cinnamon roll that became Cinnabon.

So what makes food good? Is it the ingredients, or is it the care and attention applied to those ingredients by the cook? Do great food moments arise spontaneously now and then, here and there, or can they be orchestrated on demand? Why does some food strike one person as good and another as simply strange?

If you ask me, I would say that we each carry inside us a series of criteria that any food must meet in order to qualify as "good." And that arbitrary but exacting set of parameters constitutes a palate.

Like language, a palate is formed early in life. But just like language, palates can grow and change. One's food vocabulary is almost infinitely expandable. As a college student in New England, I drank the crisp and relatively dry cider pressed from apples in Vermont, and subsequently I lost some of my enthusiasm for the overly sweet stuff that came in bottles down South.

Just as I learned new words to express the various feelings that were once summed up by the term "cool," so I learned to appreciate crumbly white cheddar, and found the pre-sliced American cheese of my youth no longer satisfied in quite the same way.

Not long ago, I sampled several brands of apple baby food at the table of my friend Jon Rowley. (Rowley is the man responsible for the Copper River salmon craze, and for several other culinary marvels). I'm not sure what prompted Jon's obsession with applesauce for babies—it came in the wake of a gift of Gravensteins from the tree in my front yard. But Jon has a way of waking up my food senses, bringing deliberate attention to the textures and flavors, aromas and colors that distinguish "Good Food" and make it stand out from the pack of mediocre stuff that surrounds it.

We sampled a jar of something called "Dutch Apple Dessert," a jar of "Organic Apple," and another brand of "100% Gravenstein Applesauce." We also had a jar of my own homemade applesauce on hand to compare. The Dutch apple dessert was bursting with the flavors of sugar and cinnamon but the taste of apple was elusive. The other brands were better—especially the one that was 100 percent Gravenstein. But when we opened the jar of my homemade applesauce and the scent came wafting off the jar, I was transfixed.

Somehow, that jar evoked the tree in my yard, a breeze through my kitchen window, and the dinner in Brusseau's sheep barn.

That night, after the bread and cheese, we sat down to plates of simply dressed farmer's market vegetables on green gypsy plates. Then came grilled salmon with blackberry sauce and corn pudding. And for dessert, we had Gravenstein apples baked in pastry, apples from the same tree that yielded the sauce in that jar. And then it occurred to me: What makes food good might be the story that goes with it.

If we are awake to what's happening, every bite we take can link us to a story. And in the language of the palate, every pantry is a veritable Scheherazade, the source of a thousand and one intriguing tales. I like Gravenstein apples not only because they are fragrant, crisp and juicy. I like them because I associate their aroma with so many good experiences I have had.

And the same might be true of every other food I like.

I still like American cheese grilled on white bread—it takes me back to my grandmother's kitchen, the Formica table top and the vinyl-covered, chrome-legged chairs, the rooster-shaped cookie jar and the cuckoo clock; it all comes back. In the same way, white cheddar evokes Vermont and goat cheese conjures memories of farmer's markets in France.

The only vital connection between these things is my own experience. What makes food good is us. Our own perceptions, heightened by knowledge and awareness, fortified by a lifetime of experience from which we might draw our own thousand and one tales of delight.

Ode to an Egg

by Michelle Wildgen
from *Tin House*

Among literary magazines, *Tin House* also pursues a minor in food writing. In this essay, Wildgen, an editor at the magazine as well as a contributor, riffs and improvises like a jazz musician on the many meanings of that most basic food item, the egg.

On this morning there was brioche and red raspberry preserve and the eggs were boiled and there was a pat of butter that melted as they stirred them and salted them lightly and ground pepper over them in the cups. They were big eggs and fresh and the girl's were not cooked quite as long as the young man's . . . he was happy with his which he diced up with the spoon and ate with only the flow of the butter to moisten them . . .

—Ernest Hemingway

The Garden of Eden was not a good book, but I was so busy reading Hemingway's descriptions of food, especially eggs, that it took me several years to notice. As do many things, the book begins with eggs. As newlyweds, Hemingway informs us, the Bournes eat eggs each morning, excited just to contemplate the manner of cooking them. The husband never abandons his joyful consumption of *oeufs au jambon* and eventually finds happiness in love and work. The wife begins to skip breakfast about midway through. Things turn out badly for her.

> Probably one of the most private things in the world is
> an egg until it is broken.
>
> —M. F. K. Fisher (1908–1992)

In English the word *egg* is something to cup in one's palm. On the page, the extra *g*, like a linguistic wink, lends the word the same oblong shape as the thing itself. *Egg* nestles against the curve of the tongue.

In its shell it is all smoothness and balance. Next to it, other kinds of beauty seem bony and embellished, and at times I think the nutmeg speckling on a blue egg is as much as we can hope for. Yet the egg lends its beauty generously—witness the way egg tempera allows itself to be saturated with color, the chalky aura that bathes a Vermeer, as though the painter has cast his light through a broken shell.

M. F. K. Fisher mused that the egg is privacy itself. As a metaphor for self-containment, only the oyster comes close, but its rough-ribboned shell lacks the egg's tranquility. The oyster must clamp itself closed, while the egg simply has not noticed anyone else.

> I had an excellent repast—the best repast possible—which
> consisted simply of boiled eggs and bread and butter. It was
> the quality of these simple ingredients that made the occa-
> sion memorable. The eggs were so good that I am ashamed
> to say how many of them I consumed . . . it might seem
> that an egg which has succeeded in being fresh has done
> all that can reasonably be expected of it. But there was a
> bloom of punctuality, so to speak, about these eggs of
> Bourg, as if it had been the intention of the very hens
> themselves that they should be promptly served.
>
> —Henry James

Those of us who did not grow up on farms retain some idealism about a fresh egg. I used to buy mine from a silent old man at a Wisconsin farmers market whose hand-lettered signs promised brown eggs, duck eggs, ayacuna eggs in yellow, pink, and blue pastels, and, if you would ask, the story of his unjust accusations and upcoming trial. He disappeared from the market, though his stand remained, staffed by children who looked to be about eleven, so I kept buying his eggs. They were smaller than supermarket eggs, each one about the size of a new potato. Bits of sticky hay clung to the shells, and the yolks were a rich orange-gold. I fed them to my skeptical mother and made a convert out of her.

> I can suck melancholy out of a song as a weasel sucks eggs.
>
> —Shakespeare, *As You Like It*

> A hen is only an egg's way of making another egg.
>
> —Samuel Butler

The Oxford Companion to Food calls the egg an "unintentional gift," which is a self-deceiving way of saying we steal them. In other animals such behavior seems especially rapacious, not to mention sneaky. The dinosaur known as *oviraptor* ("egg thief") got its name when its skeleton was discovered on a cache of fossilized eggs. Scientists assumed the dinosaur was stealing them rather than warming them and christened it accordingly. Misunderstood or not, such a creature lacks grandeur. It seems poor sport to eat the unborn. The killers we most admire—the tigers, the grizzlies—are the John Waynes of the animal world. They have no need to assume the creepy delicacy of a mongoose slithering into the henhouse.

But we humans, sly lot, are the greatest oviraptors of all, and we will never admit it. We'll never compare ourselves to the mongoose or the weasel, because it might turn our egg-love into something that feels prurient and deceitful. We believe we are in it for commerce or gourmandise, that the matter-of-fact hand beneath the hen is retrieving only what it's owed, or that the pleasure in pearls of caviar bursting against the roofs of our mouths is near-godly delectation.

We are kidding ourselves, of course; the delight we feel at the discovery of an unexpected cluster of eggs is pure animal gratitude for protein, for succulence, for easy pickings. The beachcomber who unearths a clutch of leathery turtle eggs warmed in the sand, the diner who finds a cache of scarlet pearls upon cracking the lobster shell, and the fisherman who slices open a sturgeon to discover the black burst fruit of its roe all treat the discovery as though it were a pile of gold coins. When it comes to an egg, any egg, humans are pure avarice. Hence, the egg is an animal's most vulnerable possession. The egg is its secret.

The love of eggs is a love for the tiny and tender—pinkie-sized squash, potatoes like marbles, three-week-old chickens, skinny-limbed lambs and calves—but taken one step backward. To us it feels wholesome, as though there is no kinder thing on earth than to give someone a plate of eggs, but every now and again you get a reminder what you're dealing with. You crack a shell and find the freak egg: the yolk sphere inexplicably twinned like a biology experiment, a bloody vein buried in the meat of the yolk.

> Eggs are very much like small boys. If you overheat them, or overbeat them, they will turn on you, and no amount of future love will right the wrong.
>
> —Anonymous

As befits a thing of pure potential, the egg's versatility is unparalleled. Americans cooking at home don't test this versatility as much as we might, aware that—probably in punishment for our invasion—the egg doesn't lend itself to careless treatment. Faced with graceless-ness, an egg asserts itself. Whip up mayonnaise in the food processor instead of the more gentle blender and the gluey result is most likely just what the egg thinks you deserve. Subject a custard to unmiti-gated heat without its water bath and see how it likes that. Just try skipping the tempering of beaten yolks with warm liquid before adding them to a béarnaise and watch the egg clench its proteins like fists. You will be no more successful with a chilly egg yanked from the fridge than you will with a date you have shoved into a swimming pool. It's no surprise we get our word *coddle* from the treatment of an egg. An egg demands a little respect before it yields itself, loosens up its silky insides, and draws its neighbors in.

But once granted a little kindness, the egg is the workhorse of the culinary world. Its greatest talent is to deliver other flavors while retaining its own. A scrambled egg's yolky flavor is the cushion on which chives or truffle oil lay themselves. A soufflé is no spongy messenger, but the medium itself, lending its unmistak-able flavor—it can only be called *eggy*—to cheese and chocolate alike. The whites whip up to glossy peaks more lovely and ephemeral than flower blossoms. But white and yolks are yin and yang, achieving more significance together than apart. Beaten together they become creamy and thick, a sweet butter-yellow that would cheer any depressive.

The best of us are fools for omelets. The insipid egg-white omelet, which strangles its filling in rubbery proteins, does not count. The real thing is delicate, spongy, light, and sunny yellow, laced with butter and a sprinkling of cheese. I have never mastered the classic tri-folded French omelet, and I remain convinced this is attributable to using the wrong pan. (I am fooling myself; I will have to work harder. The pretentious word *technique* suddenly seems appropriate.) Most of us have consumed innumerable omelets, but not many have had a really good one. I know I have eaten omelets that oozed strange juice, bore burned spots that stayed in my teeth like bitter leaves. The proliferation of the egg-white omelet allowed us to convince ourselves that an omelet is health food. It isn't. It shouldn't be. I ate hundreds of veggie egg-white omelets before admitting they resembled broccoli stuck to the bottom of a shoe.

I probably should have refused them, but, faced even with an inferior omelet, I always try.

> An egg is always an adventure; the next one may be different.
>
> —Oscar Wilde

Raw, they nourish the hungover; cooked, they nourish everyone. At a potluck a few years ago, I and a dozen other wine-snob gourmands abandoned our homemade foccaccia and shrimp pot stickers and stormed the deviled eggs someone had made as a joke. The egg is childhood, urban, suburban, and rural alike. This explains why omelets, fritattas, and Spanish tortillas are mainstays rather than special-occasion dishes. Yet the egg's seeming good nature also explains the occasional misstep, such as at a farm breakfast I once attended in Sheboygan, Wisconsin, where dozens of eggs were stirred up and cooked in a huge, shallow tin bowl like a hubcap over some pallid coals and then spooned onto our plates in runny clumps. This strikes me as an experience that could have been avoided.

But when dealings with an egg are successful there is nothing quite like it. When my husband had his wisdom teeth out I gave him chicken broth with finely chopped spinach. It occurred to me to try whisking beaten eggs into the hot liquid, and in a minute they formed a loose golden net suspended in the broth. This is an age-old idea but right then it felt like genius. I felt strangely capable and nourishing, like a farm wife, but sexy. Eggs will do that to you. Something similar happened when I made béarnaise (breaking it on the first try, whipping in more clarified butter until it gathered itself together again), except that time I felt rather cool and daring, as though I were descended from the French Resistance rather than Alsatian peasant stock.

The egg is sophistication and breakfast all at once. A friend who worked in a hip restaurant once served me scrambled eggs with truffle oil and porcinis at midnight on a Saturday. I was sitting at the blond-wood bar, dabbing with my toast at the soft curds of cooked egg and slicing through a fat porcini stem. Elsewhere at the bar, people were smoking cigars and drinking flights of champagne or Italian reds. I had a white burgundy because it went nicely with the truffle and the egg and as I did it struck me that wine with breakfast was not a bad idea. Not a bad idea at all.

"Only women order this dish," the bartender informed me. "It's too sexy for the men."

Until then, "sexy" was never one of the adjectives I would have ascribed to an egg. The egg is drama and succor, birth and parenthood, sex and death, the start and the finish. The egg is inevitable.

Let's Be Frank

by Sandra Tsing Loh

from *Bon Appétit*

> Humorist/composer/performance artist
> Sandra Tsing Loh can be plenty contro-
> versial, especially in her radio commen-
> taries. But there's no quarreling with her
> claim that there's only one possible
> thing to eat on a sunkissed, wind-
> whipped Southern California beach
> outing.

Over the age of 40 in Los Angeles, there are diminishing returns to staying slim. The reasons?

1. At what you've always thought was your fighting weight, the face starts looking unbelievably Leonard Nimoy-esque. 2. You have to work so much harder at it that it becomes a career—a really dull career. 3. Even if you do count carbs and flex reps with Zen-like grit, what's the best you can hope for? To join the wandering masses of thousands of Los Angeles adults currently boring others out of their skulls at cocktail parties with continual earnest updates about their diets and their workouts and . . .

Anyway, there's a major upside to letting the cheese melt where it may: summer, or more specifically, the beach in summer. If you're feeling a bit fat, feeling a bit gassy, feeling a bit un-camera-ready, there's no better place to hide. Because that's one of the great secrets about Los Angeles: No one remotely cool ever goes to the beach.

Deep into August, the cool people are busy doing their cool things, which is to say they're taking a meeting, cutting an album, doing a film. If movers and shakers are on the sand, it's never here. It's in St. Bart's or somewhere.

I once watched an unemployed actor, clearly new to town, attempting to read a script on the beach. He seemed surprised by the heat, the tar, the wind flapping his pages, and by the very un-*Baywatch*-like sight of exposed cellulite on a nearby woman in a size 14 bathing suit from Costco.

That would be me.

Because come summertime, I, a mother of two under three, am at the beach with my brood every day. For at least six hours. Eating chips and hot dogs like crazy. What kinds of hot dogs? What kind you got? Hebrew National, Farmer John, anything Ball Park—heck, even Oscar Mayer child-size dogs with Velveeta in the middle and Elmo on the front.

Because you can't kill an all-beef dog, no matter how hard you try. And try we did, growing up in the '60s and '70s in Southern California, where the height of style was Buicks and chicken fricassee. Sunday nights at the Loh household featured pigs in blankets: a tube of Pillsbury crescents, spread-eagle 'em on a cookie sheet, smear on ketchup, stick those weenies in, tug that dough closed, 375 degrees, 15 minutes, you are in heaven.

In Home Ec class at Malibu Park Junior High, I got my first recipe card: Foxy Franks. That's cut-up Oscar Mayers in a swanky brine of ketchup, soy sauce, Worcestershire sauce, and a little brown sugar, heated in a double boiler. (You're snickering now, but deep in your heart you recognize that if it were your last meal on Death Row and it was a flank of seared ahi versus a cozy little stew pot of Foxy Franks . . . Well, we'd turn our backs out of respect for you, but we would know.)

The secret is the fat grams. That's the gauntlet my fellow semi-employed writer friend Mel Green finally threw down, several Augusts ago, and there it has stayed ever since.

I remember it well. We were at Malibu on Wednesday morning, chubby and tanned, in sombreros and flip-flops, not even a whiff of employment to distract us from our ritual, painstaking, mandala-like arrangement of towels, beach chairs, the one sharp knife, the limes, the clubby fraternity of leaking coolers. The ketchup? Heinz. Mustard? French's yellow, in meaty-fist squeeze size (I love the Harley-Davidson-like heft of the grip).

The sweet Del Monte hot dog relish you shake gingerly out of the jar and sculpt along the length of the dog with a potato chip, which of course must be Lay's, plain. (Don't waste your time with Kettle Chips. There are too many flavors, it's getting way too complicated, it gives you a headache—you've got collapsing kids in a van outside, and there you stand inside in front of endless racks of gourmet chips, time itself slowing down as you ask yourself: "Yes, but would I *want* a bag of cilantro-lime-habanero-Muenster-pepper chips—with just a splash of apple vinegar? Would I? Could I? Who am I?")

Yes, it was all systems go that day, but then came the wrong turn. In a moment of ill-conceived Los Angeles waffling, I'd suddenly swerved left with unleaded franks, of turkey and chicken.

They'd looked good in the case, but now, by the light of the beach, sweating in their foil, they looked bluish. From under a tattered sun hat came a dark look I have never forgotten. Said Mel, in the quietest voice I've ever heard him use: "If it doesn't have at least 28 grams of fat in it, I'm not interested." And with that, he placed the slack rubbery wiener back into its cradle of wrinkled foil.

Lesson learned. Point taken. Ouch.

Anyway, why bother worrying? Once you go to the dark side of the nutrition label, there's a hidden lining for both cloud and stomach. I mean, sure, you're eating straight beef fat in summer, but you are also swimming/bodysurfing/flailing around in the 64-degree Pacific water. Which can only be accomplished, by humans, if your body is covered with at least an inch-thick layer of fat, like a bull seal's. Think about those hardy British who slather on suet and ford the English Channel. You *need* the back fat.

Without at least three fully loaded hot dogs, a personal "Big Grab" of chips with Hidden Valley ranch dip mix (made with full-fat sour cream), a couple of fistfuls of Toll House pull-apart-'n'-bake cookies, and a bracing swig of "The Captain" (as in Morgan's, rum, just for the heck of it), you could get *killed* out there.

And once out there, well, nothing is ultimately as euphoric as letting your gravity-challenged ham hocks fly unfettered in a buoying sea. Contrary to popular opinion, swimsuits don't make you feel fat; jeans do, with their annoying pinch and bind. Bobbing this way and that, wearing only the ocean, which happens to be very roomy, you feel at one with the universe, which, P.S., is also rumored to be quite large—indeed, like so many of us, expanding.

As gulls wheel and waves splash, you take a deep salty breath and inhale the best of California: a natural high, with just a few artificial flavors and nitrates. And you think, *Come summertime, we're the lucky ones, for once again to the dogs we go!*

Fundamental Pleasures

by Amanda Hesser
from *Women Who Eat*

The *Women Who Eat* anthology is like a kaleidoscope, refracting the many different ways women relate to food. In one of its best essays, *New York Times* food editor Amanda Hesser (author of *Cooking For Mr. Latte*) wistfully meditates on what pleases her about the very act of cooking.

I left the paper at ten of eight, walking out into the aggressive neon of Times Square, loaded down with a shopping bag filled with papers, a cookbook, and a bottle of olive oil. My eyes felt shrunken from the office's fluorescent lighting, from squinting at my computer screen. I dipped into the subway station. A scattering of people stood on the platform looking down the tunnel, down at their papers, anywhere but at each other.

I wondered, as I often do: What will they eat when they get home? For the middle-aged man with the beat-up briefcase, will it be a cold slab of lasagna, pulled from the refrigerator and eaten while standing, his fork pawing at the food? Will the woman in clunky shoes be greeted with a steaming lamb curry prepared by her husband? Or will her meal be a glass of cheap wine and a morsel of cheese, consumed on the sofa in front of the TV?

I didn't know exactly what I would be having for dinner, but I knew what I needed. My husband was away on business, and I knew our apartment would feel dead without him, so I needed to put a pan on the stove and feel heat lapping up its sides. I needed to feel the scratch of salt between my fingertips as I sprinkled it over my food. I needed my placemat on the table, the Japanese lantern above the table lit and low, the trickle of wine being poured slowly into a glass.

I buried my head in a book and waited for the subway to career under the East River to my stop just on the other side, in Brooklyn. Peas & Pickles, a local grocery, was empty. The man at the cash register was taking strawberries out of large flats and arranging them in small cartons, putting the largest ones on top. I picked up a dozen eggs, a persimmon, a bunch of thin leeks and some tarragon, and headed home, assembling the ingredients in my mental kitchen. I'd poach the egg, I thought, and melt, as the French say, the leeks in butter with a pinch of tarragon. That would be plenty.

When someone first learns to cook, some of the most basic skills—poaching an egg, sautéing a fillet of fish, and boiling pasta—can seem daunting, even infuriating. So much effort for such plain food. It can feel like it will take years to learn to compose "real" cuisine with its layering of flavors, herb oils, and reduced sauces. And it will, for most cooks at least.

And it will probably take many more—as it did for me—to realize that while preparing complex dishes and course-upon-course dinner parties is a splendid accomplishment, some of the most pleasing dishes emerge from the early stages of one's culinary life. Dressing noodles with freshly grated nutmeg, butter, and Parmesan cheese. Rolling asparagus in frothy butter. Roasting small potatoes until they caramelize on the edges and their skins wrinkle.

A few years ago, I took a new writing job—my first full-time job—and was quickly swept up in long wearying days at work. I was living in a new city with few friends and little time for the ones I had. I fought staggering waves of loneliness like I had never experienced, and when they hit I began to crave eggs and toast, orange slices and tea, the foods that my mother fed to me when I was sick. I might wilt spinach in butter and olive oil, slice romaine for a chopped salad, mash butternut squash with a little créme fraiche. Dessert was often ice cream and a cognac.

I trudged through cooking. It seemed so chore-like when the results were so mundane. Yet repetition became a powerful source of comfort. While my schedule stayed the same (maybe I even liked it, latched on to my busy-ness as a source of pride), with time—age—I changed. I wanted to slow things down elsewhere. And in the kitchen, I could. I grew to like pounding my fist on the blade of my knife to split open a clove of garlic. I enjoyed watching a piece of fish shrink at the edges in the heat of the oven. I no longer minded whisking mustard and vinegar for a vinaigrette. The meals were sound; I could recall the flavors, and began to enjoy not having worked too hard to feed myself well. I knew what I was doing, and the results had the purity and consolation of childhood memories.

I once read that M.F.K. Fisher would sometimes have fruit and a glass of cold milk for lunch. At the time, this struck me as austere, a puzzling ritual in a life lived so richly. Around that time, I visited a friend who was a chef. As we talked, she made herself a little lunch before going to work. She pulled a sweet potato out of her toaster oven, split it open and sprinkled sea salt inside. She did this with great care, then ate it slowly. Now, I understand what both women were up to.

This is a cuisine for which there are few recipes. While it is no longer acceptable to include a recipe for poaching eggs in a cookbook (unless a salsa verde or olive oil sabayon follows), everyone knows that a poached egg with a dash of salt is a combination that cannot be improved upon. The exterior of the egg sheets in the simmering water. Inside, the whites are like velvety curd and the yolk becomes its luxurious sauce. Such delectables are the great secrets of the kitchen, a testament to fundamental pleasures.

Edouard de Pomiane did his best to capture such plain treats in *Cooking with Pomiane*: "For a gourmand there is no need to produce complicated dishes with fancy names," he wrote. "Prepare for him raw materials of good quality. Transform them as little as possible and accompany them with suitable sauces and you will have produced a meal which is just right."

His pumpkin soup is cooked in a single pot and contains merely pumpkin, milk, and rice. He gives instructions for *croutes au fromage,* or grilled cheeses, and includes how and when to serve chilled white wine with them. Chives on toast are precisely that, creamed with butter and a "dusting of pepper."

Eating well, de Pomiane believed, made you a whole and "normal" person. Those who did not were likely to be "unhappy, embittered, pessimistic, disagreeable, and even dangerous." I can agree with the first part—eating well does help replenish the mind and improve one's outlook, even if it is only a post-meal high, which then fades like a sunset. The act of preparing yourself a meal is edifying, as well. *Your* hands, having left the computer keyboard or steering wheel, are put to use with their much more primal function, as tools. *You* must use your senses. And while many daily projects are left with loose ends, a meal is not. It has a beginning, middle, and end.

De Pomiane died in 1964. He would probably be frustrated by the current polarization of American cooks into those who do not have time to cook and those who love cooking so much that they can't stop themselves from pursuing the latest culinary obsessions. He would want to tidy up our kitchens and set us back on course.

But we can still turn back to him, and to his delight in carrots with cream and pork chops with rhubarb. Or we can find our own way. Occasionally, now, I will have fruit and milky coffee for lunch. Or toast with butter and jam. A piece of creamy cheese.

After shopping that evening on my way home from work, I arrived home to an empty apartment. I flicked on the kitchen light, cleared the counter, and pulled out my large knife and sauté pan. I poured myself a glass of sherry. There were no recipes to turn to. I simply knew that to soften leeks, you must cook them slowly in a thin coating of fat. There was no need for a timer. I would stand over them and watch the chemistry take place. I would drop in a little chopped tarragon at the end, then taste a spoonful to see. Rinsing the leeks, spreading the firm layers under the faucet, was the first order of business. I sliced them in half and leaned into the sink, letting the ropey stream of warm water run over my hands.

American Pie

by Peter Reinhart
from *American Pie*

In this handsome book, bread-baking maestro Reinhart chronicles his exhaustive search for the world's best pie, from Naples to New Haven to Northern California. It's his enthusiasm that really matters, and his conviction that perfecting pizza is one way of expressing one's soul.

For a long time, I thought the best pizza in the country was from Mama's in Bala Cynwyd, just outside of Philadelphia. And then something happened.

I grew up on Mama's, even worked there briefly as a delivery boy, and found warm comfort in its stringy cheese and crisp, yet floppy crust whenever I'd been rejected for a date, lost a basketball game, or got together with high-school friends for a Saturday-night poker game. My family was equally hooked, and we often picked up a Mama's pizza for dinner when my mom wanted a break from cooking, especially if going out for Chinese food, our other favorite pastime, seemed like too much trouble. We knew the owners of Pagano's Pizzeria in West Philadelphia and often went there when we wanted an actual restaurant experience to go along with our pizza, pasta, and breasted chicken (they were pioneers in this now rarely seen pressurized frying system). But as good as Pagano's pizza was, it never measured up to Mama's for deeply felt satisfaction, a culinary balm of Gilead. More than forty years after eating my first Mama's pizza, almost always made by Paul Castelucci (though I never knew his last name when I worked as a delivery boy), the business is still in the family, and the pizzas are now supervised, but not made, by Paul Jr., Paul's son. Mama's is still extremely popular, with long waiting times not only for pizza, but also for fabulous stromboli, hoagies, and cheese steaks.

My brother Fred, who now lives forty-five minutes from Mama's instead of the five minutes of our childhood, continues to make the pilgrimage whenever he needs a fix. He brought us a Mama's pizza when my wife, Susan, and I were in Philadelphia for a big food event. Susan had sprained her ankle at the airport just after we landed, forcing us to cancel our dinner plans so she could keep her foot on ice. When I called Fred to explain our plight, he said, "No problem, I'll pick up a pizza and some cheese steaks at Mama's and we'll eat in." I loved the idea. It had been years since my last Mama's pizza.

The pizza arrived ninety minutes later, accompanied by Fred and his wife, Patty. I rushed through the greetings—hug, hug, "great to see you"—while Patty comforted Susan. I was captivated by the aroma of the pizzas and cheese steaks, and my mind floated away to distant times. It was like a long-lost friend, triggering painful and joyful memories that were flashing like a deck of cards rifled in front of my eyes. I'd deal with those later. For now, as far as I was concerned, it was about opening the pizza box, unwrapping the butcher paper from the cheese steaks, and getting everyone to stop talking and start eating. We divvied up the cheese steaks, which tasted even better than I remembered them to be, and then, at last, passed around slices of the pizza. I took a bite and stopped, the pleasant image-streaming of food memories suddenly interrupted by a mental disconnect. I shook it off and took another bite expecting an automatic memory flash to kick in so I could resume my forty-year flavor retrospective. Instead, I got a blast of "Whoa!"

There was definitely something amiss. The words just came out without forethought. "Fred, they've changed the crust."

"No they haven't."

"Yes they have."

"No, they haven't. Maybe it's you."

"I don't think so. The crust is thicker and there are no air bubbles in the lip. Definitely not the Mama's I grew up with."

"I think it's you."

"No, it isn't."

Fred took another bite. "Well, it does seem a little thicker than usual. I heard they were breaking in a new pizza guy. But, I gotta tell you, it's still pretty close to usual."

"Maybe it is me," I thought. It wasn't just that the crust was a little different. The cheese and sauce certainly still resonated with old memories, and even if it wasn't the best Mama's, it was close enough that it should have elicited, within my usually tolerant margin-for-error forgiveness code, at least a sigh of pleasure. But something had changed within me. My expectations, an internal bar of standards that is both conscious and subconscious, had been violated. A slow wave of realization set in, one that I couldn't suppress even though I tried.

"Maybe," I said to myself, "it was never as good as I thought it was, just the best I'd been exposed to during my sheltered youth." I knew it was something I couldn't say out loud because Fred and Patty still lived here, while I was going back to Providence and might not have another Mama's pizza for years. Yet I couldn't shake the thought.

Since 1990, when I left the communal setting of a religious order in which everyone lived a vow of poverty and thus had limited restaurant experience, I have had the privilege of teaching and writing about food, especially bread. I've traveled around the country and beyond, belatedly pursuing knowledge about my taste passions. These passions are simple, not of the great gourmand type. I have learned that one of my inherent gifts is the ability to recognize flavors and textures of universal appeal and show people how to reproduce them. As a result of this gift, I have carved out a career as an educator, writer, and product developer. Which brings me back to pizza.

I have had a steady stream of students who have their own sets of childhood food associations that have driven them to the gates of learning. Food memories, as James Beard and M.F. K. Fisher have shown us, are powerful and compelling forces. Wherever I teach, if I want to get a lively conversation going, I need only ask, "Where do I find the best pizza around here?" Nearly everyone has a pizza story and a strong opinion. Pizza, it seems, lives in everyone's hall of fame.

In 1976, I worked in Raleigh, North Carolina, as a houseparent in a home for what we euphemistically called undisciplined teenagers; in other words, juvenile delinquents. There was a pizzeria on Hillsborough Street called Brothers Pizza and although I barely remember the details of the place, I do remember the experience of it. I took the kids there whenever we needed to decompress from the latest dramatic event in our house, and there were always, always dramas. That pizza and only that pizza among all the pizza shops in town, was a panacea, our emotional salve. It had a crispy, crackly crust, like hot buttered toast, comforting and satisfying. It was perfect. The cheese was stringy and slightly salty. Was it the best pizza I'd ever had? No, but it was "perfect" pizza, a peerless match of textures and flavors that fed more than our stomachs and palates. But if I had it now, all these years later, I imagine it would be like having a Mama's now. It would be good, perhaps the same as it always was, but it wouldn't be the pizza of 1976, when teenage boys and girls from shattered families, with broken hearts and raging hormones, felt safe enough to confess their fears to me and to one another as they ate their pizza. That pizza, out of that context, could never be that perfect again.

So here I was, years after Raleigh, in Philadelphia, realizing that I was caught in a nature versus nurture situation. Was it me or was it the pizza that had changed, or was it a little bit of both? I'm pretty sure that when I asked myself that question, I set this whole pizza quest in motion.

PIZZERIA BIANCO

A few years before what I now refer to as my "Mama's awakening," a student of mine at the California Culinary Academy in San Francisco told me about a guy named Chris Bianco, who owned Pizzeria Bianco, in Phoenix, Arizona. She had worked at his restaurant prior to coming to school and raved about his pizza. By a happy coincidence, I was headed to Phoenix for the annual conference of the International Association of Culinary Professionals, which is always held in a different city. Most of us went to Phoenix expecting to experience a blitz of great Southwest cuisine, and we weren't disappointed. But the restaurant that had the biggest buzz of all was Pizzeria Bianco, located just a short walk from the convention center in downtown Phoenix.

I was scheduled to make a presentation on bread-baking techniques at one of the conference workshops, so prior to leaving San Francisco, I asked my Phoenix student to recommend a bakery that I could partner with for making my workshop breads. She said there weren't any good bread bakeries, but that Chris Bianco made his own bread for his pizzeria, and it was easily the best in town. I called him and we arranged to bake bread together.

When I got to town, I walked over to Pizzeria Bianco with Steve Garner, a friend of mine who hosts a radio food show in Santa Rosa, California, and John Ash, one of the great chefs of America who also cohosts the show with Steve. It was three o'clock in the afternoon and the restaurant wasn't scheduled to open for another two hours. My idea was that we'd talk and plan out our bread baking, but Chris insisted on making us a couple of pizzas first.

"Okay," I said without resistance, hoping, but doubtful, that they would live up to their reputation. A few minutes later, two perfect, I mean *perfect,* pizzas landed on our table, a classic *Margherita* and a white pizza with arugula and onions, and all thought of bread baking vanished for the moment. Steve and John immediately kicked into their radio-interview mode and began grilling Chris about his pizzas. We learned that as a young man with cooking talent he had gone to Naples from the Bronx, his hometown, to learn how to make true Neapolitan pizza. When his family moved to Phoenix, he decided to make his culinary statement by trying to create the best pizza in the world. He made his own mozzarella cheese and grew his own basil and lettuce behind the restaurant. He and his brother, Marco, made their own rustic Italian bread (similar to *ciabatta*) from the pizza dough, and their mother came in to make the three desserts on the menu. Chris served five types of pizza (no substitutes, please), house salad, an appetizer course, beverages, and dessert. There was no pasta course on the menu, nor any other entrée. It was just a pizzeria, but with haute cuisine attitude. I asked him why no pasta.

"I think I actually could make the best pasta in town, and if we served it people would love it," he explained. "But then I'd have my attention divided and the pizzas might suffer. So I decided my true goal is to make the best pizza in the world. If I ever want to do pasta, I'll open a different restaurant and do it there."

Did he have plans to do just that? He smiled sheepishly and said, "No, not really. You've got to understand, I love making pizza."

We talked for quite awhile and I realized it was almost five o'clock. A crowd had been gathering outside the front door for over an hour—hot, anxious people hoping to be in the first wave to grab one of the forty-two seats and not have to wait for the second seating. (I soon learned that this is a daily ritual at Bianco.) Chris anticipated my question and said, "I don't do takeout. Can't keep up. Besides, I want them to eat the pizza the way it's meant to be eaten, right out of the oven. It's just not the same out of the box. But even so, a wood-fired oven can only handle so many pies and that's that." He excused himself to get ready for dinner.

Now we were getting dirty looks from some of the people peering through the window, wondering why we were on the inside, eating pizza, while they had to wait until the doors opened at five. More to the point, probably, they were worried our three precious seats might not be available when the doors opened. So, we made our exit, and a collective sigh of relief rose from the line.

The next morning I returned to make my bread dough and watched Chris make his pizza dough. "I don't use a mixer, just a big bowl and my hands," he said. Sure enough, he combined about fifty pounds of flour (specially flown in from the Giusto's mill in San Francisco) with salt, yeast, and water. Unlike most American pizza makers, he used no oil, true to the Neapolitan rule.

"It's really all about feel," he explained. "I have to make it by hand because it's the only way to really know when it's right. I can just feel what adjustments are needed and when it's ready."

Twenty minutes later we had finished mixing our respective doughs. Mine, using a new technique I had just learned in France, had to be chilled, but Chris's dough stayed out, covered in the bowl, to ferment slowly. Hours later he divided it into smaller pieces for either pizza or bread, shaped his loaves, and again allowed the dough to ferment, chilling the evening pizza dough in the refrigerator and leaving the bread pieces out for Marco to bake off later. The rest of the time he and his crew did all the prep, making the sauces, picking lettuce and basil from the garden, and readying themselves for the rush of people gathered at the still-locked door.

Watching Chris work helped me to realize how much I still had to learn about that simple yet complex substance called dough and, more importantly, about how dough is transformed, in the hands of a skilled *pizzaiolo* (pizza maker) into pizza. A few years passed and I got deeper and deeper into the intricacies of bread making, trying to figure out how, as I described it, to evoke the full potential of flavor from the grain. In developing pizza dough for several companies, I gradually came to understand what causes some dough to be better than others. I ate a lot of pizza along the way and tasted many toppings and, more important, heard many pizza philosophies. Whenever the subject of great pizza came up, I mentioned Bianco. At first I was met with laughter and disbelief. The idea of great pizza in Phoenix just didn't compute. But then I ran into people who knew about Pizzeria Bianco either from experience or from reading or hearing about it.

It had been a while since I'd tasted the pizza at Pizzeria Bianco, so I began to doubt my memory. Shortly after the "Mama's awakening," I ran into one of my favorite food writers, Jeffrey Steingarten, and he asked me who I thought made the best pizza. "I used to think it was Mama's in Bala Cynwyd, Pennsylvania," I told him, "but now I think it might be Pizzeria Bianco in Phoenix."

He hadn't been there but had heard of it. "How can you call it the best if you haven't tried Frank Pepe's or Sally's in New Haven, or John's or Grimaldi's in New York City?" he asked.

Of course he was right. Pizzeria Bianco might have been the best I'd ever had, but there were so many other legendary places still to try. So I did go to Pepe's, Sally's, Grimaldi's, John's, and many other places. I went to Genoa and then to Naples, into the belly of the beast, to the source, and then returned to America to immerse myself in pizza of all types: classic, modern, avant-garde, you name it. I was searching for the perfect slice. That meant I had to discover what perfection, at least pizza perfection, really is.

I had become a hunter of sorts, a pizza hunter, and I enlisted others to join me on the hunts. With Mama's no longer the benchmark, and with the memory of Pizzeria Bianco serving as a temporary beacon and standard, I sought out great pizza everywhere I traveled, and I traveled to seek out great pizza.

Some of the numerous pizza excursions I choreographed were

thwarted by circumstances: trip cancellations, a restaurant Closed sign, logistical mix-ups. But almost every time something went wrong, something else occurred to make it all right. In fact, Plan B was often better than Plan A could ever have been. As result I came up with the Reinhart Pizza Hunter's Credo, a sound axiom for anyone who decides to adopt it: It's all about the adventure, not the pizza. The pizza is just grace.

What's Been There All Along

by Min Liao

from *The Stranger*

To become a "regular" at a restaurant is a way of putting down roots, finding a sanctuary from the world. Min Liao's restaurant reviews for Seattle's alternative weekly *The Stranger* were always about more than just the food, and her final sign-off would be no exception.

I t's always the mascarpone that wrecks me, and I'm not even what you would call a dessert person.

And yet there I am every time, on a short lunch break with a long afternoon of work looming ahead, knowing perfectly well that I will render myself useless and lapse into a food coma if I continue to eat—especially if what I'm about to eat is sweet, creamy, and obscenely decadent. I am referring to the "Il Mascarpone di Ida" ($4.50), a sort of deconstructed tiramisu served in an oversized coffee cup and dusted with cocoa powder; and what I'm trying to talk about is Osteria la Spiga, a neighborhood restaurant located right between where I live and where I work.

I've been faithfully, happily eating at Osteria la Spiga for a long time, but it never occurred to me—until now, my last article for this newspaper—to actually write about it. So in a way, I'm starting with an apology, which is never a graceful thing to do. Yes, I've been holding out on you, and for that I am sorry.

While I was busy deciding what to review each week, figuring out which neighborhood to cover next and what would please my editor most, La Spiga somehow became an invisible but constant part of my everyday life. I can write about practically all of the dishes and their ingredients from memory.

This is where I go when I am too exhausted to cook on a weeknight (if I take the shortcut, I can walk there from my apartment in seven minutes exactly). This is where I go when I consider myself off-duty, and I don't feel like thinking about and describing every single thing I consume—when I just want to sit and read and mindlessly enjoy something wholesome, reliable, delicious. This has also been the site of countless lunch meetings with people from the office; where staff writers have been given their annual reviews; and where I've commiserated with co-workers about deadlines over late-afternoon lasagne.

It can be easy to miss Osteria la Spiga if you're not looking for it, since it sits on the edge of a retail plaza that includes, among other things, a UPS shipping center, a Domino's Pizza, a Burger King, and a tanning salon. This corner storefront right next door to a Great Clips franchise is not the most obvious location if you're looking for authentic specialties from Italy's Emilia-Romagna region. But check out the sheets of fresh, eggy pasta being made on the tiled countertop in the dining room; notice the precise, deliberately uncomplicated menu. When I am here, I am constantly reminded of how specific, how persistently unfancy, regional Italian cuisine can be.

While I am ashamed to say that I don't remember everything I've ever tasted here (like I said, *off-duty* . . . I never, ever took notes while eating at La Spiga), what I do recall is a blur of dishes featuring things like softly bitter escarole, or hunks of fresh fennel; tender pork loin, and even the occasional rabbit recipe; seasonal vegetables slicked with really good olive oil and stuffed, along with melting, pungent cheese, into flatbread sandwiches.

Puréed legumes are used often here, as well as Umbrian farro (a hulled-wheat grain that's like a cross between cereal and rice). There was a lovely ravioli special for a few weeks last spring— supple pasta pockets bulging with stewed lamb meat and aromatic herbs—that was simple and exquisite. I also distinctly remember a lunch entrée involving chilled tuna salad with capers and sweet onions; and, during the wintertime, there was a brilliant soup that was nourishing and flavorful, thick with black-eyed peas, I believe, and shards of silky cabbage. Earlier this summer, I sampled a velvety lasagne layered with an asparagus cream sauce; and just a couple of weeks ago, ignoring the thick summer heat, I tucked into stuffed duck breast brightened with juniper and orange zest.

While there are plenty of cozy starches to choose from, I'm also a huge fan of La Spiga's lighter dishes—various antipasti and colorful salads that make me feel like the stylish women I've seen in Rome, sipping espresso and picking at little plates in outdoor cafes (except they are leggy European hotties, and I have a stomach shaped like a bagel). The house salad is remarkable, with its Technicolor blend of romaine, frisée, radicchio, and arugula—bitter, crisp lettuces complemented by wonderfully acidic dressing and mellowed with slivers of carrots. Caprese salad is given an extra flourish: instead of raw tomato slices, thick slabs of mozzarella are interspersed with gently roasted tomatoes, practically bursting with flavor.

A wedge of aged pecorino with fig preserves and smoked scamorza cheese melted into radicchio cups are great foundations for blushing slices of Parma prosciutto fanned across a wooden board, or for the more grandiose tortelli alla lastra ($13, serves two)—impossibly soft tortelli, warm from an iron griddle, filled with buttery potato purée and served with various cured meats.

I can't mention Osteria la Spiga's iron griddle—the mighty *testo*—without properly acknowledging the piadina served to everyone instead of standard-issue rustic table bread (assorted piadina sandwiches with meats, cheeses, and vegetables are also available at lunch). Made on the premises via *testo*, this amazingly tasty (thank you, butter! thank you pork fat!) unleavened bread is a symbol of Emilia-Romagna's peasant roots.

While it's easy to get hooked on the warm triangles of piadina, trust me when I say that it's the pasta dishes you'll still be thinking about when the evening's over: you'll remember pasta details the next day and smile to yourself, just like you would in the first 24 hours after a great date. Gnocchi (dense little potato dumplings that practically dissolve on the tongue) arrive in a pond of intense tomato cream sauce. House lasagna is a fluffy mattress stacked with spinach pasta, covered in besciamella sauce. Tortelli are stuffed with impossibly smooth ricotta and puréed greens, soaking up sage butter in a deep, wide bowl. Ribbons of tagliatelle (tender, flat egg noodles with slight rippling on the edges, textured just right) are tossed with house ragù (traditional meat-and-tomato sauce, simmered and softened) or diced porcini mushrooms with cream, butter, and Parmigiano—more superb evidence that good mushrooms don't need much backup.

But as far as I'm concerned, the tagliatelle with porcini cream sauce is merely a stunt double for my absolute favorite and most-ordered dish here: tagliatelle covered in black Acqualagna truffle butter, cream, and melted Parmigiano, topped with cracked black pepper and specks of truffle (about a thumbnail's worth, which is enough). What's better than fresh noodles with butter, cream, and cheese? The truffles add an earthy, refined-mushroom character that lingers long after you've swallowed the actual pasta—a delicate, luxurious finish that tastes unlike anything else.

This seasonal dish is not currently on the menu, but when it does return, I'll probably be gone, since I'm leaving Seattle before summer's end. I am sad that I can't enjoy it one more time, and if for some reason it is permanently retired from La Spiga's menu, I'll feel terrible that I didn't write about it sooner.

In my defense, I will say that sometimes it's difficult to articulate what I love most about what's closest to me—to buckle down and actually describe the deep pleasures of routine, familiarity, and predictability. And, I will admit, I stubbornly tend to avoid what is most important sometimes—things like paying late bills, making doctors' appointments, buying cat litter, or finally getting around to saying goodbye.

Recipe Index

Acknowledgments

Grateful acknowledgment is made to all those who gave permission for written material to appear in this book. Every effort has been made to trace and contact copyright holders. If an error or omission is brought to our notice, we will be pleased to remedy the situation in future editions of this book. For further information, please contact the publisher.

"Food Porn" by Molly O'Neill. Copyright © 2003 by Molly O'Neill. Used by permission of the author. Originally appeared in *Columbia Journalism Review*, September/October, 2003. ✤ "My Time at the Times" from *Eating My Words* by Mimi Sheraton. Copyright © 2004 by Mimi Sheraton. Reprinted by permission of HarperCollins Publishers, Inc. ✤ "The Top Ten" by Patric Kuh. Copyright © 2004 by Patric Kuh. Used by permission of the author. Originally appeared in *Los Angeles Magazine*, January, 2004. ✤ "My Life as a Hand Model" by Bruce Feiler. Copyright © 2003 by Bruce Feiler. Used by permission of the author. Originally appeared in *Gourmet*, September, 2003. ✤ "The Staff and the Stuff of Life" by Laura Faye Taxel. Copyright © 2003 by Laura Faye Taxel. Reprinted by permission of the author. Originally appeared in *Northern Ohio Live*, August, 2003. ✤ "Table to the World" by John Kessler. Copyright © 2003 by *The Atlanta Journal Constitution*. Used by permission of *The Atlanta Journal Constitution*. Originally appeared in *The Atlanta Journal Constitution*, August 24, 2003. ✤ "Playing the Market" by Sara Deseran. Copyright © 2003 by Deseran. Reprinted by permission of the author. Originally appeared in *7x7*, September, 2003. ✤ "The Mother of All Markets" by Rick Nichols. Copyright © 2003 by Rick Nichols. Reprinted by permission of *The Philadelphia Inquirer*. Originally appeared in *The Philadelphia Inquirer*, May 8, 2003. ✤ "Getting the Goods" by Ann M. Bauer. Copyright © 2003 by Ann M. Bauer. Reprinted by permission of *Minnesota Monthly*. Originally appeared in *Minnesota Monthly*, November, 2003. ✤ "Learning to

Gourmet, January, 2004. ❖ "Bright Lights, Pig City" by Kathleen Purvis. Copyright © 2004 by *The Charlotte Observer*. Reprinted by permission of *The Charlotte Observer*. Originally appeared in *The Charlotte Observer*, March 17, 2004. ❖ "Barbecue, Jamaica Style" by Rand Richards Cooper. Copyright © 2003 by Rand Richards Cooper. Used by permission of the author. Originally appeared in *Bon Apetit*, July, 2003. ❖ "Breakfast" by Tim Morris. Copyright © 2003 by Tim Morris. Reprinted by permission of the author. Originally appeared in *Gastronomica*, 2003. ❖ "Appetite" from *Crazy in the Kitchen* by Louise DeSalvo. Copyright © 2004 by Louise DeSalvo. Reprinted by permission of Bloomsbury, USA and Elaine Markson Literary Agency, Inc. ❖ "Way to Go" by Jason Sheehan. Copyright © 2003 by Jason Sheehan. Used by permission of the author. Originally appeared in *WestWord*, September 25, 2003. ❖ Excerpt from *Something From The Oven* by Laura Shapiro. Copyright © 2004 by Laura Shapiro. Used by permission of Viking Penguin, a division of Penguin Group, (USA) Inc., and International Creative Management. ❖ "Stone-Ground Revival" by John T. Edge. Copyright © 2003 by John T. Edge. Reprinted by permission of *Saveur*. Originally appeared in *Saveur*, November, 2003. ❖ "Sex, Death and Oysters" by Robb Walsh. Copyright © 2004 by Robb Walsh. Reprinted by permission of *Houston Press*. Originally appeared in *Houston Press*, March 25, 2004. ❖ "The Way of the Knife" by Chad Ward. Copyright © 2003 by Chad Ward. Reprinted by permission of the author. Originally appeared on eGullet.com, December 19, 2003. ❖ "Tuscany's Soul Food" by Frances Mayes. Copyright © 2003 by Frances Mayes. Reprinted by permission of Curtis Brown, Ltd. Originally appeared in *Town & Country*, Fall, 2003. ❖ Excerpt from *Candyfreak* by Steve Almond. Copyright © 2004 by Steve Almond. Reprinted by permission of Algonquin Books of Chapel Hill. ❖ "Aboard Spaceship Adria" by Anthony Bourdain. Copyright © 2003 by Anthony Bourdain. Reprinted by permission of the author and *Food Arts*. Originally appeared in *Food Arts*, December, 2003. ❖ "A Tiger Tames New York" by Brett Anderson. Copyright © 2004 The Times–Picayune Publishing Co. All rights reserved. Used with permission of the *The Times Picayune*. Originally appeared in *The Times-Picayune*, June 17, 2003. ❖ "Alice in Italy" by Thomas

About the Editor

Holly Hughes is a writer, the former executive editor of Fodor's Travel Publications and author of *Frommer's New York City with Kids*.

Submissions for
Best Food Writing 2005

Submissions and nominations for *Best Food Writing 2005* should be forwarded no later than June 1, 2005, to Holly Hughes at *Best Food Writing 2005*, c/o Avalon Publishing Group, 245 W. 17th St., 11th floor, New York, NY 10011, or e-mailed to bestfoodwriting@avalonpub.com. We regret that, due to volume, we cannot acknowledge receipt of all submissions.

Best Food Writing 2000
Foreword by Alice Waters
1-56924-616-5
$14.95
Contributors include Maya Angelou, Eric Asimov, Anthony
Bourdain, Rick Bragg, Fran Gage, Jeffrey Steingarten, Jhumpa
Lahiri, Nigella Lawson, and Ruth Reichl.

Best Food Writing 2001
1-56924-577-0
$14.95
Contributors include Jeffrey Eugenides, Malcolm Gladwell,
David Leite, Molly O'Neill, Ruth Reichl, David Sedaris, Jeffrey
Steingarten, and Calvin Trillin.

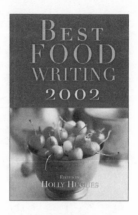

Best Food Writing 2002
1-56924-524-X
$14.95
Contributors include Anthony Bourdain, Greg Atkinson, Rand
Richards Cooper, John T. Edge, Barbara Haber, Patric Kuh, John
Mariani, Mimi Sheraton, and James Villas.

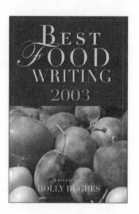

Best Food Writing 2003
1-56924-440-5
$14.95
Contributors include Susan Choi, Fran Gage, Adam Gopnik,
Amanda Hesser, David Leite, Jacques Pépin, Inga Saffron, Nigel
Slater, and John Thorne.

Please note that limited quantities are available on some previous
editions in the Best Food Writing series. Your local bookseller should
be able to help you obtain previous editions.